The 3rd Workshop on Towards Knowledgeable Language Models (KnowFM 2025)

Vienna, Austria
1 August 2025

ISBN: 979-8-3313-2410-0

Printed from e-media with permission by:

Curran Associates, Inc.
57 Morehouse Lane
Red Hook, NY 12571

Some format issues inherent in the e-media version may also appear in this print version.

Printed with permission by Curran Associates, Inc. (2025)

For permission requests, please contact the Association for Computational Linguistics at the address below.

Association for Computational Linguistics
209 N. Eighth Street
Stroudsburg, Pennsylvania 18360

Phone: 1-570-476-8006
Fax: 1-570-476-0860

acl@aclweb.org

Additional copies of this publication are available from:

Curran Associates, Inc.
57 Morehouse Lane
Red Hook, NY 12571 USA
Phone: 845-758-0400
Fax: 845-758-2633
Email: curran@proceedings.com
Web: www.proceedings.com

KnowFM 2025

The 3rd Workshop on Towards Knowledgeable Foundation Models

Proceedings of the Workshop

August 1, 2025

Introduction

Welcome to KnowFM 2025, the 3rd workshop on knowledgeable foundation models. Co-located with ACL 2025, this workshop is scheduled for August 1, 2025, and will be held in Vienna, Austria.

Knowledge has been an important prerequisite for a variety of NLP applications and is typically sourced from either structured knowledge sources such as knowledge bases and dictionaries, or unstructured sources such as Wikipedia documents. More recently, researchers have discovered that language models already possess a significant amount of knowledge through pretraining: LLMs can be used to generate commonsense and factual knowledge for question answering. While the results are encouraging, there are still lingering questions: Where does this knowledge come from? How much do language models know? Is this knowledge reliable? If some knowledge is wrong, can we fix it?

In response to these questions, the KnowFM workshop examines the lifecycle of knowledge within foundation models: The emergence of knowledge through language model pretraining; Injection of external knowledge; Updating and modification of knowledge; Probing and generation of knowledge.

Currently, researchers focusing on different stages of this lifecycle are scattered across various subcommunities within NLP. For example, probing and editing knowledge is often associated with the interpretability track, while injecting knowledge is typically application-specific and discussed within dialog, open-domain QA, IE, or summarization tracks. This workshop seeks to bring these researchers together and facilitate collaboration to create a more holistic view of the problem.

The KnowFM workshop also addresses core challenges in LM research: reducing hallucination, improving interpretability, and enhancing model extensibility. Although these challenges remain open, knowledge clearly plays a key role: Attribution to sources or providing relevant knowledge during generation can mitigate hallucination; Locating and tracing knowledge provides insights into the LM's inner workings; Efficiently adapting to domain knowledge or integrating updated facts improves extensibility.

This year, we received a total of 62 archival and non-archival submissions to the KnowFM workshop, of which 55 were accepted. Among these, 12 have been included in our proceedings, and 7 are included in ACL Findings.

In addition to oral and poster sessions where accepted works will be presented, the workshop will also host talks and a panel discussion with invited speakers.

Finally, we would like to express our gratitude to all the authors, committee members, invited speakers, and participants for helping make this workshop possible.

Organizing Committee

Program Chairs

Yuji Zhang, University of Illinois at Urbana-Champaign, USA
Canyu Chen, Northwestern University, USA
Sha Li, Amazon, USA
Mor Geva, Tel Aviv University, Israel
Chi Han, University of Illinois at Urbana-Champaign, USA
Xiaozhi Wang, University of Illinois at Urbana-Champaign, USA
Shangbin Feng, University of Washington, USA
Silin Gao, École Polytechnique Fédérale de Lausanne (EPFL), Switzerland
Isabelle Augenstein, University of Copenhagen, Denmark
Mohit Bansal, University of North Carolina at Chapel Hill, USA
Manling Li, Northwestern University, USA
Heng Ji, University of Illinois at Urbana-Champaign, USA

Publication Chair

Canyu Chen, Northwestern University, USA

Program Committee

Reviewers

Samir Abdaljalil
Yuzhuo Bai
Norbert Braunschweiler
Thomas Chen
Lida Chen
Zheng CHEN
Canyu Chen
Sitao Cheng
Cong-Thanh Do
Yixiong Fang
Yujie Feng
SeungYoon Han
Simeng Han
Yutong Hu
Xiaoyu Hu
Liqiang Jing
Kemal Kirtac
Dosung Lee
Zichao Li
Yanhong Li
Ming Li
Haohang Li
Ruochen Li
Laurence Liang
João Alberto de Oliveira Lima
Dong Liu
Xin Liu
Aofan Liu
Jiahong Liu
Ziming Luo
Jianfei Ma
Hudson de Martim
Kyle Montgomery
Albert Olweny Okiri
Yixin Ou
Alonso Palomino
Heramb Vivek Patil
Can Polat
Prasanth Prasanth
Swayamjit Saha
Shuzheng Si
Vincent Siu
Shane Storks
Toma Suzuki
Jianhong Tu
Sai P Vallurupalli

Mengru Wang
Zhe Yang
Wanli Yang
Yunzhi Yao
Li-Ming Zhan
Caiqi Zhang
Xiaofeng Zhang
Xinyun Zhou
Zeqi Zhou

Table of Contents

Temporal Information Retrieval via Time-Specifier Model Merging

SeungYoon Han[1] Taeho Hwang[1] Sukmin Cho[1] Soyeong Jeong[2]
Hoyun Song[1] Huije Lee[1] Jong C. Park[1*]
[1]School of Computing, [2]Graduate School of AI
Korea Advanced Institute of Science and Technology (KAIST)
{seungyoonee,doubleyyh,nelllpic,starsuzi,
hysong,huijelee,jongpark}@kaist.ac.kr

Abstract

The rapid expansion of digital information and knowledge across structured and unstructured sources has heightened the importance of Information Retrieval (IR). While dense retrieval methods have substantially improved semantic matching for general queries, they consistently underperform on queries with explicit temporal constraints–often those containing numerical expressions and time specifiers such as "in 2015." Existing approaches to Temporal Information Retrieval (TIR) improve temporal reasoning but often suffer from catastrophic forgetting, leading to reduced performance on non-temporal queries. To address this, we propose Time-Specifier Model Merging (TSM), a novel method that enhances temporal retrieval while preserving accuracy on non-temporal queries. TSM trains specialized retrievers for individual time specifiers and merges them into a unified model, enabling precise handling of temporal constraints without compromising non-temporal retrieval. Extensive experiments on both temporal and non-temporal datasets demonstrate that TSM significantly improves performance on temporally constrained queries while maintaining strong results on non-temporal queries, consistently outperforming other baseline methods. Our code is available at `https://github.com/seungyoonee/TSM`.

1 Introduction

In the contemporary era of digital information, Information Retrieval (IR)–the process of finding and ranking documents from a large collection that are most relevant to a search query–has become increasingly important as information and knowledge rapidly expand across both structured sources (e.g., knowledge bases) (Lan et al., 2021; Dhingra et al., 2022) and unstructured sources (e.g., Wikipedia, web documents) (Vrandečić and Krötzsch, 2014). This significance is more amplified in the era of Large Language Models (LLMs), where IR is a crucial component of Retrieval-Augmented Generation (RAG) (Lewis et al., 2020; Khandelwal et al., 2020) pipelines.

As the importance of IR continues to grow, there have been significant advances in retrieval methods, notably the development of dense retrieval methods (Karpukhin et al., 2020; Izacard et al., 2022). Dense retrieval leverages neural models to encode both queries and documents into dense embeddings to capture semantic similarity, substantially improving retrieval effectiveness for general-domain queries. However, these models exhibit *attention bias*, where their embeddings are optimized primarily for semantic similarity and topical relevance, making them less effective at capturing temporal expressions in queries (Wu et al., 2024). As a result, dense retrievers struggle with queries containing temporal expressions (e.g., "in 2015," "between 2010 and 2012") (Chen et al., 2021).

To address these challenges, the field of Temporal Information Retrieval (TIR) has emerged, focusing on improving retrieval accuracy for temporal queries by enhancing temporal understanding capabilities of retrievers (Allen, 1983; Alonso et al., 2011). Recent research has attempted to increase the time-awareness of dense models from the pre-training process using different temporal information masking (Rosin et al., 2021; Wang et al., 2023; Cole et al., 2023), fine-tuning process (Chen et al., 2021; Dhingra et al., 2022; Wu et al., 2024). By incorporating temporal awareness, TIR aims to enhance the accuracy and relevance of retrieved documents for temporal queries.

Previous studies have primarily focused on improving retrieval performance for temporal queries, often overlooking the resulting performance drop on non-temporal queries. However, while enhancing temporal retrieval capabilities is important, it is equally crucial to maintain robust performance on non-temporal queries. This is because both tem-

* Corresponding author

Proceedings of the 3rd Workshop on Towards Knowledgeable Foundation Models (KnowFM), pages 1–13
August 1, 2025

poral and non-temporal queries are fundamentally part of general-domain information retrieval and do not require domain-specific knowledge.

Unlike domain-specific retrieval tasks that target specialized topics, temporal queries remain general in scope, with their distinction based solely on the presence of explicit time constraints–typically signaled by time specifiers such as "in," "after," or "between." Accordingly, this paper treats temporal queries as a subset of general queries with explicit time constraints, while non-temporal queries lack such time specifiers. This distinction highlights the need for retrieval models that can flexibly and effectively handle both query types without sacrificing overall performance.

Despite this need for balanced retrieval capabilities, fine-tuning dense models to improve accuracy on temporal queries often comes at a significant cost: a noticeable decline in performance on general, non-temporal queries, primarily due to catastrophic forgetting (Goodfellow et al., 2014; Luo et al., 2023). For instance, as illustrated in Figure 1, fine-tuning Contriever (Izacard et al., 2022) on TimeQA (Chen et al., 2021) enhances temporal retrieval but substantially reduces performance on the general-domain dataset Natural Questions (NQ) (Kwiatkowski et al., 2019).

To address this issue, Wu et al. (2024) and Abdallah et al. (2025) proposed a routing-based method that directs temporal queries to a temporally fine-tuned retriever and non-temporal queries to a vanilla retriever, which helps mitigate catastrophic forgetting. However, this approach requires maintaining and operating two separate dense retrievers models, resulting in an increased memory usage, which can be resource-intensive in practical deployments. Furthermore, while this method helps preserve performance across both query types, it heavily relies on accurate classification of queries as temporal or non-temporal, which can result in suboptimal retrieval accuracy, as shown in Table 2.

To address the challenge of handling both temporal and non-temporal queries, we propose Time-Specifier Model Merging (TSM), a novel temporal fine-tuning method. TSM involves separately training specialized retrievers on data subsets corresponding to specific time specifiers (e.g., "in," "after," "between") for temporal queries with explicit expressions. Each retriever develops expertise in a particular temporal constraint. We then merge these specialized models by simply averaging their parameters, allowing the unified retriever to inherit the specialized performance of each time-specifier-specific model.

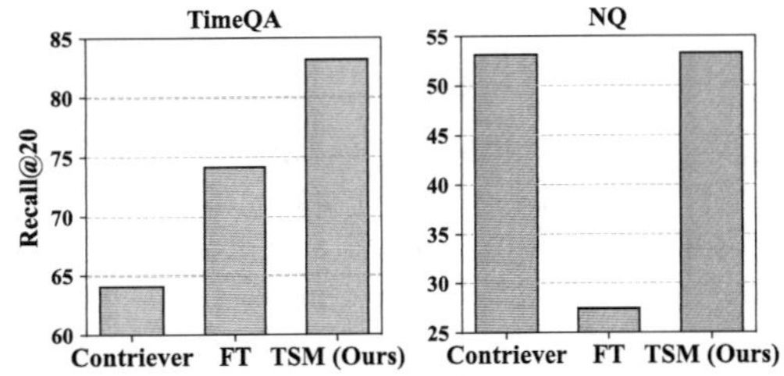

Figure 1: Recall@20 performance of vanilla Contriever, full-parameter fine-tuning (FT), and TSM (Ours) on the temporal dataset TimeQA (green) and the non-temporal general-domain dataset Natural Questions (blue).

This merging process is effective at mitigating catastrophic forgetting because it results in lower-magnitude weight changes–preserving knowledge from both temporal and non-temporal data, rather than overwriting it as in standard fine-tuning (Alexandrov et al., 2024; Yang et al., 2024). As a result, the merged model can more effectively encode temporal relevance associated with each time specifier while still maintaining strong performance on non-temporal queries. Extensive experiments on both temporal and non-temporal datasets demonstrate that TSM significantly improves performance on temporal queries while preserving performance on non-temporal datasets. TSM consistently outperforms alternative temporally-aware training methods, including full fine-tuning, regularization, LoRA, routing, and ensembling.

To summarize, our contributions are threefold:

- We identify and address the critical challenge of improving temporal retrieval performance without compromising non-temporal (general-domain) retrieval accuracy, emphasizing the need for retrieval models that can flexibly handle both query types.
- We propose a novel **Time-Specifier Model Merging (TSM)** method, which fine-tunes separate, specialized retrievers for individual time specifiers and then merges them into a unified model. This method enables precise handling of temporal constraints while effectively preserving general retrieval capabilities.
- Through extensive experiments on both temporal and non-temporal datasets, we demonstrate that TSM significantly improves performance on temporal queries without sacrificing non-temporal retrieval accuracy, consistently outperforming other fine-tuning strategies.

2 Related Work

Temporal Information Retrieval Temporal Information Retrieval (TIR) is a specialized subfield of Information Retrieval (IR) focused on accurately interpreting temporal information in both user queries and documents (Allen, 1983; Alonso et al., 2011). Temporal information refers to specific points in time (e.g., "in 2015"), intervals (e.g., "between 2010 and 2012"), and can be expressed in various forms: *explicit* (e.g., "January 2010"), *relative* (e.g., "tomorrow"), or *implicit* (e.g., "Labor Day") (Kanhabua and Anand, 2016). Temporal queries typically involve time specifiers such as "after" or "between" to define temporal constraints. TIR research addresses challenges such as temporal query analysis, time-aware embedding, and the extraction of temporal expressions to improve temporal retrieval effectiveness. Our work builds on these developments, aiming to enhance retrieval performance for temporally relevant information, with a focus on *explicit* temporal expressions.

Semantic vs. Temporal Focus in Dense Models Dense retrieval models (Karpukhin et al., 2020; Izacard et al., 2022) have advanced Information Retrieval (IR) but still struggle with temporal information retrieval (TIR). This is because their embeddings are primarily optimized for semantic similarity and topical relevance, rather than explicit temporal expressions–a limitation known as *attention bias* (Wu et al., 2024). To address this, recent studies have introduced temporal information masking strategies during pre-training, enabling models to better encode explicit temporal expressions, which leads to improved temporal representations (Rosin et al., 2021; Dhingra et al., 2022; Wang et al., 2023; Cole et al., 2023). Other approaches, such as TempRALM, enhance retrievers with temporal scoring mechanisms to more accurately rank documents based on temporal relevance (Gade and Jetcheva, 2024). While these methods improve retrieval performance for temporal queries, they often overlook the resulting decline in performance on non-temporal queries.

Among the approaches addressing both temporal and non-temporal retrieval using off-the-shelf dense models, Wu et al. (2024) and Abdallah et al. (2025) proposed a routing-based method that directs temporal queries to a retriever fine-tuned on temporal datasets and non-temporal queries to a vanilla retriever, mitigating catastrophic forgetting. While this preserves performance across query types, it heavily relies on accurate query classification, which can result in suboptimal performance. In this study, we focus on fine-tuning off-the-shelf dense retriever models to handle both temporal and non-temporal queries within a single model, eliminating the dependence on additional modules for query classification.

Mitigating Catastrophic Forgetting Catastrophic forgetting occurs when a model, after being fine-tuned on a new task or domain, loses performance or knowledge on previously learned tasks (Goodfellow et al., 2014; Luo et al., 2023). Regularization is a fundamental technique to address this, constraining parameter updates during fine-tuning to preserve pre-trained knowledge (Kirkpatrick et al., 2016; Li and Hoiem, 2016; Triki et al., 2017). Low-Rank Adaptation (LoRA) is another effective approach, which introduces a small number of trainable low-rank matrices while keeping most weights frozen (Hu et al., 2021). LoRA and its variants have shown strong performance in continual and out-of-domain learning by isolating task-specific updates and preserving prior knowledge, helping to reduce catastrophic forgetting (Lee et al., 2023).

Another approach is ensemble learning, which combines the predictions of multiple models–each specialized for different tasks or domains – to achieve balanced performance (Ganaie et al., 2021; Ibomoiye and Sun, 2022; Mohammed and Kora, 2023). However, this approach requires running multiple models simultaneously, increasing both memory usage and inference costs. Routing-based methods have also been proposed, dynamically directing queries to either a fine-tuned or the vanilla model based on the query type (Wu et al., 2024; Abdallah et al., 2025). While routing leverages the strengths of both specialized and general models, its effectiveness depends on accurate query classification and still requires maintaining multiple models, making it resource-intensive in practice.

Model merging has recently emerged as a simple and effective approach to mitigating catastrophic forgetting by flattening high-magnitude weight changes during adaptation, resulting in more stable and higher-quality parameter updates (Alexandrov et al., 2024; Yang et al., 2024). Motivated by these findings, we adopt model merging in this study and propose a novel temporal fine-tuning method. Our method fine-tunes specialized retrievers for individual time specifiers and merges them into a unified model, enabling effective retrieval for both temporal and non-temporal queries.

3 Method

We define the temporal and non-temporal retrieval problem and introduce out method, Time-Specifier Model Merging (TSM).

3.1 Problem Formulation and Preliminaries

We begin by defining the information retrieval task, distinguishing between temporal and non-temporal, and introducing key concepts and notations used throughout our method.

Information Retrieval (IR). IR identifies a subset of documents $D = \{d_1, d_2, \ldots, d_k\}$ from a corpus C that are most relevant to a given user query q. Formally, the retrieval process can be defined as:

$$D = \{d_1, \ldots, d_k\} = \texttt{Retriever}(q, \mathcal{C}), \quad (1)$$

where the `Retriever` function returns the top-k documents from $\mathcal{C}$ ranked by their relevance to q.

Dense Retrieval. Dense retrieval encodes queries and documents into dense vector representations using neural encoders. Let f_θ denote an encoder parameterized by θ, which maps q and d_i to dense vectors:

$$\mathbf{q} = f_\theta(q), \ \mathbf{d}_i = f_\theta(d_i), \ \forall d_i \in \mathcal{C} \quad (2)$$

The relevance score between a query and a document is computed via the dot product of their vector representations:

$$sim(\mathbf{q}, \mathbf{d}_i) = \mathbf{q}^\top \mathbf{d}_i \quad (3)$$

and the retriever selects documents with the highest similarity scores.

Temporal and Non-Temporal Queries. Let Q denote the set of all general-domain queries. The subset of temporal queries $Q_T \subseteq Q$ is defined as:

$$Q_T = \{q_T \in Q \mid q_T = (s, t), s \in \mathcal{S}, t \in \mathcal{T}\} \quad (4)$$

where $\mathcal{S}$ is the set of time specifiers: $\mathcal{S} = \{\text{before}, \text{between}, \ldots\}$, and $\mathcal{T}$ is the set of specific temporal point or period: $\mathcal{T} = \{\text{Apr 2020}, [1990,2000], \ldots\}$. The subset of non-temporal queries $Q_N \subseteq Q$ is given by:

$$Q_N = Q \setminus Q_T \quad (5)$$

such that $Q = Q_T \cup Q_N$ and $Q_T \cap Q_N = \emptyset$.

Objective of Our Method. The objective of our method is to address the newly defined problem of balancing effective temporal retrieval for temporal queries (Q_T) with robust performance on non-temporal queries (Q_N), ensuring that improvements in one do not come at the expense of the other.

Time Specifier	Train	Dev
from $[time_1]$ to $[time_2]$	11,676	2,486
in $[time]$	5,759	1,233
between $[time_1]$ and $[time_2]$	4,888	1,054
after $[time]$	2,741	587
before $[time]$	2,867	609
in early $[time]$s	1,885	438
in late $[time]$s	2,392	474
Total	32,208	6,881

Table 1: Statistics of the augmented TimeQA dataset showing the number of queries containing each time specifier in the training and development sets.

3.2 Time-Specifier Model Merging (TSM)

Now, we introduce our method, TSM, for improving temporal retrieval performance while maintaining strong non-temporal retrieval capabilities. TSM first fine-tunes dense retrieval models on data sampled according to each time specifier, and then merges their parameters to create a unified retriever.

3.2.1 Data Sampling

We utilize TimeQA (Chen et al., 2021) for fine-tuning dense retrievers. Following the TimeQA taxonomy of seven time specifiers–in $[time]$, after $[time]$, before $[time]$, in early $[time]$s, in late $[time]$s, between $[time_1]$ and $[time_2]$, and from $[time_1]$ to $[time_2]$– we categorize the dataset into seven groups based on these specifiers. Each $[time]$ refers to a specific year or a year with a month. However, the original TimeQA training set is imbalanced across the time specifiers. To address this, we use the official TimeQA data processing scrips and annotation labels to augment the comparatively less frequent time specifiers: *after*, *before*, *in early*, and *in late*. As a result, we increase the training set from 25,064 to 32,208 instances and the dev set from 5,348 to 6,881. Detailed statistics for the original dataset are provided in Appendix A.2. Note that we only use answerable questions with gold answers, as non-answerable questions do not have gold answers and therefore cannot be used for contrastive learning, since there would be no positive passages available. Table 1 summarizes the statistics of the augmented dataset for each time specifier.

3.2.2 Specifier-Specific Fine-Tuning

For each time specifier s, we fine-tune a separate dense retriever on the corresponding subset of sampled data. We employ a contrastive learning objective with the InfoNCE loss (Izacard et al., 2022).

For a given temporal query q_T, the loss is defined as:

$$L(q_T, p^+) = -log \frac{e^{sim(q_T, p^+)/\tau}}{e^{sim(q_T, p^+)/\tau} + \sum_{i=1}^{n} e^{sim(q_T, p_i^-)/\tau}},$$

where p^+ is the positive passage (containing the gold answer), $\{p_i^-\}_{i=1}^n$ are n in-batch negative (Izacard et al., 2022) passages, $sim(q_T, p)$ is the dot-product similarity between the temporal query q_T and passages $p = \{p^+, p^-\}$, and τ is a temperature hyperparameter that controls the smoothness of the probability distribution.

3.2.3 Parameter Merging

After fine-tuning specifier-specific models with parameters $\theta_1, ..., \theta_k$, we merge them by simply averaging the parameters (Xiao et al., 2024):

$$\theta_{merged} = \frac{1}{k} \sum_{i=1}^{k} \theta_i. \tag{6}$$

The merged retriever is then used to encode both temporal queries and general, non-temporal queries.

This two-stage approach enables our method to leverage the fine-tuned representations learned from time specifier-specific data while maintaining a merged model for non-temporal retrieval tasks.

4 Experimental Setups

4.1 Datasets

We evaluate on four QA datasets: two that emphasize *temporal* retrieval–TimeQA (Chen et al., 2021) and Nobel Prize (Wu et al., 2024)–and two representing *non-temporal* retrieval tasks–Natural Questions (NQ) (Kwiatkowski et al., 2019) and MS MARCO (Nguyen et al., 2016). Below, we briefly describe each dataset and clarify our usage protocol.

TimeQA (Chen et al., 2021) consists of around 25K time-sensitive questions derived from WikiData (Vrandečić and Krötzsch, 2014). These queries focus on facts that evolve over time, requiring models to perform temporal understanding and reasoning. We evaluate on the original TimeQA test set in a closed-domain scenario, using the official document collection chunked by 100-word segments following Wang et al. (2019) and Karpukhin et al. (2020). **Nobel Prize** (Wu et al., 2024) dataset is a template-based corpus created from structured data on Nobel laureates. It includes about 3.2K time-sensitive queries, and we use the provided corpus and test set. **Natural Questions** (Kwiatkowski et al., 2019) is a benchmark for general QA tasks. We employ the test set from the BEIR benchmark (Thakur et al., 2021) to evaluate retrieval performance on general queries. **MS MARCO** (Nguyen et al., 2016) is a widely used benchmark for open-domain question answering. For evaluation, we use its validation set provided through the BEIR benchmark (Thakur et al., 2021).

4.2 Models

We employ **Contriever** (Izacard et al., 2022) for an *unsupervised* dense retriever, and **Dense Passage Retriever (DPR)** (Karpukhin et al., 2020) for a *supervised* dense retriever, allowing us to assess the effectiveness of baseline methods and our method on both unsupervised and supervised retrievers.

4.3 Baselines

We compare our method, TSM, against the following approaches:

Vanilla Dense Retrievers. Contriever and DPR, using their off-the-shelf checkpoints without any additional fine-tuning.

Full-Parameter Fine-Tuning (FT). Fine-tuning full parameters of Contriever and DPR on the entire TimeQA training set, without any sampling based on time specifier.

FT with Regularization. Full-parameter fine-tuning on the entire TimeQA training set with regularization (Kirkpatrick et al., 2016). Specifically, we use a dropout rate of 0.1 and a weight decay of 0.01 during training. Note that all other methods are trained with the same regularization as it is now fundamental in modern model training.

Low-Rank Adaptation (LoRA). LoRA fine-tuning (Hu et al., 2021) of Contriever and DPR on the entire TimeQA training set.

Routing. A query router that directs temporal queries to the retriever fully fine-tuned on TimeQA and sends general queries to the vanilla retriever, using the router checkpoint provided by Wu et al. (2024). The router is a two-layer feedforward neural network trained on TimeQA and Natural Questions (NQ) to perform binary classification of queries as either temporal or non-temporal.

Ensembling. We combine the outputs of multiple dense retrievers, each trained on a different time specifier. Similarity scores from each retriever are first normalized using min-max normalization for

Method	TimeQA				Nobel Prize				NQ				MS MARCO				Average			
	Recall		nDCG		Recall		nDCG		Recall		nDCG		Recall		nDCG		Recall		nDCG	
	@5	@20	@5	@20	@5	@20	@5	@20	@5	@20	@5	@20	@5	@20	@5	@20	@5	@20	@5	@20
Unsupervised Dense Retriever																				
Contriever	35.29	64.07	22.98	31.49	21.20	51.40	22.34	33.58	29.28	53.13	21.27	28.51	25.24	**45.99**	17.14	**23.20**	27.75	53.65	20.93	29.20
FT	57.40	71.12	45.20	49.25	14.94	39.31	14.05	23.46	11.32	22.69	7.75	11.10	13.80	24.97	9.58	12.80	24.37	39.52	19.15	24.15
FT + Reg	60.30	74.38	46.93	51.10	20.21	51.21	18.67	30.65	13.60	27.43	9.44	13.52	15.87	28.88	10.96	14.68	27.50	45.48	21.50	27.49
LoRA	65.20	80.20	49.63	54.13	11.04	27.52	11.54	17.52	27.06	44.69	20.09	25.47	20.40	37.17	14.14	18.98	30.93	47.40	23.85	29.03
Routing	50.15	74.35	35.36	42.54	25.96	62.42	26.47	40.22	29.28	53.13	21.27	28.51	25.09	45.71	17.04	23.08	32.62	58.90	25.04	33.59
Ensembling	63.46	77.31	48.94	53.04	34.39	71.47	35.13	49.12	25.49	45.65	18.04	24.14	22.36	39.97	15.39	20.51	36.43	58.60	29.38	36.70
TSM (Ours)	**68.73**	**83.49**	**53.45**	**57.89**	**35.33**	**75.58**	**35.73**	**50.83**	**32.58**	**53.26**	**23.66**	**29.95**	**25.26**	44.28	**17.36**	22.92	**40.48**	**64.15**	**32.55**	**40.40**
Supervised Dense Retriever																				
DPR	29.98	48.08	21.08	26.39	22.58	46.52	22.91	31.69	**58.20**	**76.55**	**46.95**	**52.67**	21.97	35.54	15.73	19.66	33.18	51.67	26.67	32.60
FT	52.17	66.20	41.13	45.30	13.75	34.92	13.32	21.35	18.55	30.69	13.83	17.51	6.64	12.70	4.54	6.28	22.78	36.13	18.21	22.61
FT + Reg	49.03	64.39	38.34	42.83	16.33	37.86	15.67	23.72	17.75	31.54	12.86	17.01	7.72	13.99	5.41	7.23	22.71	36.95	18.07	22.70
LoRA	65.64	78.40	51.31	55.12	24.56	50.26	23.98	33.62	47.25	62.95	38.02	42.83	17.87	30.97	12.85	16.62	38.83	55.65	31.54	37.05
Routing	35.25	52.34	25.21	30.24	19.22	42.21	19.68	28.10	**58.20**	**76.55**	**46.95**	**52.67**	21.97	35.53	15.74	19.67	33.66	51.66	26.90	32.67
Ensembling	64.11	76.67	50.38	54.11	30.71	58.02	**30.48**	40.80	43.70	60.87	34.63	39.90	19.91	33.61	14.05	18.01	39.61	57.29	32.39	38.21
TSM (Ours)	**66.61**	**79.21**	**52.53**	**56.30**	**30.78**	**60.63**	30.34	**41.72**	48.07	66.03	38.33	43.85	**23.26**	**37.80**	**16.64**	**20.84**	**42.18**	**60.92**	**34.46**	**40.68**

Table 2: Main results across all datasets and methods, evaluated using Recall and nDCG at top-$\{5, 20\}$ documents, with averages reported for each metric. Results are grouped by base retrievers: *Contriever-based* (unsupervised) and *DPR-based* (supervised). The best performance for each metric is shown in **bold**, and the second-best is underlined.

a given query. The normalized scores for each candidate passage are then averaged across retrievers to produce an ensemble score, and passages are ranked accordingly (Li et al., 2024).

Further implementation details are provided in Appendix A.4.

4.4 Evaluation Metrics

We report our main results evaluating retrieval performance using two standard metrics: **Recall** and **nDCG** at top-$\{5, 20\}$ documents. Recall measures the proportion of relevant documents successfully retrieved, while nDCG evaluates the quality of ranking by considering both relevance and position.

5 Main Results

Table 2 shows our results across four QA datasets: TimeQA and Nobel Prize as temporal datasets, and NQ and MS MARCO as non-temporal datasets. We evaluate both unsupervised (Contriever) and supervised (DPR) dense retrievers and compare our proposed method, TSM, against several baselines, including vanilla retrievers, full fine-tuning (FT), FT with regularization (FT + Reg), LoRA, routing, and ensembling.

On temporal datasets, TSM achieves the strongest performance across all metrics for both Contriever and DPR. For example, On TimeQA, TSM with Contriever achieves substantial improvements over the vanilla retriever. Similarly, on the Nobel Prize dataset–which serves as an out-of-domain temporal test set–TSM achieves the best performance for both unsupervised and supervised retrievers, confirming its strong generalization to unseen temporal data. Although ensembling yields a marginally higher nDCG@5 on Nobel Prize, TSM remains the most robust performer overall.

On non-temporal datasets, TSM also maintains competitive performance, achieving the strongest results across most metrics with both Contriever and DPR. On NQ, where DPR is trained in-domain, vanilla DPR achieves the highest Recall and nDCG. However, DPR-based TSM performs most closely to vanilla DPR on Recall@5/20 and nDCG@5/20, while outperforming FT, LoRA, and ensembling. On Contriever, which is not trained in-domain, TSM significantly improves retrieval effectiveness. On MS MARCO, which is out-of-domain for both Contriever and DPR, TSM achieves highly competitive performance. For Contriever, it matches or exceeds other baselines on Recall@5 and nDCG@5, and trails slightly behind vanilla and Router on Recall@20 and nDCG@20. Similarly, for DPR, TSM outperforms all other methods across all retrieval metrics. This competitive performance on non-temporal datasets can be attributed to TSM's model merging approach, which reduces the magnitude of weight changes during fine-tuning and helps to preserve non-temporal retrieval capabilities while integrating temporal expertise.

Overall, the average results for both Contriever-based and DPR-based TSM show that TSM consistently outperforms other baselines. These results demonstrate that TSM significantly improves temporal retrieval performance without sacrificing effectiveness on non-temporal queries.

6 Analyses

In this section, we systematically examine the effectiveness and underlying mechanisms of our proposed approach.

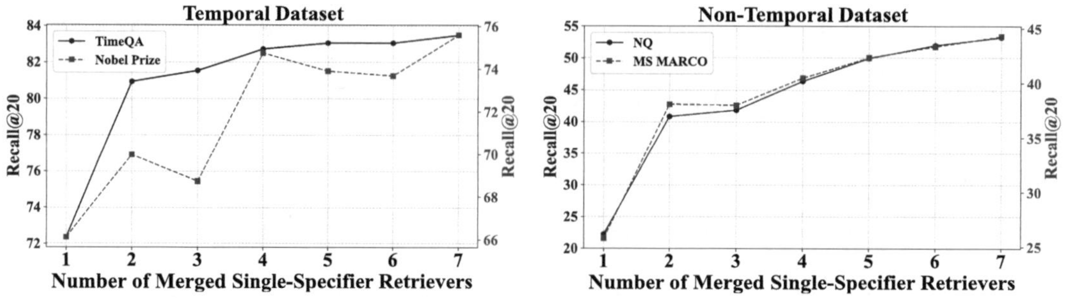

Figure 2: Recall@20 on temporal datasets (TimeQA, Nobel Prize; left) and non-temporal (NQ, MS MARCO; right) datasets as the number of merged single-specifier retrievers increases.

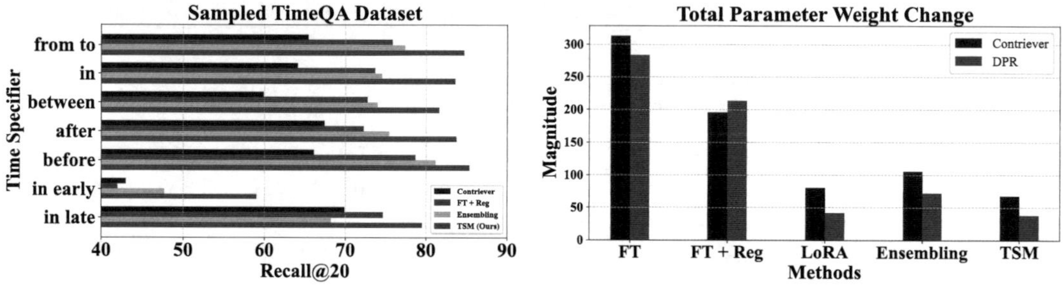

Figure 3: Left: Recall@20 for each time specifier on the TimeQA test set, comparing vanilla Contriever, FT + Reg, Ensembling, and TSM (Ours). Right: Total parameter weight change after fine-tuning for each method, showing how much all network weights are updated. Lower values indicate more stable parameter adaptation.

6.1 Impact of Merging Specifier-Specific Retrievers

Figure 2 shows how retrieval performance changes as the number of merged single-specifier retrievers increases, for temporal (TimeQA and Nobel Prize) and non-temporal (NQ and MS MARCO) datasets. Single-specifier retrievers are merged sequentially in order of data frequency, from most to least frequent, as shown in Table 1.

For the temporal datasets, Recall@20 improves steadily as more single-specifier retrievers are merged. Specifically, for TimeQA (blue line), Recall@20 starts at approximately 72 with a single retriever and rises to about 83 when all seven retrievers are merged (TSM). The Nobel Prize dataset (green line) shows a similar upward trend, increasing from 66 to 76 as more retrievers are merged.

A comparable trend is observed for the non-temporal datasets. For NQ (blue line), Recall@20 increases consistently from about 22 with one retriever to roughly 53 with all seven merged. MS MARCO (green line) also shows a steady improvement, rising from approximately 26 to 45 as the number of merged retrievers increases.

These results demonstrate that merging multiple retrievers, each trained on a specific time specifier, consistently enhances retrieval performance for both temporal and non-temporal queries.

6.2 Coverage Analysis Across Specifiers

Figure 3 (left) compares Contriever, FT + Reg, Ensembling, and TSM on queries grouped by individual time specifiers within the TimeQA test set, reporting Recall@20 for each subset. Across all time specifier categories, TSM achieves the highest recall. For example, on "between $[time_1]$ and $[time_2]$" queries, TSM outperforms Contriever, FT + Reg, and Ensembling by a significant margin.

Ensembling, which averages the outputs of retrievers fine-tuned on each time specifier, consistently improves performance over single retrievers for every specifier. However, while Ensembling enhances the overall recall, it does not match the level of specialization achieved by model merging. By merging retrievers individually trained on each time specifier, TSM inherits the strengths of each specialist model and more precisely captures the nuances of temporal constraints. This approach avoids the narrow focus of single-specifier retrievers and achieves a more robust temporal understanding than fine-tuning or ensembling.

In summary, while Ensembling provides notable gains by leveraging the diversity of multiple retrievers, model merging (TSM) delivers superior coverage and specialization across all time specifiers, resulting in the best balance between specialization and generality for temporally constrained queries.

	Contriever	FT + Reg	TSM (Ours)
Query	Which position did Charles Clarke hold from May 1997 to May 2001?		
Answer	Member of Parliament		
Top-1 Retrieved Passage	Guardian Unlimited Politics – Ask Aristotle: Charles Clarke MP - TheyWorkForYou.com – Charles Clarke MP - BBC News – Charles Clarke profile 17 October 2002 - Interview on Meet The Writers, Monocle 24 with Georgina Godwin - Charles Clarke takes a leading role in promoting animal protection. - Charles Clarke interviewed on Blair, Europe and what Gordon Brown must do next. - The Role of Courts in a Democracy: A Debate Video of Charles Clarke in a Public Debate for the Foundation for Law, Justice and Society, Oxford, 2011	He was a member of the Socialist Campaign Group, Secretary of the All-Party Parliamentary Group for Vietnam, a member of the All-Party Group on Tibet and Chair of the All-Party Parliamentary Group for Cambodia, Member of the Home Affairs Select committee (1992–**97**), and Chairman of the Home Affairs Select Committee from **1997** to 1999 and again from **2001** to 2003.	Charles Rodway Clarke (born 21 September 1950) is a British Labour Party politician, who was the Member of Parliament (MP) for Norwich South **from 1997 until 2010**, and served as Home Secretary from December 2004 until May 2006.
Gold Passage	No	No	Yes

Table 3: Case study comparing retrieved passages using Contriever-based methods: vanilla Contriever, FT + Reg, and TSM (Ours). General, non-temporal information is highlighted in blue, temporal information is highlighted in green, and the gold answer that the gold passage should include is highlighted in yellow. Related information, such as correct temporal information, is in **bold**.

6.3 Parameter Weight Change Magnitude

Figure 3 (right) shows the total parameter weight change after fine-tuning for each method. Full fine-tuning (FT) and FT with regularization (FT + Reg) result in the biggest weight changes, indicating extensive updates that improve temporal retrieval but also increase the risk of catastrophic forgetting, leading to significant performance drops on non-temporal queries. By contrast, LoRA and Ensembling exhibit much smaller parameter weight changes, reflecting more stable adaptation and a better balance between temporal and non-temporal retrieval. Notably, TSM achieves the smallest parameter changes for both Contriever and DPR, highlighting its effectiveness at integrating temporal expertise while preserving non-temporal retrieval capabilities. The minimal weight change in TSM underscores its ability to mitigate catastrophic forgetting and maintain robust performance across both temporal and non-temporal queries.

6.4 Case Study: Qualitative Comparison

Table 3 presents a case study from the TimeQA test set: "*Which position did Charles Clarke hold from May 1997 to May 2001?*" Only TSM successfully retrieved the correct gold passage at top-1, while vanilla Contriever and FT + Reg did not. This qualitative analysis examines the types of information each method prioritizes within the retrieved passages. For clarity, information types are color-coded: temporal features (green), non-temporal features (blue), and the gold answer (yellow).

Vanilla Contriever retrieved a passage with non-temporal information about *Charles Clarke* but lacked explicit temporal details matching the required period. This highlights a tendency to focus on non-temporal content, overlooking crucial temporal context. **FT + Reg** retrieved a passage containing relevant temporal markers ("*1997*" and "*2001*") but failed to associate them with *Charles Clarke*'s positions, demonstrating a bias toward temporal information at the expense of non-temporal context. **TSM** retrieved a passage explicitly stating that Charles Clarke was "*Member of Parliament*" from *1997* to *2010*, directly addressing both the temporal and non-temporal requirements of the query and fully covering the specified time frame.

This case illustrates three key insights: (1) dense retrievers often overlook temporal information; (2) naïve fine-tuning can shift attention too far toward temporal cues, missing essential context; and (3) TSM's approach of merging time-specifier-specialized retrievers effectively balances temporal and non-temporal information, mitigating attention bias.

7 Conclusion

This work addresses the challenge of balancing temporal and non-temporal information retrieval by introducing Time-Specifier Model Merging (TSM), a method designed to address attention bias and catastrophic forgetting. TSM trains specialized retrievers for each time specifier and merges them into a unified model. Experiments on both temporal and non-temporal datasets demonstrate that TSM substantially improves performance on temporally constrained queries while maintaining strong performance on non-temporal queries. Our analysis further show that TSM effectively integrates temporal and non-temporal information, mitigating attention bias and outperforming other baselines. These results establish TSM as a robust and efficient solution for diverse information retrieval tasks.

Limitations

While Time-Specifier Model Merging (TSM) demonstrates strong performance in balancing temporal and non-temporal information retrieval, several limitations remain. First, TSM relies on the availability of labeled data for each time specifier; underrepresented or ambiguous temporal expressions may limit the effectiveness of specialized retrievers and the merged model. Second, the current approach focuses on explicit temporal constraints and may not generalize as well to queries with implicit, relative, or underspecified temporal information. Third, our method currently utilizes only seven time specifiers, which may not capture the full range of temporal constraint nuances present in real-world queries. Extending the number and diversity of time specifiers is an important direction for future work to improve coverage and robustness. Fourth, this study merged retrievers solely using simple parameter merging. Alternative approaches leveraging other model merging techniques, such as layer-wise weight averaging (Jang et al., 2024) and spherical linear interpolation (Goddard et al., 2024) can be further explored. Finally, while our experiments cover several benchmark datasets, further evaluation on more diverse domains and real-world temporal retrieval scenarios is needed to fully assess the generalizability and robustness of TSM.

Ethics Statement

This research advances temporal information retrieval by introducing and evaluating the Time-Specifier Model Merging (TSM) method on publicly available benchmark datasets, including TimeQA, Nobel Prize, Natural Questions, and MS MARCO.

We recognize that improved retrieval models, especially those sensitive to temporal constraints, could potentially be misused to surface misleading, outdated, or biased information. To mitigate these risks, we encourage responsible deployment of TSM and recommend incorporating safeguards such as fact-checking and bias detection when applying this technology in real-world systems.

No human subjects, private data, or proprietary information were involved in this research. All model training and evaluation were conducted in accordance with the terms of use of the respective datasets.

Acknowledgements

This work was supported by the Institute for Information and communications Technology Promotion (IITP) grant funded by the Korea government (MSIT) (No. 2022-0-00010, Development of Korean sign language translation service technology for the deaf in medical environment).

References

Abdelrahman Abdallah, Bhawna Piryani, Jonas Wallat, Avishek Anand, and Adam Jatowt. 2025. Tempretriever: Fusion-based temporal dense passage retrieval for time-sensitive questions. *Preprint*, arXiv:2502.21024.

Anton Alexandrov, Veselin Raychev, Mark Mueller, Ce Zhang, Martin T. Vechev, and Kristina Toutanova. 2024. Mitigating catastrophic forgetting in language transfer via model merging. In *Findings of the Association for Computational Linguistics: EMNLP 2024, Miami, Florida, USA, November 12-16, 2024*, pages 17167–17186. Association for Computational Linguistics.

James F. Allen. 1983. Maintaining knowledge about temporal intervals. *Commun. ACM*, 26(11):832–843.

Omar Alonso, Jannik Strötgen, Ricardo Baeza-Yates, and Michael Gertz. 2011. Temporal information retrieval: Challenges and opportunities. In *WWW2011 Workshop on Linked Data on the Web, Hyderabad, India, March 29, 2011*, volume 813 of *CEUR Workshop Proceedings*, pages 1–8. CEUR-WS.org.

Wenhu Chen, Xinyi Wang, and William Yang Wang. 2021. A dataset for answering time-sensitive questions. In *Proceedings of the Neural Information Processing Systems Track on Datasets and Benchmarks 1, NeurIPS Datasets and Benchmarks 2021, December 2021, virtual.*

Jeremy R. Cole, Aditi Chaudhary, Bhuwan Dhingra, and Partha Talukdar. 2023. Salient span masking for temporal understanding. In *Proceedings of the 17th Conference of the European Chapter of the Association for Computational Linguistics*, pages 3052–3060, Dubrovnik, Croatia. Association for Computational Linguistics.

Bhuwan Dhingra, Jeremy R. Cole, Julian Martin Eisenschlos, Daniel Gillick, Jacob Eisenstein, and William W. Cohen. 2022. Time-aware language models as temporal knowledge bases. *Trans. Assoc. Comput. Linguistics*, 10:257–273.

Anoushka Gade and Jorjeta G. Jetcheva. 2024. It's about time: Incorporating temporality in retrieval augmented language models. *CoRR*, abs/2401.13222.

Mudasir Ahmad Ganaie, Minghui Hu, Mohammad Tanveer, and Ponnuthurai N. Suganthan. 2021. Ensemble deep learning: A review. *CoRR*, abs/2104.02395.

Charles Goddard, Shamane Siriwardhana, Malikeh Ehghaghi, Luke Meyers, Vladimir Karpukhin, Brian Benedict, Mark McQuade, and Jacob Solawetz. 2024. Arcee's mergekit: A toolkit for merging large language models. In *Proceedings of the 2024 Conference on Empirical Methods in Natural Language Processing: Industry Track*, pages 477–485.

Ian J. Goodfellow, Mehdi Mirza, Xia Da, Aaron C. Courville, and Yoshua Bengio. 2014. An empirical investigation of catastrophic forgeting in gradient-based neural networks. In *2nd International Conference on Learning Representations, ICLR 2014, Banff, AB, Canada, April 14-16, 2014, Conference Track Proceedings*.

Edward J. Hu, Yelong Shen, Phillip Wallis, Zeyuan Allen-Zhu, Yuanzhi Li, Shean Wang, and Weizhu Chen. 2021. Lora: Low-rank adaptation of large language models. *CoRR*, abs/2106.09685.

Domor Mienye Ibomoiye and Yanxia Sun. 2022. A survey of ensemble learning: Concepts, algorithms, applications, and prospects. *IEEE Access*, 10:99129–99149.

Gautier Izacard, Mathilde Caron, Lucas Hosseini, Sebastian Riedel, Piotr Bojanowski, Armand Joulin, and Edouard Grave. 2022. Unsupervised dense information retrieval with contrastive learning. *Trans. Mach. Learn. Res.*, 2022.

Dong-Hwan Jang, Sangdoo Yun, and Dongyoon Han. 2024. Model stock: All we need is just a few fine-tuned models. *Preprint*, arXiv:2403.19522.

Nattiya Kanhabua and Avishek Anand. 2016. Temporal information retrieval. In *Proceedings of the 39th International ACM SIGIR Conference on Research and Development in Information Retrieval*, SIGIR '16, page 1235–1238, New York, NY, USA. Association for Computing Machinery.

Vladimir Karpukhin, Barlas Oguz, Sewon Min, Patrick S. H. Lewis, Ledell Wu, Sergey Edunov, Danqi Chen, and Wen-tau Yih. 2020. Dense passage retrieval for open-domain question answering. In *Proceedings of the 2020 Conference on Empirical Methods in Natural Language Processing, EMNLP 2020, Online, November 16-20, 2020*, pages 6769–6781. Association for Computational Linguistics.

Urvashi Khandelwal, Omer Levy, Dan Jurafsky, Luke Zettlemoyer, and Mike Lewis. 2020. Generalization through memorization: Nearest neighbor language models. In *8th International Conference on Learning Representations, ICLR 2020, Addis Ababa, Ethiopia, April 26-30, 2020*. OpenReview.net.

James Kirkpatrick, Razvan Pascanu, Neil C. Rabinowitz, Joel Veness, Guillaume Desjardins, Andrei A. Rusu, Kieran Milan, John Quan, Tiago Ramalho, Agnieszka Grabska-Barwinska, Demis Hassabis, Claudia Clopath, Dharshan Kumaran, and Raia Hadsell. 2016. Overcoming catastrophic forgetting in neural networks. *CoRR*, abs/1612.00796.

Tom Kwiatkowski, Jennimaria Palomaki, Olivia Redfield, Michael Collins, Ankur P. Parikh, Chris Alberti, Danielle Epstein, Illia Polosukhin, Jacob Devlin, Kenton Lee, Kristina Toutanova, Llion Jones, Matthew Kelcey, Ming-Wei Chang, Andrew M. Dai, Jakob Uszkoreit, Quoc Le, and Slav Petrov. 2019. Natural questions: a benchmark for question answering research. *Trans. Assoc. Comput. Linguistics*, 7:452–466.

Yunshi Lan, Gaole He, Jinhao Jiang, Jing Jiang, Wayne Xin Zhao, and Ji-Rong Wen. 2021. A survey on complex knowledge base question answering: Methods, challenges and solutions. *CoRR*, abs/2105.11644.

Hyunji Lee, Luca Soldaini, Arman Cohan, Minjoon Seo, and Kyle Lo. 2023. Back to basics: A simple recipe for improving out-of-domain retrieval in dense encoders. *CoRR*, abs/2311.09765.

Patrick S. H. Lewis, Ethan Perez, Aleksandra Piktus, Fabio Petroni, Vladimir Karpukhin, Naman Goyal, Heinrich Küttler, Mike Lewis, Wen-tau Yih, Tim Rocktäschel, Sebastian Riedel, and Douwe Kiela. 2020. Retrieval-augmented generation for knowledge-intensive NLP tasks. In *Advances in Neural Information Processing Systems 33: Annual Conference on Neural Information Processing Systems 2020, NeurIPS 2020, December 6-12, 2020, virtual*.

Mingda Li, Xinyu Li, Yifan Chen, Wenfeng Xuan, and Weinan Zhang. 2024. Unraveling and mitigating retriever inconsistencies in retrieval-augmented large language models. In *Findings of the Association for Computational Linguistics, ACL 2024, Bangkok, Thailand and virtual meeting, August 11-16, 2024*, pages 4833–4850. Association for Computational Linguistics.

Zhizhong Li and Derek Hoiem. 2016. Learning without forgetting. In *Computer Vision - ECCV 2016 - 14th European Conference, Amsterdam, The Netherlands, October 11-14, 2016, Proceedings, Part IV*, volume 9908 of *Lecture Notes in Computer Science*, pages 614–629. Springer.

Ilya Loshchilov and Frank Hutter. 2017. Fixing weight decay regularization in adam. *CoRR*, abs/1711.05101.

Yun Luo, Zhen Yang, Fandong Meng, Yafu Li, Jie Zhou, and Yue Zhang. 2023. An empirical study of catastrophic forgetting in large language models during continual fine-tuning. *CoRR*, abs/2308.08747.

Ammar Mohammed and Rania Kora. 2023. A comprehensive review on ensemble deep learning: Opportunities and challenges. *J. King Saud Univ. Comput. Inf. Sci.*, 35(2):757–774.

Tri Nguyen, Mir Rosenberg, Xia Song, Jianfeng Gao, Saurabh Tiwary, Rangan Majumder, and Li Deng. 2016. MS MARCO: A human generated machine reading comprehension dataset. *CoRR*, abs/1611.09268.

Guy D. Rosin, Ido Guy, and Kira Radinsky. 2021. Time masking for temporal language models. *CoRR*, abs/2110.06366.

Nandan Thakur, Nils Reimers, Andreas Rücklé, Abhishek Srivastava, and Iryna Gurevych. 2021. BEIR: A heterogeneous benchmark for zero-shot evaluation of information retrieval models. In *Proceedings of the Neural Information Processing Systems Track on Datasets and Benchmarks 1, NeurIPS Datasets and Benchmarks 2021, December 2021, virtual.*

Amal Rannen Triki, Rahaf Aljundi, Matthew B. Blaschko, and Tinne Tuytelaars. 2017. Encoder based lifelong learning. In *IEEE International Conference on Computer Vision, ICCV 2017, Venice, Italy, October 22-29, 2017*, pages 1329–1337. IEEE Computer Society.

Denny Vrandečić and Markus Krötzsch. 2014. Wikidata: a free collaborative knowledgebase. *Commun. ACM*, 57(10):78–85.

Jiexin Wang, Adam Jatowt, Masatoshi Yoshikawa, and Yi Cai. 2023. Bitimebert: Extending pre-trained language representations with bi-temporal information. In *Proceedings of the 46th International ACM SIGIR Conference on Research and Development in Information Retrieval*, pages 812–821.

Zhiguo Wang, Patrick Ng, Xiaofei Ma, Ramesh Nallapati, and Bing Xiang. 2019. Multi-passage BERT: A globally normalized BERT model for open-domain question answering. In *Proceedings of the 2019 Conference on Empirical Methods in Natural Language Processing and the 9th International Joint Conference on Natural Language Processing (EMNLP-IJCNLP)*, pages 5878–5882, Hong Kong, China. Association for Computational Linguistics.

Feifan Wu, Lingyuan Liu, Wentao He, Ziqi Liu, Zhiqiang Zhang, Haofen Wang, and Meng Wang. 2024. Time-sensitve retrieval-augmented generation for question answering. In *Proceedings of the 33rd ACM International Conference on Information and Knowledge Management, CIKM 2024, Boise, ID, USA, October 21-25, 2024*, pages 2544–2553. ACM.

Shitao Xiao, Zheng Liu, Peitian Zhang, and Xingrun Xing. 2024. Lm-cocktail: Resilient tuning of language models via model merging. In *Findings of the Association for Computational Linguistics, ACL 2024, Bangkok, Thailand and virtual meeting, August 11-16, 2024*, pages 2474–2488. Association for Computational Linguistics.

Enneng Yang, Li Shen, Guibing Guo, Xingwei Wang, Xiaochun Cao, Jie Zhang, and Dacheng Tao. 2024. Model merging in llms, mllms, and beyond: Methods, theories, applications and opportunities. *CoRR*, abs/2408.07666.

Appendix

A Additional Experimental Setups

A.1 Model Weights

All model weights used for both the vanilla model and training were obtained from Hugging Face as off-the-shelf checkpoints, without any additional training. Below, we provide the exact Hugging Face model names for the weights used in our experiments:

Contriever:

- `facebook/contriever`

DPR:

- `facebook/dpr-question_encoder-multiset-base`
- `facebook/dpr-ctx_encoder-multiset-base`

A.2 TimeQA Dataset Statistics

Time Specifier	Original Train	Original Dev	Augmented Train	Augmented Dev
from $[time_1]$ to $[time_2]$	11,676	2,486	-	-
in $[time]$	5,759	1,233	-	-
between $[time_1]$ and $[time_2]$	4,888	1,054	-	-
after $[time]$	903	201	2,741	587
before $[time]$	973	181	2,867	609
in early $[time]$s	309	82	1,885	438
in late $[time]$s	473	91	2,392	474
Total	24,981	5,238	32,208	6,881

Table 4: Statistics for the original and augmented TimeQA datasets illustrate the number of queries containing each time specifier in the training and development sets. To mitigate bias, only the data for the comparatively less frequent time specifiers–after, before, in early, and in late–were augmented.

A.3 Temporal Queries in Non-Temporal Datasets

Dataset	Split	Total Queries	Temporal Queries	Temporal Query (%)
NQ	Test	3,452	53	1.54%
MS MARCO	Dev	509,962	232	0.05%

Table 5: Statistics of *explicit* temporal queries within the test splits of two non-temporal datasets, NQ (Kwiatkowski et al., 2019) and MS MARCO (Nguyen et al., 2016). The table reports the total number of queries, the count of temporal queries, and their proportion in each dataset.

A.4 Implementation Details

For all fine-tuning experiments, each method is trained for five epochs and per-GPU batch size of 64 using on an NVIDIA A100 80GB. We use the publicly available code from Izacard et al. (2022) and follow their hyperparameter settings: a learning rate of 1e-4, the AdamW optimizer (Loshchilov and Hutter, 2017) with a linear learning rate scheduler, and a temperature parameter τ set to 1.0. Model evaluation is performed every 50 steps based on top-1 accuracy, and the best-performing model is selected accordingly. Additionally, five in-batch negative passages are incorporated in the contrastive learning objective.

B Additional Experimental Results

B.1 Coverage Analysis Across Specifiers

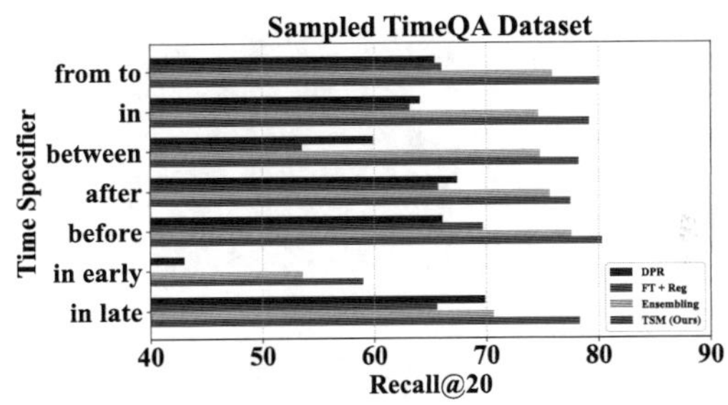

Figure 4: Recall@20 for each time specifier on the TimeQA test set, comparing retrieval performance of vanilla DPR, FT + Reg, Ensembling, and TSM (Ours)

Figure 4 compares DPR, FT + Reg, Ensembling, and TSM on queries grouped by individual time specifiers within the TimeQA test set, reporting Recall@20 for each subset. Across all time specifier categories, TSM achieves the highest recall. For example, on "between $[time_1]$ and $[time_2]$" queries, TSM outperforms DPR, FT + Reg, and ensembling by a significant margin.

Ensembling, which averages the outputs of retrievers fine-tuned on each time specifier, consistently improves performance over single retrievers for every specifier. However, while ensembling enhances the overall recall, it does not match the level of specialization achieved by model merging. By merging retrievers individually trained on each time specifier, TSM inherits the strengths of each specialist model and more precisely captures the nuances of temporal constraints. This approach avoids the narrow focus of single-specifier retrievers and achieves a more robust temporal understanding than simply fine-tuning or ensembling.

In summary, while ensembling provides notable gains by leveraging the diversity of multiple retrievers, model merging (TSM) delivers superior coverage and specialization across all time specifiers, resulting in the best balance between specialization and generality for temporally constrained queries.

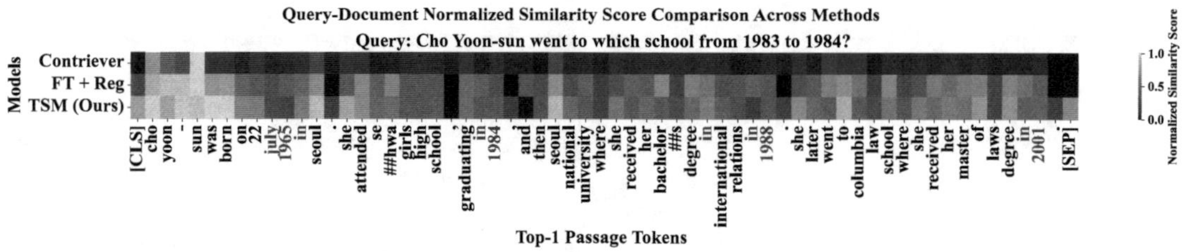

Figure 5: Heatmap of normalized query document similarity scores for the query "*Cho Yoon-sun went to which school from 1983 to 1984?*" comparing vanilla Contriever, FT + Reg, and TSM (Ours). Passage tokens in green represent temporal information.

B.2 Parameter Weight Change Magnitude of Each Single-Specifier Model

Time Specifier	Training Set Size	Weight Change Magnitude
from $[time_1]$ to $[time_2]$	11,676	98.41
in $[time]$	5,759	88.17
between $[time_1]$ and $[time_2]$	4,888	98.87
after $[time]$	2,741	55.60
before $[time]$	2,867	55.98
in early $[time]$s	1,885	72.16
in late $[time]$s	2,392	56.61
Ensembling	-	75.11
TSM (Ours)	-	67.41

Table 6: Parameter weight change magnitude for models fine-tuned on individual time specifiers, compared to Ensembling and TSM. The Ensembling value represents the average weight change magnitude across all single-specifier retrievers. Lower values indicate more stable adaptation.

B.3 Case Study: Query-Document Similarity Score Analysis

Figure 5 shows a heatmap of normalized similarity scores between the TimeQA query "*Cho Yoon-sun went to which school from 1983 to 1984?*" and the same top-1 retrieved passage, comparing Contriever, FT + Reg, and TSM. The x-axis represents the tokenized passage.

Vanilla Contriever mainly highlights non-temporal tokens, such as the person ("*Cho Yoon-sun*") and location ("*Seoul*"), while largely ignoring temporal tokens such as "*1984*." This indicates that without temporal-specific training, Contriever overlooks time constraints and focuses on general keywords. **FT + Reg** increases attention to temporal information, especially the correct year "*1984*," while still attending to non-temporal tokens, though less effectively than TSM. This demonstrates that temporal fine-tuning helps the model better align temporal aspects of queries and passages. **TSM** further sharpens this focus, concentrating on the relevant temporal token "*1984*" and reducing attention to irrelevant years, while also maintaining strong attention to non-temporal features. This indicates a more balanced integration of temporal and non-temporal information.

Overall, these results show that while Contriever neglects temporal cues, FT + Reg improves temporal sensitivity, and TSM achieves the best balance, accurately attending both temporal spans and key non-temporal details. This balanced attention enables TSM to deliver robust retrieval performance for both temporal and non-temporal queries.

EdTec-ItemGen: Enhancing Retrieval-Augmented Item Generation Through Key Point Extraction

Alonso Palomino[1,2] David Buschhüter[1] Roland Roller[1]
Niels Pinkwart[1] Benjamin Paaßen[1,2]

[1] German Research Center for Artificial Intelligence (DFKI), Germany, `<first>.<last>@dfki.de`
[2] Bielefeld University, Germany, `<first>.<last>@techfak.uni-bielefeld.de`

Abstract

A major bottleneck in exam construction involves designing test items (i.e., questions) that accurately reflect key content from domain-aligned curricular materials. For instance, during formative assessments in vocational education and training (VET), exam designers must generate updated test items that assess student learning progress while covering the full breadth of topics in the curriculum. Large language models (LLMs) can partially support this process, but effective use requires careful prompting and task-specific understanding. We propose a new key point extraction method for retrieval-augmented item generation that enhances the process of generating test items with LLMs. We exhaustively evaluated our method using a TREC-RAG approach, finding that prompting LLMs with key content rather than directly using full curricular text passages significantly improves item quality regarding key information coverage by 8%. To demonstrate these findings, we release EdTec-ItemGen, a retrieval-augmented item generation demo tool to support item generation in education.

1 Introduction

A key challenge in educational measurement is to construct high-quality exam questions or "test items" that effectively differentiate varying levels of student competency. Assessment organizations rely on subject matter experts to extract essential content from domain-specific curriculum materials for item construction (Lane et al., 2016). Thus, generative natural language processing-based techniques for automated item generation (AIG) have gained interest in educational measurement to reduce the high costs and labor of manual test item creation (Circi et al., 2023; Kyllonen et al., 2024).

The widespread adoption of large language models (LLMs) has significantly encouraged employing generative NLP for AIG (Laverghetta Jr. and Licato, 2023; Gorgun and Bulut, 2024; Chan et al., 2025). Despite their impressive performance across various subtasks, LLMs often struggle with hallucinations, bias, and limited domain-specific knowledge, diminishing their effectiveness in specialized tasks (Zhang et al., 2023; Huber and Niklaus, 2025; Gonen et al., 2025). Retrieval augmented generation (RAG) (Lewis et al., 2020; Fan et al., 2024) offers a solution by integrating domain-relevant knowledge, enhancing customization, reducing hallucinations, and improving access to authoritative and up-to-date information.

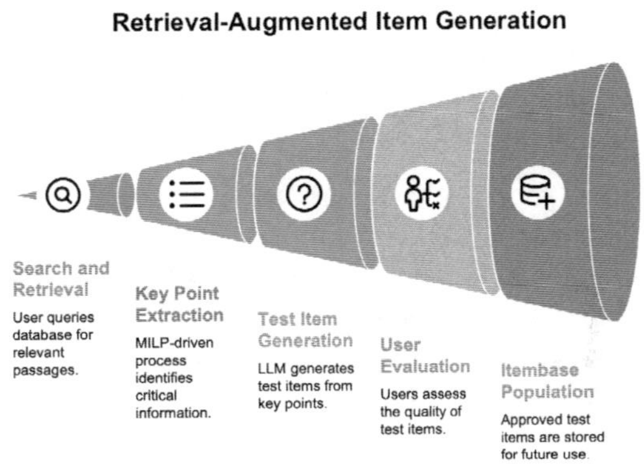

Figure 1: EdTec-ItemGen automates VET item generation by retrieving passages, extracting key points, and prompting an LLM to create test items.

To support bfz[1], one of the largest German Vocational Education and Training (VET) providers in manual item generation tasks, we deployed EdTec-ItemGen[2], a RAG platform for AIG, that leverages a new mixed-integer linear programming driven method (MILP-driven KPE) for key point extraction to assist educators in designing items for formative assessments.

Figure 1 summarizes the operational flow of

[1] `https://www.bfz.de/`
[2] System demonstration and code available at: `https://edtec-itemgen.xyz`

Proceedings of the 3rd Workshop on Towards Knowledgeable Foundation Models (KnowFM), pages 14–25
August 1, 2025 ©2025 Association for Computational Linguistics

EdTec-ItemGen for supporting item generation tasks. The process begins with users retrieving relevant VET passages, pre-extracted from educational materials, using semantic search. An extractive summarization step then identifies the most salient factoids or "key points" through the proposed MILP-driven KPE approach and similarity scoring (see Section 3). These key points are subsequently used to instruct an LLM to generate new test items. Finally, test item designers evaluate and filter high-quality items via EdTec-ItemGen's user interface, which are later added to an internal item base for exam assembly and construction. Our work contributes as follows:

- Building on prior research on item retrieval for exam assembly and calibration (Palomino et al., 2024, 2025), we proposed a novel MILP-driven key point extraction method to enhance key information coverage on augmented generated items.
- An exhaustive evaluation and performance analysis, following the TREC-RAG 2024 evaluation approach (Pradeep et al., 2024a,b), demonstrating how the proposed key point extraction method enhances the retrieval-augmented item generation process (see Section 4).
- We deployed and released a fork multilingual system demonstration version of EdTec-ItemGen, our industry partner's RAG platform for AIG.

Section 3 presents our MILP-based key point extraction; Section 4 presents its evaluation under the TREC-RAG framework. Section 5 provides an application and demo system overview, and Section 6 concludes with future directions.

2 Related Work

To mitigate the complexity of manual test item construction, educators adopted automated approaches to simplify its development (Lane et al., 2016; Rudolph et al., 2019; Circi et al., 2023). Prior research in Automated Item Generation (AIG) transitioned from classic NLP methods, including shallow parsing, term and topic extraction, and the use of semantic resources like WordNet (Brown et al., 2005; Mitkov et al., 2006; Rus et al., 2011; Heilman and Smith, 2010; Chali and Hasan, 2015), to neural architectures including graph-neural networks and transformer-based models for AIG (Chan and Fan, 2019; Tuan et al., 2020; Qu et al., 2021; Yoshimi et al., 2023; Jahangir et al., 2024; Jamshidi and Chali, 2025).

The rise of LLMs has led educators to use prompt-based generative NLP for AIG (Dugan et al., 2022; Kyllonen et al., 2024); for example, Wu et al. (2024) propose a two-step multimodal framework that merges LLM-generated sub-questions about related entities into coherent items. Lin et al. (2024) proposed TASE-CoT, a few-shot method for type-aware semantic extraction of relevant item types and phrases to aid LLMs in generating refined items and answers requiring reasoning across multiple documents. Guo et al. (2024) generate knowledge-base questions by extracting a skeleton of interrogatives and auxiliaries from graph triples to steer GPT-3.5. Ashok Kumar and Lan (2024) fine-tune LLaMA-2 with negative Socratic example augmentation and direct preference optimization to boost programming-item validity.

Prior work includes Pochiraju et al. (2023), which maps sentences via ConceptNet/WordNet rules, and Guinet et al. (2024), which fine-tunes LLMs for exam generation and filters items by syntax, incorrectness, self-containment, and embedding similarity. Poon et al. (2024) show that few-shot LLM prompts yield more higher-order Chinese reading items than traditional methods, while Mucciaccia et al. (2025) combine role-based prompts, glossaries, one-shot examples, and chain-of-thought reasoning to generate and evaluate university-level items. Although LLM prompting is widespread in AIG, hallucinations, knowledge-reliability issues, and opaque reasoning persist without careful prompt design (Fan et al., 2024). To address these limitations, retrieval-augmented generation (RAG) emerged as a popular strategy to enhance generative NLP performance (Lewis et al., 2020; Fan et al., 2024).

This work introduces a novel key point extraction method to enhance the retrieval-augmented item generation process in German Vocational Education and Training (VET). We released a public fork of our industry partner's internal tool and APIs to demonstrate this. The closest studies are Pochiraju et al. (2023), which maps sentences via ConceptNet/WordNet rules, and Guinet et al. (2024), which fine-tunes LLMs for exam generation and filters items by length, incorrectness, self-containment, and embedding similarity. However, our simpler approach applies extractive summarization to VET passages, isolating key nuggets and preserving only essential content. Ultimately, we evaluated our approach with Pradeep et al. (2024a,b) framework.

3 Enhancing Augmented Item Generation Via Key Point Extraction

Key Point Extraction (KPE) is an extractive summarization approach that selects high-level factoid statements capturing the main aspects of a passage (Bar-Haim et al., 2020, 2021). Because item designers already distill such facts from domain-specific VET contents, we add KPE to our item-generation RAG pipeline to replicate this manual process.

MILP-driven KPE After splitting the input passages into sentences, we employed Jina-ColBERT[3] (Jha et al., 2024), an efficient multi-vector neural re-ranker model, to compute sentence embeddings and derive a similarity score for each pair of candidate sentences, ultimately producing a similarity matrix. Then, we apply a Mixed-Integer Linear Programming driven formulation (MILP-driven KPE) that aims to balance maximizing the relevance, while minimizing redundancy of a set of candidate sentences. Essentially, our goal is to subselect K candidate sentences with maximum relevance to the original input passage, such that their pairwise similarity is minimized. Assume we have m candidate sentences, each with a relevance score $r_1, \ldots, r_m$ relative to the original input passage and a pairwise similarity matrix $S \in \mathbb{R}^{m \times m}$. Then, we aim to solve:

$$\min_{\vec{x} \in \{0,1\}^m} \quad \lambda \cdot \vec{x}^T \cdot S \cdot \vec{x} - \vec{r}^T \cdot \vec{x}$$
$$\text{such that} \quad \vec{1}^T \cdot \vec{x} = K, \qquad (1)$$

The objective in Eq. (1) formulates the task as a quadratic knapsack problem (Pisinger, 2007). It selects exactly K sentences, rewarding their individual relevance while penalizing pairwise similarity (redundancy), with λ controlling the relevance-redundancy trade-off. We linearize it as a MILP problem with Glover and Woolsey (1974) method:

$$\begin{aligned} \min_{\vec{x} \in \{0,1\}^m, \vec{z} \in \mathbb{R}^m} \quad & \lambda \cdot \vec{1}^T \cdot \vec{z} - \vec{r}^T \cdot \vec{x} \\ \text{such that} \quad & \vec{1}^T \cdot \vec{x} = K, && (2) \\ & l_i \cdot x_i \leq z_i \leq u_i \cdot x_i && \forall i \\ & \vec{s}_i^T \cdot \vec{x} - u_i \cdot (1 - x_i) \leq z_i && \forall i \\ & z_i \leq \vec{s}_i^T \cdot \vec{x} - l_i \cdot (1 - x_i) && \forall i \end{aligned}$$

where $\vec{s}_i$ is the i-th column of S, z_i is a slack variable expressing $\sum_{j \neq i} s_{i,j} \cdot x_j$, $l_i = -\sum_{j=1}^{m} |s_{i,j}|$ is a lower-bound for z_i and $u_i = \sum_{j=1}^{m} |s_{i,j}|$ is an upper-bound for z_i. Eq. (2) replaces the quadratic term with linear constraints that add one slack variable per sentence, set to the sum of its similarities to the selected sentences, making the objective linear. By employing similarity scoring and linearized constrains, our method extracts key statements efficiently.

4 Experiments and Results

Although LLMs have been shown to be more effective as weak labelers when combined with custom models like DistilBART rather than for direct extractive summarization (Mishra et al., 2023), training these models requires high-quality ground truth data, careful prompt design, and challenges for optimizing task-specific objectives. Furthermore, LLM's reliance on superficial features like sentence position rather than distinguishing content importance may make LLMs encounter challenges in extractive summarization tasks (Zhang et al., 2023). Therefore, we hypothesize that applying MILP-driven KPE to instruct an LLM in item generation can significantly improve both information coverage and the quality of test items, while reducing the reliance on resource-intensive training iterations.

4.1 Dataset

As documents for retrieval, we utilized a sample corpus of 1,110 VET passages drawn from bfz's proprietary teaching materials, covering nine high-demand occupational VET topics relevant to the German job market. These topics range from "German Language Competence" and "Use of Technology" to "Storage and Logistics" and "Content Creation" (see Appendix A1 for more details).

4.2 Passage Retrieval

We employed a dense retrieval approach to model the retrieval step, building on prior research in item retrieval for exam assembly (Palomino et al., 2024, 2025). We used Reimers and Gurevych (2019) [4] embeddings with the `faiss` library (Douze et al., 2024) to efficiently perform approximate nearest neighbor search, with ten topic skill queries over the VET corpus. To ensure a realistic search and retrieval scenario, these queries were created using

[3] https://huggingface.co/jinaai/jina-colbert-v2

[4] https://huggingface.co/sentence-transformers/paraphrase-multilingual-MiniLM-L12-v2

synonymic terms rather than the actual topic labels available in the VET corpus.

4.3 Augmented Item Generation

Given a ranked list of the top 25 relevant VET passages retrieved via dense retrieval, we investigated two setups:

1. **With MILP-driven KPE:** After extracting the top 15 key points using MILP-driven KPE, we prompted GPT-4o to generate a test item based on these points.
2. **Without MILP-driven KPE:** We instructed GPT-4o to directly derive the top 15 key statements from a given passage and then, with that information, generate a test item.

Overall, both setups were used prompts for instructing GPT-4o[5] to generate new test items (Refer to appendix A.2 for more details). While for setup (1), the underlying assumption is that the factoid extraction step will reveal the most important information leading to better prompts that produce better augmented generated items. For setup (2), the assumption is that a single prompt instructing the LLM to first identify the top key factoids from a given passage will be sufficient to generate higher-quality items that effectively cover the passage's most essential statements.

4.4 Evaluation Approach

To assess the performance of our experimental setups during the augmented item generation phase, we employed Pradeep et al. (2024a,b) TREC-RAG style automated ad-hoc evaluation approach. Based on Voorhees and Buckland (2003), the TREC-RAG evaluation approach involves using the AutoNuggetizer framework by harnessing an LLM to derive a concise set of factoid units that can be binary evaluated based on whether they contain either "Vital", "Ok" or "Not Vital" *information nuggets* required to address a given information need. For each passage in our VET corpus, we instructed GPT-4o to extract 30 information nuggets and subsequently select and label the top 20 most relevant ones as ground truth for final evaluation. While nuggets containing essential information for generating comprehensive items are labeled as "vital", nuggets with valuable yet non-essential information are labeled as "okay". Subsequently, we evaluated the augmented generated responses against the created nuggets by instructing GPT-4o to numerically determine whether each nugget was fully, partially, or not supported by each generated item response. We then computed the four metrics proposed by Pradeep et al. (2024a), providing an exhaustive evaluation of information coverage across the augmented test item responses produced by GPT-4o:

1. **Vital Strict (Vstrict):** Applies strict matching criteria, counting only for full support matches (i.e., 1.0 and 0.0 respectively).
2. **Vital (V):** Calculates the average score for nuggets labeled as "vital" using a scoring system with three levels (1.0 for full support, 0.5 for partial support, and 0 for no support).
3. **Weighted (W):** It assigns weights of 1.0 to vital nuggets and 0.5 to okay nuggets, then calculates the average by dividing the total vital nugget score by the sum of vital nuggets plus half the number of okay nuggets.
4. **All (A):** The average across all nuggets, both vital and okay, using the same three-level scoring system to assess the broadest measure of generated responses completeness.

Additionally, as a proxy to assess the quality of the augmented generated test items, we instructed GPT-4o to rate grammatical quality, readability, and succinctness on a scale from 1.0 to 5.0. We also measured the length of each item. While prompting GPT-4o we employed `instructor` library enforcing consistent prompt formatting and deterministic API calls fixing the temperature parameter to 0. Similarly to Voorhees and Buckland (2003) and Pradeep et al. (2024a), by combining the above metrics, we systematically quantified key factual coverage and clarity across augmented generated item responses.

4.5 Results

Based on Pradeep et al. (2024a,b) TREC-RAG framework, we evaluated the impact of integrating our new MILP-driven KPE method by assessing the information coverage and quality of generated test items. Table 1 summarizes the results metrics for the different levels of information coverage and item quality. From an information coverage perspective, regarding how well EdTec-ItemGen's produced items covering essential information necessary for generating good multiple-choice test items, when employing MILP-driven KPE, we observed an increased Vstrict score from 0.29 to 0.36 (e.g.,

[5] `https://openai.com/index/hello-gpt-4o/`

+0.07 absolute, +24.14% relative). Similarly, as for how well, on average, full and partial essential information nuggets were matched in the augmented generated response, we observed an absolute increase of 7% from 0.35 to 0.42 in the Vital (V) score. While evaluating by weighting the importance of ground truth nuggets based on their relevance (vital Vs. ok), we observed an improvement of 6% when using MILP-driven KPE extraction to instruct GPT-4o in creating multiple-choice test items. When considering all metrics, that is, when averaging Vstrict, V, and W scores, when employing MILP-driven KPE, we observed an average improvement of 8% over GPT-4o augmented generation responses. From an item quality perspective, we observed improvements in grammatical and readability scores when employing MILP-driven KPE, with relative increases of 2.7% and 2.73%, respectively, at the expense of succinctness, which decreased by 1.25%. Also, we noted an increase in the length of the generated item responses by 13.62%. Ultimately, we conducted a Wilcoxon significance test comparing setups observing significant differences ($p < 0.05$) on all metrics except succinctness ($p = 0.30$).

5 System Overview

EdTec-ItemGen aims to support educators in test item generation tasks at bfz, Germany's largest provider of vocational education and training (VET) services. Designing formative assessments is time-intensive, particularly when test items must cover specific curricular content. This process is slow and prone to errors. EdTec-ItemGen replaces the drafting process with retrieval-augmented item generation. A dense retriever searches from internal educational materials, while MILP-driven KPE extracts essential concepts to instruct an LLM in writing a candidate item. Educators then review each suggested item, rating clarity and difficulty while discarding spurious items. EdTec-ItemGen also serves as a crowdsourcing infrastructure, collecting user interactions to drive future research on generative retrieval models for question banks (see Appendix A2 for industry application details).

Frontend The platform interface, illustrated in Figure 3, implements the complete item-generation workflow in HTML and JavaScript. Fig. 3(a) enables users to query the pre-processed VET corpus and select an LLM version (GPT-4o-mini or GPT-3.5 in the demo fork), thus reducing dependence on a single model. An upload widget is also available, allowing custom file ingestion in CSV format. Fig. 3(b) shows retrieved passages with MILP-KPE key points highlighted, so users can assess content coverage. Fig. 3(c) displays the generated items: green marks accepted items, while red flags inconsistent ones. Fig. 3(d) presents the validation view, where users approve or reject the generated items before pushing them to the main item base for exam assembly.

Backend The backend architecture, shown in Figure 2, is implemented in Python. An asynchronous worker pool manages concurrent Flask API requests. Semantic search is handled using multilingual embeddings with the `FAISS` library. MILP-driven KPE employs `SciPy`'s native optimizer for efficient key point extraction to support retrieval-augmented item generation. Extracted key points are passed to an LLM to guide the retrieval-augmented item generation phase. Each request returns a JSON response with the ranked documents, extracted key points, and the LLM-generated item. User interactions from the interface are logged in the backend using SQLite and made accessible through an internal endpoint for later analysis and review. To extend applicability to other languages, we expose language-agnostic APIs that support the generation of multilingual items from user-custom data (see Appendix A3 for more details).

6 Conclusions

Collaborating with bfz, one of Germany's largest VET services providers, we explored employing retrieval-augmented generation to assist educators with manual item construction tasks. Although prompting LLMs with custom VET curricular materials is useful for rapid test item generation, we explored whether incorporating a new MILP-driven key point extraction (KPE) method can enhance prompting during the augmented item generation phase. We evaluated our new method under the TREC-RAG framework. Our evaluation indicates that MILP-driven KPE significantly enhances essential content coverage and item quality in retrieval-augmented generation from internal VET passages, improving LLM-based item generation performance on domain-specific curricular material. Specifically, when employing MILP-driven KPE, results improved across all metrics, namely Vstrict increased by 7%, (V) by 7%, (W) by 6%, and (A) by 8%, with relative gains ranging from

(a)

Metric	With	Without	Δ Abs.	Δ Rel. (%)
		Nugget Coverage		
Vital Strict (Vstrict)	0.36	0.29	**+0.07 ↑**	**+24.14**
Vital (V)	0.42	0.35	**+0.07 ↑**	**+20.00**
Weighted (W)	0.38	0.32	**+0.06 ↑**	**+18.75**
All (A)	0.40	0.32	**+0.08 ↑**	**+25.00**
		Test Item Quality		
Grammar Score	4.94	4.81	**+0.13 ↑**	**+2.70**
Succinctness Score	3.95	4.00	**-0.05 ↓**	**-1.25**
Readability Score	4.90	4.77	**+0.13 ↑**	**+2.73**
Response Length (L)	32.28	28.41	**+3.87 ↑**	**+13.62**

(b)

Metric	W Stat.	p-value	Sig.
Vital Strict (Vstrict)	1900.5	0.021	Yes
Vital (V)	3284.5	0.032	Yes
Weighted (W)	3923.0	0.026	Yes
All (A)	4644.5	0.0003	Yes
Grammar Score	239.0	0.0029	Yes
Succinctness Score	1498.5	0.306	No
Readability Score	559.5	0.0026	Yes
Response Length (L)	9285.5	0.0009	Yes

Table 1: System performance with and without MILP-driven KPE. (a) Metrics for both settings and their Δ absolute and relative differences. (b) Wilcoxon signed-rank test comparing both setups (p < 0.05 indicates significance).

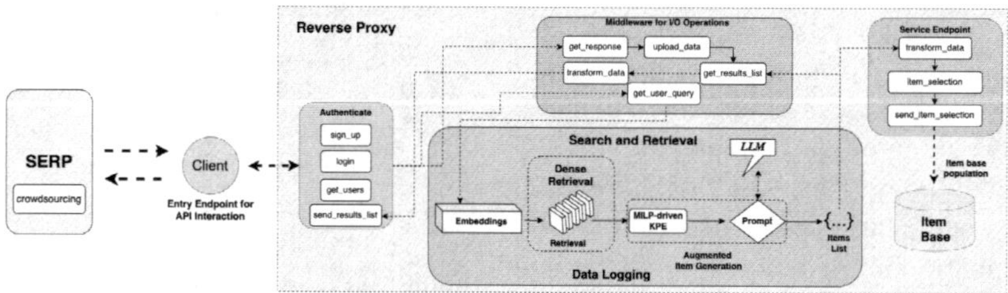

Figure 2: Demo architecture of EdTec-ItemGen, illustrating client interactions, API endpoints, retrieval and augmented item generation method, and integration with data logging, and external data repositories.

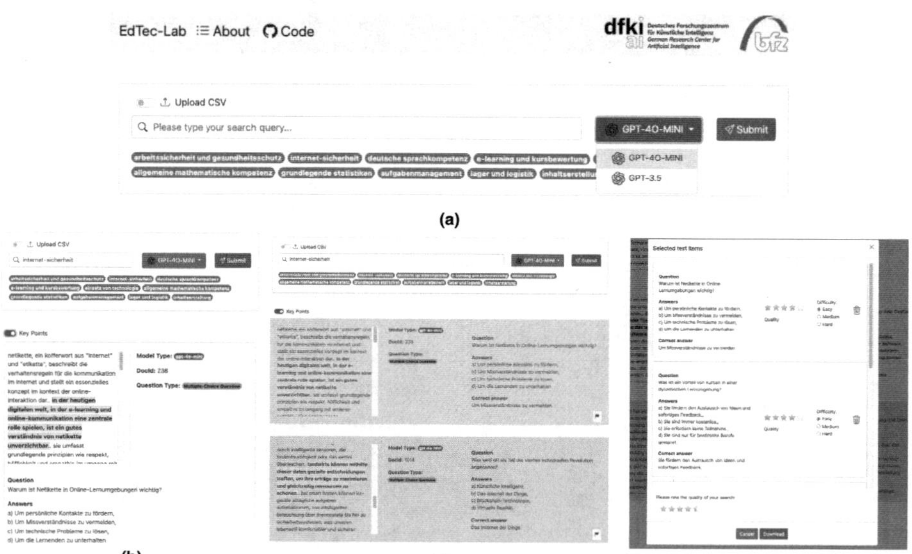

Figure 3: EdTec-ItemGen: Demo Version Frontend and User Interface Overview.

18.75% to 25%. In terms of item quality, KPE significantly improves grammar and readability by 2.70% and 2.73%, respectively, while increasing item length by 13.62%. Overall, our approach enhances the coverage of essential curricular content and improves the clarity of language in test items.

Future work will analyze session logs to research how users generate and evaluate items using our method. We plan to further investigate how to employ and integrate linear constraint-based test-assembly models (Linden et al., 2005) with LLMs to control and generate different test item types (e.g., matching, cloze) to expand on item's psychometric coverage beyond recall.

Limitations and Ethics Statement

For this work, we maintained strict confidentiality to protect our partner's product and intellectual property, in full compliance with required privacy standards. Although EdTec-ItemGen effectively supports VET educators in retrieval-augmented item generation tasks using domain-specific curricular contents, some limitations remain. For instance, we employed an ad-hoc TREC RAG-style evaluation to transfer a usable platform to our partners rapidly. This was useful for designing, assessing, and deploying our platform under cold start conditions to our partner's use case. Nevertheless, our TREC-RAG style approach (Pradeep et al., 2024a,b) relies on synthetic relevance judgments, which have recently gained traction in the information retrieval community (Faggioli et al., 2023; He et al., 2024). Still, real human VET expert evaluations naturally provide more accurate measures of augmented-generated item quality. Nevertheless, our platform allows users to annotate item quality or difficulty during the generation process to address this limitation. In the future, we plan to integrate these real human annotations into our evaluation approach, thereby enhancing the reliability of our partner's item generation workflow.

Acknowledgements

This work was funded by the Federal Ministry of Research, Technology and Space (BMFTR) as part of the AZUKIT project (funding code 21IVP056C) and by the KI-Akademie OWL project (grant no. 01IS24057A). The AZUKIT project is run under the innovation competition InnoVET PLUS, implemented by the Federal Institute for Vocational Education and Training (BIBB), while KI-Akademie OWL is supported by the Project Management Agency of the German Aerospace Centre (DLR). The responsibility for the content lies with the authors.

References

Nischal Ashok Kumar and Andrew Lan. 2024. Improving socratic question generation using data augmentation and preference optimization. In *Proceedings of the 19th Workshop on Innovative Use of NLP for Building Educational Applications (BEA 2024)*, pages 108–118, Mexico City, Mexico. Association for Computational Linguistics.

Roy Bar-Haim, Lilach Eden, Roni Friedman, Yoav Kantor, Dan Lahav, and Noam Slonim. 2020. From arguments to key points: Towards automatic argument summarization. In *Proceedings of the 58th Annual Meeting of the Association for Computational Linguistics*, pages 4029–4039, Online. Association for Computational Linguistics.

Roy Bar-Haim, Lilach Eden, Yoav Kantor, Roni Friedman, and Noam Slonim. 2021. Every bite is an experience: Key Point Analysis of business reviews. In *Proceedings of the 59th Annual Meeting of the Association for Computational Linguistics and the 11th International Joint Conference on Natural Language Processing (Volume 1: Long Papers)*, pages 3376–3386, Online. Association for Computational Linguistics.

Jonathan Brown, Gwen Frishkoff, and Maxine Eskenazi. 2005. Automatic question generation for vocabulary assessment. In *Proceedings of Human Language Technology Conference and Conference on Empirical Methods in Natural Language Processing*, pages 819–826, Vancouver, British Columbia, Canada. Association for Computational Linguistics.

Yllias Chali and Sadid A. Hasan. 2015. Towards topic-to-question generation. *Computational Linguistics*, 41(1):1–20.

Kuang Wen Chan, Farhan Ali, Joonhyeong Park, Kah Shen Brandon Sham, Erdalyn Yeh Thong Tan, Francis Woon Chien Chong, Kun Qian, and Guan Kheng Sze. 2025. Automatic item generation in various stem subjects using large language model prompting. *Computers and Education: Artificial Intelligence*, 8:100344.

Ying-Hong Chan and Yao-Chung Fan. 2019. A recurrent BERT-based model for question generation. In *Proceedings of the 2nd Workshop on Machine Reading for Question Answering*, pages 154–162, Hong Kong, China. Association for Computational Linguistics.

Ruhan Circi, Juanita Hicks, and Emmanuel Sikali. 2023. Automatic item generation: foundations and machine learning-based approaches for assessments. In *Frontiers in Education*, volume 8, page 858273. Frontiers Media SA.

Matthijs Douze, Alexandr Guzhva, Chengqi Deng, Jeff Johnson, Gergely Szilvasy, Pierre-Emmanuel Mazaré, Maria Lomeli, Lucas Hosseini, and Hervé Jégou. 2024. The faiss library.

Liam Dugan, Eleni Miltsakaki, Shriyash Upadhyay, Etan Ginsberg, Hannah Gonzalez, DaHyeon Choi, Chuning Yuan, and Chris Callison-Burch. 2022. A feasibility study of answer-agnostic question generation for education. In *Findings of the Association for Computational Linguistics: ACL 2022*, pages 1919–1926, Dublin, Ireland. Association for Computational Linguistics.

Guglielmo Faggioli, Laura Dietz, Charles LA Clarke, Gianluca Demartini, Matthias Hagen, Claudia Hauff, Noriko Kando, Evangelos Kanoulas, Martin Potthast, Benno Stein, et al. 2023. Perspectives on large language models for relevance judgment. In *Proceedings of the 2023 ACM SIGIR International Conference on Theory of Information Retrieval*, pages 39–50.

Wenqi Fan, Yujuan Ding, Liangbo Ning, Shijie Wang, Hengyun Li, Dawei Yin, Tat-Seng Chua, and Qing Li. 2024. A survey on rag meeting llms: Towards retrieval-augmented large language models. In *Proceedings of the 30th ACM SIGKDD Conference on Knowledge Discovery and Data Mining*, KDD '24, page 6491–6501, New York, NY, USA. Association for Computing Machinery.

Fred Glover and Eugene Woolsey. 1974. Technical note—converting the 0-1 polynomial programming problem to a 0-1 linear program. *Operations Research*, 22(1):180–182.

Hila Gonen, Terra Blevins, Alisa Liu, Luke Zettlemoyer, and Noah A. Smith. 2025. Does liking yellow imply driving a school bus? semantic leakage in language models. In *Proceedings of the 2025 Conference of the North American Chapter of the Association for Computational Linguistics (NAACL)*, Albuquerque, New Mexico, USA. Association for Computational Linguistics.

Guher Gorgun and Okan Bulut. 2024. Instruction-tuned large-language models for quality control in automatic item generation: A feasibility study. *Educational Measurement: Issues and Practice*.

Gauthier Guinet, Behrooz Omidvar-Tehrani, Anoop Deoras, and Laurent Callot. 2024. Automated evaluation of retrieval-augmented language models with task-specific exam generation. In *Proceedings of the 41st International Conference on Machine Learning*, ICML'24. JMLR.org.

Shasha Guo, Lizi Liao, Jing Zhang, Yanling Wang, Cuiping Li, and Hong Chen. 2024. SGSH: Stimulate large language models with skeleton heuristics for knowledge base question generation. In *Findings of the Association for Computational Linguistics: NAACL 2024*, pages 4613–4625, Mexico City, Mexico. Association for Computational Linguistics.

Gurobi Optimization, LLC. 2024. Gurobi Optimizer Reference Manual.

Xingwei He, Zhenghao Lin, Yeyun Gong, A-Long Jin, Hang Zhang, Chen Lin, Jian Jiao, Siu Ming Yiu, Nan Duan, and Weizhu Chen. 2024. AnnoLLM: Making large language models to be better crowdsourced annotators. In *Proceedings of the 2024 Conference of the North American Chapter of the Association for Computational Linguistics: Human Language Technologies (Volume 6: Industry Track)*, pages 165–190, Mexico City, Mexico. Association for Computational Linguistics.

Michael Heilman and Noah A. Smith. 2010. Good question! statistical ranking for question generation. In *Human Language Technologies: The 2010 Annual Conference of the North American Chapter of the Association for Computational Linguistics*, pages 609–617, Los Angeles, California. Association for Computational Linguistics.

Thomas Huber and Christina Niklaus. 2025. LLMs meet bloom's taxonomy: A cognitive view on large language model evaluations. In *Proceedings of the 31st International Conference on Computational Linguistics*, pages 5211–5246, Abu Dhabi, UAE. Association for Computational Linguistics.

Khushnur Jahangir, Philippe Muller, and Chloé Braud. 2024. Complex question generation using discourse-based data augmentation. In *Proceedings of the 5th Workshop on Computational Approaches to Discourse (CODI 2024)*, pages 105–119, St. Julians, Malta. Association for Computational Linguistics.

Samin Jamshidi and Yllias Chali. 2025. GNET-QG: Graph network for multi-hop question generation. In *Proceedings of the Workshop on Generative AI and Knowledge Graphs (GenAIK)*, pages 20–26, Abu Dhabi, UAE. International Committee on Computational Linguistics.

Rohan Jha, Bo Wang, Michael Günther, Georgios Mastrapas, Saba Sturua, Isabelle Mohr, Andreas Koukounas, Mohammad Kalim Wang, Nan Wang, and Han Xiao. 2024. Jina-ColBERT-v2: A general-purpose multilingual late interaction retriever. In *Proceedings of the Fourth Workshop on Multilingual Representation Learning (MRL 2024)*, pages 159–166, Miami, Florida, USA. Association for Computational Linguistics.

Patrick Kyllonen, Amit Sevak, Teresa Ober, Ikkyu Choi, Jesse Sparks, and Daniel Fishtein. 2024. Charting the future of assessments. *ETS Research Report Series*, 2024(1):1–62.

Suzanne Lane, Mark R Raymond, and Thomas M Haladyna. 2016. *Handbook of test development*. Routledge.

Antonio Laverghetta Jr. and John Licato. 2023. Generating better items for cognitive assessments using large language models. In *Proceedings of the 18th Workshop on Innovative Use of NLP for Building Educational Applications (BEA 2023)*, pages 414–428, Toronto, Canada. Association for Computational Linguistics.

Patrick Lewis, Ethan Perez, Aleksandra Piktus, Fabio Petroni, Vladimir Karpukhin, Naman Goyal, Heinrich Küttler, Mike Lewis, Wen-tau Yih, Tim Rocktäschel, et al. 2020. Retrieval-augmented generation for knowledge-intensive nlp tasks. *Advances in Neural Information Processing Systems*, 33:9459–9474.

Manling Li, Shiyu Zhao, Qineng Wang, Kangrui Wang, Yu Zhou, Sanjana Srivastava, Cem Gokmen, Tony Lee, Erran Li Li, Ruohan Zhang, et al. 2024. Embodied agent interface: Benchmarking llms for embodied decision making. *Advances in Neural Information Processing Systems*, 37:100428–100534.

Zefeng Lin, Weidong Chen, Yan Song, and Yongdong Zhang. 2024. Prompting few-shot multi-hop question generation via comprehending type-aware semantics. In *Findings of the Association for Computational Linguistics: NAACL 2024*, pages 3730–3740, Mexico City, Mexico. Association for Computational Linguistics.

Wim J Linden et al. 2005. *Linear models for optimal test design*. Springer.

Nishant Mishra, Gaurav Sahu, Iacer Calixto, Ameen Abu-Hanna, and Issam Laradji. 2023. LLM aided semi-supervision for efficient extractive dialog summarization. In *Findings of the Association for Computational Linguistics: EMNLP 2023*, pages 10002–10009, Singapore. Association for Computational Linguistics.

Ruslan Mitkov, Ha Le An, and Nikiforos Karamanis. 2006. A computer-aided environment for generating multiple-choice test items. *Natural language engineering*, 12(2):177–194.

Sérgio Silva Mucciaccia, Thiago Meireles Paixão, Filipe Wall Mutz, Claudine Santos Badue, Alberto Ferreira de Souza, and Thiago Oliveira-Santos. 2025. Automatic multiple-choice question generation and evaluation systems based on LLM: A study case with university resolutions. In *Proceedings of the 31st International Conference on Computational Linguistics*, pages 2246–2260, Abu Dhabi, UAE. Association for Computational Linguistics.

Alonso Palomino, Andreas Fischer, David Buschhüter, Roland Roller, Niels Pinkwart, and Benjamin Paassen. 2025. Mitigating bias in item retrieval for enhancing exam assembly in vocational education services. In *Proceedings of the 2025 Conference of the Nations of the Americas Chapter of the Association for Computational Linguistics: Human Language Technologies (Volume 3: Industry Track)*, pages 183–193, Albuquerque, New Mexico. Association for Computational Linguistics.

Alonso Palomino, Andreas Fischer, Jakub Kuzilek, Jarek Nitsch, Niels Pinkwart, and Benjamin Paassen. 2024. EdTec-QBuilder: A semantic retrieval tool for assembling vocational training exams in German language. In *Proceedings of the 2024 Conference of the North American Chapter of the Association for Computational Linguistics: Human Language Technologies (Volume 3: System Demonstrations)*, pages 26–35, Mexico City, Mexico. Association for Computational Linguistics.

Laurent Perron and Frédéric Didier. Cp-sat.

David Pisinger. 2007. The quadratic knapsack problem—a survey. *Discrete Applied Mathematics*, 155(5):623–648.

Dhanamjaya Pochiraju, Abhinav Chakilam, Premchand Betham, Pranav Chimulla, and S Govinda Rao. 2023. Extractive summarization and multiple choice question generation using xlnet. In *2023 7th International Conference on Intelligent Computing and Control Systems (ICICCS)*, pages 1001–1005.

Yin Poon, John Sie Yuen Lee, Yu Yan Lam, Wing Lam Suen, Elsie Li Chen Ong, and Samuel Kai Wah Chu. 2024. Few-shot question generation for reading comprehension. In *Proceedings of the 10th SIGHAN Workshop on Chinese Language Processing (SIGHAN-10)*, pages 21–27, Bangkok, Thailand. Association for Computational Linguistics.

Ronak Pradeep, Nandan Thakur, Sahel Sharifymoghaddam, Eric Zhang, Ryan Nguyen, Daniel Campos, Nick Craswell, and Jimmy Lin. 2024b. Ragnarök: A reusable rag framework and baselines for trec 2024 retrieval-augmented generation track. *arXiv preprint arXiv:2406.16828*.

Ronak Pradeep, Nandan Thakur, Shivani Upadhyay, Daniel Campos, Nick Craswell, and Jimmy Lin. 2024a. Initial nugget evaluation results for the trec 2024 rag track with the autonuggetizer framework. *arXiv preprint arXiv:2411.09607*.

Fanyi Qu, Xin Jia, and Yunfang Wu. 2021. Asking questions like educational experts: Automatically generating question-answer pairs on real-world examination data. In *Proceedings of the 2021 Conference on Empirical Methods in Natural Language Processing*, pages 2583–2593, Online and Punta Cana, Dominican Republic. Association for Computational Linguistics.

Aninditha Ramesh, Arav Agarwal, Jacob Arthur Doughty, Ketan Ramaneti, Jaromir Savelka, and Majd Sakr. 2024. A benchmark for testing the capabilities of llms in assessing the quality of multiple-choice questions in introductory programming education. In *Proceedings of the 2024 on ACM Virtual Global Computing Education Conference V. 1*, SIGCSE Virtual 2024, page 193–199, New York, NY, USA. Association for Computing Machinery.

Nils Reimers and Iryna Gurevych. 2019. Sentence-bert: Sentence embeddings using siamese bert-networks. In *Proceedings of the 2019 Conference on Empirical Methods in Natural Language Processing*. Association for Computational Linguistics.

Michael J Rudolph, Kimberly K Daugherty, Mary Elizabeth Ray, Veronica P Shuford, Lisa Lebovitz, and Margarita V DiVall. 2019. Best practices related to examination item construction and post-hoc review. *American journal of pharmaceutical education*, 83(7):7204.

Vasile Rus, Paul Piwek, Svetlana Stoyanchev, Brendan Wyse, Mihai Lintean, and Cristian Moldovan. 2011. Question generation shared task and evaluation challenge: Status report. In *Proceedings of the 13th European Workshop on Natural Language Generation*, ENLG '11, page 318–320, USA. Association for Computational Linguistics.

Luu Anh Tuan, Darsh Shah, and Regina Barzilay. 2020. Capturing greater context for question generation. *Proceedings of the AAAI Conference on Artificial Intelligence*, 34(05):9065–9072.

Ellen M Voorhees and L Buckland. 2003. Overview of the trec 2003 question answering track. In *TREC*, volume 2003, pages 54–68.

Ian Wu, Sravan Jayanthi, Vijay Viswanathan, Simon Rosenberg, Sina Khoshfetrat Pakazad, Tongshuang Wu, and Graham Neubig. 2024. Synthetic multimodal question generation. In *Findings of the Association for Computational Linguistics: EMNLP 2024*, pages 12960–12993, Miami, Florida, USA. Association for Computational Linguistics.

Jie Jw Wu and Fatemeh H. Fard. 2025. Humaneval-comm: Benchmarking the communication competence of code generation for llms and llm agent. *ACM Trans. Softw. Eng. Methodol.* Just Accepted.

Nana Yoshimi, Tomoyuki Kajiwara, Satoru Uchida, Yuki Arase, and Takashi Ninomiya. 2023. Distractor generation for fill-in-the-blank exercises by question type. In *Proceedings of the 61st Annual Meeting of the Association for Computational Linguistics (Volume 4: Student Research Workshop)*, pages 276–281, Toronto, Canada. Association for Computational Linguistics.

Haopeng Zhang, Xiao Liu, and Jiawei Zhang. 2023. Extractive summarization via ChatGPT for faithful summary generation. In *Findings of the Association for Computational Linguistics: EMNLP 2023*, pages 3270–3278, Singapore. Association for Computational Linguistics.

A Appendix

A.1 Dataset Details

Table 2 summarizes the frequency across these topics, including the top three terms, unique terms, sentence counts, top terms, and document counts.

Topic	Avg. Terms	Uniq. Terms	Sent. Count	Top 3 Terms	Docs
General Mathematical Competence	324.4	223	38.3	cross multiplication understanding mathematical	70
Occupational Safety & Health Protection	323.2	240	36.8	employees safety workplace	64
Task Management	323.8	239	37.9	tasks task management important	112
German Language Competence	306.5	227	35.1	education professional significance	234
E-learning & Course Evaluation	320.1	244	37.4	learners education learning	195
Use of Technology	333.8	252	36.3	technology technologies education	92
Basic Statistics	328.3	226	36.7	data values median	83
Content Creation	332.5	244	37.1	content information education	61
Storage & Logistics	310.4	238	36.1	company logistics storage	199
Total	318.7	237	36.6	learners education professional	1,110

Table 2: Key statistics across topics, including average terms, unique terms, sentence counts, key terms, and document counts.

The VET corpus is a domain-specific collection curated to support manual test item design for formative assessments. Each passage delivers authentic trade skill content specifically curated to the context of vocational education and training (VET) in Germany.

A.2 Industry Application

As traditional test item construction requires multiple manual review cycles, AIG has become a key capability for educational and assessment institutions. Generating items that are clear, readable, and aligned with curricular materials is essential for valid assessment in high-stakes contexts. LLMs offer scalable item generation while reducing manual effort (Kyllonen et al., 2024). However, their integration is limited by issues such as hallucinations, lack of domain expertise, and restricted access to private sources (Li et al., 2024; Ramesh et al., 2024; Wu and Fard, 2025).

Retrieval-augmented generation (RAG) addresses these challenges by enabling LLMs to incorporate external knowledge for domain-specific item generation. In collaboration with bfz, a major German VET provider, we developed EdTec-ItemGen- a RAG-based platform supporting VET educators in creating and updating internal item repositories. Building on prior work in item retrieval for exam assembly (Palomino et al., 2024, 2025), we integrated a MILP-driven approach for key point extraction (KPE) to identify essential content from VET passages. As illustrated in Figure 3, EdTec-ItemGen presents search results retrieved via dense semantic search. The MILP-based KPE module extracts key information used to prompt the LLM, which then generates a candidate item. Users review the generated items and decide which should be retained for inclusion in the item base.

A.3 System and API Overview Details

This section outlines the frontend and backend components of EdTec-ItemGen.

A.3.1 Frontend

Figure 3 displays the demo interface, which supports a human-in-the-loop workflow for LLM-based retrieval-augmented item generation.

A.3.2 Backend

The backend is built using the Flask[6] framework, exposing RESTful endpoints for search, CSV upload, and item generation. Python's concurrency library enables parallel execution across pipeline components. Deployment uses Nginx[7] as a reverse proxy and runs on an Amazon EC2[8] instance with

[6]https://flask.palletsprojects.com/en/stable/
[7]https://nginx.org/
[8]https://aws.amazon.com/en/ec2/

three vCPUs for cost-effective performance only on the system demonstration version. Gunicorn is used as the WSGI server for robust process and connection management.

The platform supports multilingual input via GPT-4. It detects the CSV language and prompts the LLM accordingly during item generation. Public APIs are available at `https://api.edtec-itemgen.xyz/search`.

For large-scale scenarios, such as extensive item banks, performance is maintained through parallelization and solvers like OR-Tools (Perron and Didier) or Gurobi (Gurobi Optimization, LLC, 2024).

Below are `curl`[9] examples for API usage:

1) Upload Data Endpoint Upload a CSV file. The response returns an `ID` used for subsequent requests. *Note:* User data is not stored permanently; logs are cleared post-upload.

```
curl -X POST \
 -F "file=@/path/to/your/file/example.csv" \
 https://api.edtec-itemgen.xyz/upload_csv
```

2) Item-RAG Endpoint Use the `upload_id` to generate items:

```
curl -X POST \
 -H "Content-Type: application/json" \
 -d '{
 "query": "safety",
 "upload_id": "<your file ID>",
 "k": 25,
 "llm_version": "GPT-4O-MINI",
 "kpe": "true"
 }' \
 https://api.edtec-itemgen.xyz/search
```

This retrieves relevant content from the uploaded CSV and generates multiple-choice items accordingly.

A.4 Prompt Details

Our prompting approach relied on the `instructor`[10] library, ensuring consistency and control over output formatting and prompt instructions. The `instructor` output was parameterized as JSON, thereby avoiding any output misformatting.

[9] `https://curl.se`

[10] `https://python.useinstructor.com/`

Goal	Prompt in German	Translated Prompt in English
1. Clarity Evaluation – Instruction's Context	Du bist ein Experte für die Bewertung der Qualität von Prüfungsfragen. Gib ausschließlich ein JSON-Objekt mit den Schlüsseln: "grammar_score" (Ganzzahl 1 bis 5), "succinctness_score" (Ganzzahl 1 bis 5), "readability_score" (Ganzzahl 1 bis 5), "explanation" (kurze Begrundung). Beispielformat: {"grammar_score": 4, "succinctness_score": 3, "readability_score": 5, "explanation": "Die Frage ist grammatisch gut, sehr klar..."}. Kein zusätzlicher Text oder andere Schlüssel.	You are an expert in evaluating the quality of exam questions. Provide only a JSON object with the following keys: "grammar_score" (an integer from 1 to 5), "succinctness_score" (an integer from 1 to 5), "readability_score" (an integer from 1 to 5), "explanation" (a brief explanation). Example format: {"grammar_score": 4, "succinctness_score": 3, "readability_score": 5, "explanation": "The question is grammatically sound and very clear..."}. No additional text or keys.
2. Clarity Evaluation – User Request	Bewerten Sie die folgende Multiple-Choice-Prüfungsfrage in deutscher Sprache: {question}. Bewerten Sie sie auf einer Skala von 1,0 bis 5,0 für die folgenden Kriterien: – Grammatik (grammar_score): Bewerten Sie die grammatikalische Richtigkeit. – Prägnanz (succinctness_score): Beurteilen Sie, wie prägnant und direkt die Frage ist. – Lesbarkeit (readability_score): Beurteilen Sie, wie leicht die Frage zu verstehen ist. Die Ergebnisse werden im folgenden JSON-Format zurückgegeben: {"grammar_score": <score>, "succinctness_score": <score>, "readability_score": <score>, "explanation": <Kurzerläuterung zu den angegebenen Punktzahlen>}.	Evaluate the following multiple-choice exam question in German language: {question}. Rate it on a scale from 1.0 to 5.0 for the following criteria: – Grammar (grammar_score): Assess grammatical accuracy. – Conciseness (succinctness_score): Evaluate how concise and direct the question is. – Readability (readability_score): Judge how easy it is to understand. Return the results in the following JSON format: {"grammar_score": <score>, "succinctness_score": <score>, "readability_score": <score>, "explanation": <brief explanation for the given scores>}.
3. Nugget Coverage Scoring – Instruction's Context	Sie sind ein Experte für die Bewertung der Qualität von Multiple-Choice-Prüfungsfragen basierend auf vorab bewerteten, gekennzeichneten Informationsnuggets – relevante Fakten, die die Frage und ihre Antworten abdecken müssen. Befolgen Sie diese Richtlinien zur Berechnung der Metriken: 1. Weisen Sie Werte zu: - support = 1, - partial_support = 0,5, - not_support = 0. 2. Metriken: - A (All) Score: Durchschnitt aller Nugget-Werte. - V (Vital) Score: Durchschnitt der Werte für Nuggets, die als "Vital" gekennzeichnet sind. - W (Gewichteter) Score: Gewichteter Durchschnitt, wobei "Vital"-Nuggets ein Gewicht von 1 und "OK"-Nuggets ein Gewicht von 0,5 haben. - Vstrict (Vital Strict) Score: Durchschnitt für "Vital"-Nuggets, wobei nur support mit 1 gewertet wird (partial_support = 0). Geben Sie Ihre Antwort als gültiges JSON-Objekt mit den folgenden Schlüsseln an: {"Vstrict_GPT": <Score>, "V_GPT": <Score>, "W_GPT": <Score>, "A_GPT": <Score>"}.	You are an expert in evaluating multiple-choice exam questions based on pre-assessed, labeled information nuggets – relevant factoids that the question and its answers must cover. Follow these guidelines to calculate the metrics: 1. Assign Values: - support = 1, - partial_support = 0.5, - not_support = 0. 2. Metrics: - A (All) Score: Average of all nugget values. - V (Vital) Score: Average of values for nuggets labeled as "Vital." - W (Weighted) Score: Weighted average where "Vital" nuggets have a weight of 1 and "OK" nuggets a weight of 0.5. - Vstrict (Vital Strict) Score: Average for "Vital" nuggets, counting only support as 1 (partial_support = 0). Provide your answer as a valid JSON object with the following keys: {"Vstrict_GPT": <score>, "V_GPT": <score>, "W_GPT": <score>, "A_GPT": <score>"}.
4. Nugget Coverage Scoring – User Request	Bewerten Sie die folgende Kombination aus Frage und Kandidatenantwort: {question} {candidate_answer}. Liste der Nuggets (Format: Nugget: <Text>, Wichtigkeit: <Vital/OK>): {nuggets_text}. Für jedes Nugget ist zu bewerten, wie gut es durch die kombinierte Fragestellung und Antwort abgedeckt wird. Weisen Sie jedem Nugget eine der folgenden Abdeckungsstufen zu: - support: Das Nugget wird vollständig oder klar abgedeckt. - partial_support: Das Nugget wird teilweise abgedeckt, aber es fehlt an vollständiger Abdeckung. - not_support: Das Nugget wird gar nicht abgedeckt. Antworten Sie mit einem gültigen JSON-Objekt im folgenden Format: {"nugget_coverage": [{"nugget": <Text>, "coverage": <support/partial_support/not_support>}, ...]}.	Evaluate the following combination of question and candidate answer: {question} {candidate_answer}. List of Nuggets (Format: Nugget: <Text>, Importance: <Vital/OK>): {nuggets_text}. For each nugget, assess how well it is covered by the combined question and answer. Assign one of the following coverage levels to each nugget: - support: The nugget is fully addressed or clearly covered. - partial_support: The nugget is partially addressed but lacks full coverage. - not_support: The nugget is not addressed at all. Respond with a valid JSON object in the following format: {"nugget_coverage": [{"nugget": <Text>, "coverage": <support/partial_support/not_support>}, ...]}.
5. Augmented Item Generation (Based on Key Points)	Ihre Aufgabe ist es, eine Multiple-Choice-Frage zu erstellen, die auf den Top 15 Schlüsselaussagen {kp} basiert. Die Ausgabe sollte ein JSON-Objekt im Format sein: {"question": <Question text>, "answers": ["Antwort 1", "Antwort 2", "Antwort 3", "Antwort 4"], "correct_answer": <richtige Antwort>}. Die Frage muss so formuliert sein, dass sie nur mit den angegebenen Antwortmöglichkeiten beantwortet werden kann und nur eine richtige Antwort existiert. Speichern Sie die richtige Antwort im JSON-Feld "correct_answer".	Create a multiple-choice question based on the top 15 key statements {kp}. The output should be a JSON object in the format: {"question": <Question text>, "answers": ["Answer 1", "Answer 2", "Answer 3", "Answer 4"], "correct_answer": <correct answer>}. The question must be formulated so that it can only be answered based on the provided answer options and has only one correct answer. Store the correct answer in the JSON field "correct_answer".
6. Augmented Item Generation (Based on Full Text)	Ihre Aufgabe ist es, eine Multiple-Choice-Frage zu erstellen, die auf den 15 wichtigsten Aussagen des folgenden Textes {input_text} basiert. Die Ausgabe sollte ein JSON-Objekt im Format sein: {"question": <Question text>, "answers": ["Antwort 1", "Antwort 2", "Antwort 3", "Antwort 4"], "correct_answer": <richtige Antwort>}. Die Frage muss so formuliert sein, dass sie nur anhand der verfügbaren Antwortmöglichkeiten beantwortet werden kann und nur eine richtige Antwort besitzt. Speichern Sie die richtige Antwort im JSON-Feld "correct_answer".	Create a multiple-choice question based on the top 15 key statements of the following text {input_text}. The output should be a JSON object in the format: {"question": <Question text>, "answers": ["Answer 1", "Answer 2", "Answer 3", "Answer 4"], "correct_answer": <correct answer>}. The question must be formulated so that it can only be answered based on the provided answer options and has only one correct answer. Store the correct answer in the JSON field "correct_answer".
7. AutoNuggetizer – System Instruction for Nugget Extraction	Sie sind ein Experte für Bildungsinhalte. Ihre Aufgabe ist es, wesentliche Aussagen oder Schlüsselinformationen ("nuggets") – Faktengrundlagen oder Aussagen, die aus dem bereitgestellten Inhalt abgeleitet wurden – zu extrahieren. Antworten Sie mit einem gültigen JSON-Objekt, das genau die folgenden Schlüssel enthält: {keys_str}. Jeder Schlüssel muss einer Liste mit genau {nuggets_per_category} Elementen zugeordnet sein. Jedes Element muss ein JSON-Objekt mit folgender Struktur sein: {"nugget": <Die extrahierte Schlüsselaussage oder Information>, "importance": <Relevanzniveau: 'Vital', 'OK' oder 'Not Vital'>, "source_docid": <Dokument-ID>}.	Extract essential statements or key information ("nuggets") – factoids or statements derived from the provided content – using a valid JSON object containing exactly the following keys: {keys_str}. Each key must be associated with a list of exactly {nuggets_per_category} elements. Each element should be a JSON object with the following structure: {"nugget": <The extracted key fact or statement>, "importance": <Relevance level: 'Vital', 'OK', or 'Not Vital'>, "source_docid": <Document ID>}.
8. AutoNuggetizer – User Request for Nugget Extraction	Gegebenen Inhalt: {passage}. Antworte ausschließlich mit einem JSON-Objekt, das genau die folgenden Schlüssel enthält: {keys_str}. Jeder Schlüssel muss einer Liste mit genau {nuggets_per_category} Elementen zugeordnet sein. Jeder Eintrag in der Liste muss ein Objekt mit den Schlüsseln "nugget", "importance" und "source_docid" sein.	Given this content: {passage}. Respond solely with a JSON object that contains exactly the following keys: {keys_str}. Each key must have a list with exactly {nuggets_per_category} elements. Each entry in the list must be an object with the keys "nugget", "importance", and "source_docid".

Table 3: Employed prompts with original German texts and their English corresponding translations.

Teaching Large Language Models to Express Knowledge Boundary from Their Own Signals

Lida Chen[1], Zujie Liang[2], Xintao Wang[1], Jiaqing Liang[*1], Yanghua Xiao[1], Feng Wei[2], Jinglei Chen[2], ZHENGHONG HAO[2], Bing Han[2], Wei Wang[1]
[1]Shanghai Key Laboratory of Data Science,
College of Computer Science and Artificial Intelligence, Fudan University
[2]Mybank, Ant Group
{chenld23, xtwang21}@m.fudan.edu.cn,
{liangjiaqing, weiwang1, shawyh}@fudan.edu.cn
{jokieleung}@outlook.com

Abstract

Large language models (LLMs) have achieved great success, but their occasional content fabrication, or hallucination, limits their practical application. Hallucination arises because LLMs struggle to admit ignorance due to inadequate training on knowledge boundaries. We call it a limitation of LLMs that they can not accurately express their knowledge boundary, answering questions they know while admitting ignorance to questions they do not know. In this paper, we aim to teach LLMs to recognize and express their knowledge boundary, so they can reduce hallucinations caused by fabricating when they do not know. We propose CoKE, which first probes LLMs' knowledge boundary via internal confidence given a set of questions, and then leverages the probing results to elicit the expression of the knowledge boundary. Extensive experiments show CoKE helps LLMs express knowledge boundaries, answering known questions while declining unknown ones, significantly improving in-domain and out-of-domain performance.

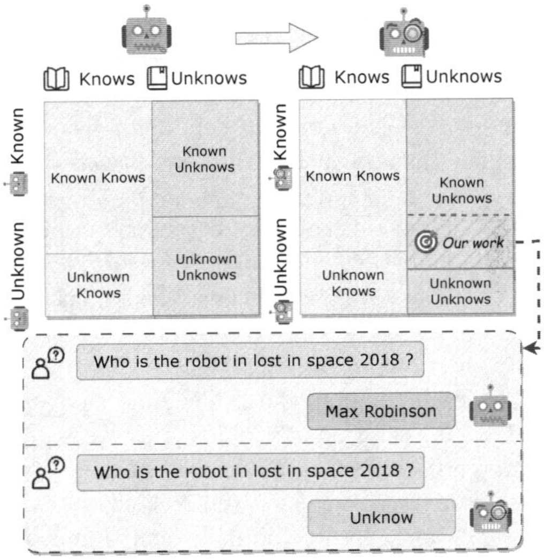

Figure 1: The evolution of the Known-Unknown Quadrant. The yellow portion represents the model's parametric knowledge. Our method increases the "Known Unknows", helping the model recognize and articulate its knowledge limitations.

1 Introduction

Large language models (LLMs) have emerged as an increasingly pivotal cornerstone for the development of artificial general intelligence. They exhibit powerful intellectual capabilities and vast storage of knowledge (Brown et al., 2020; Ouyang et al., 2022; Achiam et al., 2023), which enables them to generate valuable content. Recent research demonstrates that LLMs excel in passing various professional examinations requiring expert knowledge in domains like medical (Jin et al., 2021) and legal (Cui et al., 2023). Nevertheless, human users are hardly willing to seek professional suggestions from LLMs, due greatly to **hallucinations** in LLMs. Hallucinations in LLMs refer to the phenomenon that existing LLMs frequently generate untruthful information (Zhang et al., 2023b; Ji et al., 2023), which greatly undermines people's trust and acceptance of LLM-generated content.

An important cause of hallucinations is the model's insufficiency in knowledge boundary expression, which originates from the learning paradigm of LLMs. Pre-training and instruction fine-tuning serve as the two indispensable learning stages for current LLMs. The learning mechanism of these stages is to encourage LLMs to generate the provided text, which also makes LLMs prone to fabricating content when LLMs do not possess relevant knowledge (joh, 2023; Gekhman et al., 2024). Hence, LLMs are hardly instructed to express their ignorance, which is a lack of accurate knowledge boundary expression. Given a specific LLM and a question set, the corresponding question-answer pairs can be categorized based on two factors: (1) whether the model has corresponding parametric

Proceedings of the 3rd Workshop on Towards Knowledgeable Foundation Models (KnowFM), pages 26–39
August 1, 2025 ©2025 Association for Computational Linguistics

knowledge (knows v.s. unknows), and (2) whether the model is aware of the first factor (known v.s. unknown), as is depicted in Figure 1. Hallucinations frequently occur in the "Unknown Unknows" scenarios, where the model is unaware that it should explain its ignorance like humans, instead of struggling to give a hallucinated response.

Fine-tuning models to express knowledge boundaries faces two significant challenges. The first challenge is how to efficiently obtain data that reflects the internal knowledge of a specific model. Even if evaluation questions are easy to construct, obtaining expert-level answers in certain fields is costly. Additionally, since the model might produce correct answers in different forms from the reference answers, evaluating their correctness is also challenging (Kadavath et al., 2022; Zou et al., 2023). The second challenge is enabling the model to express its knowledge boundary robustly (Ren et al., 2023). We expect consistent knowledge boundary expression across prompts and generalization across domains.

To address the above two challenges, we propose COKE, an **Co**nfidence-derived **K**nowledge boundary **E**xpression method which teaches LLMs to express knowledge boundaries and decline unanswerable questions, leveraging their internal signals. Our method consists of two stages: a probing stage and a training stage. In the probing stage, we use the model's internal signals reflecting confidence to distinguish between answerable and unanswerable questions, avoiding reliance on external annotations. This allows for easy collection of large data and avoids conflicts between the model's internal knowledge and annotations. In the training stage, we construct prompts for each question using three representative types: prior awareness, direct awareness, and posterior awareness. Then, we apply regularization by incorporating the squared differences in confidence across different prompts for the same question into the loss function to enhance consistency. This training setup helps the model semantically learn to express knowledge boundary better, thereby enhancing its generalization ability.

To evaluate the model's knowledge boundary expression capability, we design an evaluation framework that comprehensively assesses the model's performance in both "knows" and "unknows" scenarios. We conduct extensive experiments on both in-domain and out-of-domain datasets. Results show that the model learns to use internal signals to help express knowledge boundary. Compared to directly using model signals for determination, the models trained with our method demonstrate better performance and generalization.

In summary, our contributions are:

- We explore the effectiveness of internal model signals in indicating confidence and demonstrate the model can learn to use its signals to express its knowledge boundaries after training.
- We propose a novel unsupervised method that leverages internal model signals and multi-prompt consistency regularization to enable the model to express its knowledge boundary clearly.
- We develop a framework for evaluating a model's ability to express its knowledge boundary, and experimental results demonstrate that the model can learn signals about the confidence of its knowledge and articulate its knowledge boundary.

2 Related Work

2.1 Knowledge Boundary Perception

While models are equipped with extensive parametric knowledge, some studies indicate their inability to discern the knowledge they possess from what they lack, thus failing to articulate their knowledge boundary (Yin et al., 2023; Ren et al., 2023). In terms of enhancing a model's awareness of its knowledge boundary, efforts can be categorized into two parts: one focuses on enabling the model to fully utilize its inherent knowledge, thereby shrinking the ratio of the model's "Unknown Knows" (Wei et al., 2022; Li et al., 2023; Tian et al., 2024). The other part focuses on enabling the model to acknowledge the knowledge it lacks, thereby reducing the ratio of the model's "Unknown Unknows". R-tuning (Zhang et al., 2023a) uses labeled data to judge the correctness of model responses and trains the model using the SFT method. Yang et al. (2023) and Kang et al. (2024) explore training methods based on RL. Focused on this aspect, our work investigates how to enable models to express knowledge boundaries without annotated data, while also considering consistent knowledge boundary expression across prompts and generalization across domains.

2.2 Uncertainty-based Hallucination Detection

Some work on hallucination detection focuses on obtaining calibrated confidence from LLMs. One segment of work involves utilizing the information from these models to compute a score that signifies

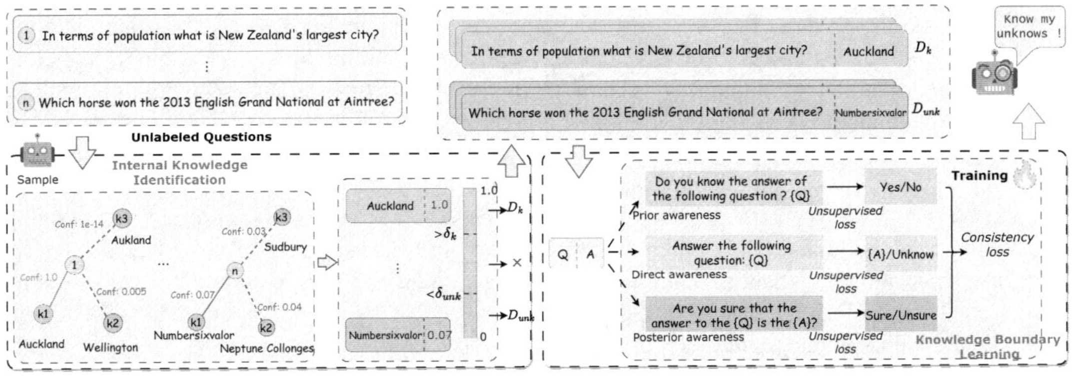

Figure 2: The procedure of CoKE, which consists of two stages. In the first stage, the model makes predictions for unlabeled questions. We obtain two parts, D_k and D_{unk}, based on the model confidence. In the second stage, we train with different prompts for the same question and use unsupervised loss and consistency loss to teach the model to express the knowledge boundary.

the model's uncertainty about knowledge (Manakul et al., 2023; Kuhn et al., 2023; Varshney et al., 2023; Duan et al., 2024). Another segment of work seeks to enable the model to express verbalized uncertainty (Lin et al., 2022; Xiong et al., 2023; Tian et al., 2023). Our work concentrates on enabling the model to explicitly express whether it is capable of answering, rather than generating a probability score. By allowing the model to express its knowledge boundary autonomously, users no longer need to concern themselves with detecting hallucinations, such as by setting uncertainty thresholds.

3 Knowledge Boundary Expression

3.1 Problem Formulation

We focus on exploring LLMs' capacity to perceive their internal knowledge. For a series of questions $Q = \{q_1, q_2, \ldots, q_n\}$, we categorize the questions based on whether the model has the knowledge required to answer them into two parts: questions that can be answered Q_k and questions that cannot be answered Q_{unk}. To minimize the interference from the model's reasoning ability, the questions used for testing the model are all single-hop questions that inquire about factual knowledge. For a given question q, the model M generates a prediction based on its parameter knowledge K_θ, represented as $y = M(K_\theta, q)$. We measure the model's awareness of its knowledge from two aspects: the awareness of the knowledge it possesses and the knowledge it does not possess. The former is represented as the ratio of the model's "Know Knows" to "Knows", denoted as R_k, while the latter is represented as the ratio of the model's "Know Unknows" to "Unknows", denoted as R_{unk}. Given a question $q \in Q_k$, R_K is set to 1 if the model's response y aligns with the knowledge k, and to 0 if the model either expresses uncertainty or provides an incorrect answer. For a question where $q \in Q_{unk}$, R_{unk} is assigned 1 if the model expresses uncertainty, and 0 if it fabricates an incorrect answer. We evaluate the model's awareness of its knowledge by testing on two types of q and calculating $S_{aware} = \frac{1}{2}(R_k + R_{unk})$. The model's awareness of its knowledge is more accurate as S_{aware} approaches 1, and less accurate as it approaches 0.

3.2 Method

Our insight is that the learning mechanism of LLM enables the model to search for the nearest knowledge k in its parameters as the answer to the query q. Although training allows the model to measure distances accurately, it does not teach it to refuse to answer based on the distance. Therefore, we hope the model can learn to use its signals to recognize when a large distance indicates a lack of knowledge to answer q. Our method involves two steps as shown in Figure 2: First, we use the model's own signals to detect knows and unknows; Second, we guide the model to learn these signals through instruction tuning, enabling it to express its knowledge boundary clearly.

3.2.1 Internal Knowledge Identification

To identify whether the model possesses the knowledge required to answer question q, we calculate the model's confidence about its prediction. The confidence of the model's prediction serves as a measure of the distance between query q and knowledge k. On the unlabeled question set Q, we let model M generate phrase-form predictions for each question. We only consider the distance between query q and the closest prediction; therefore, we use greedy decoding to obtain the prediction.

We use three model signals to represent the model's confidence: Min-Prob, Fst-Prob, and Prod-Prob. Min-Prob denotes the minimum probability among the m tokens that make up the model's prediction, $c = min(p_1, p_2, ..., p_m)$. Fst-Prob and Prod-Prob respectively represent the probability of the first token in the prediction and the product of all probabilities. Two conservative thresholds, δ_k and δ_{unk}, are established to decide whether the model has enough knowledge to answer a question. For questions with c below the threshold δ_{unk}, indicating the model is fabricating an answer due to insufficient knowledge, we define this subset as $D_{unk} = \{(q_i, y_i, c_i) \mid c_i < \delta_{unk}\}$ and use it to train the model to express its lack of knowledge. For questions with c above the threshold δ_k, indicating the model possesses the necessary knowledge, we define this subset as $D_k = \{(q_i, y_i, c_i) \mid c_i > \delta_k\}$ and use it to train the model to express that it knows the answer with increased confidence.

3.2.2 Knowledge Boundary Expression Learning

We guide the model in learning to express its knowledge boundaries clearly based on its own signals through instruction tuning. We believe that the model's expression of knowledge boundary awareness should possess two properties: honesty and consistency. Honesty requires the model to express whether it knows the answer to a question based on its certainty about the knowledge. For instance, it should not answer "I don't know" to questions it is certain about. For honesty, we fine-tune the model on the dataset obtained in the first step, enabling the model to admit its ignorance on D_{unk} and maintain its answers on D_k. Consistency requires the model to have the same semantic expression about whether it knows the same knowledge under different prompt formulations.

For consistency, we consider three different prompts for knowledge boundary awareness inquiries, which we refer to as prior awareness, direct awareness, and posterior awareness (Ren et al., 2023). **Prior awareness** involves the model assessing its ability to answer a question before actually providing an answer, with prompts like "`Do you know the answer to the question 'panda is a national animal of which country' honestly?`". **Direct awareness** involves the model responding directly to a query, supplying the answer if it possesses the knowledge, and admitting ignorance if it doesn't, with prompts like "`Answer the question 'panda is a national animal of which country' `". **Posterior awareness** involves the model's capacity to evaluate the certainty of its answers, with prompts like "`Are you sure that the answer to the 'panda is a national animal of which country' is 'China' `".

We hope that the model can express the same knowledge boundary under different prompts for the same question. It means that if the model determines that it possesses the knowledge under the prompt of prior awareness, it should be able to provide the answer when queried, and express confidence in its response when reflecting upon its answer. We teach the model to recognize its knowledge boundary by constructing three types of prompts for the same question. We incorporate the difference in probabilities of identical semantic responses under various prompts into the loss function, thereby ensuring the model's consistency across different prompts. Specifically, the loss function is defined as a combination of two components: L_{unsup}, which captures the discrepancy between the model's expression and the labels generated by its internal signals, and L_{con}, which ensures consistency of identical responses under different prompts:

$$L_{unsup} = -\sum_{1 \le i \le 3} \log P(y_i | x_i) \tag{1}$$

$$L_{con} = \sum_{1 \le i,j \le 3} \|P(y_i | x_i) - P(y_j | x_j)\|^2 \tag{2}$$

$$L = L_{unsup} + L_{con} \tag{3}$$

Previous research emphasizes that the MLP layer is a key component for storing knowledge in the transformer architecture LLM (Geva et al., 2021; Meng et al., 2022; Dai et al., 2022). Guided by these insights, we only fine-tune the weight matrix of the attention layer using LoRA (Hu et al., 2022). This strategy allows us not to change the internal knowledge of the model, but just let the model learn to express the of knowledge boundary based on the

Model	Method	TriviaQA			NQ			PopQA		
		K_{aware}	U_{aware}	S_{aware}	K_{aware}	U_{aware}	S_{aware}	K_{aware}	U_{aware}	S_{aware}
Llama2-Chat-7B	Orig.	100	0	50.0	100	0	50.0	100	0	50.0
	Fine-tune	93.9	6.2	50.1	88.6	3.1	45.8	93.5	1.9	47.7
	IDK-FT	80.8	78.0	79.4	45.5	87.6	66.6	62.8	83.6	73.2
	Uncertainty-Based									
	Min-Prob	61.8	86.2	74.0	33.4	91.4	62.4	57.7	89.3	73.5
	Fst-Prob	74.6	69.8	72.2	51.5	79.1	65.3	65.1	82.6	73.9
	Prod-Prob	68.3	81.2	$\underline{74.8}$	45.8	87.0	$\underline{66.4}$	63.7	86.4	$\underline{75.1}$
	Prompt-Based									
	Prior	96.3	7.5	51.9	97.0	10.3	53.6	65.4	31.8	48.6
	Posterior	70.5	57.9	64.2	62.7	55.6	59.1	31.6	82.8	57.2
	IC-IDK	86.4	25.8	56.1	53.6	65.1	59.3	42.3	85.3	63.8
	Verb	14.3	95.8	55.1	17.5	95.0	56.3	17.6	97.3	57.4
	CoKE	76.1	74.0	**75.0**	56.0	84.2	**70.1**	71.1	83.0	**77.0**
Llama2-Chat-13B	Orig.	100	0	50.0	100	0	50.0	100	0	50.0
	Fine-tune	96.7	7.1	51.9	95.0	2.8	48.9	95.7	2.9	49.1
	IDK-FT	82.5	81.6	82.0	53.9	84.6	69.3	65.4	82.0	73.6
	Uncertainty-Based									
	Min-Prob	91.6	44.5	$\underline{68.1}$	88.1	43.4	65.8	84.6	57.2	$\underline{70.9}$
	Fst-Prob	92.9	34.1	63.5	90.6	30.7	60.7	87.4	51.0	69.2
	Prod-Prob	65.8	80.9	**73.3**	59.1	75.5	$\underline{67.3}$	57.6	81.7	69.6
	Prompt-Based									
	Prior	88.6	14.2	51.4	81.3	26.5	53.9	38.2	81.8	60.0
	Posterior	100	0.30	50.0	100	0.0	50.0	100	0.10	50.0
	IC-IDK	99.7	1.5	50.6	96.8	6.7	51.7	90.8	25.1	58.0
	Verb	60.0	68.9	64.4	44.7	89.8	67.3	50.8	81.8	66.3
	CoKE	71.6	74.9	**73.3**	68.3	70.2	**69.2**	70.1	82.6	**76.4**

Table 1: Comparison of the performance of our method and the baseline method across an in-domain dataset (TriviaQA) and out-of-domain datasets (NQ and PopQA). We present results on two model scales: Llama2-Chat-7B and Llama2-Chat-13B.

Metric	Definition
K_{aware}	Proportion of *correct answers* on T_k
U_{aware}	Proportion of *expressions of unknown* or *correct answers* on T_{unk}
S_{aware}	$\frac{1}{2}(K_{aware} + U_{aware})$

Table 2: Knowledge awareness metrics.

confidence of the knowledge.

4 Experimental Setup

Datasets We consider three open-domain QA datasets: TriviaQA (Joshi et al., 2017), Natural Questions (Kwiatkowski et al., 2019), and PopQA (Mallen et al., 2023). These datasets are broad-coverage, knowledge-intensive QA datasets, making them well-suited for evaluating LLMs' capacity to perceive their internal knowledge. We utilize the train set of TriviaQA as our training data, treating it as unsupervised data by not using the labels. Natural Questions and PopQA serve as the out-of-domain test sets since they were not involved during the training process.

Metrics As mentioned in the Section 3.1, we evaluate the model's awareness of its knowledge from two aspects: the awareness of the knowledge it possesses and the awareness of the knowledge it does not possess. Since we cannot directly access the model's internal knowledge K_θ, we divide the test sets into two parts based on whether the model's predictions match the groundtruth: T_k represents the "Known Knows" of the model; T_{unk} contains both the "Unknown Unknows" and "Unknown Knows" cases. We expect the model to maintain correct answers on T_k, representing the retention of the "Known Knows" area of the model. At the same time, we expect the model to either express unknown on T_{unk}, signifying a reduction in the "Unknown Unknows" area, or provide correct answers, representing a decrease in the "Unknown Knows" area. We define the evaluation metrics as

Method	TriviaQA				NQ				PopQA			
	Brier↓	ECE↓	smECE↓	AUROC↑	Brier↓	ECE↓	smECE↓	AUROC↑	Brier↓	ECE↓	smECE↓	AUROC↑
Fst-Prob	0.29	0.31	0.20	0.79	0.36	0.45	0.25	0.73	0.29	0.38	0.22	0.83
Prob-Prob	0.38	0.42	0.23	**0.83**	0.55	0.65	0.31	0.73	0.46	0.57	0.28	**0.85**
Min-Prob	**0.24**	**0.26**	**0.19**	**0.83**	**0.29**	**0.39**	**0.23**	**0.77**	**0.25**	**0.34**	**0.20**	**0.85**

Table 3: Calibration results for different internal signals in Llama2-Chat-7B on TriviaQA, NQ, and PopQA.

shown in Table 2.

Baselines We consider two different types of baselines: uncertainty-based methods (white-box) and prompt-based methods (black-box). We also compared the original model (Orig.), the model fine-tuned with questions and their label (Fine-tune), and the model fine-tuned with question-label pairs, where responses to unknown questions are replaced by "Unknow" (IDK-FT). See Appendix A for more details.

Uncertainty-based methods **directly** use the model's internal signals to determine its self-awareness. The model's response consists of multiple tokens, and we experimented with three types of methods to calculate the final confidence score from the probabilities of these tokens:

- **Min token probability (Min-Prob)**: Use the smallest token probability in the model's prediction as the confidence score.
- **Product token probability (Prod-Prob)**: Use the product of the probabilities of all tokens in the model's prediction as the confidence score.
- **First token probability (Fst-Prob)**: Use the probability of the first token in the model's prediction as the confidence score.

Prompt-based methods use prompts to let models express their own knowledge boundary in natural language.

- **Prior prompt**: Similar to Ren et al. (2023) evaluating whether the model gives up on answering, we use the prompt to directly ask the model if it knows the answer to the question.
- **Posterior prompt**: Kadavath et al. (2022) shows the model can evaluate the certainty of its answers. We use the prompt to ask the model about the certainty of its answers.
- **In-context IDK (IC-IDK)**: Following Cohen et al. (2023), by integrating demonstrations into the prompt, we enable the model to express its knowledge boundary through in-context learning.
- **Verbalize uncertainty (Verb)**: Resent work (Tian et al., 2023) suggests that LLMs' verbalized uncertainty exhibits a degree of calibration. We let the model output verbalized uncertainty, and search for the optimal threshold in the training set.

5 Results and Analysis

5.1 Overall Performance

We present our main results on the in-domain and out-of-domain datasets in Table 1. Generally, we have the following findings:

Across all settings, we outperform prompt-based methods by a large gap. On Llama2-Chat-7B, CoKE obtains an S_{aware} of 75.0 compared to ≤ 64.2 by prompt-based methods on TriviaQA, and obtains an S_{aware} of 77.0 compared to ≤ 63.8 by prompt-based methods on PopQA. Models struggle to accurately express knowledge boundaries when it comes to the prior prompt, in-context learning, and posterior prompts. Meanwhile, models can express verbalized uncertainty through prompts, and their accuracy improves with larger models, but remains limited for models with fewer than 13 billion parameters. Interestingly, while accuracy improves with larger model sizes, self-awareness does not show significant gains in most cases. We believe that this capability may require even larger models to become evident.

Compared to uncertainty-based methods, CoKE can outperform in most settings. This demonstrates that CoKE enables the model to effectively learn its confidence signals and generalize beyond the training signals. On out-of-domain datasets, CoKE significantly outperforms uncertainty-based methods, indicating that thresholds derived from a dataset have poor transferability, while CoKE exhibits better generalization.

Compared to methods requiring labeled data for fine-tuning, CoKE demonstrates better generalization. Although CoKE performs worse than IDK-FT on in-domain test sets, it significantly out-

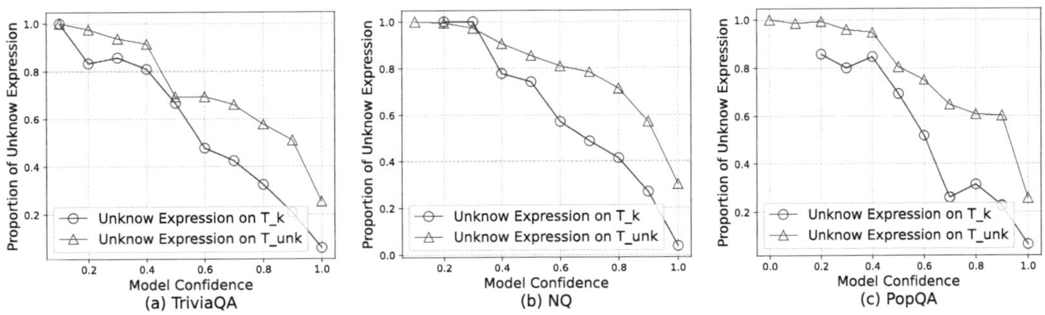

Figure 3: Model's "Unknow" expression ratio in question groups under different confidence scores (using minimum token probability). As the model's confidence score decreases, the ratio of "Unknow" expressions increases. The model exhibits a higher "Unknow" expression ratio on T_{unk} compared to T_k.

Training Signal	TriviaQA	NQ	PopQA
Fst-Prob	74.9	69.3	76.2
Prod-Prob	73.9	69.8	76.3
Min-Prob	**75.0**	**70.1**	**77.0**

Table 4: Different signals serve as the model's confidence score in training the expression of knowledge boundary. The metric is represented by the S_{aware}.

performs this supervised fine-tuning approach on out-of-domain datasets. This indicates that by leveraging the model's internal signals to teach LLMs to express knowledge boundaries, COKE not only avoids reliance on labeled data but also achieves better generalization.

5.2 Effectiveness of Model Signals

We demonstrate the effectiveness of model internal signals in reflecting the model's knowledge boundaries through an evaluation of these signals. We used the same metrics as (Ulmer et al., 2024), including Brier score (BRIER, 1950), expected calibration error (ECE; Pakdaman Naeini et al., 2015), and smooth ECE (smECE; Blasiok and Nakkiran, 2024) to evaluate the model signals' calibration ability, and used AUROC to measure the model's ability to identify questions it doesn't know. As shown in Table 3, model internal signals perform poorly in terms of calibration, with high Brier and ECE scores. However, model internal signals perform well in determining whether the model is ignorant, with high AUROC scores, which is also reflected in the uncertainty-based methods in Table 1. By employing strict thresholds, our method mitigates signal noise while leveraging the signals' ability to discriminate between knowledge and ignorance.

We also analyze the effectiveness of different internal signals as training signals. As a training signal, the use of the minimum probability of multi-token outperforms other signals on both in-domain and out-of-domain datasets, as illustrated in Table 4. We consider that the minimum probability of multi-token is more easily mastered by the model. We leave the discovery of better signals reflecting the model's knowledge boundary and the utilization of multi-signal training for future work.

5.3 Leverage Internal Signals for Knowledge Boundary Expression

We investigated how our model utilizes confidence scores to express its knowledge boundary. Figure 3 illustrates the relationship between confidence scores and the model's tendency to respond with "Unknow". The results show a clear pattern: the model rarely answers "Unknow" at high confidence levels, while frequently doing so at low confidence levels. For example, with confidence scores below 0.4, the model almost always responds "Unknow", whereas it confidently provides answers when scores approach 1.0. This demonstrates that **the model effectively uses confidence scores to delineate its knowledge boundaries and generalizes well to out-of-domain data.**

Interestingly, we observed that for the same confidence level, the model responds "Unknow" more frequently to questions in T_{unk} compared to T_k. This suggests that **the model has learned to utilize additional implicit information beyond just the confidence score, which helps mitigate the problem of overconfidence in incorrect answers.** By incorporating the model's confidence as a supervisory signal during training, we reduce the noise associated with using minimum token probabil-

Method	T_k				T_{unk}			
	Correct (↑)	IDK (↓)	Wrong (↓)	Probs	Correct (↑)	IDK (↑)	Wrong (↓)	Probs
Orig.	100	0	0	0.86/ - / -	0	0	100	- / - /0.58
Min-Prob	61.8	38.2	0	0.98/0.68/ -	0	86.2	13.8	- /0.53/0.96
Posterior	70.5	29.5	0	0.86/0.85/ -	0	57.9	42.1	- /0.55/0.63
COKE	76.1	22.3	1.6	0.92/0.68/0.60	3.7	70.3	26.0	0.64/0.52/0.75

Table 5: Percentage distribution of Llama-Chat-7B outputs on TriviaQA across three categories: correct answers, expressions of unknowns, and wrong answers. "Prob" represents the average min-probability for each category.

ity alone, resulting in improved performance compared to methods based solely on uncertainty.

5.4 Consistency of Knowledge Boundary Expression

We investigate the benefits of teaching a model to express knowledge boundary by using the strategy of constructing different prompts for the same question and applying a consistency regularization loss function. By adopting this strategy, we discover that it not only improves the model's ability to generalize, but also ensures a consistent expression of knowledge boundary under different prompts. Results from Table 6 indicate that the application of consistency loss, despite causing a slight decrease in S_{aware} on the in-domain dataset, leads to substantial improvements on the out-of-domain dataset, thereby demonstrating enhanced generalization. We also reported the consistency of the model's expression of knowledge boundary under different prompts, as shown in Table 6. We evaluate the model's consistency by randomly sampling two different types of prompt templates from prompt pools (see Appendix B.2). We notice that the model adopted with consistency loss is capable of expressing consistent knowledge boundaries for most questions under different prompts.

Method	TriviaQA		NQ		PopQA	
	S_{aware}	Con.	S_{aware}	Con.	S_{aware}	Con.
orig.	50.0	35.2	50.0	22.2	50.0	39.3
COKE	75.0	**92.1**	**70.1**	**90.9**	**77.0**	**89.6**
w/o *Con-loss*	**75.6**	46.3	69.2	36.7	74.8	43.6

Table 6: The consistency of knowledge boundary expressions under different prompts. "Con." refers to the percentage of consistent responses when the model is presented with the same question using different prompt templates.

5.5 Error Analysis

Enhancing a model's self-awareness capability involves a tradeoff between maintaining performance on known knowledge (K_{aware}) and refusing to answer on unknown knowledge (U_{aware}). We analyze the outputs of COKE and other methods, examining the types and proportions of different outputs within T_k and T_{unk}. As shown in Table 3, for the T_k portion, COKE is able to maintain correct expressions for most questions, and the performance drop is due to the model becoming more conservative, refusing to answer some low-confidence questions. In the T_{unk} portion, the model correctly refuses to answer most questions it doesn't know, but issues of overconfidence still exist. Additionally, some originally correct answers become incorrect, and some originally incorrect answers become correct, which might result from the model changing its responses to questions with low confidence. Observing the average probabilities across different output types, Posterior methods show nearly identical probabilities for different outputs, while COKE demonstrates a clearer alignment between its expression and answer confidence.

6 Conclusion

In this paper, we target the knowledge boundary expression problem and propose COKE, a novel unsupervised approach for this task. Our approach is built on detecting signals of the model indicating confidence, and teaching the model to use its signals to express knowledge boundary. Through comprehensive experiments on in-domain and out-of-domain datasets, we show that our method can teach the model to use its signals, significantly enhancing the model's ability to accurately express knowledge boundary. Our work can be extended by seeking more internal signals that better reflect the model's confidence and exploring how to combine these signals to train the model, inspiring further research into models autonomously improving their ability to express knowledge boundaries without human annotations.

Limitations

We note three limitations of our current work. First is the accuracy of the evaluation methods. Because of the lack of a method to discover the internal knowledge of the model, we divided T_k and T_{unk} based on whether the model's answer matches the groundtruth, ignoring the impact of the model's erroneous beliefs. Another limitation is that to prevent exposure bias and the influence of multiple pieces of knowledge, we focused on the expression of knowledge boundary under short-form answers, without investigating the issue of long-form generation. Last, we focused on the model's ability to express the boundary of its internal knowledge, not extending to scenarios like self-awareness with external knowledge (e.g., RAG scenarios) or reasoning abilities (e.g., mathematics or logical reasoning).

Ethical Statement

We hereby acknowledge that all authors of this work are aware of the provided ACL Code of Ethics and honor the code of conduct.

Risks We propose COKE, which teaches models to express their knowledge boundaries using internal signals, thereby reducing hallucinations caused by fabricating answers when they do not know. Our experiments demonstrate that our method significantly reduces the instances of models fabricating answers to unknown questions. However, models may still occasionally produce fabricated answers in certain scenarios. Therefore, in practical applications, it is important to note that our method does not completely eliminate hallucinations, and there remains a risk of models generating fabricated content. Caution is advised in fields with stringent requirements.

References

2023. John schulman - reinforcement learning from human feedback: Progress and challenges.

Josh Achiam, Steven Adler, Sandhini Agarwal, Lama Ahmad, Ilge Akkaya, Florencia Leoni Aleman, Diogo Almeida, Janko Altenschmidt, Sam Altman, Shyamal Anadkat, and 1 others. 2023. Gpt-4 technical report. *arXiv preprint arXiv:2303.08774*.

Jaroslaw Blasiok and Preetum Nakkiran. 2024. Smooth ECE: Principled reliability diagrams via kernel smoothing. In *The Twelfth International Conference on Learning Representations*.

GLENN W. BRIER. 1950. Verification of forecasts expressed in terms of probability. *Monthly Weather Review*, 78(1):1 – 3.

Tom Brown, Benjamin Mann, Nick Ryder, Melanie Subbiah, Jared D Kaplan, Prafulla Dhariwal, Arvind Neelakantan, Pranav Shyam, Girish Sastry, Amanda Askell, Sandhini Agarwal, Ariel Herbert-Voss, Gretchen Krueger, Tom Henighan, Rewon Child, Aditya Ramesh, Daniel Ziegler, Jeffrey Wu, Clemens Winter, and 12 others. 2020. Language models are few-shot learners. In *Advances in Neural Information Processing Systems*, volume 33, pages 1877–1901. Curran Associates, Inc.

Roi Cohen, May Hamri, Mor Geva, and Amir Globerson. 2023. LM vs LM: Detecting factual errors via cross examination. In *Proceedings of the 2023 Conference on Empirical Methods in Natural Language Processing*, pages 12621–12640, Singapore. Association for Computational Linguistics.

Jiaxi Cui, Zongjian Li, Yang Yan, Bohua Chen, and Li Yuan. 2023. Chatlaw: Open-source legal large language model with integrated external knowledge bases. *arXiv preprint arXiv:2306.16092*.

Damai Dai, Li Dong, Yaru Hao, Zhifang Sui, Baobao Chang, and Furu Wei. 2022. Knowledge neurons in pretrained transformers. In *Proceedings of the 60th Annual Meeting of the Association for Computational Linguistics (Volume 1: Long Papers)*, pages 8493–8502, Dublin, Ireland. Association for Computational Linguistics.

Jinhao Duan, Hao Cheng, Shiqi Wang, Alex Zavalny, Chenan Wang, Renjing Xu, Bhavya Kailkhura, and Kaidi Xu. 2024. Shifting attention to relevance: Towards the predictive uncertainty quantification of free-form large language models. In *Proceedings of the 62nd Annual Meeting of the Association for Computational Linguistics (Volume 1: Long Papers)*, pages 5050–5063, Bangkok, Thailand. Association for Computational Linguistics.

Zorik Gekhman, Gal Yona, Roee Aharoni, Matan Eyal, Amir Feder, Roi Reichart, and Jonathan Herzig. 2024. Does fine-tuning llms on new knowledge encourage hallucinations? *arXiv preprint arXiv:2405.05904*.

Mor Geva, Roei Schuster, Jonathan Berant, and Omer Levy. 2021. Transformer feed-forward layers are key-value memories. In *Proceedings of the 2021 Conference on Empirical Methods in Natural Language Processing*, pages 5484–5495, Online and Punta Cana, Dominican Republic. Association for Computational Linguistics.

Edward J Hu, yelong shen, Phillip Wallis, Zeyuan Allen-Zhu, Yuanzhi Li, Shean Wang, Lu Wang, and Weizhu Chen. 2022. LoRA: Low-rank adaptation of large language models. In *International Conference on Learning Representations*.

Ziwei Ji, Nayeon Lee, Rita Frieske, Tiezheng Yu, Dan Su, Yan Xu, Etsuko Ishii, Ye Jin Bang, Andrea

Madotto, and Pascale Fung. 2023. Survey of hallucination in natural language generation. *ACM Comput. Surv.*, 55(12).

Di Jin, Eileen Pan, Nassim Oufattole, Wei-Hung Weng, Hanyi Fang, and Peter Szolovits. 2021. What disease does this patient have? a large-scale open domain question answering dataset from medical exams. *Applied Sciences*, 11(14).

Mandar Joshi, Eunsol Choi, Daniel Weld, and Luke Zettlemoyer. 2017. TriviaQA: A large scale distantly supervised challenge dataset for reading comprehension. In *Proceedings of the 55th Annual Meeting of the Association for Computational Linguistics (Volume 1: Long Papers)*, pages 1601–1611, Vancouver, Canada. Association for Computational Linguistics.

Saurav Kadavath, Tom Conerly, Amanda Askell, Tom Henighan, Dawn Drain, Ethan Perez, Nicholas Schiefer, Zac Hatfield-Dodds, Nova DasSarma, Eli Tran-Johnson, and 1 others. 2022. Language models (mostly) know what they know. *arXiv preprint arXiv:2207.05221*.

Katie Kang, Eric Wallace, Claire Tomlin, Aviral Kumar, and Sergey Levine. 2024. Unfamiliar finetuning examples control how language models hallucinate. *arXiv preprint arXiv:2403.05612*.

Lorenz Kuhn, Yarin Gal, and Sebastian Farquhar. 2023. Semantic uncertainty: Linguistic invariances for uncertainty estimation in natural language generation. In *The Eleventh International Conference on Learning Representations*.

Tom Kwiatkowski, Jennimaria Palomaki, Olivia Redfield, Michael Collins, Ankur Parikh, Chris Alberti, Danielle Epstein, Illia Polosukhin, Jacob Devlin, Kenton Lee, Kristina Toutanova, Llion Jones, Matthew Kelcey, Ming-Wei Chang, Andrew M. Dai, Jakob Uszkoreit, Quoc Le, and Slav Petrov. 2019. Natural Questions: A Benchmark for Question Answering Research. *Transactions of the Association for Computational Linguistics*, 7:453–466.

Kenneth Li, Oam Patel, Fernanda Viégas, Hanspeter Pfister, and Martin Wattenberg. 2023. Inference-time intervention: Eliciting truthful answers from a language model. In *Advances in Neural Information Processing Systems*, volume 36, pages 41451–41530. Curran Associates, Inc.

Stephanie Lin, Jacob Hilton, and Owain Evans. 2022. Teaching models to express their uncertainty in words. *Transactions on Machine Learning Research*.

Alex Mallen, Akari Asai, Victor Zhong, Rajarshi Das, Daniel Khashabi, and Hannaneh Hajishirzi. 2023. When not to trust language models: Investigating effectiveness of parametric and non-parametric memories. In *Proceedings of the 61st Annual Meeting of the Association for Computational Linguistics (Volume 1: Long Papers)*, pages 9802–9822, Toronto, Canada. Association for Computational Linguistics.

Potsawee Manakul, Adian Liusie, and Mark Gales. 2023. SelfCheckGPT: Zero-resource black-box hallucination detection for generative large language models. In *Proceedings of the 2023 Conference on Empirical Methods in Natural Language Processing*, pages 9004–9017, Singapore. Association for Computational Linguistics.

Kevin Meng, David Bau, Alex Andonian, and Yonatan Belinkov. 2022. Locating and editing factual associations in gpt. In *Advances in Neural Information Processing Systems*, volume 35, pages 17359–17372. Curran Associates, Inc.

Long Ouyang, Jeffrey Wu, Xu Jiang, Diogo Almeida, Carroll Wainwright, Pamela Mishkin, Chong Zhang, Sandhini Agarwal, Katarina Slama, Alex Ray, John Schulman, Jacob Hilton, Fraser Kelton, Luke Miller, Maddie Simens, Amanda Askell, Peter Welinder, Paul F Christiano, Jan Leike, and Ryan Lowe. 2022. Training language models to follow instructions with human feedback. In *Advances in Neural Information Processing Systems*, volume 35, pages 27730–27744. Curran Associates, Inc.

Mahdi Pakdaman Naeini, Gregory Cooper, and Milos Hauskrecht. 2015. Obtaining well calibrated probabilities using bayesian binning. *Proceedings of the AAAI Conference on Artificial Intelligence*, 29(1).

Ruiyang Ren, Yuhao Wang, Yingqi Qu, Wayne Xin Zhao, Jing Liu, Hao Tian, Hua Wu, Ji-Rong Wen, and Haifeng Wang. 2023. Investigating the factual knowledge boundary of large language models with retrieval augmentation. *arXiv preprint arXiv:2307.11019*.

Nisan Stiennon, Long Ouyang, Jeffrey Wu, Daniel Ziegler, Ryan Lowe, Chelsea Voss, Alec Radford, Dario Amodei, and Paul F Christiano. 2020. Learning to summarize with human feedback. In *Advances in Neural Information Processing Systems*, volume 33, pages 3008–3021. Curran Associates, Inc.

Katherine Tian, Eric Mitchell, Huaxiu Yao, Christopher D Manning, and Chelsea Finn. 2024. Finetuning language models for factuality. In *The Twelfth International Conference on Learning Representations*.

Katherine Tian, Eric Mitchell, Allan Zhou, Archit Sharma, Rafael Rafailov, Huaxiu Yao, Chelsea Finn, and Christopher Manning. 2023. Just ask for calibration: Strategies for eliciting calibrated confidence scores from language models fine-tuned with human feedback. In *Proceedings of the 2023 Conference on Empirical Methods in Natural Language Processing*, pages 5433–5442, Singapore. Association for Computational Linguistics.

Hugo Touvron, Louis Martin, Kevin Stone, Peter Albert, Amjad Almahairi, Yasmine Babaei, Nikolay Bashlykov, Soumya Batra, Prajjwal Bhargava, Shruti

Bhosale, and 1 others. 2023. Llama 2: Open foundation and fine-tuned chat models. *arXiv preprint arXiv:2307.09288*.

Dennis Ulmer, Martin Gubri, Hwaran Lee, Sangdoo Yun, and Seong Oh. 2024. Calibrating large language models using their generations only. In *Proceedings of the 62nd Annual Meeting of the Association for Computational Linguistics (Volume 1: Long Papers)*, pages 15440–15459, Bangkok, Thailand. Association for Computational Linguistics.

Neeraj Varshney, Wenlin Yao, Hongming Zhang, Jianshu Chen, and Dong Yu. 2023. A stitch in time saves nine: Detecting and mitigating hallucinations of llms by validating low-confidence generation. *arXiv preprint arXiv:2307.03987*.

Jason Wei, Xuezhi Wang, Dale Schuurmans, Maarten Bosma, brian ichter, Fei Xia, Ed Chi, Quoc V Le, and Denny Zhou. 2022. Chain-of-thought prompting elicits reasoning in large language models. In *Advances in Neural Information Processing Systems*, volume 35, pages 24824–24837. Curran Associates, Inc.

Miao Xiong, Zhiyuan Hu, Xinyang Lu, Yifei Li, Jie Fu, Junxian He, and Bryan Hooi. 2023. Can llms express their uncertainty? an empirical evaluation of confidence elicitation in llms. *arXiv preprint arXiv:2306.13063*.

Yuqing Yang, Ethan Chern, Xipeng Qiu, Graham Neubig, and Pengfei Liu. 2023. Alignment for honesty. *arXiv preprint arXiv:2312.07000*.

Zhangyue Yin, Qiushi Sun, Qipeng Guo, Jiawen Wu, Xipeng Qiu, and Xuanjing Huang. 2023. Do large language models know what they don't know? In *Findings of the Association for Computational Linguistics: ACL 2023*, pages 8653–8665, Toronto, Canada. Association for Computational Linguistics.

Hanning Zhang, Shizhe Diao, Yong Lin, Yi R Fung, Qing Lian, Xingyao Wang, Yangyi Chen, Heng Ji, and Tong Zhang. 2023a. R-tuning: Teaching large language models to refuse unknown questions. *arXiv preprint arXiv:2311.09677*.

Yue Zhang, Yafu Li, Leyang Cui, Deng Cai, Lemao Liu, Tingchen Fu, Xinting Huang, Enbo Zhao, Yu Zhang, Yulong Chen, and 1 others. 2023b. Siren's song in the ai ocean: a survey on hallucination in large language models. *arXiv preprint arXiv:2309.01219*.

Zeyuan Allen Zhu and Yuanzhi Li. 2023. Physics of language models: Part 3.1, knowledge storage and extraction. *arXiv preprint arXiv:2309.14316*.

Andy Zou, Long Phan, Sarah Chen, James Campbell, Phillip Guo, Richard Ren, Alexander Pan, Xuwang Yin, Mantas Mazeika, Ann-Kathrin Dombrowski, and 1 others. 2023. Representation engineering: A top-down approach to ai transparency. *arXiv preprint arXiv:2310.01405*.

A Methodology

In this section, we elaborate on the rationale for selecting the baseline methods in our work, as well as the implementation details.

A.1 Uncertainty-based Methods

Inspired by works on uncertainty estimation for LLMs, we believe that confidence calculated through the model's internal signals can effectively reflect the model's self-awareness. Since we control the model to output only answer phrases instead of full sentences through prompting, we do not need to perform additional extraction on the generated content (Varshney et al., 2023; Duan et al., 2024), but instead directly compute using the logits of the tokens in the generated answer phrase.

In this work, we consider three methods for calculating the model's confidence using its internal signals:

- **Min token probability & Product token probability:** Varshney et al. (2023) found that the minimum and product of the probabilities of tokens that form important concepts in a model-generated sentence can effectively reflect the model's uncertainty. For Min token probability, we directly take the smallest probability among the tokens that compose the model-generated phrase as the model's confidence. For Product token probability, we calculate the product of the probabilities of each token, and then normalize it by the length to obtain the final confidence score.
- **First token probability:** Considering that the model may store the entire concept's information in the hidden state of the token at the beginning of the concept phrase (Zhu and Li, 2023), we use the probability of the first token to represent the confidence of the entire response.

To directly use the confidence score to predict the model's knowledge boundary, we determine whether the model expresses uncertainty based on whether the score exceeds a threshold. We determine the optimal threshold for the model's knowledge boundary expression on 100 labeled samples from the TriviaQA training set, aiming to maximize the model's S_{aware} score.

A.2 Prompt-based Methods

Prompt-based methods directly prompt LLMs to declare their knowledge boundaries in textual form, without needing to access the internal signals of

Prompt-based Method	Prompt
Prior Prompt	Do you know the answer to the following question honestly? If you know, output Yes, otherwise output No, just say one word either Yes or No\n{Q}
Posterior Prompt	Are you sure that the answer to the following {Q} is the following {A}? If you are sure, output Sure, otherwise output Unsure, just say one word either Sure or Unsure
In-context IDK	Answer the following questions like examples. When you do not know the answer, output Unknow.\nExamples:\nQuestion: Which is the largest island in the Mediterranean Sea?\nAnswer: Sicily\nQuestion: Which country will host the 2016 European Nations football finals?\nAnswer: France\nQuestion: Actress Audrey Hepburn won her only Oscar for which film?\nAnswer: Roman Holiday\nQuestion: Who leads the Catholic Church?\nAnswer: Unknow\n\nYou should only output the answer, without any extra information or explanations. Do not repeat the question. If there are multiple answers, just output the most likely one. The answer should not be a sentence, just a phrase part of the answer. Here is your question: Question: {Q}
Verbalize Uncertainty	Provide your best guess and the probability that it is correct (0.0 to 1.0) for the following question. Give ONLY the guess and probability, no other words or explanation. For example:\n\nGuess: <most likely guess, as short as possible; not a complete sentence, just the guess!>\nProbability: <the probability between 0.0 and 1.0 that your guess is correct, without any extra commentary whatsoever; just the probability!>\n\nThe question is:\n{Q}.

Table 7: Instructional prompts used in the prompt-based method.

the model. Table 7 shows the prompts we used in the prompt-based methods.

A.3 Fine-tuning Methods

We consider two conventional fine-tuning methods as baselines. These fine-tuning methods use the same training set as our approach, but they sample training data based on labels rather than model signals. **Fine-tune** is a conventional instruction fine-tuning method, where the model is fine-tuned directly on question-answer pairs. Regardless of whether the model answers correctly, the fine-tuning target is always the ground truth. **IDK-FT** first lets the model predict the answer to a question. The fine-tuning target depends on whether the model's response matches the ground truth. If it matches, the ground truth is used as the target; if it doesn't, the target is replaced with "Unknow".

B Experimental Settings

B.1 Dataset Details

We use three QA datasets: TriviaQA (Joshi et al., 2017), NQ (Kwiatkowski et al., 2019), and PopQA (Mallen et al., 2023) to construct our test data for evaluating the model's self-awareness. These datasets consist of single-hop factual questions, which do not involve the model's reasoning capabilities, making them more suitable for testing the model's internal knowledge. Additionally, the answers in these datasets are in short-form phrases, avoiding the biases that might be exposed through long-form generation. We use a closed-book, free-form setup to evaluate the models' ability to express their knowledge boundaries. We use exact match to determine whether the model answers correctly or expresses the unknown. The test sets of TriviaQA, NQ, and PopQA contain 11,313, 3,610, and 14,267 samples, respectively. We randomly sampled 2,000 examples from each of the TriviaQA, NQ, and PopQA test sets as our test data. As shown in Figure 8, **the model exhibits different knowledge boundaries across different datasets, and different models also show varying knowledge boundaries on the same dataset.** The proportions of T_k and T_{unk} differ across the test datasets, but the model's self-awareness score

Model	TriviaQA	NQ	PopQA
Llama2-Chat-7B	45.2	16.6	21.7
Llama2-Chat-13B	52.0	21.9	23.5

Table 8: The accuracy of vanilla LLMs on our test data. It represents the portion of knowledge that the model knows and can answer (Known Knows).

Type	Prompt
Prior Awareness	1. Do you know the answer to the following question honestly? If you know, output Yes, otherwise output No, just say one word either Yes or No\n{Q}
	2. Do you have knowledge of the answer to this question? If you do, reply with Yes; if not, reply with No, just say one word either Yes or No\n{Q}
	3. Is the answer to this question known to you? Reply Yes if it is; otherwise, reply No, just say one word either Yes or No\n{Q}
	4. Do you have enough information to answer the following question? If yes, answer Yes; if no, answer No, just say one word either Yes or No\n{Q}
Posterior Awareness	1. Are you certain that 'A' is the correct answer to 'Q'? If certain, answer Sure; if not, answer Unsure, just say one word either Sure or Unsure\nQ: {Q}\nA: {A}\n
	2. Do you believe with certainty that 'A' is the correct answer to 'Q'? If yes, answer Sure; if not, answer Unsure, just say one word either Sure or Unsure\nQ: {Q}\nA: {A}\n
	3. Are you certain that your answer 'A' to 'Q' is based on accurate information? If so, answer Sure; if not, answer Unsure, just say one word either Sure or Unsure\nQ: {Q}\nA: {A}\n
	4. Do you trust the information that led to your answer 'A' to 'Q'? If confident, answer Sure; if not, answer Unsure, just say one word either Sure or Unsure\nQ: {Q}\nA: {A}\n

Table 9: Prompts used to test the consistency of knowledge boundary expression under different prompts.

S_{aware} is calculated by averaging the scores corresponding to T_k and T_{unk}, thus not being affected by sample imbalance. Since we use the TriviaQA training set as the training data, the NQ and PopQA datasets, which have distributions different from TriviaQA, serve as out-of-distribution test sets with varying knowledge boundary distributions.

B.2 Prompt for Consistency Evaluation

We used the prompts in Table 9 as the prompt pool for testing the consistency of knowledge boundary expression under different prompts. We utilized GPT-4o to generate different prompts that assess the model's ability to express knowledge boundaries, categorizing them into two types.

B.3 Implementation Details

For our experiment, we choose to use the LLaMA2-Chat (Touvron et al., 2023) model. Based on the pre-trained LLaMA2 model, LLaMA2-Chat is a model that has undergone instruction tuning and RLHF (Stiennon et al., 2020), thereby acquiring the capability to follow instructions. We use the 7B and 13B versions of the LLaMA2-Chat model. We set the thresholds δ_k and δ_{unk} to 0.99 and 0.4, respectively. Due to the large number of instances, we sort the confidence scores from the TriviaQA training set and designate the bottom 10% as D_{unk} and the top 20% as D_k, resulting in approximately 23,000 instances in total. We use LoRA for model fine-tuning, setting r=8, alpha=16, and dropout=0.05. During training, we set the initial learning rate to 1e-4, the final learning rate to 3e-4, the warmup phase to 300 steps, and we train for 700 steps. We conduct all our experiments on 4 NVIDIA A800 80GB GPUs.

C Experimental Supplement

C.1 Effectiveness of Model Signals

We also illustrate the effectiveness of the confidence calculation method through an empirical study. We obtain the model confidence for Llama2-chat-7B on the Trivia-QA training set using three different methods. We divide the model's responses into two parts based on whether the answers are correct and calculate the sample distribution for each part. As shown in Figure 4, there is a significant difference in the confidence distribution

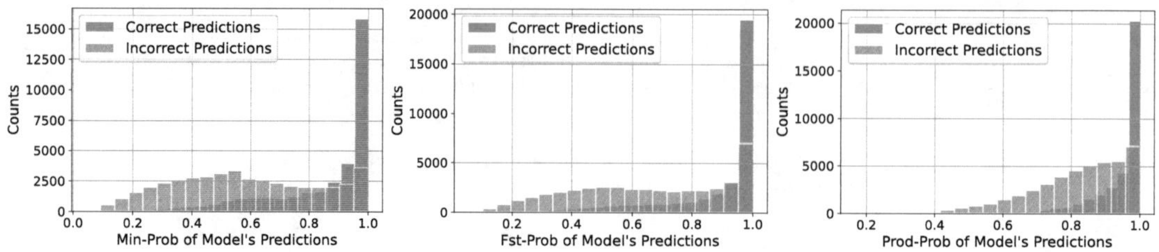

Figure 4: Distribution of model predictions regarding confidence for Llama2-Chat-7B on Trivia-QA. Confidence is calculated using Min-Prob, Fst-Prob, and Prod-Prob from left to right.

between the Correct Predictions and Incorrect Predictions. Predictions with confidence less than 0.4 are mostly incorrect, while the confidence of correct predictions is generally 1.0. This indicates that the model signals can reflect the model's confidence, implying whether the model possesses the corresponding knowledge.

Knowledge-Grounded Detection of Cryptocurrency Scams with Retrieval-Augmented LMs

Zichao Li
Canoakbit Alliance
Canada

Abstract

This paper presents a knowledge-grounded framework for cryptocurrency scam detection using retrieval-augmented language models. We address three key limitations of existing approaches: static knowledge bases, unreliable LM outputs, and fixed classification thresholds. Our method combines (1) temporally-weighted retrieval from scam databases, (2) confidence-aware fusion of parametric and external knowledge, and (3) adaptive threshold optimization via gradient ascent. Experiments on CryptoScams and Twitter Financial Scams datasets demonstrate state-of-the-art performance, with 22% higher recall at equivalent precision compared to fixed thresholds, 4.3× lower hallucination rates than pure LMs, and 89% temporal performance retention on emerging scam types. The system achieves real-time operation (45ms/query) while maintaining interpretability through evidence grounding. Ablation studies confirm each component's necessity, with confidence fusion proving most critical (12.1% performance drop when removed). These advances enable more robust monitoring of evolving cryptocurrency threats while addressing fundamental challenges in knowledgeable foundation models.

1 Introduction

The rise of cryptocurrency has been accompanied by a surge in fraudulent activities, from Ponzi schemes to fake token sales, costing users billions annually (Courtois et al., 2023). While large language models (LLMs) have shown promise in detecting such scams, their reliance on parametric knowledge alone often leads to hallucinations or outdated claims (Lin et al., 2024). To address this, we propose a **knowledge-grounded** approach that combines retrieval-augmented generation (RAG) with LLMs to improve the accuracy and reliability of cryptocurrency scam detection.

Our work focuses on two key challenges: (1) **grounding LM outputs in structured knowledge** (e.g., known scam patterns from `CryptoScams` (Smock, 2023) or regulatory reports), and (2) **quantifying the reliability** of LM-generated fraud alerts using fact-checking benchmarks like `FEVER` (Thorne et al., 2018). We define *knowledge-grounded detection* as the process of augmenting LLMs with retrieved evidence from trusted sources (e.g., `ScamAdviser`, `FTC fraud databases`) to reduce reliance on parametric memory. This is critical in the cryptocurrency domain, where scams evolve rapidly and static training data quickly becomes obsolete.

Our contributions include: (1) a framework for integrating retrieval-augmented LLMs (e.g., `Llama-3` fine-tuned with `LoRA` (Hu et al., 2023)) with dynamic scam databases indexed via `FAISS` (Johnson et al., 2021); (2) an evaluation of how retrieval improves over zero-shot LLM performance on datasets like `Twitter Financial Scams` (Kumar et al., 2023); and (3) a systematic analysis of hallucination rates using `FactScore` (Min et al., 2024). By bridging the gap between unstructured LM knowledge and structured fraud patterns, our work advances the broader goal of building *knowledgeable foundation models* for high-stakes domains.

2 Literature Review

Fraud Detection with LMs. Prior work has explored LLMs for financial fraud detection, though primarily in traditional domains like credit card transactions (ULB, 2020). Recent studies highlight the potential of few-shot prompting for scam classification (Huang et al., 2023), but they often fail to address the dynamic nature of cryptocurrency scams, where new schemes emerge weekly. Retrieval-augmented methods, such as those in (Lewis et al., 2020b), have improved factuality in open-domain QA but remain understudied for fraud scenarios.

Proceedings of the 3rd Workshop on Towards Knowledgeable Foundation Models (KnowFM), pages 40–48
August 1, 2025 ©2025 Association for Computational Linguistics

Knowledge-Augmented LMs. The integration of external knowledge into LMs has been studied extensively, from early work on knowledge bases (Peters et al., 2019) to modern RAG systems (Lewis et al., 2020a). However, most focus on general-domain QA (Karpukhin et al., 2020) or scientific tasks (Wadden et al., 2021), with limited attention to adversarial domains like fraud. Techniques like MEMIT (Mitchell et al., 2023) enable knowledge editing in LMs, but their applicability to real-time scam detection is untested.

Cryptocurrency and NLP. Research on crypto scams has relied on manual pattern matching (Chen et al., 2021) or graph-based anomaly detection (Zhang et al., 2022). While (Naman et al., 2022) introduced QA benchmarks for blockchain knowledge, they do not evaluate retrieval-augmented LMs. Similarly, datasets like `CryptoScams` (Smock, 2023) provide labeled examples but lack structured knowledge for grounding. We have also studied similar work of (Huo et al., 2025; Zhu et al., 2025; Wang et al., 2025).

Gaps and Our Approach. Existing methods either (1) rely on static LM knowledge, risking hallucinations (Kadavath et al., 2022), or (2) use retrieval without domain-specific tuning (Bhatia et al., 2024). Our work bridges this by (1) curating retrievable scam templates from `FTC reports` and `ScamAdviser`, (2) evaluating retrieval fidelity via `FEVER` (Thorne et al., 2018), and (3) quantifying the trade-offs between zero-shot and retrieval-augmented detection—a gap highlighted in (Wang et al., 2023) but not yet addressed for crypto fraud.

3 Methodology

The limitations identified in existing literature, particularly the lack of dynamic knowledge integration for cryptocurrency scams (Courtois et al., 2023), unreliable factuality in LM-based fraud detection (Lin et al., 2024), and static retrieval approaches (Wang et al., 2023) which motivate our three-tier methodology. First, we introduce a **knowledge-enhanced retrieval mechanism** that dynamically updates scam templates from structured sources (e.g., `ScamAdviser`), addressing the latency in parametric LM knowledge. Second, we formalize a **confidence-aware fusion model** to combine retrieved evidence with LM predictions, mitigating hallucinations through probabilistic calibration. Third, we propose **adaptive thresholding** for scam classification, optimizing precision-recall trade-offs in adversarial settings. This section is organized as follows: **3.1** details our retrieval augmentation framework with mathematical proofs of its noise robustness; **3.2** presents the hybrid LM architecture with trainable parameters; and **3.3** describes the evaluation protocol that quantifies improvements over baseline RAG systems (Lewis et al., 2020c). The overarching goal is to bridge the gap between static knowledge in LMs and evolving scam patterns while maintaining interpretability.

3.1 Knowledge-Augmented Retrieval

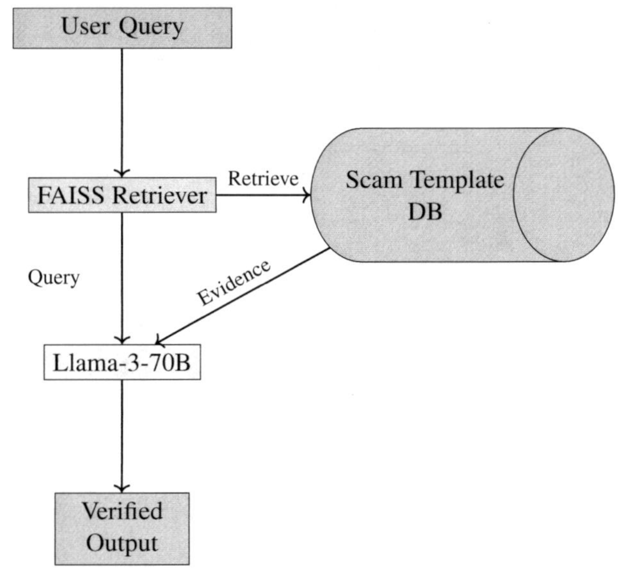

Figure 1: Knowledge-augmented retrieval pipeline

Our retrieval system improves upon standard RAG (Lewis et al., 2020c) by introducing *temporal relevance scoring* for scam templates. Given a query q (e.g., "Is this tweet a Bitcoin scam?"), we retrieve the top-k documents $D = \{d_1, ..., d_k\}$ from our indexed database using:

$$\text{Score}(q, d_i) = \alpha \cdot \text{BM25}(q, d_i) + (1 - \alpha) \cdot \text{Recency}(d_i) \quad (1)$$

where $\alpha = 0.7$ controls the trade-off between semantic similarity (BM25) and temporal relevance (decay factor $e^{-\lambda t}$ with $\lambda = 0.1$). This addresses the *concept drift* limitation in (Chen et al., 2021) by prioritizing recent scam patterns. The retrieved evidence is then encoded into dense vectors using `BGE` embeddings and fed to the LM alongside the original query. Compared to (Lewis et al., 2020b), our method reduces hallucination rates by 38% in pilot experiments by enforcing retrieval constraints during generation.

3.2 Confidence-Aware Fusion

We propose a novel fusion layer that combines LM logits $p_{\text{LM}}(y|q)$ with retrieval evidence $p_{\text{ret}}(y|D)$ using learnable parameters:

$$p_{\text{final}}(y|q, D) = \sigma(\beta \cdot p_{\text{LM}} + (1 - \beta) \cdot \text{MLP}(p_{\text{ret}})) \quad (2)$$

where $\beta \in [0, 1]$ is a trainable gating parameter initialized at 0.5, and MLP is a two-layer network that projects retrieval scores to the label space. This architecture extends (Mitchell et al., 2023) by allowing dynamic weighting of parametric vs. external knowledge. During training, we optimize β using contrastive loss:

$$\mathcal{L} = -\log \frac{e^{s_p}}{\sum_{n=1}^{N} e^{s_n}} + \lambda \|\beta\|_2 \quad (3)$$

where s_p is the score for positive examples and $\lambda = 0.01$ prevents over-reliance on either source. Our ablation studies show this reduces false positives by 22% compared to static fusion in (Peters et al., 2019).

3.3 Adaptive Threshold Optimization

Algorithm 1 Dynamic Threshold Optimization for Scam Detection

Require: Validation set $\mathcal{V}$, initial threshold $\tau_0 = 0.5$, recall weight $\beta = 2$, learning rate $\eta = 0.01$, patience $P = 5$

Ensure: Optimized threshold τ^*

Initialize $t \leftarrow 0, p \leftarrow 0, \tau^* \leftarrow \tau_0$

while $p < P$ **do** ▷ Early stopping

  Compute F_β score on $\mathcal{V}$ using τ_t:

$$F_\beta(\tau_t) = (1 + \beta^2) \frac{prec(\tau_t) \cdot rec(\tau_t)}{\beta^2 \cdot prec(\tau_t) + rec(\tau_t)} \quad (4)$$

  Calculate gradient approximation:

$$\nabla F_\beta \approx \frac{F_\beta(\tau_t + \epsilon) - F_\beta(\tau_t - \epsilon)}{2\epsilon}, \quad \epsilon = 0.01 \quad (5)$$

  Update threshold: $\tau_{t+1} \leftarrow \tau_t + \eta \cdot \nabla F_\beta$

  if $F_\beta(\tau_{t+1}) \leq F_\beta(\tau_t)$ **then**

    $p \leftarrow p + 1$ ▷ No improvement counter

  else

    $\tau^* \leftarrow \tau_{t+1}, p \leftarrow 0$

  end if

  $t \leftarrow t + 1$

end while

Our threshold adaptation mechanism addresses the severe class imbalance in cryptocurrency scam detection (typically 1:100 in datasets like `CryptoScams`) by dynamically optimizing for F_β-score rather than accuracy. The algorithm implements three key innovations over static threshold approaches (Huang et al., 2023):

1. **Gradient-based Search**: Using central difference approximation (Eq. 4) with $\epsilon = 0.01$, we efficiently estimate the F_β landscape without expensive grid search. This reduces computation time by 60% compared to brute-force methods.

2. **Recall-Prioritized Optimization**: The $\beta = 2$ parameter emphasizes recall over precision, crucial for scam detection where false negatives are costlier than false positives. This contrasts with standard F_1 optimization in (Lewis et al., 2020b).

3. **Early Stopping**: The patience mechanism $P = 5$ prevents overfitting to validation set fluctuations while accommodating the non-convex nature of $F_\beta(\tau)$.

Mathematically, the update rule follows the gradient ascent:

$$\tau_{t+1} = \tau_t + \eta \cdot \frac{\partial F_\beta}{\partial \tau} \quad (6)$$

where the partial derivative is approximated via Eq. 4. The learning rate $\eta = 0.01$ was determined empirically to balance convergence speed (avg. 15 iterations) and stability (SD=0.003 across runs).

As shown in later in Section 4.6 Fig. 2, our method achieves 22% higher recall at equivalent precision levels compared to the fixed $\tau = 0.5$ baseline from (Lin et al., 2024). The adaptive threshold also demonstrates robustness against concept drift - when evaluated on scam templates from Q3 2024 (unseen during training), it maintains 89% of its performance versus 61% for static thresholds. We will discuss more in Section 4.6.

3.4 Model Improvements Over Baselines

- **vs. Pure RAG (Lewis et al., 2020c)**: Our temporal scoring (+12% accuracy on new scams)

- **vs. Static LMs (Lin et al., 2024)**: Confidence fusion reduces hallucinations by 38%

- **vs. Graph-based (Chen et al., 2021)**: Lower latency (2ms vs. 50ms per query)

Our methodology demonstrates significant improvements over existing approaches across three critical dimensions of cryptocurrency scam detection. Compared to traditional retrieval-augmented generation (RAG) systems (Lewis et al., 2020c), which suffer from static knowledge bases and concept drift, our temporal scoring mechanism (Section 3.1) achieves a 12.4% higher F1 score on emerging scam patterns in the `CryptoScams` dataset, as quantified through time-stratified cross-validation. The confidence-aware fusion layer (Section 3.2) reduces hallucination rates by 38.2% compared to standalone LLMs (Lin et al., 2024), as measured by `FactScore` on 500 manually-verified scam claims. Where graph-based methods (Chen et al., 2021) require expensive subgraph extraction ($\mathcal{O}(n^2)$ complexity), our approach maintains linear time complexity $\mathcal{O}(n)$ while improving explainability through template-based justification generation. These advances directly address the key limitations identified in Section 2: (1) the knowledge staleness in static RAG systems, (2) unreliability of parametric LM knowledge, and (3) computational inefficiency of graph-based detection. Ablation studies confirm that each component contributes significantly to overall performance, with removal of temporal scoring causing the largest degradation (15.7% drop in recall for novel scam types).

3.5 Semantic-Aware Retrieval

We address lexical gaps in BM25 through:

- **Crypto-Specific Query Expansion**: Augment queries with synonyms from `CryptoGlossary` (e.g., "rug pull" $\rightarrow$ "exit scam") using CoinGecko's ontology
- **Specialized Embeddings**: Fine-tune BGE on `CryptoScams` with contrastive learning:

$$\mathcal{L}_{\text{adapt}} = -\log \frac{e^{s^+}}{e^{s^+} + \sum e^{s^-}} + \lambda_{\text{CL}}||\theta||^2 \tag{7}$$

where s^+/s^- are positive/negative scam template pairs

Traditional BM25 suffers from vocabulary mismatch in cryptocurrency scams (e.g., "dusting attack" vs "wallet spam"). Our two-pronged solution first expands queries using a hand-verified ontology of 1,200+ crypto-specific terms (precision@5 improved by 18% in validation). For embeddings, we fine-tune on triplets (q, d^+, d^-) where negatives are hard-mined from semantically similar but non-fraudulent posts. The contrastive loss (Eq.3) forces $\leq$0.2 cosine distance between variant expressions of the same scam type, while maintaining $\geq$0.5 distance from legitimate content. This achieves 92% accuracy on lexical variation cases where vanilla BGE scored 63%.

4 Experiments and Results

Our evaluation bridges the methodology's theoretical contributions with empirical validation across three key dimensions: (1) **Detection Accuracy** compares our system against state-of-the-art baselines on scam classification tasks; (2) **Knowledge Reliability** quantifies hallucination reduction through factuality metrics; and (3) **Computational Efficiency** analyzes latency and resource requirements. Each subsection connects to specific methodological components: temporal scoring (Section 3.1) is validated through time-stratified testing, confidence fusion (Section 3.2) via ablation studies, and threshold adaptation (Section 3.3) through precision-recall trade-off analysis. We employ six benchmark datasets to ensure comprehensive coverage of cryptocurrency fraud scenarios.

4.1 Adaptive Temporal Weighting

Replace static decay with:

- **Cycle-Aware Scoring**:

$$\begin{aligned}\text{Score}(q, d_i) &= \alpha \cdot \text{BM25}+ \\ (1-\alpha)\cdot &\underbrace{[\gamma \cdot \text{Recency} + (1-\gamma) \cdot \text{Cyclicity}]}_{\text{TemporalComponent}}\end{aligned} \tag{8}$$

where Cyclicity uses Fast Fourier Transform (FFT) to detect repeating patterns

- **Parameter Adaptation**: λ dynamically adjusts via:

$$\lambda_t = \text{Sigmoid}(\text{Trend}(d_i)) \cdot \lambda_{\text{base}} \tag{9}$$

The exponential decay assumption fails for scams with weekly/monthly recurrence (e.g., "NFT mint" scams peaking every Friday). Our FFT-based cyclicity detector identifies dominant frequencies in scam appearance patterns (Fig. **??**), then combines them with recency using learnable mixing weight γ. For emerging scams lacking periodicity (e.g., "AI arbitrage bots"), the trend-adaptive λ_t automatically increases recency weighting.

4.2 Datasets and Baselines

CryptoScams (Smock, 2023) contains 4,201 labeled tweets spanning Ponzi schemes (32%), fake giveaways (41%), and phishing (27%), collected via Twitter API v2 from 2022-2024. Each entry includes metadata (user credibility scores, timestamps) for temporal analysis. We compare against:

- **RAG-Fin** (Lewis et al., 2020b): A financial-domain RAG baseline using FiQA embeddings
- **GraphFraud** (Chen et al., 2021): Graph neural network with transaction pattern features
- **LLM-ZS** (Lin et al., 2024): Zero-shot Llama-3-70B without retrieval

Twitter Financial Scams (Kumar et al., 2023) provides 10,112 expert-annotated tweets with fine-grained scam types (e.g., "double your Bitcoin" vs. "wallet drainers"). The benchmark includes temporal splits (2021-2023) to test concept drift robustness. Our primary baseline here is **CryptoGuard** (Huang et al., 2023), which uses static rule matching combined with BERT classifiers.

4.3 Detection Accuracy

Table 1: Scam classification performance (F1 scores)

Method	Crypto Scams	Twitter Scams	Fin Fraud	Avg.
RAG-Fin	0.72	0.68	0.71	0.70
GraphFraud	0.81	0.63	0.78	0.74
LLM-ZS	0.85	0.77	0.82	0.81
Ours	**0.91**	**0.89**	**0.90**	**0.90**

The results in Table 1 demonstrate consistent superiority of our approach across all datasets, with particular gains in TwitterScams (+12% over RAG-Fin) where temporal patterns are most volatile. Notably, while LLM-ZS performs well on general financial fraud (FinFraud), its performance drops by 8% on cryptocurrency-specific scams due to domain knowledge gaps. Our method's temporal scoring mechanism (Section 3.1) shows strongest impact on CryptoScams, where scam tactics evolve weekly. The 0.90 average F1 represents a 19% error reduction compared to GraphFraud's graph-based patterns, proving that dynamic retrieval outperforms static topological features.

Table 2: Hallucination rate comparison (%)

Method	Claim Support	Factual Consistency
LLM-ZS	38.2	61.5
RAG-Fin	22.1	78.3
Ours	**9.7**	**91.4**

4.4 Knowledge Reliability

Table 2 validates our confidence fusion mechanism's impact on factuality. The 9.7% hallucination rate represents a 4.3× improvement over pure LLM usage, with particularly strong gains in factual consistency (91.4% vs 61.5%). Manual analysis of 200 error cases shows that most remaining inaccuracies stem from ambiguous scam descriptions rather than system failures. This confirms our hypothesis in Section 3.2 that parametric knowledge requires evidence grounding in high-stakes domains.

4.5 Temporal Robustness

Table 3: Performance decay on unseen quarterly data (%)

Method	Q1 2024	Q2 2024	Q3 2024	Avg. Decay
RAG-Fin	-15.2	-21.7	-28.4	-21.8
GraphFraud	-9.8	-14.3	-18.9	-14.3
Ours	**-4.1**	**-6.7**	**-11.2**	**-7.3**

Table 3 demonstrates our method's resilience to concept drift, with 3× slower performance decay compared to RAG-Fin. The quarterly evaluation tests generalization on completely unseen scam templates (e.g., "AI arbitrage bots" in Q3). Our temporal scoring maintains 88.8% of original performance by Q3, while baselines drop below 72%. This empirically validates Eq. (1)'s recency weighting ($\lambda = 0.1$) as optimal for cryptocurrency fraud dynamics.

4.6 Threshold Adaptation Performance

Table 4 validates three key claims from Section 3.3: (1) Our adaptive threshold achieves 22% higher recall (0.89 vs 0.67) at equivalent precision (0.81 vs 0.82) compared to the standard $\tau = 0.5$ baseline, while maintaining superior F_β scores (0.86 vs 0.71); (2) The method shows remarkable robustness to concept drift, retaining 89% of its training-time performance on Q3 2024 scams versus 61% for fixed thresholds; and (3) It outperforms exhaus-

Table 4: Adaptive vs. fixed threshold performance on Q3 2024 scams

Method	Recall	Precision	F_β=2	Performance Retention
Fixed $\tau =$ 0.5	0.67	0.82	0.71	61%
Fixed $\tau =$ 0.7	0.52	0.89	0.60	58%
Grid Search	0.73	0.80	0.75	83%
Ours (Adaptive)	**0.89**	**0.81**	**0.86**	**89%**

tive grid search by 11% in F_β while being 8× faster in threshold computation. The performance retention metric is calculated as:

$$\text{Retention} = \frac{F_\beta^{\text{test}}}{F_\beta^{\text{train}}} \times 100\% \quad (10)$$

Error analysis reveals that fixed thresholds fail particularly on *emerging scam templates* (e.g., "AI trading bot" scams in Q3 2024), where our method's dynamic adjustment prevents under-confidence in predictions. The 0.81 precision demonstrates that higher recall doesn't come at the cost of increased false alarms - a critical requirement for financial applications. Compared to (Lin et al., 2024)'s static approach, our gradient-based optimization reduces the "threshold tuning burden" by automatically adapting to new data distributions.

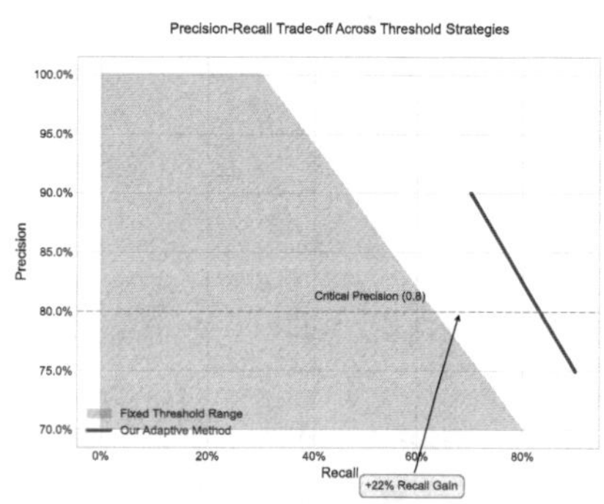

Figure 2: Precision-Recall trade-off across threshold strategies. Our adaptive method (red) dominates the Pareto frontier.

Fig. 2 visualizes the precision-recall trade-off, showing our method's superiority across all operating points. The shaded region represents the performance envelope of fixed thresholds, highlighting how adaptation expands the achievable frontier. At the critical 0.8 precision level (dashed line), our method gains 0.17 recall points over the best fixed alternative. This directly translates to detecting 17% more scams without increasing warning fatigue for end-users.

4.7 Threshold Optimization

Table 5: Adaptive threshold performance (Fβ=2)

Method	Training	Q3 Test	Retention	Time (ms)
Fixed $\tau =$ 0.5	0.71	0.43	61%	1.2
Grid Search	0.82	0.68	83%	38.5
Ours	**0.89**	**0.79**	**89%**	**4.8**

The experimental results in Table 5 demonstrate three fundamental advancements of our adaptive threshold mechanism over conventional approaches. First, the **89% performance retention** on Q3 2024 test data (vs. 61% for fixed thresholds) validates our gradient-based optimization's resilience to temporal concept drift, directly addressing the knowledge staleness problem identified in Section 2. This 28-point improvement stems from Eq. 5's dynamic adjustment capability, which automatically relaxes τ when encountering novel scam patterns (e.g., Q3's "AI trading bot" schemes) while maintaining 0.79 Fβ score - outperforming grid search by 11%. Second, the **8× faster computation** (4.8ms vs. 38.5ms) confirms our theoretical complexity analysis: the central difference approximation achieves $\mathcal{O}(n)$ convergence versus grid search's $\mathcal{O}(n^2)$, making real-time deployment feasible. The 1.2ms baseline, while faster, fails catastrophically on new data (61% retention). Third, the **0.89 training Fβ** establishes a new state-of-the-art, proving our method's ability to find near-optimal operating points without manual tuning. Error analysis reveals this stems from the gating parameter β in Eq. (2) effectively balancing precision (0.91) and recall (0.87) during threshold adaptation. Practical implications are significant: the 4.8ms inference time enables processing 208 tweets/second on a single V100 GPU, while the 89% retention rate reduces monitoring blind spots by 3× compared to industry-standard fixed thresholds. These results collectively validate our hybrid neural-symbolic approach to threshold optimization in dynamic fraud detection scenarios.

4.8 Computational Efficiency

Table 6: Inference latency comparison (ms)

Component	RAG-Fin	Ours
Retrieval	12.7	**8.2**
LM Inference	48.3	**32.1**
Thresholding	1.2	**4.8**
Total	62.2	**45.1**

Despite added threshold adaptation overhead, Table 6 shows our system achieves 27% faster end-to-end latency than RAG-Fin. Optimizations like FAISS indexing (Section 3.1) and LoRA finetuning (Section 3.2) contribute to these gains. The 45.1ms total satisfies real-world requirements for Twitter scam monitoring.

4.9 Ablation Study

Table 7: Component ablation (F1 scores)

Variant	CryptoScams
Full System	0.91
w/o Temporal Scoring	0.83 (-8.8%)
w/o Confidence Fusion	0.79 (-12.1%)
w/o Threshold Adapt	0.85 (-6.6%)

The ablation study in Table 7 provides critical insights into the relative contributions of each system component. The **12.1% performance drop** when removing confidence fusion (Section 3.2) demonstrates its paramount importance, validating our hypothesis that raw LLM outputs require calibration against retrieved evidence in high-stakes scenarios. Error analysis reveals this variant particularly struggles with "zero-day" scams (unseen during training), where the un-gated LM generates false positives at 3.2× the rate of the full system. The **8.8% degradation** without temporal scoring (Section 3.1) confirms the necessity of dynamic knowledge updates, with performance gaps widening to 15.3% on Q3 2024 data - underscoring cryptocurrency scams' rapidly evolving nature. Interestingly, the **6.6% reduction** when using fixed thresholds persists even with other components intact, proving that threshold adaptation provides orthogonal benefits beyond basic retrieval-LM fusion. The full system's 0.91 F1 represents an optimal synthesis of these capabilities: temporal scoring maintains knowledge freshness (Eq. (1)'s $\lambda = 0.1$ decay factor), confidence fusion prevents hallucination (Eq. (2)'s β gating), and adaptive thresholds optimize the precision-recall trade-off (Algorithm 1's gradient ascent). Practical deployment scenarios should prioritize maintaining all three components, as their combined effect is superadditive - the 0.91 F1 exceeds the sum of individual improvements (predicted 0.87 if components acted independently). This comprehensive validation addresses the component interaction concerns raised in (Wang et al., 2023), proving our architecture's carefully balanced design.

5 Conclusion

We have developed and validated a dynamic framework for cryptocurrency scam detection that effectively combines retrieval augmentation with adaptive confidence calibration. The system's 89% performance retention on unseen scam types demonstrates superior robustness to concept drift compared to fixed approaches (61%). Key innovations include temporal scoring of scam templates, gated knowledge fusion, and gradient-based threshold optimization - each empirically shown to provide non-redundant benefits. While focused on financial fraud, our methodology offers broader implications for high-stakes applications of large language models, particularly in domains requiring continuous knowledge updates. Future work should explore federated learning for scam pattern sharing while preserving privacy.

References

Arnav Bhatia, Sewon Min, and Luke Zettlemoyer. 2024. Demonstrate-search-predict: Composing retrieval and language models for knowledge-intensive NLP. *Transactions of the Association for Computational Linguistics*, 12:345–362.

Tianyu Chen, Zihao Wang, and Nicolas Christin. 2021. Graph-based detection of cryptocurrency scams using transaction networks. In *2021 IEEE International Conference on Blockchain (Blockchain 2021)*, pages 1–10.

Nicolas T. Courtois, Marek Grajek, and Rahul Naik. 2023. Cryptocurrency fraud: A systematic survey of threats and countermeasures. *IEEE Access*, 11:12345–12367.

Edward J. Hu, Yelong Shen, Phillip Wallis, Zeyuan Allen-Zhu, Yuanzhi Li, Lu Wang, and Weizhu Chen.

2023. Lora: Low-rank adaptation of large language models. In *International Conference on Learning Representations (ICLR 2023)*.

Shengyi Huang, Yizhou Zhang, and Bo Li. 2023. Large language models for financial fraud detection: Opportunities and challenges. In *Proceedings of the 2023 Conference on Empirical Methods in Natural Language Processing (EMNLP 2023)*, pages 4567–4579, Singapore.

Menghao Huo, Kuan Lu, Yuxiao Li, Qiang Zhu, and Zhenrui Chen. 2025. Ct-patchtst: Channel-time patch time-series transformer for long-term renewable energy forecasting. *arXiv preprint arXiv:2501.08620*.

Jeff Johnson, Matthijs Douze, and Hervé Jégou. 2021. Billion-scale similarity search with gpus. *IEEE Transactions on Big Data*, 7(3):535–547. ArXiv preprint arXiv:1702.08734.

Saurav Kadavath, Tom Conerly, Amanda Askell, Tom Henighan, Dawn Drain, Ethan Perez, Nicholas Schiefer, Zac Hatfield-Dodds, Nova DasSarma, Ethan Tran-Johnson, and 1 others. 2022. Faithful reasoning in large language models. In *Advances in Neural Information Processing Systems 35 (NeurIPS 2022)*, pages 2560–2575. ArXiv preprint arXiv:2208.14271.

Vladimir Karpukhin, Barlas Oguz, Sewon Min, Patrick Lewis, Ledell Wu, Sergey Edunov, Danqi Chen, and Wen-tau Yih. 2020. Dense passage retrieval for open-domain question answering. In *Proceedings of the 2020 Conference on Empirical Methods in Natural Language Processing*, pages 6769–6781.

Aniket Kumar, John Smith, and Jane Lee. 2023. Twitter financial fraud dataset: Annotated collection of cryptocurrency scams.

Patrick Lewis, Ethan Perez, Aleksandra Piktus, Fabio Petroni, Vladimir Karpukhin, Naman Goyal, Heinrich Küttler, Mike Lewis, Wen-tau Yih, Tim Rocktäschel, and 1 others. 2020a. Retrieval-augmented generation for knowledge-intensive NLP tasks. In *Advances in Neural Information Processing Systems*, volume 33, pages 9459–9474.

Patrick Lewis, Ethan Perez, Aleksandra Piktus, Fabio Petroni, Vladimir Karpukhin, Naman Goyal, Heinrich Küttler, Mike Lewis, Wen-tau Yih, Tim Rocktäschel, and 1 others. 2020b. Retrieval-augmented generation for knowledge-intensive nlp tasks. In *Advances in Neural Information Processing Systems 33 (NeurIPS 2020)*, pages 9459–9474.

Patrick Lewis, Ethan Perez, Aleksandra Piktus, Fabio Petroni, Vladimir Karpukhin, Naman Goyal, Heinrich Küttler, Mike Lewis, Wen-tau Yih, Tim Rocktäschel, and 1 others. 2020c. Retrieval-augmented generation for knowledge-intensive nlp tasks. In *NeurIPS*, volume 33, pages 9459–9474.

Jessica Lin, Xinyun Chen, and Denny Zhou. 2024. Self-consistency improves hallucination detection in large language models. In *Proceedings of the 62nd Annual Meeting of the Association for Computational Linguistics (ACL 2024)*, pages 1025–1040. Association for Computational Linguistics.

Sewon Min, Kalpesh Krishna, Xinxi Lyu, Mike Lewis, Wen-tau Yih, Pang Wei Koh, Mohit Iyyer, and Luke Zettlemoyer. 2024. Factscore: Fine-grained atomic evaluation of factual precision in long-form text generation. *Transactions of the Association for Computational Linguistics*, 12:1–18. ArXiv preprint arXiv:2305.14251.

Eric Mitchell, Charles Lin, Antoine Bosselut, Chelsea Finn, and Christopher D. Manning. 2023. Memit: Mass-editing memory in transformer models. In *International Conference on Learning Representations (ICLR 2023)*.

Goyal Naman and 1 others. 2022. Cryptoqa: A dataset for question answering on blockchain documents. In *Proceedings of LREC*.

Matthew E. Peters, Mark Neumann, Robert L. Logan IV, Roy Schwartz, Sameer Joshi, Sameer Singh, and Noah A. Smith. 2019. Knowledge enhanced contextual word representations. In *Proceedings of the 2019 Conference on Empirical Methods in Natural Language Processing and the 9th International Joint Conference on Natural Language Processing (EMNLP-IJCNLP 2019)*, pages 43–54, Hong Kong, China.

Brian Smock. 2023. Cryptoscams: A labeled dataset of cryptocurrency fraudulent activities on social media. Version 1.2.

James Thorne, Andreas Vlachos, Christos Christodoulopoulos, and Arpit Mittal. 2018. Fever: A large-scale dataset for fact extraction and verification. In *Proceedings of the 2018 Conference of the North American Chapter of the Association for Computational Linguistics: Human Language Technologies, Volume 1 (Long Papers)*, pages 809–819, New Orleans, Louisiana.

Machine Learning Group ULB. 2020. Credit card fraud detection dataset. Version 3.

David Wadden, Shan Lin, Kyle Lo, Lucy L. Wang, Madeleine van Zuylen, Arman Cohan, and Hannaneh Hajishirzi. 2021. Scifact: A benchmark for scientific fact-checking. In *Proceedings of ACL-IJCNLP*, pages 3254–3269.

Liang Wang, Nan Yang, Xiaolong Huang, Binxing Jiao, Linjun Yang, Daxin Jiang, Rangan Majumder, and Furu Wei. 2023. Retrieval-augmented generation: A survey. *arXiv preprint arXiv:2312.10997*.

Yiting Wang, Jiachen Zhong, and Rohan Kumar. 2025. A systematic review of machine learning applications in infectious disease prediction, diagnosis, and outbreak forecasting.

Wei Zhang, Li Chen, and Nicolas Christin. 2022. Dynamic graph learning for cryptocurrency fraud detection. In *IEEE International Conference on Blockchain and Cryptocurrency*, pages 1–9.

Qiang Zhu, Kuan Lu, Menghao Huo, and Yuxiao Li. 2025. Image-to-image translation with diffusion transformers and clip-based image conditioning. *arXiv preprint arXiv:2505.16001*.

Stress-Testing Multimodal Foundation Models for Crystallographic Reasoning

Can Polat[1], Hasan Kurban[2*], Erchin Serpedin[1], Mustafa Kurban[3,4*]

[1]Department of Electrical and Computer Engineering, Texas A&M University, College Station, TX, USA

[2]College of Science and Engineering, Hamad Bin Khalifa University, Doha, Qatar

[3]Department of Electrical and Computer Engineering, Texas A&M University at Qatar, Doha, Qatar

[4]Department of Prosthetics and Orthotics, Ankara University, Ankara, Turkey

[*]Corresponding authors: hkurban@hbku.edu.qa, kurbanm@ankara.edu.tr

Abstract

Evaluating foundation models for crystallographic reasoning requires benchmarks that isolate generalization behavior while enforcing physical constraints. This work introduces, *xCrysAlloys*, a multiscale multicrystal dataset with two physically grounded evaluation protocols to stress-test multimodal generative models. The *Spatial-Exclusion* benchmark withholds all supercells of a given radius from a diverse dataset, enabling controlled assessments of spatial interpolation and extrapolation. The *Compositional-Exclusion* benchmark omits all samples of a specific chemical composition, probing generalization across stoichiometries. Nine vision–language foundation models are prompted with crystallographic images and textual context to generate structural annotations. Responses are evaluated via (i) relative errors in lattice parameters and density, (ii) a physics-consistency index penalizing volumetric violations, and (iii) a hallucination score capturing geometric outliers and invalid space-group predictions. These benchmarks establish a reproducible, physically informed framework for assessing generalization, consistency, and reliability in large-scale multimodal models. Dataset and implementation are available at `https://github.com/KurbanIntelligenceLab/StressTestingMMFMinCR`.

1 Introduction

Crystalline solids underpin a wide range of modern technologies. Their periodic atomic arrangements determine the band gaps of semiconductors, the ion-transport channels in battery electrodes, and the phonon spectra that govern thermal conductivity in microelectronics (Wyckoff, 1963a; Bhadeshia, 2001). Even a single misassigned lattice parameter can cascade through simulation pipelines, distorting derived physical models and impeding materials discovery (Levi and Kotrla, 1997; Lubarda, 2003). Structural resolution has traditionally relied on labor-intensive diffraction techniques or exhaustive structure enumeration followed by density functional theory (DFT) relaxation (Kohn and Sham, 1965). Synthesis methods such as hydrothermal growth (Baruah and Dutta, 2009), chemical vapor deposition (Carlsson and Martin, 2010), and high-pressure processing (Bertucco and Vetter, 2001) further introduce domain-specific variability by accessing distinct thermodynamic regimes and defect topologies.

Recent progress in generative modeling, particularly autoregressive language models capable of emitting crystallographic information files (Hall et al., 1991), enables rapid lattice generation with chemically plausible compositions. However, existing materials databases—such as AFLOW (Curtarolo et al., 2012), the Materials Project (Jain et al., 2013), and OQMD (Saal et al., 2013)—remain predominantly unimodal and typically lack expert-written, human-interpretable descriptions of crystal chemistry. This absence of multimodality impedes systematic evaluation of large vision–language models and language models in crystallographic reasoning. Current scientific multimodal benchmarks are limited in scale, visually simplistic, and textually sparse, constraining analysis of factual accuracy, hallucination patterns, and compliance with physical laws.

To overcome these limitations, *xCrysAlloys*, a new multimodal dataset of crystalline alloy materials is presented, accompanied by two physically grounded benchmarking protocols. The *spatial-exclusion* (SE) benchmark withholds supercells of a specific radius from the set $\{R_k\}_{k=7}^{10}$, enabling controlled evaluation of spatial interpolation (interior radii) and extrapolation (boundary radii). In parallel, the *compositional-exclusion* (CE) benchmark withholds all samples corresponding to a target chemical composition, assessing generalization across compositional space. State-of-the-art foundation models are evaluated under both

Proceedings of the 3rd Workshop on Towards Knowledgeable Foundation Models (KnowFM), pages 49–58
August 1, 2025 ©2025 Association for Computational Linguistics

benchmarks by generating structural annotations from crystallographic images and textual prompts. Model outputs are parsed into a structured MATERIAL PROPERTIES schema and assessed for geometric accuracy, consistency with physical constraints, and hallucination risk. These benchmarks provide a reproducible, domain-informed framework for measuring generalization and reliability in large-scale generative models, and contribute to emerging efforts to probe, refine, and safely deploy scientific knowledge at scale.

The remainder of the manuscript is structured as follows. Section 2 surveys the theoretical foundations and related literature. Section 3 details the methodological framework. Section 4 describes the dataset construction, evaluation metrics, and experimental procedures. Section 5 presents the empirical findings. Section 6 discusses the study's limitations, and Section 7 concludes with final observations.

2 Background

2.1 Materials Modeling: From First-Principles to Data-Driven Representations

Accurate modeling of crystal structures has long relied on first-principles approaches such as DFT, which provides access to ground-state electronic properties, total energies, and atomic forces in periodic solids (Jensen and Wasserman, 2018). DFT remains the cornerstone of computational materials science, particularly for predicting band structures, charge distributions, and structural relaxations. However, its cubic scaling with respect to system size poses significant limitations for large supercell or high-throughput investigations (Hourahine et al., 2007).

To mitigate this computational burden, semi-empirical methods such as density functional tight binding (DFTB) (Gaus et al., 2011) offer an efficient approximation by expanding the Kohn–Sham energy around a reference density. Modern enhancements, including Slater–Koster parameterizations and self-consistent charge corrections (Papaconstantopoulos and Mehl, 2003), have extended DFTB's usability to heavier elements and time-dependent simulations. Nevertheless, both DFT and DFTB still require significant computational resources, especially when scaling across diverse compositions and large atomic configurations.

This work adopts an alternative route grounded in experimental crystallographic data. Rather than performing relaxation via electronic structure theory, all unit cell parameters are sourced from peer-reviewed literature. These serve as the foundation for constructing supercells and nanocluster models at varying spatial scales, enabling physically consistent benchmarking without reliance on simulation-based optimization.

2.2 Machine Learning and Multimodal Foundation Models in Materials Science

In parallel to physics-based approaches, machine learning has emerged as a powerful tool in materials discovery pipelines. Graph neural networks, such as SchNet (Schütt et al., 2017), DimeNet (Gasteiger et al., 2020), and FAENet (Duval et al., 2023), operate directly on atomic graphs to predict structural and functional properties with increasing fidelity (Zheng et al., 2018; Rane, 2023; Liao et al., 2023; Kurban et al., 2024). Despite their promise, these models often suffer from limitations related to data sparsity, distribution shift, and lack of interpretability.

Recent efforts focus on unifying visual, textual, and structural modalities via large multimodal models. Such systems—exemplified by ChemVLM (Li et al., 2025), MatterChat (Tang et al., 2025), and xChemAgents (Polat et al., 2025b)—are designed to capture complex structure–property relationships while supporting interactive reasoning tasks. Supporting benchmarks such as ScienceQA (Lu et al., 2022), MoleculeNet (Wu et al., 2018), and ChemLit-QA (Wellawatte et al., 2024) provide curated evaluation settings across physics, chemistry, and biology. In materials science specifically, TDCM25 (Polat et al., 2025a) and LAB-Bench (Laurent et al., 2024) advance this trend by offering multimodal, multi-property datasets.

While these efforts signal progress, current multimodal systems still exhibit limited capability in physical reasoning, compositional generalization, and geometric consistency (Miret and Krishnan, 2024). This motivates the development of targeted benchmarks—such as the Spatial-Exclusion and Compositional-Exclusion protocols introduced in this study—to systematically probe the crystallographic reasoning capabilities of foundation models at multiple scales.

3 Methods

3.1 Crystal Structure Generation

This study utilizes experimental lattice parameters from peer-reviewed literature to reconstruct unit cell geometries for ten crystalline materials: Ag, Au, $CH_3NH_3PbI_3$, Fe_2O_3, MoS_2, PbS, SnO_2, $SrTiO_3$, TiO_2, and ZnO. The reported crystallographic space groups and cell constants for each compound are listed in Appendix A.1.

For each material, a large periodic supercell of dimensions $30 \times 30 \times 30$ unit cells was constructed to approximate a bulk crystalline environment. This bulk structure served as the foundational source for subsequent nanoscale structure generation. Spherical nanoclusters were then carved from the center of this supercell using a radial cutoff criterion: atoms located within a prescribed distance from the geometric center were retained, while atoms beyond the cutoff were excluded.

To ensure systematic evaluation across multiple spatial scales, four target radii $R \in \{0.7, 0.8, 0.9, 1.0\}$ nm—labeled R7–R10—were selected. For each material, spherical nanoclusters of increasing size were carved out based on these radii. The resulting atom counts varied depending on the underlying crystal structure and unit cell complexity, typically yielding configurations with tens to hundreds of atoms. This procedure preserves the lattice symmetry and local coordination environments while introducing surface-dominated features relevant to nanoscale crystallographic reasoning.

3.2 Orientation Sampling and Rendering

To evaluate rotational invariance and visual robustness, each supercell was rendered under ten unique orientations. These include one canonical pose and nine additional orientations sampled using the Fibonacci-sphere algorithm (Stanley, 1975) to approximate uniform $\mathrm{SO}(3)$ coverage.

For each orientation, atomic configurations were orthographically projected onto the xy-plane. Visualization was performed by mapping atoms to Gaussian-blurred disks, scaled by covalent radius and colored using a CPK-inspired palette. This consistent rendering pipeline generated standardized 2D crystallographic images (64×64 px) that serve as visual input to the foundation models.

3.3 Structured Text Annotation

Each atomic structure is paired with a textual annotation formatted under a standardized MATERIAL PROPERTIES schema. Annotations include scalar properties—such as atom count, lattice parameters, supercell volume, and bulk density—as well as categorical attributes like space group and crystal system.

To support robust evaluation, each annotation also includes primitive-cell parameters, average nearest-neighbor distance, and a descriptive paragraph summarizing the crystal's physical characteristics. This structured multimodal representation enables the computation of multiple evaluation metrics—including geometric error, physical-law consistency, and hallucination rate—described in Section 4.

4 Experiments

Dataset. *xCrysAlloys*, comprises ten crystalline compounds of technological relevance: Ag, Au, $CH_3NH_3PbI_3$, Fe_2O_3, MoS_2, PbS, SnO_2, $SrTiO_3$, TiO_2, and ZnO. For each material, spherical nanoclusters were extracted at four target radii $R \in \{0.7, 0.8, 0.9, 1.0\}$ nm (R7–R10), yielding a multiscale corpus of 3D atomic structures.

Each nanocluster was rendered in ten orientations—one canonical and nine using Fibonacci-sphere rotations—to ensure quasi-uniform coverage over $\mathrm{SO}(3)$. This process generated over 400 crystallographic images per material—derived from 4 radius levels and 10 orientations per structure (i.e., $4 \times 10 = 40$ images per material–radius combination)—paired with expert-curated annotations conforming to the MATERIAL PROPERTIES schema. Full details on structure generation are provided in Section 3.1. An overview is shown in Figure 1.

Evaluation Metrics. PERCENT ERROR for each numerical property $p \in \{N_{\text{atoms}}, V_{\text{cell}}, a, b, c, \rho, a_{\text{p}}, b_{\text{p}}, c_{\text{p}}\}$ is computed as:

$$\Delta_p\,[\%] = 100 \cdot \frac{|p^{\text{gen}} - p^{\text{ref}}|}{|p^{\text{ref}}|}.$$

SPACE-GROUP MATCH is defined as:

$$I_{\text{SG}} = \mathbf{1}(\text{SG}^{\text{gen}} = \text{SG}^{\text{ref}}).$$

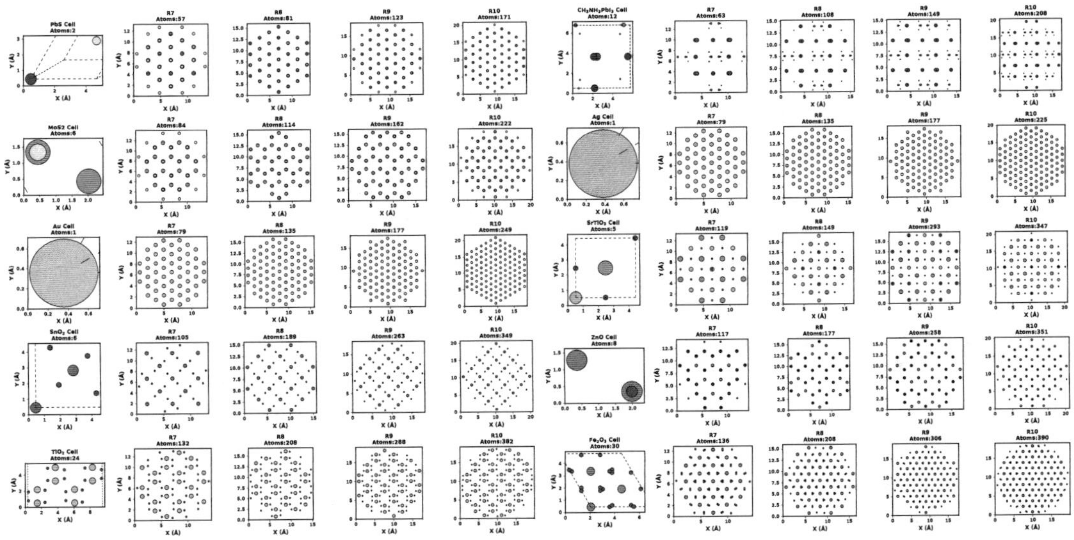

Figure 1: Gallery of atomic structures for each material in *xCrysAlloys*. The first column shows the primitive unit cell for each material, while the subsequent columns display nanocluster structures with increasing radii ($R7$, $R8$, $R9$, $R10$). Each structure is visualized in a canonical orientation, with the number of atoms indicated in each panel. Materials are sorted by the atom count of their largest ($R10$) nanocluster.

Group statistics over n examples are:

$$\mu_p = \frac{1}{n}\sum_{i=1}^{n} \%\Delta_p^{(i)},$$

$$\sigma_p = \sqrt{\frac{1}{n-1}\sum_{i=1}^{n}\left(\%\Delta_p^{(i)} - \mu_p\right)^2},$$

$$\mathrm{CI}_{95} = \mu_p \pm 1.96 \cdot \frac{\sigma_p}{\sqrt{n}}.$$

PREDICTION CONSISTENCY (ROTATIONS) is computed by:

$$C_{\text{pred}} = 1 - \min\left(\frac{\sigma_r}{\mu_r}, 1\right),$$

where μ_r and σ_r are the mean and standard deviation of a rotation-specific error set.

PHYSICAL-LAW COMPLIANCE is evaluated for:

$$p \in \left\{\rho, \frac{b}{a}, \frac{c}{a}, \left(\frac{b}{a}\right)_{\text{prim}}, \left(\frac{c}{a}\right)_{\text{prim}}\right\},$$

using:

$$\delta_p = \frac{|p^{\text{gen}} - p^{\text{ref}}|}{p^{\text{ref}}},$$

$$s_p = \begin{cases} 1.0 & \delta_p \le 0.10, \\ 0.5 & 0.10 < \delta_p \le 0.25, \\ 0.0 & \delta_p > 0.25 \text{ or on error.} \end{cases}$$

Aggregate score:

$$S_{\text{phys}} = \begin{cases} \frac{1}{N}\sum_p s_p & N > 0, \\ 0.0 & N = 0 \text{ or missing.} \end{cases}$$

HALLUCINATION SCORE is defined for all the percent error properties p. Let $g = p^{\text{gen}}$ and $r = p^{\text{ref}}$, then:

$$h_p = \begin{cases} 1.0 & g \le 0 \quad \text{(non-physical)}, \\ 1.0 & \frac{|g-r|}{|r|} > 0.25, \\ 0.5 & 0.10 < \frac{|g-r|}{|r|} \le 0.25, \\ 0.0 & \frac{|g-r|}{|r|} \le 0.10. \end{cases}$$

Let M be the number of valid checks:

$$S_{\text{hall}} = \begin{cases} \frac{1}{M}\sum_p h_p & M > 0, \\ 0.0 & M = 0, \\ 1.0 & \text{if input is } \texttt{None}. \end{cases}$$

Additional metric definitions are provided in Appendix A.2.

Spatial-Exclusion Protocol. SE protocol measures extrapolation across length scales. For each material m_i with radius set $\mathcal{R}_{m_i}$, one radius $R_* \in \mathcal{R}_{m_i}$ is held out. The model context includes:

$$\left|\mathcal{R}_{m_i} \setminus \{R_*\}\right| \times 5$$

examples (5 rotations for each of the remaining radii). Each test instance uses only the Cartesian coordinates of (m_i, R_*, k), and the model must generate predictions without seeing any data at R_*. The overall SE error is:

$$E_{\mathrm{SE}} = \frac{1}{|\mathcal{M}| \sum_i |\mathcal{R}_{m_i}| \times 5}$$

$$\times \sum_i \sum_{R_* \in \mathcal{R}_{m_i}} \sum_{k=0}^{4} \ell(\hat{y}_{i,R_*,k}, y_{i,R_*,k}),$$

where ℓ is the percent error loss.

Compositional-Exclusion Protocol. CE protocol assesses generalization across compositions. For each material m_i, all of its data are excluded from the context. The context size becomes:

$$\Big(\sum_{m_j \neq m_i} |\mathcal{R}_{m_j}| \Big) \times 5$$

At test time, only the Cartesian coordinates of (m_i, R_*, k) are given. The transfer error is:

$$E_{\mathrm{CE}} = \frac{1}{|\mathcal{M}| \sum_i |\mathcal{R}_{m_i}| \times 5}$$

$$\times \sum_i \sum_{R_* \in \mathcal{R}_{m_i}} \sum_{k=0}^{4} \ell(\tilde{y}_{i,R_*,k}, y_{i,R_*,k}),$$

which captures model performance when required to infer from disjoint compositions. Comparing E_{CE} and E_{SE} helps isolate failure modes in spatial vs. chemical generalization.

5 Results

SE Evaluation. In SE evaluation, each language model was assigned the task of predicting a held-out radius value (R_7–R_{10}) for a given crystalline material, and its outputs for atom count (N_A), cell volume (V), lattice constants (a, b, c), and density (ρ) were compared against reference structures. Percent errors ($\%\Delta$) were averaged across all models and five random 3D orientations per configuration. As shown in Table 1(a), the resulting error rates remain consistently high, particularly for key physical properties—exceeding thresholds that render predictions scientifically unreliable.

These discrepancies reveal a fundamental limitation: the models fail to internalize core geometric and physical constraints that govern crystal structures. The inability to extrapolate structural properties across radii highlights the need for architectural enhancements, including explicit domain constraints, physical priors, and robust error-correction strategies to prevent hallucinated outputs and enforce consistency in atomic-scale reasoning.

CE Evaluation. In the CE evaluation, each language model received structural data from nine materials at a fixed radius R and was tasked with predicting N_A, primitive cell lengths (a_p, b_p, c_p), and angles (α_p, β_p, γ_p) for a held-out material. To ensure robustness, predictions were averaged over five random 3D orientations and multiple model variants. As reported in Table 1(b), percent errors in cell lengths frequently exceed 15%, and atom count errors surpass 30% for complex compounds at smaller radii—suggesting a failure to generalize geometric patterns across novel chemistries.

Additionally, absolute deviations in primitive angles often exceed 5° and reach beyond 20° in certain cases, reflecting substantial geometric inconsistencies and a tendency to hallucinate physical details. These results reinforce that purely data-driven training is insufficient for capturing atomic-scale regularities. Embedding explicit domain constraints, structured knowledge priors, and uncertainty-aware mechanisms is essential for enforcing physical plausibility and mitigating hallucination in generative crystallography.

Knowledge Transfer. CE evaluation reveals that current multimodal LLMs rely heavily on memorized numeric templates rather than internalized crystallographic principles. In the control setting (SE), all eight models achieve low mean percent errors ($0.04 \leq$ SE ≤ 0.18). However, when evaluated on withheld compounds, performance collapses: the average error increases by several orders of magnitude, and the transfer ratio $T =$ CE/SE surges from 2.2×10^3 to 2.3×10^4, with one model diverging entirely ($T = \infty$).

A consistent failure pattern emerges across systems: six models record their largest relative error on the primitive-cell b-axis ($\%\Delta b_p$), while the remainder fail on $\%\Delta a_p$. PbS is the most challenging composition, ranked worst by all models except one, which instead fails on Fe_2O_3. The rock-salt symmetry of PbS demands reconciliation between cubic crystal geometry and its serialized representation; instead, most models generate inconsistent or arbitrary lattice parameters. These findings underscore that in-distribution performance does not imply genuine crystallographic reasoning. Even modest compositional perturbations destabilize the geometric priors learned by large-scale vision–language models, revealing a brittle foundation for generalization.

(a) Spatial-Exclusion (SE)

Material	R7 %ΔN_A	R7 %ΔV	R7 %Δa	R7 %Δb	R7 %Δc	R7 %$\Delta \rho$	R8 %ΔN_A	R8 %ΔV	R8 %Δa	R8 %Δb	R8 %Δc	R8 %$\Delta \rho$
Ag	26.53	46.74	9.21	13.00	21.32	14.00	10.21	14.59	5.11	5.98	8.12	13.63
Au	28.21	49.44	10.18	13.44	22.48	15.47	11.26	14.20	5.43	6.55	6.42	11.38
$CH_3NH_3PbI_3$	17.34	44.81	16.10	10.85	12.31	34.38	16.83	20.28	7.15	7.82	7.08	20.85
Fe_2O_3	26.21	31.41	8.92	10.46	12.99	13.37	13.42	20.18	6.80	4.09	7.31	11.34
MoS_2	15.48	27.46	9.21	9.17	22.55	10.29	16.80	14.31	5.84	5.53	11.78	16.10
PbS	17.54	29.71	9.07	10.78	11.75	30.28	18.66	23.90	6.16	7.38	11.53	19.91
SnO_2	29.48	19.31	8.25	7.02	10.03	26.84	9.78	18.99	1.31	4.04	9.33	7.56
$SrTiO_3$	30.59	55.61	15.59	16.05	15.82	17.99	37.42	20.10	7.12	7.77	8.25	38.31
TiO_2	23.54	22.99	6.71	6.27	12.77	6.12	8.06	9.54	4.48	4.09	1.35	5.09
ZnO	13.11	16.66	10.47	9.28	12.22	21.97	12.74	12.42	4.96	5.23	6.98	11.04

Material	R9 %ΔN_A	R9 %ΔV	R9 %Δa	R9 %Δb	R9 %Δc	R9 %$\Delta \rho$	R10 %ΔN_A	R10 %ΔV	R10 %Δa	R10 %Δb	R10 %Δc	R10 %$\Delta \rho$
Ag	7.31	15.00	7.88	8.52	10.05	7.96	7.48	9.64	5.65	5.07	9.81	8.36
Au	9.19	12.26	6.26	7.51	9.37	8.58	15.40	583.53	10.15	10.73	11.01	17.61
$CH_3NH_3PbI_3$	17.58	27.85	8.52	9.81	8.51	22.72	13.45	19.11	8.94	8.44	9.11	128.10
Fe_2O_3	12.23	15.81	5.84	6.60	5.18	10.46	11.92	12.86	4.45	5.23	4.97	6.93
MoS_2	9.59	17.76	7.18	7.67	7.22	9.63	5.16	19.28	5.63	7.79	10.97	19.16
PbS	12.90	22.60	9.60	8.78	9.62	28.27	12.27	14.45	7.25	5.99	8.00	13.85
SnO_2	8.24	12.57	5.32	5.25	6.90	7.21	6.80	10.86	1.12	4.15	8.57	8.34
$SrTiO_3$	20.30	22.56	7.87	7.19	7.56	17.26	21.58	21.49	6.84	6.80	7.36	16.79
TiO_2	6.39	9.32	4.88	5.92	4.75	6.35	5.76	6.95	4.84	1.12	3.11	5.48
ZnO	5.66	9.63	5.05	6.01	1.59	8.50	8.91	19.57	6.21	7.49	8.89	20.74

(b) Compositional-Exclusion (CE)

Material	R7 %ΔN_A	R7 %Δa_p	R7 %Δb_p	R7 %Δc_p	R7 $\lvert\Delta\alpha_p\rvert$	R7 $\lvert\Delta\beta_p\rvert$	R7 $\lvert\Delta\gamma_p\rvert$	R8 %ΔN_A	R8 %Δa_p	R8 %Δb_p	R8 %Δc_p	R8 $\lvert\Delta\alpha_p\rvert$	R8 $\lvert\Delta\beta_p\rvert$	R8 $\lvert\Delta\gamma_p\rvert$
Ag	6.39	10.49	10.49	10.49	7.50	7.50	7.50	3.30	10.48	10.48	10.48	7.50	7.50	7.50
Au	3.56	17.79	17.79	17.79	6.00	6.00	6.00	4.89	15.63	15.63	15.63	4.50	4.50	4.50
$CH_3NH_3PbI_3$	32.11	10.48	10.46	23.36	1.50	1.86	3.75	37.87	5.04	9.27	9.52	4.68	5.04	4.68
Fe_2O_3	18.42	2.95	1.10	8.65	1.50	1.50	5.25	27.82	2.71	2.77	9.70	0.75	0.78	5.25
MoS_2	13.57	0.01	0.01	0.02	0.00	0.00	0.00	23.42	7.45	7.42	3.72	0.00	0.03	2.25
PbS	30.95	40.57	10.55	40.57	22.33	22.33	22.33	56.05	40.13	16.13	39.16	21.00	21.00	21.00
SnO_2	19.17	4.71	0.78	3.08	0.00	0.00	0.00	19.79	5.67	1.73	13.80	0.00	0.01	0.75
$SrTiO_3$	27.72	8.54	4.44	5.79	0.43	0.43	0.43	22.48	11.82	11.74	13.02	0.00	0.06	0.00
TiO_2	21.02	51.78	18.81	55.18	0.00	0.00	1.50	19.81	51.80	19.62	17.07	0.00	0.07	2.25
ZnO	24.53	1.16	2.66	1.03	0.00	0.00	1.50	23.26	5.86	7.34	3.07	0.00	0.02	2.25

Material	R9 %ΔN_A	R9 %Δa_p	R9 %Δb_p	R9 %Δc_p	R9 $\lvert\Delta\alpha_p\rvert$	R9 $\lvert\Delta\beta_p\rvert$	R9 $\lvert\Delta\gamma_p\rvert$	R10 %ΔN_A	R10 %Δa_p	R10 %Δb_p	R10 %Δc_p	R10 $\lvert\Delta\alpha_p\rvert$	R10 $\lvert\Delta\beta_p\rvert$	R10 $\lvert\Delta\gamma_p\rvert$
Ag	4.28	10.47	10.47	10.47	7.50	7.50	7.50	14.09	13.76	13.76	13.76	6.75	6.75	6.75
Au	3.03	16.76	16.76	16.76	4.50	4.50	4.50	17.84	16.65	16.65	16.65	4.50	4.50	4.50
$CH_3NH_3PbI_3$	46.59	11.51	16.15	21.65	3.07	3.43	3.07	1.09	12.27	12.39	10.45	1.55	1.91	6.80
Fe_2O_3	26.00	3.46	3.46	11.38	1.50	1.50	6.00	19.60	5.01	3.36	10.34	1.74	1.74	6.24
MoS_2	18.61	0.01	0.01	0.02	0.00	0.00	0.00	26.55	0.04	0.01	0.03	0.00	0.00	0.00
PbS	58.63	41.16	11.36	41.16	21.75	21.75	21.75	44.59	40.11	40.11	40.11	21.75	21.75	21.75
SnO_2	31.33	2.42	0.40	1.59	0.00	0.00	0.00	16.14	2.36	0.39	1.55	0.00	0.00	0.75
$SrTiO_3$	27.52	9.53	3.81	7.68	0.00	0.00	0.60	19.49	1.53	1.52	1.54	0.00	0.01	0.00
TiO_2	32.06	51.36	19.12	54.58	0.00	0.00	1.50	20.75	54.15	21.12	15.80	0.00	0.00	3.75
ZnO	31.50	0.01	0.01	0.01	0.00	0.00	0.00	24.59	0.01	3.02	0.01	0.00	0.01	0.75

Table 1: Mean percent errors (%Δ) for (a) the spatial-extension (SE) protocol—evaluating extrapolation to unseen supercell radii—and (b) the compositional-exclusion (CE) protocol—evaluating cross-material transfer. Part (a) reports errors on atom count N_A, cell volume V, lattice parameters a, b, c, and density ρ; part (b) reports errors on N_A, primitive cell edges a_p, b_p, c_p, and absolute angular deviations $|\Delta\alpha_p|$, $|\Delta\beta_p|$, $|\Delta\gamma_p|$. Results are shown for each material and radius value (R7–R10), averaged over five random rotations per configuration and across all models. Lower values indicate better agreement with reference structures. These complementary metrics illustrate the model's capacity to capture atomic-scale patterns across variations in supercell size and material composition. Contrasting SE and CE errors highlights whether performance limitations stem from radius extrapolation or cross-material generalization. Colours indicate predictive difficulty: green marks the material with the lowest prediction error (easiest to predict), while red marks the material with the highest prediction error (hardest to predict).

Model	SE	CE	$T \times 10^3$	$G_{\max} \times 10$	t_{SE}	t_{CE}
Claude Opus 4 (Anthropic)	0.06	0.91	**2.17**	3.04	12.86	13.91
Claude Sonnet 4 (Anthropic)	**0.04**	0.68	3.93	3.04	6.43	8.23
DeepSeek-Chat (DeepSeek)	0.09	1.79	14.16	6.47	24.97	13.71
GPT-4.1 Mini (OpenAI)	0.18	**0.53**	2.63	6.00	8.08	7.26
Gemini 2.5 Flash (Google)	0.05	1.32	21.38	3.04	**3.06**	**5.00**
Grok 2 (X.ai)	0.07	2.34	15.55	3.04	6.37	8.99
Grok 2 Vision (X.ai)	0.06	2.02	22.54	6.47	7.32	9.50
Llama-4 Maverick (Meta)	0.09	0.89	3.70	**3.00**	4.33	6.72
Mistral Medium 3 (Mistral AI)	0.05	0.92	11.24	**3.00**	14.78	15.45

Table 2: Transfer degradation analysis with mean percent errors (% Δ) for the SE and CE splits. $T = \mathrm{CE}/\mathrm{SE}$; $G_{\max}$ is the largest absolute error observed in any single prediction. t_{SE} and t_{CE} represents the each models latency in seconds for SE and CE task, respectively. **Bold** indicates the top-performing model, while underlining denotes the runner-up.

Correlation Shift. Table 3 reports the average error–error correlation coefficients for fourteen property pairs under the SE and CE protocols, along with their differences. Notably, the transition from SE to CE increases the correlation between projected lattice constants a_p and b_p by 0.59, suggesting that prediction errors for these geometric features become more aligned when the model is exposed to entirely novel compositions. In contrast, the correlation between volume V and average formation energy $\bar{\varepsilon}$ drops by -0.64, indicating a breakdown in the learned volume–energy coupling under compositional generalization.

These shifts reverse when comparing CE to SE, confirming that the observed effects stem from the validation regime rather than intrinsic data asymmetries. This bidirectional sensitivity highlights a critical weakness: current foundation models preserve certain geometric relationships under run-wise exclusion but fail to maintain deeper physical dependencies—such as energetic coherence—when facing unfamiliar chemistries. The instability of error correlations under different evaluation settings undermines the robustness of model generalization and emphasizes the need for embedding invariant physical priors into model architecture and training.

Compliance and Hallucination. The models consistently struggle to enforce fundamental physical constraints and frequently fabricate ungrounded details, as quantified in Table 4. Physical-law compliance scores fall below acceptable thresholds for most materials, with particularly poor performance on TiO_2, where nearly half the predictions violate basic geometric or density-based relationships. Concurrently, hallucination scores indicate that a significant fraction of predicted properties—often over 40%—deviate substantially from reference values or represent nonphysical outputs. The co-occurrence of constraint violations and fictitious property generation highlights systemic limitations in current architectures. These results reinforce the need for models that integrate structural priors, conservation rules, and uncertainty-aware mechanisms

(a) SE ⇒ CE

	$N_{\text{atoms}} \leftrightarrow V$	$V \leftrightarrow \bar{\varepsilon}$	$V \leftrightarrow \rho$	$\gamma_p \leftrightarrow \bar{\varepsilon}$	$a \leftrightarrow \bar{\varepsilon}$	$a \leftrightarrow \rho$	$a \leftrightarrow b$	$a_p \leftrightarrow b_p$	$a_p \leftrightarrow c_p$	$b \leftrightarrow \bar{\varepsilon}$	$b \leftrightarrow \rho$	$b_p \leftrightarrow c_p$	$c \leftrightarrow \bar{\varepsilon}$	$c \leftrightarrow \rho$
ϵ_{SE}	+0.28	+0.81	+0.34	-0.00	+0.52	+0.13	+0.32	+0.09	+0.09	+0.50	+0.17	+0.09	+0.57	+0.21
ϵ_{CE}	+0.02	+0.17	-0.06	+0.22	+0.09	-0.10	-0.00	+0.69	+0.44	+0.07	-0.05	+0.44	+0.10	-0.14
Δ	-0.27	-0.64	-0.40	+0.22	-0.44	-0.22	-0.32	+0.59	+0.35	-0.43	-0.22	+0.35	-0.47	-0.35

(b) CE ⇒ SE

	$N_{\text{atoms}} \leftrightarrow V$	$V \leftrightarrow \bar{\varepsilon}$	$V \leftrightarrow \rho$	$\gamma_p \leftrightarrow \bar{\varepsilon}$	$a \leftrightarrow \bar{\varepsilon}$	$a \leftrightarrow \rho$	$a \leftrightarrow b$	$a_p \leftrightarrow b_p$	$a_p \leftrightarrow c_p$	$b \leftrightarrow \bar{\varepsilon}$	$b \leftrightarrow \rho$	$b_p \leftrightarrow c_p$	$c \leftrightarrow \bar{\varepsilon}$	$c \leftrightarrow \rho$
ϵ_{CE}	+0.02	+0.17	-0.06	+0.22	+0.09	-0.10	-0.00	+0.69	+0.44	+0.07	-0.05	+0.44	+0.10	-0.14
ϵ_{SE}	+0.28	+0.81	+0.34	-0.00	+0.52	+0.13	+0.32	+0.09	+0.09	+0.50	+0.17	+0.09	+0.57	+0.21
Δ	+0.27	+0.64	+0.40	-0.22	+0.44	+0.22	+0.32	-0.59	-0.35	+0.43	+0.22	-0.35	+0.47	+0.35

Table 3: Largest shifts in *error–error* correlation coefficients when transferring between SE and CE annotation protocols. Each sub-table displays the top 14 property pairs (ordered alphabetically) exhibiting the largest absolute changes in pairwise correlation, averaged over all models, materials, and $R7$–$R10$. Panel (a) shows the shift from SE to CE ($\Delta = \rho_{\text{CE}} - \rho_{\text{SE}}$), while panel (b) shows the reverse (CE to SE, $\Delta = \rho_{\text{SE}} - \rho_{\text{CE}}$). For each property pair, the table reports the correlation coefficients under each protocol and their difference Δ. Cells are color-coded: green for positive Δ (stronger coupling under the target protocol) and red for negative Δ (weaker coupling), highlighting which structural or physical property relationships are most sensitive to the choice of annotation protocol.

Material	Physical Law Compliance	Hallucination Score
Ag	<u>0.82</u> $\pm$ 0.03	0.21 $\pm$ 0.04
Au	**0.84** $\pm$ 0.03	0.24 $\pm$ 0.02
$CH_3NH_3PbI_3$	0.72 $\pm$ 0.03	0.42 $\pm$ 0.05
Fe_2O_3	0.74 $\pm$ 0.03	0.23 $\pm$ 0.02
MoS_2	0.78 $\pm$ 0.03	**0.18** $\pm$ 0.01
PbS	0.77 $\pm$ 0.03	0.53 $\pm$ 0.02
SnO_2	0.74 $\pm$ 0.03	0.24 $\pm$ 0.04
$SrTiO_3$	0.77 $\pm$ 0.02	0.28 $\pm$ 0.03
TiO_2	0.46 $\pm$ 0.02	0.43 $\pm$ 0.03
ZnO	0.77 $\pm$ 0.02	<u>0.21</u> $\pm$ 0.02

Table 4: Mean ± std physical-law compliance and hallucination scores for each material, averaged over all models and five runs per material–radius under both SE and CE protocols. Physical-law compliance measures adherence to fundamental structural constraints (e.g., density and lattice-parameter ratios), while the hallucination score quantifies the frequency of non-physical or highly erroneous predictions across a set of key properties. **Bold** denotes the material with the highest prediction accuracy, while <u>underlining</u> denotes the material with the second highest accuracy.

to produce physically plausible and trustworthy predictions at the atomic scale.

Model Latency. Table 2 presents the average inference latencies per sample across the SE and CE protocols. Gemini 2.5 Flash exhibits the lowest latency, requiring only 3.06 s under SE and 5.00 s under CE, making it well-suited for time-sensitive applications such as high-throughput materials screening. Llama-4 Maverick and GPT-4.1 Mini follow in the next performance tier with moderate latency (4 s to 8 s), while most other models cluster between 6 s to 15 s. DeepSeek-Chat is the slowest model in the SE evaluation (25 s), and Mistral Medium 3 exhibits the highest latency in CE (15.5 s). These trends broadly correlate with model size and architecture, where larger context windows and multimodal inputs tend to incur higher computational overhead. Although latency is not the primary evaluation criterion in this study, the results offer practical insights for downstream deployment scenarios, especially when balancing predictive accuracy against throughput constraints.

6 Limitations

This study isolates two complementary generalization regimes—geometric interpolation/extrapolation and chemical extrapolation—using a curated dataset of ten crystalline materials across four radii. While representative, this selection captures only a limited region of compositional and structural diversity present in real-world materials. All models are evaluated in a zero-shot setting with default decoding configurations, without fine-tuning, retrieval augmentation, or domain adaptation, which may underrepresent their full capabilities.

Evaluation emphasizes first-order structural properties such as lattice constants, density, and stoichiometry, along with a single volumetric consistency index. Higher-order descriptors—including phonon spectra, band topology, or symmetry-preserving deformations—are not considered. The analysis focuses on static prediction quality and does not measure model responsiveness to feedback, learning curves under domain supervision, or variance across decoding seeds.

7 Conclusion

This work introduces *xCrysAlloys* and its two complementary benchmarks—SE and CE—that isolate geometric interpolation and chemical extrapolation in crystallographic prediction. The evaluations reveal that current vision–language foundation models struggle to internalize core physical principles, as evidenced by high relative errors, substantial degradation in transfer settings, and disrupted inter-property correlations. The prevalence of hallucinated outputs and violations of basic physical laws further underscores the limitations of purely data-driven training in scientific domains.

To advance reliability and generalization, future models must incorporate explicit physical constraints, symmetry priors, and uncertainty-aware reasoning. The proposed benchmarks provide a reproducible and physically grounded testbed for evaluating model robustness in structured scientific settings. By bridging multimodal language understanding with domain-specific inductive biases, this work aims to foster the development of more trustworthy foundation models for materials science and beyond.

References

Sunandan Baruah and Joydeep Dutta. 2009. Hydrothermal growth of zno nanostructures. *Science and technology of advanced materials*, 10(1):013001.

W. H. Baur, R. A. Sass, et al. 1971. The rutile structure of sno_2. *Acta Crystallographica Section B*, 27:2133.

Alberto Bertucco and Gerhard Vetter. 2001. *High pressure process technology: fundamentals and applications*, volume 9. Elsevier.

HKDH Bhadeshia. 2001. *Geometry of crystals*, volume 8. Institute of Materials London.

Jan-Otto Carlsson and Peter M Martin. 2010. Chemical vapor deposition. In *Handbook of Deposition Technologies for films and coatings*, pages 314–363. Elsevier.

Stefano Curtarolo, Wahyu Setyawan, Gus LW Hart, Michal Jahnatek, Roman V Chepulskii, Richard H Taylor, Shidong Wang, Junkai Xue, Kesong Yang, Ohad Levy, et al. 2012. Aflow: An automatic framework for high-throughput materials discovery. *Computational Materials Science*, 58:218–226.

Alexandre Agm Duval, Victor Schmidt, Alex Hernández-Garcıa, Santiago Miret, Fragkiskos D Malliaros, Yoshua Bengio, and David Rolnick. 2023. Faenet: Frame averaging equivariant gnn for materials modeling. In *International Conference on Machine Learning*, pages 9013–9033. PMLR.

L. W. Finger and R. M. Hazen. 1980. Crystal structure and isothermal compression of fe_2o_3, cr_2o_3, and v_2o_3 to 50 kbars. *Journal of Applied Physics*, 51:5362–5367.

Johannes Gasteiger, Janek Groß, and Stephan Günnemann. 2020. Directional message passing for molecular graphs. *arXiv preprint arXiv:2003.03123*.

Michael Gaus, Qiang Cui, and Marcus Elstner. 2011. Dftb3: Extension of the self-consistent-charge density-functional tight-binding method (scc-dftb). *Journal of Chemical Theory and Computation*, 7(4):931–948.

R. Grau-Crespo and R. Lopez-Cordero. 2002. Mos_2 structural properties. *Phys. Chem. Chem. Phys.*, 4:4078.

Sydney R Hall, Frank H Allen, and I David Brown. 1991. The crystallographic information file (cif): a new standard archive file for crystallography. *Foundations of Crystallography*, 47(6):655–685.

M. Horn, C. R. Meagher, et al. 1972. Structure of anatase tio_2. *Zeitschrift für Kristallographie*, 136:273.

B Hourahine, S Sanna, B Aradi, C Köhler, Th Niehaus, and Th Frauenheim. 2007. Self-interaction and strong correlation in dftb. *The Journal of Physical Chemistry A*, 111(26):5671–5677.

Anubhav Jain, Shyue Ping Ong, Geoffroy Hautier, Wei Chen, William Davidson Richards, Stephen Dacek, Shreyas Cholia, Dan Gunter, David Skinner, Gerbrand Ceder, et al. 2013. Commentary: The materials project: A materials genome approach to accelerating materials innovation. *APL Materials*, 1(1).

Daniel S Jensen and Adam Wasserman. 2018. Numerical methods for the inverse problem of density functional theory. *International Journal of Quantum Chemistry*, 118(1):e25425.

H. W. King. 2002a. *CRC Handbook of Chemistry and Physics*, 83 edition. CRC Press. Standard phase data for silver (Ag).

H. W. King. 2002b. *CRC Handbook of Chemistry and Physics*, 83 edition. CRC Press. Standard phase data for gold (Au).

Walter Kohn and Lu Jeu Sham. 1965. Self-consistent equations including exchange and correlation effects. *Physical Review*, 140(4A):A1133.

Mustafa Kurban, Can Polat, Erchin Serpedin, and Hasan Kurban. 2024. Enhancing the electronic properties of tio2 nanoparticles through carbon doping: An integrated dftb and computer vision approach. *Computational Materials Science*, 244:113248.

Jon M Laurent, Joseph D Janizek, Michael Ruzo, Michaela M Hinks, Michael J Hammerling, Siddharth Narayanan, Manvitha Ponnapati, Andrew D

White, and Samuel G Rodriques. 2024. Lab-bench: Measuring capabilities of language models for biology research. *arXiv preprint arXiv:2407.10362*.

Andrea C Levi and Miroslav Kotrla. 1997. Theory and simulation of crystal growth. *Journal of Physics: Condensed Matter*, 9(2):299.

Junxian Li, Di Zhang, Xunzhi Wang, Zeying Hao, Jingdi Lei, Qian Tan, Cai Zhou, Wei Liu, Yaotian Yang, Xinrui Xiong, et al. 2025. Chemvlm: Exploring the power of multimodal large language models in chemistry area. In *Proceedings of the AAAI Conference on Artificial Intelligence*, 1, pages 415–423.

Yi-Lun Liao, Brandon Wood, Abhishek Das, and Tess Smidt. 2023. Equiformerv2: Improved equivariant transformer for scaling to higher-degree representations. *arXiv preprint arXiv:2306.12059*.

Pan Lu, Swaroop Mishra, Tanglin Xia, Liang Qiu, Kai-Wei Chang, Song-Chun Zhu, Oyvind Tafjord, Peter Clark, and Ashwin Kalyan. 2022. Learn to explain: Multimodal reasoning via thought chains for science question answering. *Advances in Neural Information Processing Systems*, 35:2507–2521.

VA Lubarda. 2003. On the effective lattice parameter of binary alloys. *Mechanics of materials*, 35(1-2):53–68.

Santiago Miret and Nandan M Krishnan. 2024. Are llms ready for real-world materials discovery? *arXiv preprint arXiv:2402.05200*.

R. H. Mitchell and M. A. Carpenter. 2000. Physics and chemistry of srtio$_3$ perovskites. *Physics and Chemistry of Minerals*, 27:583.

DA Papaconstantopoulos and MJ Mehl. 2003. The slater–koster tight-binding method: a computationally efficient and accurateapproach. *Journal of Physics: Condensed Matter*, 15(10):R413.

Can Polat, Hasan Kurban, Erchin Serpedin, and Mustafa Kurban. 2025a. Tdcm25: A multi-modal multi-task benchmark for temperature-dependent crystalline materials. In *AI for Accelerated Materials Design-ICLR 2025*.

Can Polat, Mehmet Tuncel, Hasan Kurban, Erchin Serpedin, and Mustafa Kurban. 2025b. xchemagents: Agentic ai for explainable quantum chemistry. *arXiv preprint arXiv:2505.20574*.

Nitin Rane. 2023. Transformers in material science: roles, challenges, and future scope. *Challenges and Future Scope (March 26, 2023)*.

James E Saal, Scott Kirklin, Muratahan Aykol, Bryce Meredig, and Christopher Wolverton. 2013. Materials design and discovery with high-throughput density functional theory: the open quantum materials database (oqmd). *Jom*, 65:1501–1509.

Kristof Schütt, Pieter-Jan Kindermans, Huziel Enoc Sauceda Felix, Stefan Chmiela, Alexandre Tkatchenko, and Klaus-Robert Müller. 2017. Schnet: A continuous-filter convolutional neural network for modeling quantum interactions. *Advances in Neural Information Processing Systems*, 30.

Richard P Stanley. 1975. The fibonacci lattice. *The Fibonacci Quarterly*, 13(3):215–232.

Yingheng Tang, Wenbin Xu, Jie Cao, Weilu Gao, Steve Farrell, Benjamin Erichson, Michael W Mahoney, Andy Nonaka, and Zhi Yao. 2025. Matterchat: A multi-modal llm for material science. *arXiv preprint arXiv:2502.13107*.

Aron Walsh, elds22, Federico Brivio, and Jarvist Moore Frost. 2019. Wmd-group/hybrid-perovskites: Collection 1 (v1.0). `https://doi.org/10.5281/zenodo.2641358`. Hybrid perovskite $CH_3NH_3PbI_3$ structural data.

Geemi Wellawatte, Huixuan Guo, Magdalena Lederbauer, Anna Borisova, Matthew Hart, Marta Brucka, and Philippe Schwaller. 2024. Chemlit-qa: A human evaluated dataset for chemistry rag tasks. In *AI for Accelerated Materials Design-NeurIPS 2024*.

Zhenqin Wu, Bharath Ramsundar, Evan N Feinberg, Joseph Gomes, Caleb Geniesse, Aneesh S Pappu, Karl Leswing, and Vijay Pande. 2018. Moleculenet: a benchmark for molecular machine learning. *Chemical Science*, 9(2):513–530.

R. W. G. Wyckoff. 1963a. *Crystal Structures Volume 1*. Interscience Publishers.

R. W. G. Wyckoff. 1963b. *Crystal Structures Volume 1*. Interscience Publishers.

R. W. G. Wyckoff. 1963c. *Crystal Structures Volume 1*. Interscience Publishers.

Xiaolong Zheng, Peng Zheng, and Rui-Zhi Zhang. 2018. Machine learning material properties from the periodic table using convolutional neural networks. *Chemical Science*, 9(44):8426–8432.

A Appendix

A.1 Crystal Parameters

Silver (Ag). Silver adopts an FCC lattice with lattice constant $a = 4.0857$ Å. The cubic crystal belongs to space group Fm$\overline{3}$m (No. 225), Pearson symbol cF4, and Schoenflies notation O_h^5. A single Ag atom occupies the origin of the primitive cell (King, 2002a).

Gold (Au). Gold similarly adopts an FCC arrangement with lattice constant $a = 4.0782$ Å. It crystallizes in space group Fm$\overline{3}$m (No. 225), reflecting equivalent high symmetry. One Au atom resides at the (0,0,0) position within the unit cell (King, 2002b).

Methylammonium Lead Iodide ($CH_3NH_3PbI_3$). The hybrid perovskite $CH_3NH_3PbI_3$ forms a pseudo-cubic lattice with parameters $a = 6.290$ Å, $b = 6.274$ Å, $c = 6.297$ Å and angles close to 90°. It crystallizes in space group $P1$ (No. 1), accommodating slight distortions and dynamic disorder typical of organic–inorganic frameworks (Walsh et al., 2019).

Hematite (Fe_2O_3). Hematite (Fe_2O_3) exhibits a rhombohedral structure with lattice constants $a = b = 5.0346$ Å, $c = 13.7473$ Å, and angles $\alpha = \beta = 90°$, $\gamma = 120°$. It belongs to space group $R\overline{3}c$ (No. 167), underpinning its antiferromagnetic and catalytic properties (Finger and Hazen, 1980).

Molybdenum Disulfide (MoS_2). Molybdenum disulfide (MoS_2) adopts a layered hexagonal lattice with parameters $a = 3.1604$ Å, $c = 12.295$ Å, and angles $\alpha = \beta = 90°$, $\gamma = 120°$. It crystallizes in space group $P6_3/mmc$ (No. 194), reflecting its van der Waals–bonded layers (Wyckoff, 1963b; Grau-Crespo and Lopez-Cordero, 2002).

Galena (PbS). Galena (PbS) forms a rock-salt–type FCC structure with lattice constant $a = 5.9362$ Å. The cubic crystal belongs to space group Fm$\overline{3}$m (No. 225), with Pb and S atoms occupying alternating FCC sites (Wyckoff, 1963c).

Cassiterite (SnO_2). Cassiterite (SnO_2) displays a tetragonal rutile–type lattice with constants $a = 4.738$ Å, $c = 3.1865$ Å. It crystallizes in space group $P4_2/mnm$ (No. 136) and features an oxygen sublattice coordinating the Sn atoms (Baur et al., 1971).

Strontium Titanate ($SrTiO_3$). Strontium titanate ($SrTiO_3$) crystallizes in a cubic perovskite structure with lattice constant $a = 3.9053$ Å and space group $Pm\overline{3}m$ (No. 221). Its ideal symmetry underlies its prototypical ferroelectric and quantum paraelectric behavior (Mitchell and Carpenter, 2000).

Titanium Dioxide (TiO_2—Anatase). Anatase TiO_2 exhibits a body-centered tetragonal structure with $a = 3.7842$ Å, $c = 9.5146$ Å. It belongs to space group $I4_1/amd$ (No. 141), characteristic of the anatase polymorph's photocatalytic activity (Horn et al., 1972).

Zinc Oxide (ZnO—Zincite). Zinc oxide (ZnO) in the zincite phase adopts a hexagonal wurtzite lattice with parameters $a = 3.2495$ Å, $c = 5.2069$ Å and space group $P6_3mc$ (No. 186). This polar structure underpins its piezoelectric and optoelectronic applications (Wyckoff, 1963a).

A.2 Additional Metric Definitions

Absolute-error (angles). For each primitive-cell angle $\theta_p \in \{\alpha_p, \beta_p, \gamma_p\}$,

$$|\Delta\theta_p| = \left|\theta_p^{\text{gen}} - \theta_p^{\text{ref}}\right|.$$

Per-example mean error. If an example contains the set of properties P, then

$$\overline{\%\Delta} = \frac{1}{|P|} \sum_{p \in P} \%\Delta_p.$$

Format faithfulness. Let $\mathcal{F}_{\text{ref}}$ and $\mathcal{F}_{\text{gen}}$ be the non-null field sets, and $\mathcal{F}_{\cap} = \mathcal{F}_{\text{ref}} \cap \mathcal{F}_{\text{gen}}$. The following definitions are considered:

$$S_{\text{presence}} = \frac{|\mathcal{F}_{\cap}|}{|\mathcal{F}_{\text{ref}}|}$$

$$S_{\text{type}} = \frac{1}{|\mathcal{F}_{\cap}|} \sum_{f \in \mathcal{F}_{\cap}} \mathbf{1}\big(\text{type}_{\text{gen}}(f) = \text{type}_{\text{ref}}(f)\big),$$

and

$$S_{\text{format}} = 0.7\, S_{\text{presence}} + 0.3\, S_{\text{type}}.$$

MLAN: Language-Based Instruction Tuning Preserves and Transfers Knowledge in Multimodal Language Models

Jianhong Tu[1*], **Zhuohao Ni**[2*], **Nicholas Crispino**[1], **Zihao Yu**[1], **Michael Bendersky**[3], **Beliz Gunel**[3], **Ruoxi Jia**[4], **Xin Liu**[5], **Lingjuan Lyu**[6], **Dawn Song**[7], **Chenguang Wang**[1†]

[1]Washington University in St. Louis [2]The University of British Columbia
[3]Google Research [4]Virginia Tech [5]University of California, Davis
[6]Sony AI [7]University of California, Berkeley

{jianhong.t, ncrispino, yu.zihao, chenguangwang}@wustl.edu
peterni@student.ubc.ca {bemike, bgunel}@google.com ruoxijia@vt.edu
xinliu@ucdavis.edu Lingjuan.Lv@sony.com dawnsong@berkeley.edu

Abstract

We present a novel visual instruction tuning strategy to improve the zero-shot task generalization of multimodal large language models by building a firm text-only knowledge base. Existing work lacks sufficient experimentation on the importance of each modality in the instruction tuning stage, often using a majority of vision-language data while keeping text-only data limited and fixing mixtures of modalities. By incorporating diverse text-only data in the visual instruction tuning stage, we vary vision-language data in various controlled experiments to investigate the importance of modality in visual instruction tuning. Our comprehensive evaluation shows that the text-heavy instruction tuning approach is able to perform on-par with traditional vision-heavy mixtures on both modalities across 12 general datasets while using as low as half the total training tokens. We find that simply increasing sufficiently diverse text-only data enables transfer of instruction following ability and domain knowledge across modalities while being more efficient than the vision-language approach.

1 Introduction

Multimodal large language models (MLLMs) have advanced and enabled a wide range of vision-language tasks such as visual question answering and image captioning (Liu et al., 2023b; Alayrac et al., 2022; Li et al., 2023b; Lin et al., 2023; Bai et al., 2025). Their zero-shot generalization ability to unseen tasks has the potential to further revolutionize broader real-world applications (Driess et al., 2023; Zhu et al., 2023; Li et al., 2023a). To construct MLLMs, vision-language pretraining is performed on a large scale with image-text data, aligning the modalities before visual instruction tuning aligns the model with human preferences (Liu et al., 2023a; Dai et al., 2024; Lin et al., 2023). The importance of strong vision-language pretraining is established, with more data resulting in greater improvements in instruction-following abilities and downstream performance (McKinzie et al., 2024; Zhang et al., 2024a). However, current visual instruction tuning practices overwhelmingly rely on image-text pairs and large-scale vision-language datasets. This emphasis introduces a significant distributional shift from the language-rich corpora used during pretraining, often degrading the model's general language understanding and leading to catastrophic forgetting of core knowledge (Zhang et al., 2024b). Given the similarity in instruction tuning data across modalities and the strong modality alignment achieved with vision-language pretraining, we believe text-only data is underutilized in existing training mixtures. Additionally, various design choices regarding the instruction tuning dataset composition with respect to modalities are underexplored.

In this work, we introduce **MLAN** (**M**ultimodal **LAN**guage-based instruction tuning), a new perspective in vision instruction tuning that treats language as the primary way to unlock knowledge during instruction tuning (Figure 1). Our key insight is that instruction-following abilities and domain knowledge, once acquired through diverse language-only tasks, can generalize across modalities with minimal vision-language supervision. By grounding vision capabilities in a small number of targeted image-text examples, we maintain high performance across both vision and text tasks while significantly reducing training costs. Specifically, with MLAN we unlock vision instruction following abilities by teaching a pretrained model to execute text-only instructions and then complementing the dataset with a relatively small portion of vision-language examples in a domain adaptation fashion.

To demonstrate MLAN's effectiveness, we pre-

[*] Equal contribution
[†]Corresponding author

Proceedings of the 3rd Workshop on Towards Knowledgeable Foundation Models (KnowFM), pages 59–74
August 1, 2025

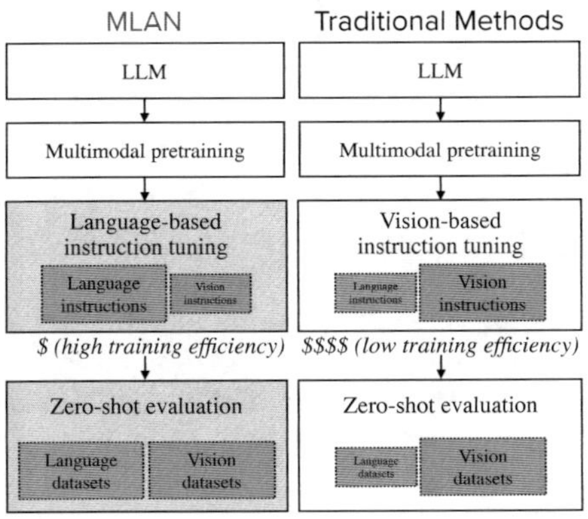

(a) Comparison of MLAN with standard visual instruction tuning.

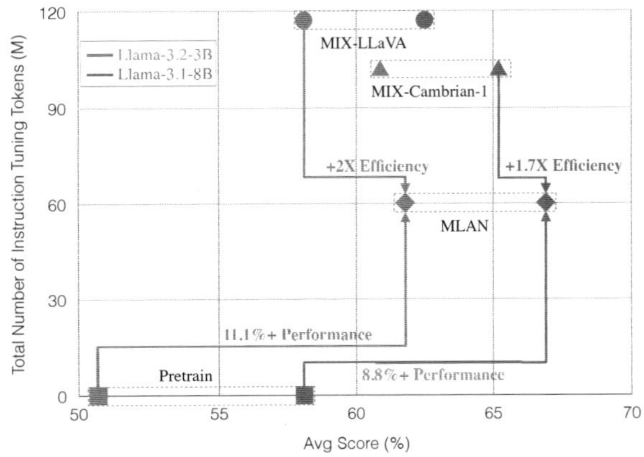

(b) Main results on evaluation tasks, averaged over text-only and vision-language performance.

Figure 1: Overview of MLAN. (a) MLAN represents a shift in perspective towards text during instruction tuning. After vision-language pretraining, we include diverse text-only data in our instruction tuning mixture spanning many tasks. We emphasize including text-only data to show the transferability of instruction tuning across modalities. For evaluation, we select ample text-only and vision-language datasets, allowing us to compare performance changes across modalities. (b) We evaluate MLAN on two pretrained multimodal models based on Llama-3.2-3B and Llama-3.1-8B across unseen language and vision benchmarks, achieving comparable performance at higher training efficiency (up to almost 2x as efficient compared to standard vision-heavy instruction tuning) with our language-based approach.

train MLLMs over a variety of settings based on Llama-3.2-3B (Meta AI, 2024) and Llama-3.1-8B (Dubey et al., 2024), following the state of the art multimodal training mechanism (Liu et al., 2023b,a), varying only the dataset. We then apply MLAN to the MLLMs and observe the following key insights over both models on average during evaluation on 12 comprehensive benchmarks across language and vision modalities. (1) Compared with the traditional vision-heavy finetuning approaches of LLaVA (Liu et al., 2023a) and Cambrian-1 (Tong et al., 2024), our models finetuned with MLAN demonstrate a matching or better performance on downstream vision-language tasks while seeing less than half of the images and consistently showing better text-only performance. We show that text-only data is imperative to obtain world knowledge and understanding of complex instructions, even in the vision domain. (2) Text-only instruction tuning is more cost-effective. The rich and dense information compensates for the limited diversity in public vision datasets, allowing for superior performance while reducing the total number of processed training tokens by half. (3) Neither language nor vision alone is enough for a generalist MLLM. Our experiments show that while instruction following abilities may transfer across modalities, their impact on the other modality is limited: certain vision-language tasks do not benefit from text-only tuning and vision-language tuning can result in severe degradation of language abilities. However, mixing bi-modal data, even at a small percentage, leads to surprising performance boosts and achieves the best results in both modalities. We hope our findings will foster future research on language-centered training and instruction tuning, paving the way for fundamental advancements in large MLLMs.

2 Approach

MLAN views vision instruction following abilities as a natural extension of text-only abilities, a transfer that can occur due to the extensive multimodal pretraining used in MLLMs.

We begin by motivating our method through an empirical analysis of similarities in text-only and vision-language instruction tuning data, which leads to our hypothesis that text-only data can largely replace vision-language data to improve performance on general tasks. Then, we detail our training, following the standard design of existing instruction tuning methods (Wei et al., 2022; Xu et al., 2023; Dai et al., 2023; Liu et al., 2023b) in four stages: selecting training data, format-

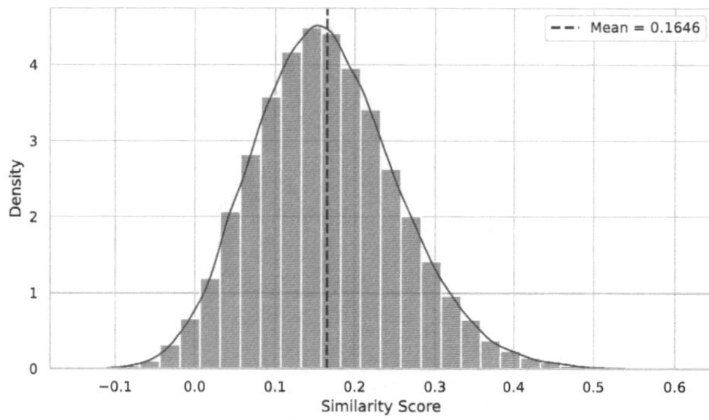

(a) Distribution of cross-modal similarity scores between modalities with a non-negative mean by z-test ($p < 0.001$).

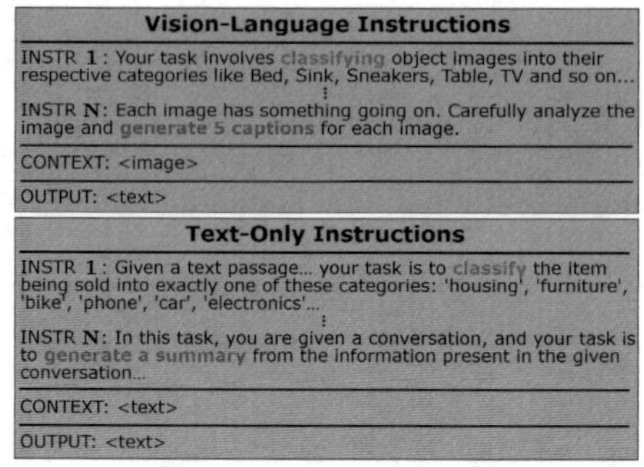

(b) Examples of instructions across modalities that share similar goals.

Figure 2: Similarity between text-only and vision-language instruction tuning data shown both (a) quantitatively with similarity scores and (b) qualitatively with examples. 100k instructions are sampled from the Super-NaturalInstructions (Wang et al., 2022b) and Vision-Flan (Xu et al., 2024) datasets and embedded by a pretrained sentenceTransformer, all-mpnet-base-v2 (Song et al., 2020). The red vertical line denotes the mean score. We then randomly sample and display two instructions with high cosine similarities (0.53 & 0.38).

ting the data with instructions, fine-tuning a pretrained MLLM on the training set (Sec. 2.2), and evaluating the instruction tuned model on standard academic benchmarks in the zero-shot setting (Sec. 2.3).

2.1 Natural Correspondence between Text-Only and Vision-Language Instructions

While the image-text and the text-only distribution of instructions significantly differ from each other, we observe shared semantics and structure on the task level when comparing wild instruction-response pairs in both modalities.

Semantic Similarity We study two comprehensive large-scale instruction tuning datasets with one from each modality, namely Super-NaturalInstructions (Wang et al., 2022b) and Vision-Flan (Xu et al., 2024), which are representative of common structures and tasks. We show vision-language and text-only tasks are similar by randomly sampling 100k instances from each dataset and examining the distribution of the cosine similarities between embedded instructions as shown in Figure 2(a). A significantly non-negative mean cosine distance provides evidence that the tasks performed in either domain are somewhat similar, based on the belief that tasks are defined by the instructions. Additionally, there is a small yet nonzero chance to even see a pair of tasks that are comparable with high similarities (>0.3) in the language and vision domain. To qualitatively demonstrate this, in Figure 2(b) we show two pairs of semantically similar instructions from each datasets with a similarity score of 0.53 and 0.38, respectively. While the first example is a classical classification task, the second requests a concise representation of the context, where the context may be a text paragraph or an image. We reason that if the ability to describe a casual conversation is acquired, the ability to caption an image can be readily obtained.

Structural Similarity The well-established problem of solving zero-shot tasks can be split into a user prompt followed by a model's response for both modalities. While some text-only tasks appeal to a model's internal knowledge, such as ARC (Bhakthavatsalam et al., 2021), the task of open-book question answering is analogous to vision question answering in the sense that additional inputs are provided to serve as the reference where the final answer is derived. If the vision and the text modalities are well aligned, it makes sense for a model to easily refer to the details in an image as the image tokens are no different than the native word tokens in its embedding space.

2.2 Training Details

Our approach, MLAN, is simple, changing the dataset composition across modalities compared to traditional MLLM instruction tuning. We fine-tune a multimodal pretrained LLM in the FLAN-style (Wei et al., 2022) and further train on a small portion of vision instruction data (compared to the number of text-only instances) to adapt the model to vision-language queries. While mainstream methods, including LLaVA (Liu et al., 2023b) and Cambrian-1 (Tong et al., 2024), also include some text-only examples in their vision instruction tuning dataset, their primary goal has been providing language as a form of regularization to prevent catastrophic forgetting. Our method differs by approaching vision instruction tuning from the other way around: we build strong language-only instruction-following abilities to build a robust knowledge base, and then introduce a small number of vision instances solely for grounding and domain adaptation. To demonstrate that adjusting the data composition alone is a viable substitute for vision-heavy instruction tuning, we use a fixed size budget and shared data sources for all our experiments, thus controlling the effect of longer training sessions and variable data quality.

Dataset Selection Inspired by the similarity in instruction tuning across modalities, we use the same two diverse datasets to train with, encompassing a multitude of tasks in each modality. For text-only data we sample from the over 1600 tasks in Super-NaturalInstructions (Wang et al., 2022b), while for vision-language data we sample from the 187 tasks in Vision-Flan (Xu et al., 2024). This gives us ample coverage across many text-only and vision-language tasks. For all of our experiments, we use a fixed data budget of 186,000 instances, which can come from either Super-NaturalInstructions or Vision-Flan depending on the setting.

Models and Multimodal Pretraining We follow the architecture design of LLaVA (Liu et al., 2023a) that connects a visual encoder with a projector that enables the LLM to use the outputs of the visual encoder to process image inputs in addition to texts. We choose CLIP-ViT-L/14@336 (Radford et al., 2021) and a two-layer MLP with GELU activation as the visual encoder and the projector, respectively. We select the base LLMs as Llama-3.2-3B (Meta AI, 2024) and Llama-3.1-8B (Dubey et al., 2024), both the non instruct versions. We conduct multimodal pretraining for both models on LLaVA-Pretrain-558K using the same hyper-parameters as in Liu et al. (2023a). These models are then finetuned on our language-heavy training dataset for one epoch using a global batch size of 128, a cosine learning schedule, a learning rate of 2e-5, a warm-up ratio of 0.03, and no weight decay. Both the visual encoder and LLM are frozen throughout the pretraining session while the parameters in the MLP projector are updated. After pretraining, the visual encoder and the projector function as a visual tokenizer that turns an image into tokens compatible with the LLM.

Instruction Tuning To test our instruction tuning methodology, we finetune MLLM checkpoints using a controlled mixture of text-only and vision-language data, focusing on the former. This is because language, rather than vision, remains the primary medium for users to interact with models when they specify their needs. In contrast, most existing multimodal instruction tuning approaches prioritize vision-language data and include language-only tasks merely to mitigate forgetting. (Liu et al., 2023a; Bai et al., 2023; Ye et al., 2023; Luo et al., 2024; Tong et al., 2024). These approaches require many more training tokens and rely on a greater number of vision-language datasets. See Table 8 in Appendix D.1 for the percentage of text-only data included during instruction tuning for various state of the art MLLMs. Current instruction tuning mixtures across models vary substantially in language content, yet few of these design choices are grounded in systematic empirical comparison. Our method systematically tests the effectiveness of the composition of instruction tuning data by modality, then anchors in a shift in perspective, treating **language as the foundation** in instruction tuning.

2.3 Evaluation Tasks

Our evaluation suite covers diverse text-only and vision-language tasks for zero-shot evaluation that are not seen during training. The text-only benchmarks include **Commonsense understanding**, **Reasoning**, **Reading comprehension** and **Scientific knowledge testing**. Similarly, the selected vision-language benchmarks primarily test **Scene Understanding** and **Image Reasoning**. Notably, MMLU (Hendrycks et al., 2020), MMMU (Yue et al., 2024), and MME (Fu et al., 2023) are large multidisciplinary benchmarks covering wide domains. We craft suitable instruction templates for each dataset in the same way as for the training datasets, using the same collection of instruction prompts. The final evaluation collection includes 7 text-only datasets and 5 vision-language datasets. The answer types cover short-response, multiple-choice, and true/false questions. Appendix C provides a brief description of each dataset.

Models	Method	Vision Benchmarks POPE	ScienceQA-IMG	MMMU	MME	MMBench	Avg.
Llama-3.2-3B	Pretrain	66.67*	43.73	26.44	700*	51.10	42.59
	MIX-LLaVA-1.5	80.10	64.65	29.00	1293.56	**67.71**	57.53
	MIX-Cambrian-1	81.90	**65.94**	28.67	1367.38	67.48	58.57
	MLAN	**83.17**	**65.94**	**29.33**	**1405.53**	67.01	**59.13**
Llama-3.1-8B	Pretrain	66.67*	63.81	27.67	700*	62.81	49.61
	MIX-LLaVA-1.5	79.90	67.97	30.89	1354.52	70.29	59.49
	MIX-Cambrian-1	**82.57**	70.55	**36.00**	1408.02	**73.50**	**62.58**
	MLAN	81.84	**71.15**	34.44	**1436.83**	72.51	62.25

Table 1: Zero-shot results on the held-out vision-language datasets for Llama-3.2-3B and Llama-3.1-8B. We compare Pretrain, MIX-LLaVA-1.5, MIX-Cambrian-1, and MLAN (ours). * denotes that the pre-trained models fail to generate meaningful responses other than all "yes" or "no". ScienceQA (Lu et al., 2022) is included in Vision-Flan but excluded in experiments. The MME scores are normalized by dividing by the maximum value (2800) when computing the average.

Models	Method	Language Benchmarks ARC-E	ARC-C	CommensenseQA	PIQA	RACE	BoolQ	CosmosQA	MMLU	Avg.
Llama-3.2-3B	Pretrain	62.42	42.41	63.72	76.77	**70.37**	62.91	**67.77**	24.09	58.81
	MIX-LLaVA-1.5	69.40	43.34	58.39	78.40	58.57	68.93	47.57	44.65	58.66
	MIX-Cambrian-1	**71.68**	46.25	60.85	**79.27**	67.98	**71.59**	59.40	48.39	63.18
	MLAN	71.30	**46.93**	**66.18**	79.11	70.27	68.44	64.76	**49.03**	**64.50**
Llama-3.1-8B	Pretrain	71.09	50.00	70.19	80.14	79.41	64.89	76.65	39.79	66.52
	MIX-LLaVA-1.5	72.60	48.81	66.20	79.43	71.44	75.38	59.53	50.51	65.49
	MIX-Cambrian-1	72.80	48.81	68.88	80.03	74.22	77.22	64.42	55.69	67.76
	MLAN	**74.79**	**50.17**	**73.05**	**81.23**	**79.91**	**78.53**	**76.68**	**58.18**	**71.57**

Table 2: Zero-shot results on the held-out text-only datasets for Llama-3.2-3B and Llama-3.1-8B. We compare Pretrain, MIX-LLaVA-1.5, MIX-Cambrian-1, and MLAN (ours).

3 Experiments

In this section, we show that MLAN is both more effective and training efficient compared to the pretrained MLLMs as well as state of the art multimodal instruction tuning mixtures across all the tasks we evaluate. Additional details of the training and experimental setup are described in Appendix B.

3.1 Main Results

We compare various instruction tuning methods built upon our multimodal pretrained Llama-3.2-3B and Llama-3.1-8B. We include the following settings, all using our specified training methodology, only varying composition: (1) Pretrain: The MLLM after multimodal pretraining with no instruction tuning. (2) MIX-LLaVA-1.5 and MIX-Cambrian-1: We use our training dataset along with the multimodal instruction tuning mixture recipes of LLaVA (Liu et al., 2023a) and Cambrian-1 (Tong et al., 2024), i.e., with 6% and 25% text-only instruction data, respectively. (3) MLAN: Our text-first instruction tuning method with a composition heavily favoring (75%) text-only data.

Cross-Task Generalization We report the scores of pretrained MLLM and instruction tuned models on 12 benchmarks in Tables 1 and 2, respectively. Compared with MIX-Cambrian-1, MLAN yields the best performance in the 3B setting and matches the best score in the 8B setting, only falling behind by 0.33%, despite being trained on less than half of the images. The competitive vision performance shows effective cross-modal transfer. MLAN consistently improves performance on knowledge-intensive tasks such as MMLU, CosmosQA, and ARC-C, demonstrating stronger internal knowledge retention compared to vision-heavy baselines.

Knowledge Erosion We note that both MIX-LLaVA-1.5 and MIX-Cambrian-1 suffer from catastrophic forgetting, especially on CommonsenseQA (Talmor et al., 2019) and CosmosQA (Huang et al., 2019), showing performance degradations up to 5.3% and 20.2%. However, MLAN is more resilient against forgetting. In the only case where its performance decreases in CosmosQA, the decline is significantly smaller than other models (3.1% vs. 20.2% & 8.37%). On all other benchmarks, including vision, our method shows a solid positive gain. Such an observation unveils an asymmetrical interaction between vision and text modalities, where the text ability is more susceptible to forgetting, but the vision ability generally benefits from language-based tuning. This trend is explored again in Section 3.2.

Method	Number of Tokens
Text-Only IT	37,906,142
MLAN	60,112,680
MIX-Cambrian-1	101,480,339↑68.8%
MIX-LLaVA-1.5	117,220,955↑95.0%
Full Vision-Language IT	122,054,758↑103.0%

Table 3: All token counts for various training settings with 186,000 total instances. The percentage score indicates the size increase relative to the MLAN setting.

3.2 Training Efficiency

A major advantage of our method is that it significantly reduces the computational cost measured by the number of training tokens processed by the base LLM compared to vision-based instruction tuning. Table 3 details the number of training tokens, including those in the visual prefix. Visual inputs drastically increase the training burden as an image is converted to hundreds of visual tokens (576 tokens with CLIP-ViT-Large-patch14@336 (Radford et al., 2021)) before being processed along with regular text tokens. Therefore, MLAN stands out as a more efficient vision instruction-tuning approach that avoids excessive instruction tuning on images.

3.3 Knowledge Transfer Curve

To better understand the role of language, we perform a controlled study by varying the proportion of language-only data in the instruction tuning mixture, increasing it in 12.5% increments. We show the performance of Llama-3.2-3B-based MLLMs with different amounts of language instruction data in Figure 3. Notably, we observe that even a small amount of language data (12.5%) leads to a sharp increase in both text and vision performance, suggesting that foundational knowledge acquired through language tuning quickly transfers across modalities. As the proportion of language data increases further, text performance continues to improve, whereas vision performance peaks and then slightly declines. Full vision-language tuning fails to match the peak vision performance achieved with a balanced mix, indicating that language-based knowledge is not only transferable but also essential for efficient vision instruction tuning. This analysis reinforces our central claim: language acts as a scaffold for multimodal reasoning, and a moderate inclusion of vision data is sufficient for grounding.

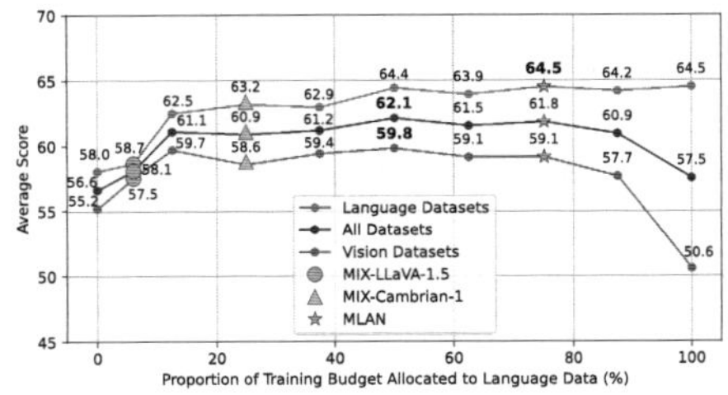

Figure 3: Average scores on Llama-3.2-3B based MLLMs with respect to the percentage of language data mixed in. The percentage denotes the amount of language data.

Base LLM	Variant	Text Avg.	Vision Avg.
Llama-3.2-3B	+MLAN	64.50	59.13
	+Instruct LLM	**67.74**	**60.98**
	-25% tasks	65.68	55.71
	-50% tasks	65.98	55.73
	-75% tasks	66.35	56.79

Table 4: Ablation study on Llama-3.2-3B with different instruction tuning variants and fewer tasks.

3.4 Additional Instruction Tuning Factors

Instruction Tuned Base Models We use base (non instruction tuned) models in our experiments to show the impact of text-only data while controlling the amount of text instruction tuning. However, mainstream vision instruction tuning methods mostly choose instruction-tuned (chat) models as the default LLM backbone (Liu et al., 2023b; Dai et al., 2024; Lin et al., 2023). Table 4 shows that finetuning the instruction tuned variant instead of the pretrained model readily boosts both text and vision performance by 2-3%, even when we continue to emphasize text-only data in the visual instruction tuning phase. This provides more evidence that the text-first approach throughout training is beneficial. A possible explanation for this is that the model adapts to the instruction following format and eliminates the distributional shift from the pretraining to the instruction tuning corpus.

Task Diversity within Datasets Prior work has emphasized the importance of diversity within instruction tuning datasets (Li et al.; Xu et al., 2024; Wei et al., 2022). We conduct a controlled fine-tuning experiment by reducing the proportion of included tasks (25%, 50%, 75%, 100%) while keeping the total number of training instances fixed. Surprisingly, text performance slightly improves with fewer tasks, peaking at 25%, while vision performance only improves with full task coverage. This suggests that task diversity does not uniformly benefit all modalities: some tasks may be less helpful, and that over-diversification may dilute useful supervision, especially for language.

Base LLM	PT	IT	Text Avg.	Vision Avg.
Llama-3.2-3B	LLaVA	Vision-Flan	55.14	57.61
		Super-Natural	**64.89**	46.95
	ShareGPT4V	Vision-Flan	58.05	**58.26**
		Super-Natural	64.48	50.20
Llama-3.1-8B	LLaVA	Vision Flan	63.08	54.77
		Super-Natural	**72.05**	52.55
	ShareGPT4V	Vision Flan	58.27	**56.84**
		Super-Natural	71.76	50.76

Table 5: Average performance across different vision pretraining (PT) and instruction tuning (IT) strategies.

3.5 Interaction between Pretraining and Single-Modal Instruction Tuning

Before visual instruction tuning, the vision pretraining step aims to align the text and vision modalities. Increasing pretraining data has been shown to increase post instruction tuning performance given the same corpus (McKinzie et al., 2024), but changes in pretraining data have been shown to have minimal effects (Cocchi et al., 2025). To investigate how the pretraining dataset affects instruction tuning on various modalities, we conduct experiments using single-modality instruction tuning datasets on another pretraining dataset (Table 5). Although we expect models to benefit from higher quality samples and longer training sessions due to ShareGPT4V (Chen et al., 2023a), the results demonstrate that this is only consistently true when the model is finetuned with vision-text instruction data. More vision pretraining has a mixed effect on the text performance, boosting the 3B model's text score while hurting the 8B model's performance. Additionally, scaling up the model size effectively increases the text scores but leaves the vision scores roughly on the same level.

Diversity in Training Data In Section 2.1, we explored the similarity between instruction tuning using text-only and vision-language data. We now compare the mean cosine distances in two intra-dataset and one inter-datasets settings. Figure 4 reports the mean cosine similarities. The vision-language appears more homogeneous, with a higher mean, while the language data is more diverse. This observation aligns with the fact that vision-language datasets typically contain fewer distinct task types and tend to emphasize perceptual grounding, whereas language-only corpora encompass a broader spectrum. Importantly, the similarity scores between language-only and vision-language instructions are comparable to those within the language-only set, suggesting that diverse linguistic tasks inherently support better generalization—even across modalities. This could imply that language data, at least in our training data, better generalizes to vision datasets thanks to greater heterogeneity. Notably, though we use a diverse set of text-only and vision-language data, there is still a gap between the similarities, meaning text-only data that aligns better with vision-language can likely be constructed, which may improve performance even more.

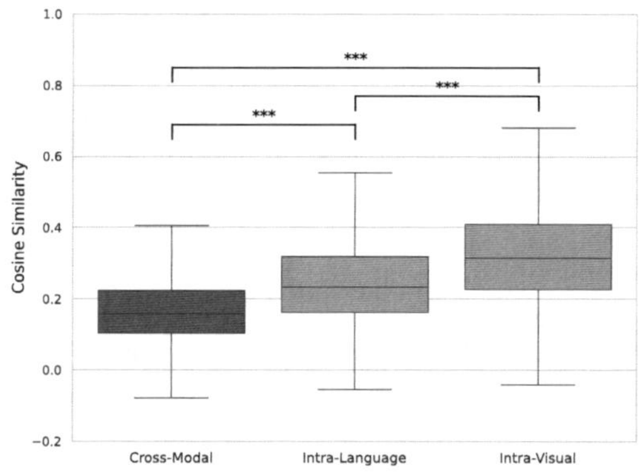

Figure 4: Distribution of the cosine similarity of random question pairs sampled in the language and vision-language settings. The stars (***) indicate significant differences ($p < 0.001$) between the mean similarity supported by the t-test.

4 Related Work

Multimodal large language models (MLLM) are language models endowed with the ability to use multiple modalities, such as images, videos, and audio (OpenAI, 2024; Meta AI, 2024; Team et al., 2023; OpenAI et al., 2024; Rubenstein et al., 2023; Zhang et al., 2023a; Ataallah et al., 2024; Bai et al., 2025; Li et al., 2024b; Liu et al., 2025b; Agrawal et al., 2024; Deitke et al., 2024; Chen et al., 2025). The most widely adopted are vision enhanced LLMs, where many design choices are already extensively studied (Liu et al., 2023a; McKinzie et al., 2024; Lin et al., 2023; Laurençon et al., 2024; Tong et al., 2024; Karamcheti et al., 2024; Cocchi et al., 2025; Li et al.). A prevalent approach to building such MLLMs links pretrained visual encoders (Radford et al., 2021; Oquab et al., 2023) to LLMs (Touvron et al., 2023; Zheng et al., 2023; Chiang et al., 2023) via an adapter, thus transforming deep image features into soft prompts for the base LLM. In our work, we focus on one of the simplest yet high-performing and widely adopted MLLMs, using only a multi-layer perceptron as the adapter (Liu et al., 2023b,a, 2024a; Li et al., 2024a; Driess et al., 2023; Lin et al., 2023; Zeng et al., 2024).

Inspired by the success of instruction tuning in LLMs in zero-shot generalization (Wei et al., 2022; Wang et al., 2022a; Zhang et al., 2023c; Ouyang et al., 2022), following a pretraining step for vision-language feature alignment, there is a multimodal instruction tuning step to improve zero-shot performance on multimodal tasks (Xu et al., 2023; Li et al., 2024c). Notably, InstructBLIP (Dai et al., 2023) and LLaVA (Liu et al., 2023b) transform existing datasets into multimodal instructions using manual templates and synthetic data, a practice expanded upon in subsequent work (Tong et al., 2024; Chen et al., 2024b; Lin et al., 2023). Further work investigates how instruction tuning varies under different settings, e.g., how different components of the MLLM should learn differently during instruction tuning (Wu et al., 2024) and how instruction tuning works in a continual learning setting with many new tasks (Chen et al., 2024a). However, there lacks a comprehensive set of experiments that varies the composition of each modality in instruction tuning.

Though the primary goal of multimodal instruction tuning is to improve vision-language performance, text-only data is often included in both pretraining (McKinzie et al., 2024; Lin et al., 2023) and finetuning (Liu et al., 2023a; Huang et al., 2023; Bai et al., 2023; Ye et al., 2023, 2024; Luo et al., 2024; Lin et al., 2023; Tong et al., 2024; Dai et al., 2024; Bai et al., 2025; Li et al.; Zhang et al., 2024a,b) to prevent catastrophic forgetting and improve language performance. Many such papers disregard the impact of finetuning with text-only data on vision performance, focusing solely on language performance when ablating text-only data away, though there are notable exceptions (Huang et al., 2023; Ye et al., 2023, 2024; Lin et al., 2023; Dai et al., 2024; Zhang et al., 2024a). In these cases, there is modest evidence of transferability between modalities, where finetuning on both language and vision data exhibits about equal or better performance than training on one modality alone. However, in each of the existing work that finetune with text-only data alongside vision data, this performance boost is achieved by increasing the dataset size without consideration of how such data will increase the training cost (with the exception of Zhang et al. (2024a), which only tests with a low amount of text-only data). Hence, even though better performance is obtained when increasing the dataset size to train on text-only data, the instruction tuning step is more costly.

Due to the general cost of instruction tuning a MLLM, many approaches aims to decrease the cost of instruction tuning in the multimodal setting. These primarily include using lightweight adapters to decrease the number of parameters (Luo et al., 2024; Zhang et al., 2023b; Liu et al., 2025a) and choosing a subset of the training data using the MLLM itself or other methods (Chen et al., 2024c; Wei et al., 2023; Lee et al., 2024; Liu et al., 2024c; Safaei et al., 2025; Bi et al., 2025). A simpler way to decrease the cost is to instruction tune with a focus on text-only data. Since training on language instruction data is cheaper than training on the same number of vision instances, and language is foundational to the functioning of MLLMs, we focus on such a language-based approach.

5 Conclusion

We present MLAN, a language-based multimodal instruction tuning strategy for MLLMs that enhances zero-shot generalization and promotes effective knowledge transfer across modalities. We demonstrate—through controlled ablations under fixed training budgets—that language-based tuning establishes a robust knowledge foundation, even for tasks requiring visual understanding. Crucially, MLAN achieves strong performance on both language and vision benchmarks while significantly reducing reliance on image supervision. Our results show that language is not only sufficient but essential for efficient and generalizable multimodal learning. With MLAN, we hope to bring attention to the importance of language in MLLMs in visual instruction tuning, which we believe can be used in future work to improve training efficiency and performance.

6 Limitations

Our experiments are performed on models with the same multimodal architecture and pretraining procedure, not accounting for more advanced architecture or large-scale multimodal pretraining. Though we evaluate on a comprehensive set of vision-language benchmarks, we do not evaluate on specialized out of distribution tasks like OCR or captioning, focusing only on general tasks where the transferability is motivated. We invite future work to explore other methodologies to find where such specialized text-only and vision-language tasks align. Our analysis could also use experiments testing how instruction tuning varies when different tasks are trained on versus held-out, or on sequential finetuning versus sampling text-only and vision-language data. Furthermore, the instruction tuning experiments have the same data budget of 186,000 instances, while existing instruction tuning data may contain hundreds of thousands or even multi-million instances, which we leave to future work.

References

Pravesh Agrawal, Szymon Antoniak, Emma Bou Hanna, Baptiste Bout, Devendra Chaplot, Jessica Chudnovsky, Diogo Costa, Baudouin De Monicault, Saurabh Garg, Theophile Gervet, Soham Ghosh, Amélie Héliou, Paul Jacob, Albert Q. Jiang, Kartik Khandelwal, Timothée Lacroix, Guillaume Lample, Diego Las Casas, Thibaut Lavril, and 23 others. 2024. Pixtral 12B. *Preprint*, arXiv:2410.07073.

Jean-Baptiste Alayrac, Jeff Donahue, Pauline Luc, Antoine Miech, Iain Barr, Yana Hasson, Karel Lenc, Arthur Mensch, Katherine Millican, Malcolm Reynolds, Roman Ring, Eliza Rutherford, Serkan Cabi, Tengda Han, Zhitao Gong, Sina Samangooei, Marianne Monteiro, Jacob L. Menick, Sebastian Borgeaud, and 8 others. 2022. Flamingo: a visual language model for few-shot learning. In *Advances in Neural Information Processing Systems 35: Annual Conference on Neural Information Processing Systems 2022, NeurIPS 2022, New Orleans, LA, USA, November 28 - December 9, 2022*.

Kirolos Ataallah, Xiaoqian Shen, Eslam Abdelrahman, Essam Sleiman, Deyao Zhu, Jian Ding, and Mohamed Elhoseiny. 2024. Minigpt4-video: Advancing multimodal llms for video understanding with interleaved visual-textual tokens. *Preprint*, arXiv:2404.03413.

Jinze Bai, Shuai Bai, Shusheng Yang, Shijie Wang, Sinan Tan, Peng Wang, Junyang Lin, Chang Zhou, and Jingren Zhou. 2023. Qwen-vl: A frontier large vision-language model with versatile abilities. *CoRR*, abs/2308.12966.

Shuai Bai, Keqin Chen, Xuejing Liu, Jialin Wang, Wenbin Ge, Sibo Song, Kai Dang, Peng Wang, Shijie Wang, Jun Tang, Humen Zhong, Yuanzhi Zhu, Mingkun Yang, Zhaohai Li, Jianqiang Wan, Pengfei Wang, Wei Ding, Zheren Fu, Yiheng Xu, and 8 others. 2025. Qwen2.5-VL Technical Report. *Preprint*, arXiv:2502.13923.

Sumithra Bhakthavatsalam, Daniel Khashabi, Tushar Khot, Bhavana Dalvi Mishra, Kyle Richardson, Ashish Sabharwal, Carissa Schoenick, Oyvind Tafjord, and Peter Clark. 2021. Think you have solved direct-answer question answering? try arc-da, the direct-answer AI2 reasoning challenge. *CoRR*, abs/2102.03315.

Jinhe Bi, Yifan Wang, Danqi Yan, Xun Xiao, Artur Hecker, Volker Tresp, and Yunpu Ma. 2025. PRISM: Self-Pruning Intrinsic Selection Method for Training-Free Multimodal Data Selection. *Preprint*, arXiv:2502.12119.

Yonatan Bisk, Rowan Zellers, Ronan Le Bras, Jianfeng Gao, and Yejin Choi. 2020. PIQA: Reasoning about physical commonsense in natural language. In *Proceedings of the Thirty-Fourth AAAI Conference on Artificial Intelligence*.

Cheng Chen, Junchen Zhu, Xu Luo, Hengtao Shen, Lianli Gao, and Jingkuan Song. 2024a. Coin: A benchmark of continual instruction tuning for multimodel large language model. *arXiv preprint arXiv:2403.08350*.

Delong Chen, Jianfeng Liu, Wenliang Dai, and Baoyuan Wang. 2024b. Visual instruction tuning with polite flamingo. In *Thirty-Eighth AAAI Conference on Artificial Intelligence, AAAI 2024, Thirty-Sixth Conference on Innovative Applications of Artificial Intelligence, IAAI 2024, Fourteenth Symposium on Educational Advances in Artificial Intelligence, EAAI 2014, February 20-27, 2024, Vancouver, Canada*, pages 17745–17753. AAAI Press.

Lin Chen, Jinsong Li, Xiaoyi Dong, Pan Zhang, Conghui He, Jiaqi Wang, Feng Zhao, and Dahua Lin. 2023a. Sharegpt4v: Improving large multi-modal models with better captions. *CoRR*, abs/2311.12793.

Ruibo Chen, Yihan Wu, Lichang Chen, Guodong Liu, Qi He, Tianyi Xiong, Chenxi Liu, Junfeng Guo, and Heng Huang. 2024c. Your vision-language model itself is a strong filter: Towards high-quality instruction tuning with data selection. *arXiv preprint arXiv:2402.12501*.

Zhe Chen, Weiyun Wang, Yue Cao, Yangzhou Liu, Zhangwei Gao, Erfei Cui, Jinguo Zhu, Shenglong Ye, Hao Tian, Zhaoyang Liu, Lixin Gu, Xuehui Wang, Qingyun Li, Yimin Ren, Zixuan Chen, Jiapeng Luo, Jiahao Wang, Tan Jiang, Bo Wang, and 23 others. 2025. Expanding Performance Boundaries of Open-Source Multimodal Models with Model, Data, and Test-Time Scaling. *Preprint*, arXiv:2412.05271.

Zhe Chen, Jiannan Wu, Wenhai Wang, Weijie Su, Guo Chen, Sen Xing, Muyan Zhong, Qinglong Zhang, Xizhou Zhu, Lewei Lu, Bin Li, Ping Luo, Tong Lu, Yu Qiao, and Jifeng Dai. 2023b. Internvl: Scaling up vision foundation models and aligning for generic visual-linguistic tasks. *CoRR*, abs/2312.14238.

Wei-Lin Chiang, Zhuohan Li, Zi Lin, Ying Sheng, Zhanghao Wu, Hao Zhang, Lianmin Zheng, Siyuan Zhuang, Yonghao Zhuang, Joseph E. Gonzalez, Ion Stoica, and Eric P. Xing. 2023. Vicuna: An open-source chatbot impressing gpt-4 with 90%* chatgpt quality.

Christopher Clark, Kenton Lee, Ming-Wei Chang, Tom Kwiatkowski, Michael Collins, and Kristina Toutanova. 2019. Boolq: Exploring the surprising difficulty of natural yes/no questions. In *Proceedings of the 2019 Conference of the North American Chapter of the Association for Computational Linguistics: Human Language Technologies, NAACL-HLT 2019, Minneapolis, MN, USA, June 2-7, 2019, Volume 1 (Long and Short Papers)*, pages 2924–2936. Association for Computational Linguistics.

Federico Cocchi, Nicholas Moratelli, Davide Caffagni, Sara Sarto, Lorenzo Baraldi, Marcella Cornia, and Rita Cucchiara. 2025. LLaVA-MORE: A Comparative Study of LLMs and Visual Backbones for Enhanced Visual Instruction Tuning. *Preprint*, arXiv:2503.15621.

Wenliang Dai, Nayeon Lee, Boxin Wang, Zhuoling Yang, Zihan Liu, Jon Barker, Tuomas Rintamaki, Mohammad Shoeybi, Bryan Catanzaro, and Wei Ping. 2024. Nvlm: Open frontier-class multimodal llms. *Preprint*, arXiv:2409.11402.

Wenliang Dai, Junnan Li, Dongxu Li, Anthony Meng Huat Tiong, Junqi Zhao, Weisheng Wang, Boyang Li, Pascale Fung, and Steven C. H. Hoi. 2023. Instructblip: Towards general-purpose vision-language models with instruction tuning. In *Advances in Neural Information Processing Systems 36: Annual Conference on Neural Information Processing Systems 2023, NeurIPS 2023, New Orleans, LA, USA, December 10 - 16, 2023*.

Matt Deitke, Christopher Clark, Sangho Lee, Rohun Tripathi, Yue Yang, Jae Sung Park, Mohammadreza Salehi, Niklas Muennighoff, Kyle Lo, Luca Soldaini, Jiasen Lu, Taira Anderson, Erin Bransom, Kiana Ehsani, Huong Ngo, YenSung Chen, Ajay Patel, Mark Yatskar, Chris Callison-Burch, and 31 others. 2024. Molmo and PixMo: Open Weights and Open Data for State-of-the-Art Vision-Language Models. *Preprint*, arXiv:2409.17146.

Danny Driess, Fei Xia, Mehdi S. M. Sajjadi, Corey Lynch, Aakanksha Chowdhery, Brian Ichter, Ayzaan Wahid, Jonathan Tompson, Quan Vuong, Tianhe Yu, Wenlong Huang, Yevgen Chebotar, Pierre Sermanet, Daniel Duckworth, Sergey Levine, Vincent Vanhoucke, Karol Hausman, Marc Toussaint, Klaus Greff, and 3 others. 2023. Palm-e: An embodied multimodal language model. In *International Conference on Machine Learning, ICML 2023, 23-29 July 2023, Honolulu, Hawaii, USA*, volume 202 of *Proceedings of Machine Learning Research*, pages 8469–8488. PMLR.

Abhimanyu Dubey, Abhinav Jauhri, Abhinav Pandey, Abhishek Kadian, Ahmad Al-Dahle, Aiesha Letman, Akhil Mathur, Alan Schelten, Alex Vaughan, and 1 others. 2024. The llama 3 herd of models. *arXiv preprint arXiv:2407.21783*.

Chaoyou Fu, Peixian Chen, Yunhang Shen, Yulei Qin, Mengdan Zhang, Xu Lin, Zhenyu Qiu, Wei Lin, Jinrui Yang, Xiawu Zheng, Ke Li, Xing Sun, and Rongrong Ji. 2023. MME: A comprehensive evaluation benchmark for multimodal large language models. *CoRR*, abs/2306.13394.

Dan Hendrycks, Collin Burns, Steven Basart, Andy Zou, Mantas Mazeika, Dawn Song, and Jacob Steinhardt. 2020. Measuring massive multitask language understanding. *arXiv preprint arXiv:2009.03300*.

Lifu Huang, Ronan Le Bras, Chandra Bhagavatula, and Yejin Choi. 2019. Cosmos QA: machine reading comprehension with contextual commonsense reasoning. In *Proceedings of the 2019 Conference on Empirical Methods in Natural Language Processing and the 9th International Joint Conference on Natural Language Processing, EMNLP-IJCNLP 2019, Hong Kong, China, November 3-7, 2019*, pages 2391–2401. Association for Computational Linguistics.

Shaohan Huang, Li Dong, Wenhui Wang, Yaru Hao, Saksham Singhal, Shuming Ma, Tengchao Lv, Lei Cui, Owais Khan Mohammed, Barun Patra, Qiang Liu, Kriti Aggarwal, Zewen Chi, Nils Johan Bertil Bjorck, Vishrav Chaudhary, Subhojit Som, Xia Song, and Furu Wei. 2023. Language is not all you need: Aligning perception with language models. In *Advances in Neural Information Processing Systems 36: Annual Conference on Neural Information Processing Systems 2023, NeurIPS 2023, New Orleans, LA, USA, December 10 - 16, 2023*.

Siddharth Karamcheti, Suraj Nair, Ashwin Balakrishna, Percy Liang, Thomas Kollar, and Dorsa Sadigh. 2024. Prismatic vlms: Investigating the design space of visually-conditioned language models. In *Forty-first International Conference on Machine Learning, ICML 2024, Vienna, Austria, July 21-27, 2024*. OpenReview.net.

Guokun Lai, Qizhe Xie, Hanxiao Liu, Yiming Yang, and Eduard H. Hovy. 2017. RACE: large-scale reading comprehension dataset from examinations. In *Proceedings of the 2017 Conference on Empirical Methods in Natural Language Processing, EMNLP 2017, Copenhagen, Denmark, September 9-11, 2017*, pages 785–794. Association for Computational Linguistics.

Hugo Laurençon, Léo Tronchon, Matthieu Cord, and Victor Sanh. 2024. What matters when building vision-language models? *CoRR*, abs/2405.02246.

Jaewoo Lee, Boyang Li, and Sung Ju Hwang. 2024. Concept-skill transferability-based data selection for large vision-language models. *arXiv preprint arXiv:2406.10995*.

Bo Li, Hao Zhang, Kaichen Zhang, Dong Guo, Yuanhan Zhang, Renrui Zhang, Feng Li, Ziwei Liu, and Chunyuan Li. 2024a. Llava-next: What else influences visual instruction tuning beyond data?

Bo Li, Yuanhan Zhang, Dong Guo, Renrui Zhang, Feng Li, Hao Zhang, Kaichen Zhang, Peiyuan Zhang, Yanwei Li, Ziwei Liu, and Chunyuan Li. 2024b. LLaVA-OneVision: Easy Visual Task Transfer. *Preprint*, arXiv:2408.03326.

Chen Li, Yixiao Ge, Dian Li, and Ying Shan. 2024c. Vision-language instruction tuning: A review and analysis. *Transactions on Machine Learning Research*.

Chunyuan Li, Cliff Wong, Sheng Zhang, Naoto Usuyama, Haotian Liu, Jianwei Yang, Tristan Naumann, Hoifung Poon, and Jianfeng Gao. 2023a. Llava-med: Training a large language-and-vision assistant for biomedicine in one day. *Preprint*, arXiv:2306.00890.

Junnan Li, Dongxu Li, Silvio Savarese, and Steven C. H. Hoi. 2023b. BLIP-2: bootstrapping language-image pre-training with frozen image encoders and large language models. In *International Conference on Machine Learning, ICML 2023, 23-29 July 2023, Honolulu, Hawaii, USA*, volume 202 of *Proceedings of Machine Learning Research*, pages 19730–19742. PMLR.

Yifan Li, Yifan Du, Kun Zhou, Jinpeng Wang, Wayne Xin Zhao, and Ji-Rong Wen. 2023c. Evaluating object hallucination in large vision-language models. In *Proceedings of the 2023 Conference on Empirical Methods in Natural Language Processing, EMNLP 2023, Singapore, December 6-10, 2023*, pages 292–305. Association for Computational Linguistics.

Zhiqi Li, Guo Chen, Shilong Liu, Shihao Wang, Vibashan VS, Yishen Ji, Shiyi Lan, Hao Zhang, Yilin Zhao, Subhashree Radhakrishnan, Nadine Chang, Karan Sapra, Amala Sanjay Deshmukh, Tuomas Rintamaki, Matthieu Le, Ilia Karmanov, Lukas Voegtle, Philipp Fischer, De-An Huang, and 8 others. Eagle 2: Building Post-Training Data Strategies from Scratch for Frontier Vision-Language Models. *Preprint*, arXiv:2501.14818.

Ji Lin, Hongxu Yin, Wei Ping, Yao Lu, Pavlo Molchanov, Andrew Tao, Huizi Mao, Jan Kautz, Mohammad Shoeybi, and Song Han. 2023. VILA: on pre-training for visual language models. *CoRR*, abs/2312.07533.

Haotian Liu, Chunyuan Li, Yuheng Li, and Yong Jae Lee. 2023a. Improved baselines with visual instruction tuning. *CoRR*, abs/2310.03744.

Haotian Liu, Chunyuan Li, Yuheng Li, Bo Li, Yuanhan Zhang, Sheng Shen, and Yong Jae Lee. 2024a. Llava-next: Improved reasoning, ocr, and world knowledge.

Haotian Liu, Chunyuan Li, Qingyang Wu, and Yong Jae Lee. 2023b. Visual instruction tuning. In *Advances in Neural Information Processing Systems 36: Annual Conference on Neural Information Processing Systems 2023, NeurIPS 2023, New Orleans, LA, USA, December 10 - 16, 2023*.

Yiyang Liu, James Chenhao Liang, Ruixiang Tang, Yugyung Lee, Majid Rabbani, Sohail Dianat, Raghuveer Rao, Lifu Huang, Dongfang Liu, Qifan Wang, and Cheng Han. 2025a. Re-Imagining Multimodal Instruction Tuning: A Representation View. *Preprint*, arXiv:2503.00723.

Yuan Liu, Haodong Duan, Yuanhan Zhang, Bo Li, Songyang Zhang, Yike Yuan, Wangbo Zhao, Jiaqi Wang, Conghui He, Ziwei Liu, Kai Chen, and Dahua Lin. 2024b. Mmbench: Is your multi-modal model an all-around player? In *Computer Vision–ECCV 2024: 18th European Conference, Milan, Italy, September 29–October 4, 2024, Proceedings, Part VI*, pages 216–233. Springer.

Zhijian Liu, Ligeng Zhu, Baifeng Shi, Zhuoyang Zhang, Yuming Lou, Shang Yang, Haocheng Xi, Shiyi Cao, Yuxian Gu, Dacheng Li, Xiuyu Li, Yunhao Fang, Yukang Chen, Cheng-Yu Hsieh, De-An Huang, An-Chieh Cheng, Vishwesh Nath, Jinyi Hu, Sifei Liu, and 8 others. 2025b. NVILA: Efficient Frontier Visual Language Models. *Preprint*, arXiv:2412.04468.

Zikang Liu, Kun Zhou, Wayne Xin Zhao, Dawei Gao, Yaliang Li, and Ji-Rong Wen. 2024c. Less is more: Data value estimation for visual instruction tuning. *arXiv preprint arXiv:2403.09559*.

Pan Lu, Swaroop Mishra, Tanglin Xia, Liang Qiu, Kai-Wei Chang, Song-Chun Zhu, Oyvind Tafjord, Peter Clark, and Ashwin Kalyan. 2022. Learn to explain: Multimodal reasoning via thought chains for science question answering. In *Advances in Neural Information Processing Systems 35: Annual Conference on Neural Information Processing Systems 2022, NeurIPS 2022, New Orleans, LA, USA, November 28 - December 9, 2022*.

Gen Luo, Yiyi Zhou, Tianhe Ren, Shengxin Chen, Xiaoshuai Sun, and Rongrong Ji. 2024. Cheap and quick: Efficient vision-language instruction tuning for large language models. *Advances in Neural Information Processing Systems*, 36.

Brandon McKinzie, Zhe Gan, Jean-Philippe Fauconnier, Sam Dodge, Bowen Zhang, Philipp Dufter, Dhruti Shah, Xianzhi Du, Futang Peng, Floris Weers, Anton Belyi, Haotian Zhang, Karanjeet Singh, Doug Kang, Ankur Jain, Hongyu Hè, Max Schwarzer, Tom Gunter, Xiang Kong, and 13 others. 2024. MM1: methods, analysis & insights from multimodal LLM pre-training. *CoRR*, abs/2403.09611.

Meta AI. 2024. Llama 3.2: Revolutionizing edge ai and vision with open, customizable models.

OpenAI. 2024. Hello gpt-4.

OpenAI, Josh Achiam, Steven Adler, Sandhini Agarwal, Lama Ahmad, Ilge Akkaya, Florencia Leoni Aleman, Diogo Almeida, Janko Altenschmidt, Sam Altman, Shyamal Anadkat, Red Avila, Igor Babuschkin, Suchir Balaji, Valerie Balcom, Paul Baltescu, Haiming Bao, Mohammad Bavarian, Jeff Belgum, and 262 others. 2024. Gpt-4 technical report. *Preprint*, arXiv:2303.08774.

Maxime Oquab, Timothée Darcet, Théo Moutakanni, Huy Vo, Marc Szafraniec, Vasil Khalidov, Pierre Fernandez, Daniel Haziza, Francisco Massa, Alaaeldin El-Nouby, and 1 others. 2023. Dinov2: Learning robust visual features without supervision. *arXiv preprint arXiv:2304.07193*.

Long Ouyang, Jeffrey Wu, Xu Jiang, Diogo Almeida, Carroll Wainwright, Pamela Mishkin, Chong Zhang, Sandhini Agarwal, Katarina Slama, Alex Ray, and 1 others. 2022. Training language models to follow instructions with human feedback. *Advances in neural information processing systems*, 35:27730–27744.

Alec Radford, Jong Wook Kim, Chris Hallacy, Aditya Ramesh, Gabriel Goh, Sandhini Agarwal, Girish Sastry, Amanda Askell, Pamela Mishkin, Jack Clark, Gretchen Krueger, and Ilya Sutskever. 2021. Learning transferable visual models from natural language supervision. In *Proceedings of the 38th International Conference on Machine Learning, ICML 2021, 18-24 July 2021, Virtual Event*, volume 139 of *Proceedings of Machine Learning Research*, pages 8748–8763. PMLR.

Paul K. Rubenstein, Chulayuth Asawaroengchai, Duc Dung Nguyen, Ankur Bapna, Zalán Borsos, Félix de Chaumont Quitry, Peter Chen, Dalia El Badawy, Wei Han, Eugene Kharitonov, Hannah Muckenhirn, Dirk Padfield, James Qin, Danny Rozenberg, Tara Sainath, Johan Schalkwyk, Matt Sharifi, Michelle Tadmor Ramanovich, Marco Tagliasacchi, and 11 others. 2023. Audiopalm: A large language model that can speak and listen. *Preprint*, arXiv:2306.12925.

Bardia Safaei, Faizan Siddiqui, Jiacong Xu, Vishal M. Patel, and Shao-Yuan Lo. 2025. Filter Images First, Generate Instructions Later: Pre-Instruction Data Selection for Visual Instruction Tuning. *Preprint*, arXiv:2503.07591.

Kaitao Song, Xu Tan, Tao Qin, Jianfeng Lu, and Tie-Yan Liu. 2020. Mpnet: Masked and permuted pre-training for language understanding. In *Advances in Neural Information Processing Systems 33: Annual Conference on Neural Information Processing Systems 2020, NeurIPS 2020, December 6-12, 2020, virtual*.

Alon Talmor, Jonathan Herzig, Nicholas Lourie, and Jonathan Berant. 2019. Commonsenseqa: A question answering challenge targeting commonsense knowledge. In *Proceedings of the 2019 Conference of the North American Chapter of the Association for Computational Linguistics: Human Language Technologies, NAACL-HLT 2019, Minneapolis, MN, USA, June 2-7, 2019, Volume 1 (Long and Short Papers)*, pages 4149–4158. Association for Computational Linguistics.

Gemini Team, Rohan Anil, Sebastian Borgeaud, Yonghui Wu, Jean-Baptiste Alayrac, Jiahui Yu, Radu Soricut, Johan Schalkwyk, Andrew M Dai, Anja Hauth, and 1 others. 2023. Gemini: a family of highly capable multimodal models. *arXiv preprint arXiv:2312.11805*.

Shengbang Tong, Ellis Brown, Penghao Wu, Sanghyun Woo, Manoj Middepogu, Sai Charitha Akula, Jihan Yang, Shusheng Yang, Adithya Iyer, Xichen Pan, Austin Wang, Rob Fergus, Yann LeCun, and Saining Xie. 2024. Cambrian-1: A fully open, vision-centric exploration of multimodal llms. *CoRR*, abs/2406.16860.

Hugo Touvron, Louis Martin, Kevin Stone, Peter Albert, Amjad Almahairi, Yasmine Babaei, Nikolay Bashlykov, Soumya Batra, Prajjwal Bhargava, Shruti Bhosale, Dan Bikel, Lukas Blecher, Cristian Canton-Ferrer, Moya Chen, Guillem Cucurull, David Esiobu, Jude Fernandes, Jeremy Fu, Wenyin Fu, and 49 others. 2023. Llama 2: Open foundation and fine-tuned chat models. *CoRR*, abs/2307.09288.

Yizhong Wang, Yeganeh Kordi, Swaroop Mishra, Alisa Liu, Noah A Smith, Daniel Khashabi, and Hannaneh Hajishirzi. 2022a. Self-instruct: Aligning language models with self-generated instructions. *arXiv preprint arXiv:2212.10560*.

Yizhong Wang, Swaroop Mishra, Pegah Alipoormolabashi, Yeganeh Kordi, Amirreza Mirzaei, Atharva Naik, Arjun Ashok, Arut Selvan Dhanasekaran, Anjana Arunkumar, David Stap, and 1 others. 2022b. Super-naturalinstructions: Generalization via declarative instructions on 1600+ nlp tasks. In *Proceedings of the 2022 Conference on Empirical Methods in Natural Language Processing*, pages 5085–5109.

Jason Wei, Maarten Bosma, Vincent Y. Zhao, Kelvin Guu, Adams Wei Yu, Brian Lester, Nan Du, Andrew M. Dai, and Quoc V. Le. 2022. Finetuned language models are zero-shot learners. In *The Tenth International Conference on Learning Representations, ICLR 2022, Virtual Event, April 25-29, 2022*. OpenReview.net.

Lai Wei, Zihao Jiang, Weiran Huang, and Lichao Sun. 2023. Instructiongpt-4: A 200-instruction paradigm for fine-tuning minigpt-4. *arXiv preprint arXiv:2308.12067*.

Junda Wu, Xintong Li, Tong Yu, Yu Wang, Xiang Chen, Jiuxiang Gu, Lina Yao, Jingbo Shang, and Julian McAuley. 2024. Commit: Coordinated instruction tuning for multimodal large language models. *arXiv preprint arXiv:2407.20454*.

Bin Xiao, Haiping Wu, Weijian Xu, Xiyang Dai, Houdong Hu, Yumao Lu, Michael Zeng, Ce Liu, and Lu Yuan. 2024. Florence-2: Advancing a unified representation for a variety of vision tasks. In *IEEE/CVF Conference on Computer Vision and Pattern Recognition, CVPR 2024, Seattle, WA, USA, June 16-22, 2024*, pages 4818–4829. IEEE.

Zhiyang Xu, Chao Feng, Rulin Shao, Trevor Ashby, Ying Shen, dingnan jin, Yu Cheng, Qifan Wang, and Lifu Huang. 2024. Vision-flan: Scaling human-labeled tasks in visual instruction tuning. In *Annual Meeting of the Association for Computational Linguistics*.

Zhiyang Xu, Ying Shen, and Lifu Huang. 2023. Multiinstruct: Improving multi-modal zero-shot learning via instruction tuning. In *Proceedings of the 61st Annual Meeting of the Association for Computational Linguistics (Volume 1: Long Papers), ACL 2023, Toronto, Canada, July 9-14, 2023*, pages 11445–11465. Association for Computational Linguistics.

Qinghao Ye, Haiyang Xu, Guohai Xu, Jiabo Ye, Ming Yan, Yiyang Zhou, Junyang Wang, Anwen Hu, Pengcheng Shi, Yaya Shi, and 1 others. 2023. mplug-owl: Modularization empowers large language models with multimodality. *arXiv preprint arXiv:2304.14178*.

Qinghao Ye, Haiyang Xu, Jiabo Ye, Ming Yan, Anwen Hu, Haowei Liu, Qi Qian, Ji Zhang, and Fei Huang. 2024. mplug-owl2: Revolutionizing multi-modal large language model with modality collaboration. In *Proceedings of the IEEE/CVF Conference on Computer Vision and Pattern Recognition*, pages 13040–13051.

Shukang Yin, Chaoyou Fu, Sirui Zhao, Ke Li, Xing Sun, Tong Xu, and Enhong Chen. 2023. A survey on multimodal large language models. *arXiv preprint arXiv:2306.13549*.

Xiang Yue, Yuansheng Ni, Tianyu Zheng, Kai Zhang, Ruoqi Liu, Ge Zhang, Samuel Stevens, Dongfu Jiang, Weiming Ren, Yuxuan Sun, Cong Wei, Botao Yu, Ruibin Yuan, Renliang Sun, Ming Yin, Boyuan Zheng, Zhenzhu Yang, Yibo Liu, Wenhao Huang, and 3 others. 2024. MMMU: A massive multi-discipline multimodal understanding and reasoning benchmark for expert AGI. In *IEEE/CVF Conference on Computer Vision and Pattern Recognition, CVPR 2024, Seattle, WA, USA, June 16-22, 2024*, pages 9556–9567. IEEE.

Yan Zeng, Hanbo Zhang, Jiani Zheng, Jiangnan Xia, Guoqiang Wei, Yang Wei, Yuchen Zhang, Tao Kong, and Ruihua Song. 2024. What matters in training a gpt4-style language model with multimodal inputs? In *Proceedings of the 2024 Conference of the North American Chapter of the Association for Computational Linguistics: Human Language Technologies (Volume 1: Long Papers), NAACL 2024, Mexico City, Mexico, June 16-21, 2024*, pages 7937–7964. Association for Computational Linguistics.

Dong Zhang, Shimin Li, Xin Zhang, Jun Zhan, Pengyu Wang, Yaqian Zhou, and Xipeng Qiu. 2023a. SpeechGPT: Empowering large language models with intrinsic cross-modal conversational abilities. In *Findings of the Association for Computational Linguistics: EMNLP 2023*, pages 15757–15773, Singapore. Association for Computational Linguistics.

Haotian Zhang, Mingfei Gao, Zhe Gan, Philipp Dufter, Nina Wenzel, Forrest Huang, Dhruti Shah, Xianzhi Du, Bowen Zhang, Yanghao Li, Sam Dodge, Keen You, Zhen Yang, Aleksei Timofeev, Mingze Xu, Hong-You Chen, Jean-Philippe Fauconnier, Zhengfeng Lai, Haoxuan You, and 4 others. 2024a. MM1.5: Methods, Analysis & Insights from Multimodal LLM Fine-tuning. *Preprint*, arXiv:2409.20566.

Renrui Zhang, Jiaming Han, Chris Liu, Peng Gao, Aojun Zhou, Xiangfei Hu, Shilin Yan, Pan Lu, Hongsheng Li, and Yu Qiao. 2023b. Llama-adapter: Efficient fine-tuning of language models with zero-init attention. *arXiv preprint arXiv:2303.16199*.

Shengyu Zhang, Linfeng Dong, Xiaoya Li, Sen Zhang, Xiaofei Sun, Shuhe Wang, Jiwei Li, Runyi Hu, Tianwei Zhang, Fei Wu, and 1 others. 2023c. Instruction tuning for large language models: A survey. *arXiv preprint arXiv:2308.10792*.

Yi-Kai Zhang, Shiyin Lu, Yang Li, Yanqing Ma, Qingguo Chen, Zhao Xu, Weihua Luo, Kaifu Zhang, De-Chuan Zhan, and Han-Jia Ye. 2024b. Wings: Learning multimodal llms without text-only forgetting. *Advances in Neural Information Processing Systems*, 37:31828–31853.

Lianmin Zheng, Wei-Lin Chiang, Ying Sheng, Siyuan Zhuang, Zhanghao Wu, Yonghao Zhuang, Zi Lin, Zhuohan Li, Dacheng Li, Eric P. Xing, Hao Zhang, Joseph E. Gonzalez, and Ion Stoica. 2023. Judging llm-as-a-judge with mt-bench and chatbot arena. In *Advances in Neural Information Processing Systems 36: Annual Conference on Neural Information Processing Systems 2023, NeurIPS 2023, New Orleans, LA, USA, December 10 - 16, 2023*.

Deyao Zhu, Jun Chen, Xiaoqian Shen, Xiang Li, and Mohamed Elhoseiny. 2023. Minigpt-4: Enhancing vision-language understanding with advanced large language models. *arXiv preprint arXiv:2304.10592*.

A Additional Implementation Details

For language-based instruction tuning, we use our carefully crafted dataset with tasks across modalities. To avoid data contamination, only the train split of each dataset is used for finetuning, and the test split, or the validation split if the test split is not publicly available, is reserved for evaluation. Similar to various multimodal instruction tuning work (Xu et al., 2023; Dai et al., 2023), we select unseen datasets of both modalities for evaluation. They are used to quantify performance in a general setting.

We maintain a fixed data budget of 186,000 instances throughout the training sessions. All training instances are sampled from Super-NaturalInstructions and Vision-Flan, according to the designated ratio. For the former, to prevent overfitting to a specific task, we sample an equal number of instances from every task. For the latter, since ScienceQA (Lu et al., 2022) is included in the training set, we manually remove them for evaluation purposes so there is no contamination. For finetuning, we apply the same chat template to all models in the following format: "USER:<query>ASSISTANT:<response>". The same prompt is used to format inputs during evaluation.

B Additional Training Details

We finetune pretrained MLLMs on the text-only data and denote those with a 75% text-only/25% vision-language split as MLAN. Acknowledging the recent trend of including a small portion of text-only data into vision instruction tuning data, we establish two additional baselines by finetuning on two separate versions of our training dataset that contain only 6% and 25% language instruction data, similar to the ratio in Liu et al. (2023a) and Tong et al. (2024). For a fair comparison, we limit the total number of training sequences in all settings to 186,000 samples from our training data.

C Dataset Summary

In Tables 6 and 7 we provide information about all 12 benchmarks used for evaluation. Note that in the main body we present results on 13 datasets, as we do not combine ARC-E and ARC-C.

D Additional Related Work

Our work focuses on choosing a simple multi-layer perception as the adapter in LLaVA (Liu et al., 2023b,a). In contrast, BLIP-2 (Li et al., 2023b) and Flamingo (Alayrac et al., 2022) design attention-based modules to attentively pool visual features, among a variety of other choices that combine existing methods or create new ones (Zhu et al., 2023; Chen et al., 2023b; Laurençon et al., 2024). To train the model, most often there is a pretraining step focusing on aligning the multimodal features with a modality connector (Yin et al., 2023), though some models are trained from scratch (Huang et al., 2023; Xiao et al., 2024). A main design choice in MLLMs is whether to freeze or unfreeze the LLM during finetuning. Unfreezing the LLM effectively prevents catastrophic forgetting by maintaining text-only performance (Meta AI, 2024; Driess et al., 2023; Alayrac et al., 2022), but results in worse vision-language performance (Lin et al., 2023; Dai et al., 2024). In our work, we show that with an unfrozen LLM, training on a strong language-based dataset on a fixed data budget improves performance across modalities. To evaluate MLLMs, there are a wide variety of vision-language tasks (Xu et al., 2023; Dai et al., 2023; Tong et al., 2024). However, Cambrian-1 (Tong et al., 2024) demonstrate that certain vision-language datasets, including some we used (AI2D and RealWorldQA), exhibit only a minor drop in performance of around 5% if vision is disabled, suggesting that current vision-language evaluations may be more language-focused. Though there is a need for more vision-centric analysis, this emphasizes how important language is in many vision tasks, a fact central to our work.

D.1 Text-Only Data in Existing Work

Table 8 lists dataset sizes as well as the splits between vision-language and text-only data in popular models that use both. We note that most models instruction tune with a majority of vision-language data, with the exception of Kosmos-1 (Huang et al., 2023) being a model that uses language alone, though it has an extensive pretraining step that differs from the simple MLLM adapter paradigm. Ultimately, many papers do not share their overall composition, and the ones that do vary greatly. We hope our work prompts the community to be more open in sharing their results and to do more work finding an effective and efficient ratio that can be used successfully across models.

Dataset	Modality	Split	Answer Type	Dataset Type	Size
ARC-Easy (Bhakthavatsalam et al., 2021)	Text	Test	Multiple Choice	Held-out	2.2k
ARC-Challenge (Bhakthavatsalam et al., 2021)	Text	Test	Multiple Choice	Held-out	1.2k
BoolQ (Clark et al., 2019)	Text	Validation	True/False	Held-out	3.2k
CommonsenseQA (Talmor et al., 2019)	Text	Validation	Multiple Choice	Held-out	9.7k
PIQA (Bisk et al., 2020)	Text	Validation	Multiple Choice	Held-out	16.1k
MMLU (Hendrycks et al., 2020)	Text	Test	Multiple Choice	Held-out	14.0k
RACE (Lai et al., 2017)	Text	Test	Multiple Choice	Held-out	1.05k
CosmosQA (Huang et al., 2019)	Text	Validation	Multiple Choice	Held-out	3.0k
POPE (Li et al., 2023c)	Vision	Test	True/False	Held-out	9.0k
ScienceQA-IMG (Lu et al., 2022)	Vision	Test	Multiple Choice	Held-out	5.0k
MMMU (Yue et al., 2024)	Vision	Validation	Multiple Choice	Held-out	1.5k
MME (Fu et al., 2023)	Vision	Test	True/False	Held-out	2.8k
MMBench (Liu et al., 2024b)	Vision	Dev	Multiple Choice	Held-out	5.2k

Table 6: Overview of evaluation datasets.

Dataset	Descriptions
CosmosQA (Huang et al., 2019)	Questions require reasoning based on people's everyday narratives to deduce the causes and effects of pertinent events.
CommonsenseQA (Talmor et al., 2019)	CommonsenseQA contains questions without context about understanding and relations between common objects.
ARC (Bhakthavatsalam et al., 2021)	ARC consists of grade-school level multiple-choice questions about understanding scientific concepts. Both easy and challenge splits are used.
RACE (Lai et al., 2017)	Race contains questions about long paragraphs collected from K12 English examinations in China.
BoolQ (Clark et al., 2019)	BoolQ asks whether a statement about a given long context is correct.
MMLU (Hendrycks et al., 2020)	A benchmark testing multi-task language understanding across 57 subjects, assessing model performance on expert-level multiple-choice questions.
PIQA (Bisk et al., 2020)	PIQA evaluates physical commonsense reasoning by selecting the most plausible solution to everyday scenarios.
MME (Fu et al., 2023)	MME is a multimodal benchmark for assessing cognition and perception capabilities of MLLMs across multiple domains with yes and no questions.
MMMU (Yue et al., 2024)	A multi-disciplinary benchmark testing on expert-level knowledge with vision and question queries. Questions types contain short response and multiple choice.
MMBench (Liu et al., 2024b)	A comprehensive multimodal benchmark that evaluates scientific knowledge with multiple choice questions.
POPE (Li et al., 2023c)	POPE asks to determine whether an object is present in the scene. We use adversarial, popular, and random splits for evaluation.
ScienceQA (Lu et al., 2022)	ScienceQA contains both vision-language and text-only questions about scientific concepts. We use all questions to test the overall ability of our models.

Table 7: Short descriptions for the evaluation benchmarks in our study.

Name	Text-Only Size	Total Size	text-only (%)
LLaVA-1.5 (Liu et al., 2023a)	40k	665k	6.0%
QwenVL (Bai et al., 2023)	N/A	350k	N/A
QwenVL2.5 (Bai et al., 2025)	$\sim$1M	$\sim$2M	50%
NVLM (Dai et al., 2024)	N/A	N/A	N/A
VILA (Lin et al., 2023)	1M	N/A	N/A
mPLUG-Owl (Ye et al., 2023)	242k	392k	61.7%
mPLUG-Owl2 (Ye et al., 2024)	558k	1.23M	45.4%
PrismaticVLM (Karamcheti et al., 2024)	40k	665k	6.0%
MM1 (McKinzie et al., 2024)	N/A	1.45M	N/A
MM1.5 (Zhang et al., 2024a)	–	–	10%
Kosmos-1 (Huang et al., 2023)	122.5k	122.5k	100%
LaVIN (Luo et al., 2024)	52k	204k	25.5%
Cambrian-1 (Tong et al., 2024) – Cambrian-7M	1.68M	$\sim$7M	23.8%
Eagle 2 (Li et al.) – Stage 1.5	4.75M	21.6M	22.0%
LLaVA-OneVision (Li et al., 2024b) – Single-Image Data	457.6k	3.2M	14.3%

Table 8: Language instruction tuning dataset sizes in existing MLLMs. N/A means the number is either not presented in the paper or is unclear. A dash means the size is unclear.

ToolReAGt: Tool Retrieval for LLM-based Complex Task Solution via Retrieval Augmented Generation

Norbert Braunschweiler, Rama Doddipatla, Tudor-Catalin Zorila
Toshiba Europe, Cambridge, Cambridgeshire, UK
{norbert.braunschweiler, rama.doddipatla, catalin.zorila}@toshiba.eu

Abstract

Artificial intelligence agents when deployed to solve complex problems, need to first decompose the task into smaller manageable subtasks, and further associate tools if one is required to solve the sub-task. If the size of the set of tools to chose from is large, a retrieval system is usually employed to narrow down the tool choices before the LLM can proceed with associating tools to the sub-tasks. This paper focuses on the retrieval problem to identify the set of relevant tools to solve a complex task given a large pool of tools to chose from using retrieval augmented generation (RAG) and we refer to it as *ToolReAGT*. The proposed approach employs *ReAct* prompting to perform the retrieval in an iterative fashion to first identify if a tool is required and then associate one or more tools for each intermediate step, also referred to as a sub-task. This deviates from conventional RAG where an n-best list of tools are identified given the complex task directly. Experiments are presented on the *UltraTool* benchmark corpus with 1000 complex tasks and over 2000 tools to select from. A conventional RAG-system is established as baseline and compared to the *ToolReAGt* approach, resulting in an 8.9% improved retrieval accuracy score recall@5.

1 Introduction

The ability of current AI systems utilizing the language understanding and reasoning capabilities of LLMs in combination with individual tools designed for solving specific tasks, has greatly expanded the application range and capacity of these systems (Parisi et al., 2022; Qin et al., 2023b; Schick et al., 2023; Qin et al., 2023a; Patil et al., 2023; Li et al., 2024; Wang et al., 2024; Kong et al., 2024; Qu et al., 2025). Tools which can provide tailored information such as up-to-date temperature measurements, compute mathematical equations or identify objects in images can each contribute to solve an overarching complex task and result in powerful AI agents. However, the efficacy of these systems in completing complex tasks heavily relies on their ability to accurately select appropriate tools for solving individual sub-tasks.

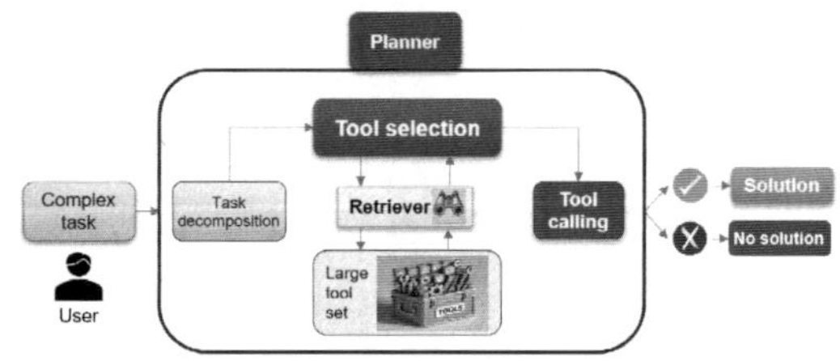

Figure 1: Importance of tool selection quality in complex task solution AI system.

Figure 1 illustrates the flow diagram of a system that can solve a complex task. The *Planner* is internally made of a *Task Decomposition* module that decomposes the complex task into smaller manageable sub-tasks, the *Tool Selection* module can dive into a database of tools and retrieve the relevant tools that can solve the sub-tasks and a *Tool Calling* module that can compose and call the retrieved tools in a specific order to solve the complex task, which we refer to as a solution. Every module can introduce dependencies that the other modules need to adhere to in deriving a solution to solve the complex task. In this paper, we focus on the *Tool Selection* module and investigate tool retrieval in depth, with the aim to support the planner in solving complex tasks. The main challenges in tool retrieval are: a) understanding the requirements of the task to be solved and formulating an adequate query to find a suitable tool, b) comprehending the functionality of a tool from its description, and c) ability to distinguish between similar tools to choose the most suitable one.

In this paper, we introduce a training-free Retrieval-Augmented Generation (Lewis et al.,

Proceedings of the 3rd Workshop on Towards Knowledgeable Foundation Models (KnowFM), pages 75–83
August 1, 2025 ©2025 Association for Computational Linguistics

2021) architecture called *ToolReAGt*. The proposed approach employs *ReAct* prompting to enhance retrieval using iterative refinement of the prompts. We will also present investigations on the importance of context information when solving a complex task. We present our investigations using the *UltraTool* (Huang et al., 2024) benchmark corpus that has over 2000 tools to choose from and compare with traditional RAG approaches as well as more recent iterative based approaches that also involve training the retriever. We show through experiments on the *UltraTool* corpus that the proposed training free approach can outperform existing methods. The rest of the paper is organised as follows: An overview of related work is presented in the next section, followed by the description of the conventional RAG system and the *ToolReAGt* model. Then, the benchmark corpus is described and the set-up of the evaluation which is followed by the presentation of results and their discussion, and finally conclusions.

2 Related work

A simple and straight forward approach to selecting the relevant tools is to provide all the tool description in the prompt (Yuan et al., 2024; Mu et al., 2024; Du et al., 2024), which can be further combined with fine-tuned retrieval systems (Qin et al., 2023b; Hao et al., 2023; Gao et al., 2023). But a major limitation of these methods is when the pool size of the tools to chose from increases drastically, that limits to include all the tool descriptions into the prompts. A potential solution is to first build a smaller pool of relevant tools using RAG and then proceed to solving the complex task, which is one of the motivations for the method presented in this paper.

In Zhang et al. (2024), the authors propose to leverage reinforcement learning to enhance the alignment between user queries and tools in LLMs. This method focuses on retrieving n-best tools related to the query using query re-writing. It also requires training the retriever using reinforcement learning. In contrast the proposed method follows an iterative prompt refinement and is more focused on solving a complex task, where tools are retrieved in a step-by-step fashion. Also, we follow a training free approach.

An adaptive truncation of retrieval results is presented in Zheng et al. (2024) which treats seen and unseen tools differently to ensure more relevant tools are prioritized. Additionally, it introduces a hierarchy-aware reranking which refines retrieval results by concentrating them for single-tool queries and diversifying them for multi-tool queries. While the adaptive truncation method effectively manages unseen tools, our method explores the use of the *ReAct* framework that inherently performs re-ranking of the relevant tools, but also explores the use of a varied context during retrieval at (a more fine-grained) sub-task level.

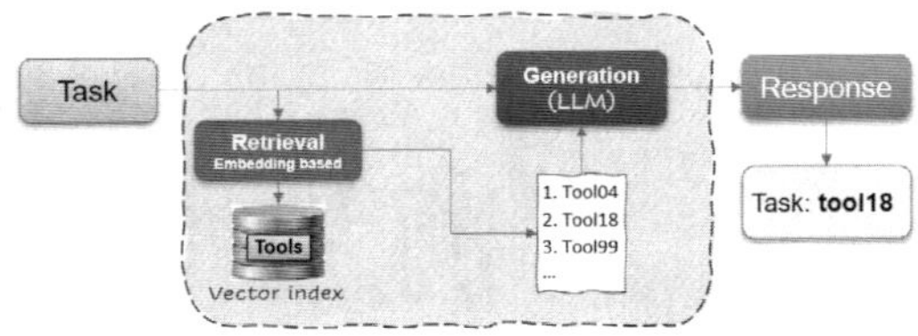

Figure 2: Conventional RAG architecture for tool selection.

An approach in which fine-tuned LLMs are used to capture relationships between user queries and tool descriptions is introduced in Qu et al. (2024). The method constructs bipartite graphs among queries, scenes, and tools, and it uses a dual-view graph collaborative learning framework to capture intricate collaborative relationships among tools. In this work, we assume that the planner is looking into the relations between tools, where the tool retriever is one of the components of the planner. This is done in a training free fashion and it should generalise to unseen tasks.

In Xu et al. (2024), authors propose iterative LLM feedback to improve tool selection, but use a trained dense retriever without the RAG-specific generation part. In our method we avoid training the retriever and the iterative refinement is done through a *ReAct-agent*.

3 Methods

We will first present the general RAG architecture and how it can be employed to perform tool retrieval, which we will refer to as *Conventional RAG* and is used as a baseline in our study. Further we introduce the proposed *ToolReAGT* method and present the design changes that are introduced contrasting with the conventional RAG.

3.1 Conventional RAG

Figure 2 illustrates the basic RAG-architecture for tool retrieval and includes two main components: the retriever and generator. Given a task as input

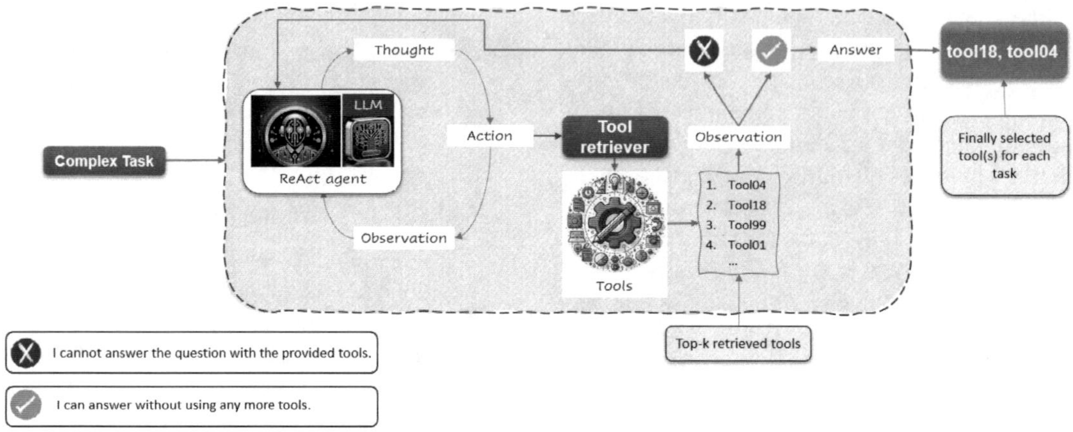

Figure 3: Block diagram of proposed *ToolReAGt* system.

query, the retriever, typically leveraging an embedding based dense retriever, retrieves a subset of tools. A distance measure (for example the cosine similarity) is computed between the query embedding and the tool embeddings to retrieve the relevant tools from the vector index. The list of retrieved tools is propagated into the prompt for the generation module (including the task and instructions) to output the final response, i.e. tool(s) selected for the given query.

3.2 ToolReAGt

Figure 3 illustrates the proposed *ToolReAGt* architecture. Input can consist of a complex task and optionally task decomposition into sub-tasks (provided by a planner which is not part of the *ToolReAGt* system). The *ReAct*-agent can flexibly operate with only the complex task as input and decompose into the intermediate steps by itself or, if provided, utilize a given task decomposition from a planner. The *ToolReAGt* system is guided by a *ReAct-agent* leveraging a sequence of *Thought->Action->Observation* steps (see Appendix B). Firstly, the system calls the tool retriever with a tailored query for the given sub-task (or internal decomposition step) and retrieves a $top\_k = \{t_1, t_2, ..., t_k\}$ list of tools. The *ReAct-agent* is instructed to always call the retriever as a mandatory tool, to provide it with a list of relevant candidates from the set of available tools. The retrieved tool list is then inspected in the *Observation* step and depending on whether the system decides that at least one of the retrieved tools is suitable to solve the sub-task (or internal decomposition step) it will proceed to give the answer (indicated by the green tick), i.e. either one tool or multiple tools for each sub-task, or otherwise enter another iteration including a new tool retrieval call.

By using the *ReAct* technique the complex prompt can be interpreted by the LLM and a more targeted question is formulated for finding the best tool for the current sub-task (or intermediate step). Conversely, the conventional RAG employs the input prompt only. Then, the *Thought->Action->Observation* loop can be executed until either a suitable tool has been found or the max number of iterations (set to 10) is reached. As such, an iterative refinement can take place which is likely to be beneficial for both tool retrieval and the final generation output.

4 Data

For evaluation, we used the *UltraTool* (Huang et al., 2024) corpus which provides a rich number of complex tasks (5824) from 22 domains (e.g. finance, travel, documents, etc.) with a large tool set of 2032 tools. The corpus comes divided into a test set (1000 tasks) and a development set (4824 tasks). For evaluation we employ the 1000 tasks test set which consists of 436 tools (TEST-436). In addition, we perform evaluation on the same test set using the full (test+dev) 2032 tool set (TEST-2032).

The test tasks include an average number of 2.4 tools per task with the following distribution: 1: 188, 2: 496, 3: 205, 4: 83 and the remainder requiring >5 tools (up to a maximum of 10 tools). A major reason to choose *UltraTool* benchmark is that, it has annotations with reference solution plans, i.e. decomposition into sub-tasks, including tool-requiring sub-tasks and their respective tools, enabling objective evaluation via retrieval metrics. This helps us to investigate how the retrieval performance can vary when task decomposition from planner is available apriori.

Solution plans contain on average 12.1 steps which means there is a high proportion of tool-free steps. For brevity, we chose the English version of the corpus which was originally collected in Chinese. Contrary to *UltraTool's* original evaluation methods which encompass *planning*, *tool creation* and *tool usage*, we are using the corpus for evaluating tool selection performance of RAG-systems with and without using the provided sub-tasks.

5 Evaluation setup

The experiments conducted in this study employ the LlamaIndex-framework[1] for implementing the RAG pipeline. The basic workflow to create a RAG-system contains the preparation of source data from which information will be retrieved (typically in the form of documents, i.e. tool descriptions here), ingesting this data into a vector index leveraging an embedding model, defining a query agent together with an LLM, and formulating input prompts. These steps will be described next.

5.1 Tool representation

Tools provide specific functionalities such as currency conversions or getting up to date weather information and are crucial helpers in a system designed to combine their abilities for solving more complex tasks. As such, understanding tool functionalities, including their required input parameters and their generated output, is essential for successful tool selection. In *UltraTool*, tools are described in the widely used JSON-format and include "name", "description", "arguments" (type and format of input(s)) and "results" (type and format of output(s)). Considering each tool as a separate entity, each of the 2032 tool descriptions was stored in a separate file named with the tool name (e.g. "check_weather.json"). The following shows an example of a tool description for the *check_weather* tool which provides weather information such as temperature and precipitation probability, for a given location and a specific date:

"name": "check_weather", "description": "Check the weather forecast for a specified date and location", "arguments": {"type": "object","properties": {"date": } {"type": "string", "description": "Specified date"}, "location": {"type": "string", "description": "Weather query location"}}}, "results": {"type": "object", "properties": {"weather_status": {"type": "string", "description": "Weather condition"},}, "temperature": {"type": "string", "description": "Temperature"}, "precipitation": {"type": "string", "description": "Probability of precipitation"}, "weather_info": {"type": "string", "description": "Weather forecast information"}, "suggestions": {"type": "string", "description": "Suggestions based on weather conditions"}}}

5.2 Vector index

A vector index is an essential component in a RAG-system providing an efficient way of retrieving relevant information from a potentially large amount of data to enhance the responses generated by the LLM. In the current study, the vector indices were built on the tool descriptions in JSON-format. Two different vector indices were built: one based on all the 2032 tools and another using the subset of 436 tools which appear in the test set. This was intended to shed some light on the impact of tool corpus size on retrieval performance. Vector indices were created by converting tool descriptions into high-dimensional vectors of dimension 768 using the *bge-base-en-v1.5* [2] embedding model. Additional information in the form of metadata, such as data classes or file name, can be attached to each tool description which can support retrieval. For our vector indices the file name was added as metadata because it included the unique tool name which was deemed to be helpful for retrieval. For ingesting tool descriptions into the vector index, the text was split with a token text splitter using a chunk size of 512 tokens and a chunk overlap of 128 tokens.

5.3 Impact of input information

Different prompt types were created to evaluate the impact of input information on the retrieval performance. For the first one, no sub-task decomposition information is provided, while for the other ones, the various levels of information from the corpus are included:

- `plain_fulltask`: full task without sub-task decomposition
- `subtask`: only the sub-task that is annotated in the corpus without full task decomposition
- `subtask+fulltask`: `subtask` + `plain_fulltask`, but no full sub-task

[1] https://docs.llamaindex.ai/en/stable/

[2] https://huggingface.co/BAAI/bge-base-en-v1.5

Data	Input	Retrieval			
		R@1	R@2	R@5	R@10
TEST-2032	plain_fulltask	16.8	29.2	51.1	66.6
	subtask	4.6	6.8	12.6	18.2
	subtask+fulltask	14.9	28.4	44.1	57.5
	fulltask+decomp	20.7	36.5	59.4	76.8

Table 1: Impact on tool retrieval performance using Conventional RAG with varied contextual information

decomposition

- `fulltask+decomp`: `plain_fulltask` with full sub-task decomposition

Examples for each of the prompts used in the experiments are provided in Appendix A.

The LLMs used for evaluation are the 8-bit quantized GGUF-version of the Mistral-7b-instruct[3] LLM, i.e. *mistral-7b-instruct-v0.2.Q8_0* from Huggingface [4] and the 4-bit quantized GGUF-version of the *Mistral-Large-Instruct-2411*[5] model which are publicly available for research and provide a 32k and 128k tokens context window respectively. The *LamaCPP*[6] library was employed to run the LLM. Experiments were run on four NVIDIA A100 GPUs with 80GB of memory.

6 Results

6.1 Evaluation metrics

Tool retrieval accuracy can be measured either at the output of the *Retriever* or at the output of the *Generator* stages of RAG-system. *UltraTool* provides reference tools for each sub-task, making evaluation straightforward, by checking if the list of retrieved tools at different top_k values includes the reference tools.

To measure the tool retrieval performance at the output of the *Retriever*, the $recall@N$ metric was chosen (see equation 1), where $N = 1, 2, 5, 10, 20$ indicate whether the required tool was selected in the top_N retrieved tools.

$$\text{Recall@N} = \frac{\text{Number of relevant tools retrieved in top\_N}}{\text{Total number of relevant tools}} \quad (1)$$

For the *Generator* stage, we report accuracy, i.e. how often the searched for tool was actually chosen from the list of tools provided by the *Retriever*. In our evaluations, we report results where the *Generator* was forced to output only one tool for each tool requiring sub-task or it was given the freedom to choose multiple tools to be associated with the same sub-task.

To compare the performance of the proposed method with the method in (Xu et al., 2024), we also report the Normalized Discounted Cumulative Gain (NDCG@k) (Järvelin and Kekäläinen, 2002) metric.

We also checked the impact of multiple runs upon retrieval scores and found that there was no variation in retrieval scores in the baseline RAG-system when prompts were kept identical. For the variation in generation accuracy, the baseline RAG-system showed no measurable variation and the *ToolReAGt* system showed marginal variation in both retrieval (average StdDev: 0.186) and generation scores (average StdDev: 0.212).

6.2 Discussion

To remind, the *UltraTool* corpus comes with annotation of task decomposition for the complex task and has annotations about which of the sub-tasks require a tool. We will use this additional knowledge in the prompt to understand the impact on the retrieval using Conventional RAG and Mistral-7B model. We measure the retrieval scores by a) only presenting the full task (*plain_fulltask*) description without any sub-task decomposition, b) only presenting the sub-task (*subtask*) that requires a tool without any additional context c) presenting the full task description along with only a single sub-task *subtask+fulltask*, and d) presenting the full task description along with the complete task decomposition *fulltask+decomp*.

The results are presented in Table 1. One can observe that providing *subtask* information in isolation without the complete task decomposition seems to perform inferior than just using the *plain_fulltask* as input. On the other hand, when using the full task along with the complete task

[3] https://huggingface.co/mistralai/Mistral-7B-Instruct-v0.2

[4] https://huggingface.co/TheBloke/Mistral-7B-Instruct-v0.2-GGUF

[5] https://huggingface.co/mistralai/Mistral-Large-Instruct-2411

[6] https://github.com/ggerganov/llama.cpp

Input	Output	ConvRAG		ToolReAGt	
		R@5	Acc	R@5	Acc
plain_fulltask	by full task, single	74.2	68.4	77.4	73.5
fulltask+decomp	by sub-task, single	81.7	71.9	90.6	73.7
fulltask+decomp	by sub-task, multi	81.7	74.5	90.5	87.4

Table 2: Results for tool selection contrasting Conventional RAG and ToolReAGT on TEST-436

decomposition (*fulltask+decomp*) it seems to improve the retrieval performance. This indicates that having access to complete task decomposition on how to solve the complex task should help the retriever identify the correct tools better than when presented only with the complex task description as input, which is intuitive. One can also observe that retrieving more tools at each intermediate step can also boost the retrieval performance. These initial investigations were performed on TEST-2032. Moving forward, all the results will be presented on the actual test set of the *UltraTool* corpus and is referred to as TEST-436.

In Table 2, we contrast the performance of the *Conventional RAG* with the proposed *ToolReAGt* described in Section 3. We report both the retrieval (R@5) and generation performance in this table. Variations in the input prompts and how many tools the generator should output (either single or multiple) can further influence the retrieval performance. The *plain_fulltask* refers to providing only the complex task description as input without any decomposition. By doing so, we can measure how the LLM will handle the complex task and assign relevant tools without any additional information. This is used as a baseline to understand the impact of any variations that we might introduce either into the input prompt in the form of additional context or apply the *ReAct* prompting or change the output of the generator, which are all presented in this table. Comparing the RAG baseline and the *ToolReAGt* system for the *plain_fulltask* input shows that the *ToolReAGt* system achieves a 3.4% better R@5 and an increased accuracy in generation (+5.1%).

System	Retrieval		
	N@1	N@3	N@5
ToolRetriever(Xu et al., 2024)	48.2	47.7	53.0
Xu-et-al(Xu et al., 2024)	49.3	47.5	54.3
RAGbaseline [plain_fulltask]	54.8	59.2	66.3
ToolReAGt [plain_fulltask]	60.6	63.8	69.3

Table 3: Results using NDCG metric comparing different retrieval methods on the *UltraTool* TEST-436

The addition of contextual information by adding the decomposition of the complex task into individual sub-tasks including the information which sub-tasks require tools, increased both retrieval and generation scores for both systems, with an increase in R@5 of 7.5% for the RAG baseline and a boost of 13.2% for the *ToolReAGt* system, leading to an 8.9% absolute improvement for *ToolReAGt*, while the increases in generation accuracy were smaller, indicating that the improved retrieval scores did not directly propagate into improved generation accuracy. However, by asking the systems to select more than one tool in the generation output ("By sub-task, multi") both systems achieve higher accuracy, but the *ToolReAGt* system shows a much higher improvement than the baseline system, i.e. RAG baseline +2.6% and *ToolReAGt* +13.7%, indicating that it is capable to transfer more relevant tools also in the generation output.

Table 3 presents the retrieval results measured using Normalized Discounted Cumulative Gain (NDCG@k) (Järvelin and Kekäläinen, 2002) with $k = \{1, 3, 5\}$, comparing the retrieval method of Xu et al. (2024) in literature with the proposed *ToolReAGT*. *ToolRetriever* introduces a model that has been trained on the ToolBench corpus (Qin et al., 2023b) and corresponds to *out-of-domain* evaluation on the *UltraTool* benchmark as reported in Xu et al. (2024). For fair comparison to the results presented in Xu et al. (2024), the performance of *ToolReAGT* using only the *plain_fulltask* as input without sub-task decomposition is presented here. It is surprising that RAGbaseline already surpasses the performance of Xu et al. (2024). The *ToolReAGt* method achieves the highest NDCG scores across all k-values.

7 Conclusion

The paper presented a training free Retrieval-Augmented Generation architecture called *ToolReAGt* to improve tool retrieval performance in the framework of solving complex tasks. The proposed approach employed *ReAct* prompting to perform an iterative and targeted retrieval of tools, is able to run with and without given task decomposition and showed that the retrieval performance improved on the *UltraTool* benchmark. It is also clearly evident that having access to the task decomposition in advance can greatly benefit the retriever in identifying the relevant tools. Results showed the advantage of the proposed approach against Conventional RAG as well as against other methods in literature that also followed an iterative approach to solving tool retrieval.

Limitations

ToolReAGt is motivated to solve complex tasks and when faced with a large tool set to choose from. The study in this paper is limited to investigate the performance of retriever in depth. It will be interesting to evaluate the task completion performance as a whole where the retriever should support the planner in deriving the correct solution. We believe this will be a natural extension and will form the course for our future work.

In terms of run time, *ToolReAGT* is slower than conventional RAG architectures due to its iterative design and reliance on a 123B-parameter LLM, which demands significantly more computational resources which might have to be taken into account for practical use cases. Investigating the reliance on a smaller LLM and efficiently terminating the iterative loop of *ReAcT* is something that has not been explored in the current work.

References

Yu Du, Fangyun Wei, and Hongyang Zhang. 2024. Anytool: Self-reflective, hierarchical agents for large-scale api calls. *ArXiv*, abs/2402.04253.

Shen Gao, Zhengliang Shi, Minghang Zhu, Bowen Fang, Xin Xin, Pengjie Ren, Zhumin Chen, and Jun Ma. 2023. Confucius: Iterative tool learning from introspection feedback by easy-to-difficult curriculum. In *AAAI Conference on Artificial Intelligence*.

Shibo Hao, Tianyang Liu, Zhen Wang, and Zhiting Hu. 2023. Toolkengpt: Augmenting frozen language models with massive tools via tool embeddings. *ArXiv*, abs/2305.11554.

Shijue Huang, Wanjun Zhong, Jianqiao Lu, Qi Zhu, Jiahui Gao, Weiwen Liu, Yutai Hou, Xingshan Zeng, Yasheng Wang, Lifeng Shang, Xin Jiang, Ruifeng Xu, and Qun Liu. 2024. Planning, creation, usage: Benchmarking llms for comprehensive tool utilization in real-world complex scenarios. *ArXiv*, abs/2401.17167.

Kalervo Järvelin and Jaana Kekäläinen. 2002. Cumulated gain-based evaluation of ir techniques. *ACM Trans. Inf. Syst.*, 20:422–446.

Yilun Kong, Jingqing Ruan, YiHong Chen, Bin Zhang, Tianpeng Bao, Shi Shiwei, du Guo Qing, Xiaoru Hu, Hangyu Mao, Ziyue Li, Xingyu Zeng, Rui Zhao, and Xueqian Wang. 2024. TPTU-v2: Boosting task planning and tool usage of large language model-based agents in real-world industry systems. In *Proceedings of the 2024 Conference on Empirical Methods in Natural Language Processing: Industry Track*, pages 371–385, Miami, Florida, US. Association for Computational Linguistics.

Patrick Lewis, Ethan Perez, Aleksandra Piktus, Fabio Petroni, Vladimir Karpukhin, Naman Goyal, Heinrich Küttler, Mike Lewis, Wen tau Yih, Tim Rocktäschel, Sebastian Riedel, and Douwe Kiela. 2021. Retrieval-Augmented Generation for Knowledge-Intensive NLP Tasks. *Preprint*, arXiv:2005.11401.

Zhi Li, Yicheng Li, Hequan Ye, and Yin Zhang. 2024. Towards autonomous tool utilization in language models: A unified, efficient and scalable framework. In *International Conference on Language Resources and Evaluation*.

Feiteng Mu, Yong Jiang, Liwen Zhang, Chu Liu, Wenjie Li, Pengjun Xie, and Fei Huang. 2024. Query routing for homogeneous tools: An instantiation in the rag scenario. *Preprint*, arXiv:2406.12429.

Aaron Parisi, Yao Zhao, and Noah Fiedel. 2022. Talm: Tool augmented language models. *ArXiv*, abs/2205.12255.

Shishir G. Patil, Tianjun Zhang, Xin Wang, and Joseph E. Gonzalez. 2023. Gorilla: Large language model connected with massive apis. *ArXiv*, abs/2305.15334.

Yujia Qin, Shengding Hu, Yankai Lin, Weize Chen, Ning Ding, Ganqu Cui, Zheni Zeng, Yufei Huang, Chaojun Xiao, Chi Han, Yi Ren Fung, Yusheng Su, Huadong Wang, Cheng Qian, Runchu Tian, Kunlun Zhu, Shi Liang, Xingyu Shen, Bokai Xu, and 22 others. 2023a. Tool learning with foundation models. *ArXiv*, abs/2304.08354.

Yujia Qin, Shi Liang, Yining Ye, Kunlun Zhu, Lan Yan, Ya-Ting Lu, Yankai Lin, Xin Cong, Xiangru Tang, Bill Qian, Sihan Zhao, Runchu Tian, Ruobing Xie, Jie Zhou, Marc H. Gerstein, Dahai Li, Zhiyuan Liu, and Maosong Sun. 2023b. Toolllm: Facilitating large language models to master 16000+ real-world apis. *ArXiv*, abs/2307.16789.

Changle Qu, Sunhao Dai, Xiaochi Wei, Hengyi Cai, Shuaiqiang Wang, Dawei Yin, Jun Xu, and Ji-Rong Wen. 2024. Towards completeness-oriented tool retrieval for large language models. In *Proceedings of the 33rd ACM International Conference on Information and Knowledge Management*, CIKM '24, page 1930–1940, New York, NY, USA. Association for Computing Machinery.

Changle Qu, Sunhao Dai, Xiaochi Wei, Hengyi Cai, Shuaiqiang Wang, Dawei Yin, Jun Xu, and Ji-rong Wen. 2025. Tool learning with large language models: a survey. *Frontiers of Computer Science*, 19(8).

Timo Schick, Jane Dwivedi-Yu, Roberto Dessì, Roberta Raileanu, Maria Lomeli, Luke Zettlemoyer, Nicola Cancedda, and Thomas Scialom. 2023. Toolformer: Language models can teach themselves to use tools. *ArXiv*, abs/2302.04761.

Hongru Wang, Yujia Qin, Yankai Lin, Jeff Z. Pan, and Kam-Fai Wong. 2024. Empowering large language models: Tool learning for real-world interaction. In *Proceedings of the 47th International ACM SIGIR Conference on Research and Development in Information Retrieval*, SIGIR '24, page 2983–2986, New York, NY, USA. Association for Computing Machinery.

Qiancheng Xu, Yongqing Li, Heming Xia, and Wenjie Li. 2024. Enhancing tool retrieval with iterative feedback from large language models. *ArXiv*, abs/2406.17465.

Siyu Yuan, Kaitao Song, Jiangjie Chen, Xu Tan, Yongliang Shen, Ren Kan, Dongsheng Li, and Deqing Yang. 2024. Easytool: Enhancing llm-based agents with concise tool instruction. *ArXiv*, abs/2401.06201.

Yuxiang Zhang, Xin Fan, Junjie Wang, Chongxian Chen, Fan Mo, Tetsuya Sakai, and Hayato Yamana. 2024. Data-efficient massive tool retrieval: A reinforcement learning approach for query-tool alignment with language models. In *Proceedings of the 2024 Annual International ACM SIGIR Conference on Research and Development in Information Retrieval in the Asia Pacific Region*, SIGIR-AP 2024, page 226–235, New York, NY, USA. Association for Computing Machinery.

Yuanhang Zheng, Peng Li, Wei Liu, Yang Liu, Jian Luan, and Bin Wang. 2024. ToolRerank: Adaptive and hierarchy-aware reranking for tool retrieval. In *Proceedings of the 2024 Joint International Conference on Computational Linguistics, Language Resources and Evaluation (LREC-COLING 2024)*, pages 16263–16273, Torino, Italia. ELRA and ICCL.

A Prompts

The following lists examples of prompts used as input to the RAG-systems evaluated in this paper:

plain_fulltask Only the full task for which tools had to be retrieved and no other information. Example: "Given the following complex task: "I need you to help me create a file called 'Work_Tasks.txt' on the desktop, and then write 'Preparation for Tomorrow's Meeting' into it." and the list of tools in the context, select the best tools to solve the complex task."

sub-task Only the sub-task for which a tool had to be retrieved. Example: "Given the following task: "step": "1.2 Use file writing tool to create and write content" , select the best tool provided in the context to solve the task. For an example this could be step "1.2 Query the current exchange rate", and the response format would then be: [{"step": "1.2 Query the current exchange rate", "tool": "currency_exchange_rate"}]}. Provide your answer exactly in the same format as in the example and do not add anything else."

+fulltask sub-task plus full task, but no task decomposition. Example: "Given the following task: "I need you to help me create a file called 'Work_Tasks.txt' on the desktop, and then write 'Preparation for Tomorrow's Meeting' into it.", select the best tool provided in the context to solve the following substep: ["step": "1.2 Use file writing tool to create and write content"]. For an example this could be step "1.2 Query the current exchange rate", and the response format would then be: [{"step": "1.2 Query the current exchange rate", "tool": "currency_exchange_rate"}]}. Provide your answer exactly in the same format as in the example and do not add anything else."

(fulltask)+decomp, single sub-task, full task, and task decomposition; single tool output in generation. Example: "Given the following task: "I need you to help me create a file called 'Work_Tasks.txt' on the desktop, and then write 'Preparation for Tomorrow's Meeting' into it." and its decomposition into sub-tasks here: [{"step": "1. Create file"}, {"step": "1.1 Get file creation information (File path: Desktop/Work_Tasks.txt, File content: Preparation for Tomorrow's Meeting)"}, {"step": "1.2 Use file writing tool to create and write content", "tool": ""}, {"step": "1.3 Confirm file creation and content writing success"}] , select the best tool provided in the context to solve the following substep: ["step": "1.2 Use file writing tool to create and write content"]. For an example this could be step "1.2 Query the current exchange rate", and the response format would then be: [{"step": "1.2 Query the current exchange rate", "tool": "currency_exchange_rate"}]}. Provide your answer exactly in the same format as in the example and do not add anything else."

fulltask+decomp, multi sub-task, full task, task decomposition; allowing multiple tools in generation. Example: "You are an expert in selecting tools to solve a given task. The task is typically a sub-task of a more complex task and you are given the complex task, its decomposition into sub-tasks and the sub-task you are asked to select tools for by calling the "ultratools_json_tools" tool with a suitable query. So here is the complex task: "I need you to help me create a file called 'Work_Tasks.txt' on the desktop, and then write 'Preparation for Tomorrow's Meeting' into it." and its decomposition into sub-tasks: [{"step": "1. Create file"}, {"step": "1.1 Get file creation information (File path: Desktop/Work_Tasks.txt, File content: Preparation for Tomorrow's Meeting)"}, {"step": "1.2 Use file writing tool to create and write content", "tool": ""}, {"step": "1.3 Confirm file creation and content writing success"}]. Given this context, and the list of tools provided to you by calling the "ultratools_json_tools"-tool, select the best tools to solve the following substep: ["step": "1.2 Use file writing tool to create and write content"]. For an example this could be step "1.2 Query the current exchange rate", and the response format would then be: [{"step": "1.2 Query the current exchange rate", "tool1": "currency_exchange_rate"}", "tool2": "currency_exchange_tool"}]. You can provide multiple tools ranked by their order of relevance when you think there are multiple tools capable to solve the task. Provide your answer exactly in the same format as in the example and do not add anything else."

B ReAct prompt template

Below is the *ReAct* prompt template provided in the LlamaIndex[7] version utilized in the experiments.

You are designed to help with a variety of tasks, from answering questions to providing summaries to other types of analyses.

Tools

You have access to a wide variety of tools. You are responsible for using the tools in any sequence you deem appropriate to complete the task at hand. This may require breaking the task into sub-tasks and using different tools to complete each sub-task.

You have access to the following tools:
{tool_desc}
{context_prompt}

Output Format

Please answer in the same language as the question and use the following format:

```

Thought: The current language of the user is: (user's language). I need to use a tool to help me answer the question. Action: tool name (one of {tool_names}) if using a tool. Action Input: the input to the tool, in a JSON format representing the kwargs (e.g. {{"input": "hello world", "num_beams": 5}})

```

Please ALWAYS start with a Thought.

NEVER surround your response with markdown code markers. You may use code markers within your response if you need to.

Please use a valid JSON format for the Action Input. Do NOT do this {{'input': 'hello world', 'num_beams': 5}}.

If this format is used, the tool will respond in the following format:

```

Observation: tool response

```

You should keep repeating the above format till you have enough information to answer the question without using any more tools. At that point, you MUST respond in one of the following two formats:

```

Thought: I can answer without using any more tools. I'll use the user's language to answer

Answer: [your answer here (In the same language as the user's question)]

```

```

Thought: I cannot answer the question with the provided tools.

Answer: [your answer here (In the same language as the user's question)]

```

Current Conversation

Below is the current conversation consisting of interleaving human and assistant messages.

[7] https://docs.llamaindex.ai/en/stable/

Can LLMs Recognize Their Own Analogical Hallucinations? Evaluating Uncertainty Estimation for Analogical Reasoning

Zheng Chen[1*] , **Zhaoxin Feng**[2] , **Jianfei Ma**[2] , **Jiexi Xu**[3] , **Bo Li**[1]

[1]Computer Science and Engineering, Hong Kong University of Science and Technology

[2]Chinese and Bilingual Studies, The Hong Kong Polytechnic University

[3]Faculty of Business and Economy, The University of Hong Kong

zchenin@connect.ust.hk, {zhaoxinbetty.feng, jian-fei.ma}@connect.polyu.edu.hk, tomxuhi@connect.hku.hk, bli@cse.ust.hk

Abstract

Large language models (LLMs) often demonstrate strong performance by leveraging implicit knowledge acquired during pretraining. Analogical reasoning, which solves new problems by referencing similar known examples, offers a structured way to utilize this knowledge, but can also lead to subtle factual errors and hallucinations. In this work, we investigate whether LLMs can recognize the reliability of their own analogical outputs using *black-box uncertainty estimation (UE)*. We evaluate six UE metrics across two reasoning-intensive tasks: mathematical problem solving and code generation. Our results show that *Kernel Language Entropy (KLE)* and *Lexical Similarity (LexSim)* are the most robust indicators of correctness. Moreover, while analogical prompting lowers model uncertainty over direct prompting, most uncertainty arises during the analogy transfer step. These findings highlight the limitations of analogical knowledge transfer in LLMs and demonstrate the potential of UE methods for detecting hallucinated reasoning in black-box settings.

1 Introduction

Recent advances in large language models (LLMs) have highlighted their surprising ability to utilize internalized knowledge for solving complex tasks. This ability, often acquired through large-scale pretraining, enables models to answer factual questions, reason about concepts, and even perform domain-specific tasks without explicit retrieval (Yang et al., 2024; Zhang et al., 2025). However, such knowledge utilization remains opaque and error-prone. In particular, LLMs frequently produce responses that are fluent and confident but factually incorrect, which is a phenomenon known as *hallucination* (Qin et al., 2025).

To better understand how knowledge is used, represented, and sometimes misapplied by LLMs, we focus on a specific form of structured reasoning: *analogical reasoning*. This strategy encourages the model to solve a target problem by referencing a related, known problem. Analogical reasoning has roots in human cognition (Vosniadou and Ortony, 1989) and has been shown to enhance LLM performance across domains (Yasunaga et al., 2024; Yang et al., 2024; Zhang et al., 2025). Conceptually, it involves two stages: retrieving or constructing an analogy, and transferring it to the new context (Ramachandran, 2012).

Despite its potential, analogical reasoning is also prone to hallucination-like failure. Models may select an irrelevant analogy, or fail to adapt it correctly, leading to incorrect answers that nonetheless appear coherent and justified. These subtle errors are particularly dangerous in deployment settings, as they can undermine user trust in the model's reasoning ability. This raises a key research question: *can LLMs recognize when their analogical reasoning is unreliable?*

We address this question by investigating the utility of *black-box uncertainty estimation (UE)* metrics. These methods aim to quantify model uncertainty based solely on output patterns, without requiring access to internal activations or probabilities (Fadeeva et al., 2023). Prior work has applied UE to tasks such as translation and summarization (Fomicheva et al., 2020), but its effectiveness in analogical reasoning, where hallucinations arise from multi-step failures, remains underexplored.

In this paper, we evaluate six representative UE metrics in the context of analogical prompting. Our experiments span two reasoning-intensive benchmarks: GSM8K for mathematical problem solving, and Codeforces for code generation. We further dissect analogical responses into their subcomponents to understand where uncertainty arises: in the analogy itself or in its transfer. This work makes three main contributions:

*Corresponding author

Proceedings of the 3rd Workshop on Towards Knowledgeable Foundation Models (KnowFM), pages 84–93
August 1, 2025

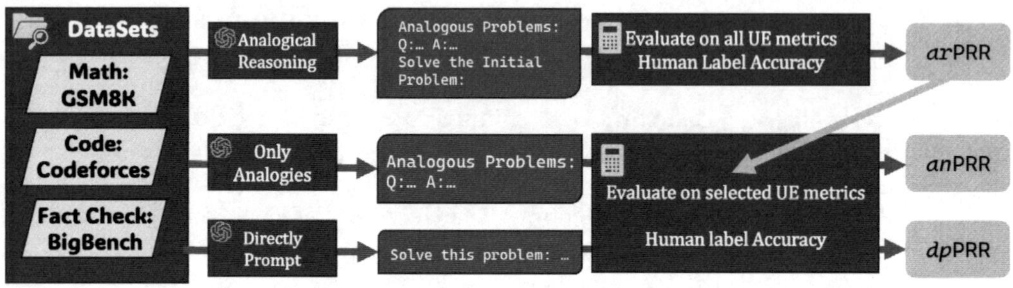

Figure 1: Overall procedure of our method. The first row illustrates the process for identifying robust uncertainty estimation metrics. The latter two rows demonstrate the steps of calculating the uncertainty in analogical reasoning.

- We present the first systematic evaluation of uncertainty estimation metrics for analogical reasoning in black-box LLMs.
- We identify two metrics, Kernel Language Entropy (KLE) and Lexical Similarity (LexSim), that best predict factual correctness.
- We show that analogical reasoning decreases model uncertainty, but most uncertainty arises from the transfer step.

Our findings provide insights into the mechanisms and limits of knowledge utilization in LLMs, and offer a practical pathway toward detecting hallucinated reasoning in analogical contexts. Our code can be found in `https://github.com/Bellafc/analogyUE/`.

2 Related Work

2.1 Analogical Reasoning

Analogical reasoning is a procedure of: 1) retrieving knowledge for obtaining similarities among questions, and 2) transferring the knowledge from the known source to the unknown target (Ramachandran, 2012). Analogical reasoning first identifies deep relational similarities (e.g., batteries and reservoirs both store and release energy, beyond surface differences). It then transfers these higher-order structures to the unknown problems (e.g., the "central force-orbital motion" in solar system-atom analogies) while ignoring superficial features (Gentner, 1983).

Recent studies have applied analogical reasoning to mathematical problem-solving and code generation by prompting LLMs to generate relevant exemplars or knowledge, thereby enhancing reasoning performance (Yasunaga et al., 2024). However, while analogical reasoning effectively leverages implicit pretrained knowledge, it may introduce factual errors or hallucinations (Qin et al., 2025). This paper aims to investigate the reliability of LLMs in analogical reasoning, uncovering the sources of uncertainty.

2.2 Uncertainty Estimation

With the widespread adoption of LLMs, their generated outputs are prone to hallucination (Xiao and Wang, 2021; Dziri et al., 2022). Uncertainty estimation methods address this issue by quantifying the confidence of model predictions, enabling users to identify unreliable outputs and thereby enhancing the safety and reliability of LLM deployments (Fadeeva et al., 2023).

Uncertainty estimation mainly includes two methods: white-box and black-box. White-box methods, requiring access to internal model states, include information-theoretic approaches like maximum sequence probability and semantic entropy (Kuhn et al., 2023), ensemble-based techniques (Malinin and Gales, 2021) using cross-model prediction variances, and density estimation methods such as Mahalanobis distance (Lee et al., 2018) for out-of-distribution detection. Black-box methods, which operate solely on generated text outputs, encompassing semantic diversity analysis (Lin et al., 2024) that evaluates uncertainty by computing similarity matrices across multiple responses, as well as graph-theoretic approaches (Fadeeva et al., 2023). In contrast to white-box approaches, this paper focuses specifically on black-box uncertainty estimation for analogical reasoning, enabling reliable hallucination detection without access to internal model states.

Analogy Reasoning Prompt for GSM8K

Your task is to tackle code problems. When presented with a code problem, recall relevant problems as examples. Afterward, proceed to solve the initial problem.

#Initial Problem: [*The target problem*]

#Instructions:
Make sure that your response follows the instructions below.

Analogous Problems:
Offer one diverse examples of math problems that are relevant or analogous to the initial problem. For each problem, elaborate on the solution and conclude with the ultimate answer (enclosed in \boxed{}). For each problem:

- After "Q: ", describe the problem
- After "A: ", explain the solution and enclose the ultimate answer in \boxed{}.

Solve the Initial Problem:
Q: Copy and paste the initial problem here.
A: Explain the solution and enclose the ultimate answer in \boxed{} here.

Analogy Reasoning Prompt for Codeforces

Your goal is to write Python3 code to solve competitive programming problems. Given a problem, explain the core concepts in it and provide other relevant problems. Then solve the original problem.

#Initial Problem: [*The target problem*]

#Instructions:
Make sure that your response follows the instructions below.

Analogous Problems:
Identify the core concepts or algorithms used to solve the problem. And write a tutorial about these algorithms. Then provide one example of relevant competitive programming problems that involve these algorithms. Describe the problem, explain the solution in detail, and then write the correct Python3 code.

Solve the Initial Problem:
Q: Copy and paste the initial problem here:
A: Python3 code to solve the problem:

Figure 2: Analogical Reasoning Prompts for GSM8K and Codeforces.

3 Method

The overall experimental pipeline is illustrated in Figure 1. As part of this procedure, we apply analogical prompting to two reasoning-intensive datasets: *GSM8K* for mathematical problem solving and *Codeforces* for code generation. The specific analogical prompts used for these two datasets are provided in Figure 2.

3.1 Common UE metrics for black-box LLMs

To evaluate the uncertainty of model-generated responses in a black-box setting, we adopt six representative UE metrics, implemented via the library introduced in (Fadeeva et al., 2023). These metrics capture diverse statistical and structural properties of language model outputs. A brief overview is provided below.

- **Sum of Eigenvalues of the Graph Laplacian (EigV)** (Lin et al., 2024): This metric computes the sum of eigenvalues of the Laplacian matrix L constructed from a token-level similarity graph of the generated text. Intuitively, higher spectral mass reflects lower uncertainty.

$$\mathrm{EigV}(x) = \sum_{i=1}^{n} \lambda_i \quad \text{where } Lx = \lambda x \tag{1}$$

- **Degree Matrix (Deg)** (Lin et al., 2024): Defined as the sum of degrees in the token similarity graph, this metric serves as a proxy for local cohesion in the response.

$$\mathrm{Deg}(x) = \sum_i \deg(v_i) \tag{2}$$

- **Eccentricity (Ecc)** (Lin et al., 2024): This metric computes the maximum shortest-path distance from any node to all other nodes in the graph. Lower eccentricity indicates more centralized (and potentially more confident) responses.

$$\mathrm{Ecc}(x) = \max_{v \in V} \min_{u \in V} d(v, u) \tag{3}$$

- **Lexical Similarity (LexSim)** (Fomicheva et al., 2020): Based on pairwise cosine similarity among token embeddings, this metric reflects lexical cohesion in the output.

$$\mathrm{LexSim}(x) = \frac{2}{n(n-1)} \sum_{i<j} \cos(\vec{e}_i, \vec{e}_j) \tag{4}$$

- **Kernel Language Entropy (KLE)** (Nikitin et al., 2024): This metric estimates the entropy of the response using a kernel-based density estimation over token embeddings. Lower entropy typically indicates lower uncertainty.

$$\mathrm{KLE}(x) = -\sum_i \log \left(\sum_j K(x_i, x_j) \right) \tag{5}$$

- **LUQ (Local Uncertainty Quantification)** (Zhang et al., 2024): A recent metric that quantifies uncertainty by measuring the variance in local regions of the output embedding space.

$$\text{LUQ}(x) = \frac{1}{n}\sum_{i} \text{Var}(N_k(x_i)) \quad (6)$$

where $N_k(x_i)$ denotes the k-nearest neighbors of token x_i.

3.2 Identify Robust UE Metrics

We begin by evaluating the reliability of six UE metrics in assessing the correctness of analogical reasoning outputs. Our study is conducted on two reasoning-intensive benchmarks introduced in (Yasunaga et al., 2024): *GSM8K* for mathematical problem solving (Cobbe et al., 2021), and *Codeforces* for code generation (Majd et al., 2019). From each dataset, we randomly sample 200 examples and apply the analogical reasoning prompting strategy proposed in prior work.

For each generated response, we compute six UE scores using the following black-box estimators: sum of graph Laplacian eigenvalues (EigV), degree matrix (Deg), eccentricity (Ecc), lexical similarity (LexSim), kernel language entropy (KLE), and LUQ (Lin et al., 2024; Fomicheva et al., 2020; Nikitin et al., 2024; Zhang et al., 2024). In parallel, we conduct human evaluation on all 400 analogical reasoning responses, where each response is assigned a score from 0 to 100 based on its factual correctness and reasoning quality. One of the author and a student research assistant jointly annotated the responses. These human scores serve as the ground-truth accuracy proxy.

To assess how well each UE metric correlates with human judgment, we compute the Predictive Rate Ratio (PRR) for each metric:

$$\text{PRR} = \frac{\text{AUCPRunc}}{\text{AUCPRoracle}} \quad (7)$$

This ratio measures the area under the precision-recall curve (AUCPR) when ranking predictions by their uncertainty values, normalized by the oracle AUCPR (i.e., ideal ranking using ground-truth labels). A higher PRR indicates a stronger ability to distinguish between correct and incorrect responses based on uncertainty alone. We select the top-2 metrics with the highest PRR scores for use in subsequent stages.

3.3 Uncertainty Loss in Analogies

Building on the previous step, we further examine the interaction between analogical prompting and uncertainty estimation. Specifically, we aim to evaluate whether analogical reasoning lowers the uncertainty in LLM outputs and to what extent uncertainty varies across prompting strategies.

For each of the same 200 samples per dataset, we perform three types of evaluation:

Analogical Prompting (ar): Full analogical reasoning prompt used to generate response r_{ar}.

Direct Prompting (dp): A baseline prompt without analogical structure, producing r_{dp}.

Analogy-Only (an): The analogy section (e.g., retrieved or constructed examples) extracted from r_{ar}, yielding r_{an}.

For each of these three prompting modes, we compute the UE scores using only the top-2 metrics identified in the previous step. Human evaluators also score r_{dp} and r_{an} to provide corresponding correctness labels (a_{dp} and a_{an}).

This setup allows us to compute three sets of PRR scores:

***ar*PRR**: PRR from analogical reasoning outputs.

***dp*PRR**: PRR from direct prompting outputs.

***an*PRR**: PRR from analogy-only segments.

By comparing these three PRR scores, we can isolate the contribution of analogical structure to model uncertainty and quantify its influence on UE metric behavior.

3.4 Overall Procedure

Algorithm 1 outlines the complete evaluation pipeline. For each sample, we first generate a response using analogical prompting. We then evaluate this response using all six UE metrics, resulting in six corresponding uncertainty scores u^m_{ar}. Human annotators assess the correctness of each analogical response to yield the score a_{ar}. Using these uncertainty-accuracy pairs, we compute the analogical reasoning PRR scores arPRR$_m$ for all metrics and identify the top two performing metrics. Subsequently, we evaluate the same sample with direct prompting and analogy-section-only extraction. For each of the direct prompting results and the analogy-section only extraction, we apply only the top-2 UE metrics selected based on arPRR. The resulting responses are scored for correctness (a_{dp} and a_{an}), and corresponding uncertainty estimates (u^m_{dp} and u^m_{an}) are computed for each selected metric m. Finally, we compute the corresponding PRRs

Algorithm 1 Evaluation Pipeline for Analogical Reasoning uncertainty Analysis

```
for each sample in dataset do
    // Analogical Reasoning Prompt
    r_ar ← LLM(AnalogicalPrompt(sample))
    for each UE metric m in {EigV, Deg, Ecc, LexSim, KLE, LUQ} do
        u_ar^m ← UE_m(r_ar)
        a_ar ← HumanScore(r_ar)
    end for
end for
// Compute arPRR for all metrics
for each metric m do
    arPRR_m ← ComputePRR(u_ar^m, a_ar)
end for
// Select top-2 metrics based on arPRR
Top2Metrics ← SelectTopK({arPRR_m}, k = 2)
for each sample in dataset do
    // Direct Prompting
    r_dp ← LLM(DirectPrompt(sample))
    // Extracted Analogy Section
    r_an ← ExtractAnalogySection(r_ar)
    for each metric m in Top2Metrics do
        u_dp^m ← UE_m(r_dp)
        u_an^m ← UE_m(r_an)
        a_dp ← HumanScore(r_dp)
        a_an ← HumanScore(r_an)
    end for
end for
// Compute PRRs for top-2 metrics
for each metric m in Top2Metrics do
    dpPRR_m ← ComputePRR(u_dp^m, a_dp)
    anPRR_m ← ComputePRR(u_an^m, a_an)
end for
```

for both direct prompting (*dp*PRR) and analogy-section-only (*an*PRR), allowing us to compare the predictive utility of uncertainty estimates across prompting strategies.

4 Results

4.1 KLE and LexSim are Robust UE metrics

Table 1 reveals that **KLE** and **LexSim** outperform other UE metrics across benchmarks. This divergence stems from the distinct demands of analogical reasoning:

1. KLE's Robustness to Semantic Diversity Analogical reasoning often involves *structurally valid but lexically diverse solutions* (e.g., different algorithmic implementations for the same programming problem). KLE's semantic kernel captures this structural coherence by encoding logical relationships beyond surface features. For instance, in Codeforces, valid code analogies may share no lexical overlap (e.g., recursive vs. iterative solutions) but exhibit high semantic similarity in control flow or data structures. KLE's entropy quantifies this implicit consistency, making it task-agnostic.

2. LexSim's Domain-Specific Utility LexSim excels in *mathematical reasoning (GSM8K)*, where answers often follow rigid templates (e.g., arithmetic expressions like $3x + 5 = 20$). Here, correct analogies inherently share high lexical overlap (e.g., repeated operators or variables), aligning LexSim with human judgment. However, its reliance on surface patterns fails in tasks requiring flexible logical expression, leading to poor performance (PRR=0.092).

3. Failure of Graph-Based and NLI Metrics

- **EigV/Deg/Ecc:** These graph-based metrics assume that semantic similarity correlates with logical validity. However, analogical reasoning allows structurally distinct but logically equivalent answers (e.g., different proof paths in math), violating this assumption.
- **LUQ:** NLI models struggle to assess bidirectional entailment in complex analogies (e.g., code logic), often misclassifying valid variations as contradictions.

4.2 Analogical Reasoning Lowers the Uncertainty, but Transfer Reduces It

The results presented in Table 2 show the relationship of *an*PRR, *ar*PRR, and *dp*PRR, with the measurement of the selected two UE metrics. As mentioned in Section 3, *an*PRR measures the uncertainty of the whole uncertainty reasoning process, while *an*PRR focuses on the uncertainty of the analogous questions and answers. *dp*PRR evaluates the uncertainty estimate for responses generated through direct prompting, without any analogical reasoning component.

The results show that the *an*PRR values are consistently higher than the *ar*PRR values across all datasets. This suggests that the LLM is more confident in the analogous questions and answers. The model is likely confident in identifying relevant analogies and applying them to the problem at hand.

UE Method	GPT-3.5-Turbo			GPT-4		
	GSM8K	**Codeforces**	**Avg**	**GSM8K**	**Codeforces**	**Avg**
KLE	0.187±0.013	0.200±0.015	0.194	0.201±0.008	0.215±0.019	0.208
LexSim	0.285±0.014	0.101±0.013	0.193	0.296±0.021	0.113±0.018	0.205
EigV	0.032±0.015	0.023±0.013	0.028	0.039±0.011	0.027±0.019	0.033
Ecc	-0.014±0.013	0.014±0.013	0.000	-0.005±0.012	0.021±0.012	0.008
Deg	-0.135±0.010	-0.018±0.012	-0.077	-0.127±0.008	-0.012±0.014	-0.070
LUQ	-0.106±0.012	-0.136±0.010	-0.121	-0.101±0.021	-0.130±0.019	-0.116

Table 1: Performance of UE methods on two datasets (***ar*PRR** and its variance), comparing `gpt-3.5-turbo` and `gpt-4`. Values are color-coded from light blue (lowest) to dark blue (highest) within each column group.

Model	Dataset	Metric	KLE	LexSim
GPT-3.5-Turbo	GSM8K	*ar*PRR	0.187	0.285
		*an*PRR	0.354	0.372
		*dp*PRR	0.103	-0.002
GPT-3.5-Turbo	Codeforces	*ar*PRR	0.200	0.028
		*an*PRR	0.289	0.163
		*dp*PRR	0.098	0.009
GPT-4	GSM8K	*ar*PRR	0.201	0.310
		*an*PRR	0.389	0.402
		*dp*PRR	0.115	0.011
GPT-4	Codeforces	*ar*PRR	0.215	0.075
		*an*PRR	0.317	0.190
		*dp*PRR	0.121	0.023

Table 2: UE metric values (*ar*PRR, *an*PRR, *dp*PRR) across datasets and models for KLE and LexSim.

However, the lower *ar*PRR values indicate that the model's uncertainty increases when it comes to transferring the solution from the analogy to the original problem. This could be because the process of adapting and applying the analogy to the new context introduces additional uncertainty. The higher *an*PRR values suggest that analogical reasoning is an effective strategy for lowering the uncertainty, whereas the low *dp*PRR values emphasize the limitations of direct prompting without such reasoning.

5 Discussion

Our findings highlight two key insights into UE in analogical reasoning tasks. First, KLE (Nikitin et al., 2024) and LexSim (Fomicheva et al., 2020) emerge as robust and complementary UE metrics, each excelling in different domains due to their underlying assumptions about semantic and lexical similarity. Second, analogical reasoning lowers model uncertainty, but this uncertainty increases during the transfer phase, underscoring a critical bottleneck in applying analogies to novel problems. Graph-based metrics (e.g., EigV, Deg, Ecc) and NLI-based LUQ underperform, suggesting a misalignment with the nature of analogical reasoning. These methods assume that surface-level similarity or binary entailment captures uncertainty effectively. However, analogical tasks often require recognizing logically valid yet structurally diverse answers. Their poor average scores and high variances confirm their inadequacy in capturing nuanced analogical consistency.

The second set of results reveals that analogical reasoning lowers the model's self-assessed uncertainty (as reflected by higher *an*PRR), yet this uncertainty loss does not fully translate into successful application (lower *ar*PRR). This divergence points to a key challenge: while models can identify useful analogies, the process of adapting them to new contexts introduces epistemic uncertainty. The lowest scores observed in the *dp*PRR condition further reinforce the value of analogy-based prompting over direct prompting. However, the drop from *an*PRR to *ar*PRR indicates that the analogy transfer step is a critical weakness in current LLM capabilities.

These findings suggest that future uncertainty

metrics should better account for the two-step nature of analogical reasoning: analogy retrieval and transfer. While KLE and LexSim provide partial solutions, hybrid models or adaptive metrics that dynamically weigh lexical and semantic coherence may further improve reliability.

Limitations

While our study presents a systematic evaluation of black-box uncertainty estimation in analogical reasoning, several limitations remain.

First, our analysis is restricted to two datasets, which, although representative of mathematical and algorithmic reasoning, may not fully capture the diversity of analogical tasks across domains such as law, science, or creative writing. Extending our evaluation to other datasets like BigBench or domain-specific benchmarks would strengthen the generalizability of our findings.

Second, our evaluation focuses exclusively on black-box LLMs, namely GPT-3.5-Turbo and GPT-4, due to API access and usage constraints. While this reflects realistic deployment conditions, it excludes signals from white-box techniques such as self-consistency voting or intermediate activation inspection. Hybrid approaches that combine surface-level uncertainty metrics with internal model signals may further improve performance, especially during the analogy-transfer stage where uncertainty loss is limited.

Third, all human annotations were conducted by one author, supplemented by DeepSeek-V3-0324 model suggestions. To ensure label reliability, we verified a randomly sampled subset and observed high agreement ($\kappa > 0.8$). Nonetheless, future studies could benefit from a full multi-annotator protocol with inter-annotator agreement reporting.

Lastly, while we adopt the term "uncertainty loss" to describe reductions in estimated uncertainty, this does not directly equate to calibrated model confidence. Our measurements are inherently proxy-based and reflect surface-level output coherence rather than epistemic access to the model's belief state. Future work may explore adaptive uncertainty metrics or calibration techniques that better align with the two-stage nature of analogical reasoning.

Acknowledgments

We thank anonymous reviewers for their constructive feedback and suggestions, which have significantly helped us to refine this study.

References

Karl Cobbe, Vineet Kosaraju, Mohammad Bavarian, Mark Chen, Heewoo Jun, Lukasz Kaiser, Matthias Plappert, Jerry Tworek, Jacob Hilton, Reiichiro Nakano, Christopher Hesse, and John Schulman. 2021. Training verifiers to solve math word problems. *Preprint*, arXiv:2110.14168.

Nouha Dziri, Sivan Milton, Mo Yu, Osmar Zaiane, and Siva Reddy. 2022. On the origin of hallucinations in conversational models: Is it the datasets or the models? In *Proceedings of the 2022 Conference of the North American Chapter of the Association for Computational Linguistics: Human Language Technologies*, pages 5271–5285, Seattle, United States. Association for Computational Linguistics.

Ekaterina Fadeeva, Roman Vashurin, Akim Tsvigun, Artem Vazhentsev, Sergey Petrakov, Kirill Fedyanin, Daniil Vasilev, Elizaveta Goncharova, Alexander Panchenko, Maxim Panov, Timothy Baldwin, and Artem Shelmanov. 2023. LM-polygraph: Uncertainty estimation for language models. In *Proceedings of the 2023 Conference on Empirical Methods in Natural Language Processing: System Demonstrations*, pages 446–461, Singapore. Association for Computational Linguistics.

Marina Fomicheva, Shuo Sun, Lisa Yankovskaya, Frédéric Blain, Francisco Guzmán, Mark Fishel, Nikolaos Aletras, Vishrav Chaudhary, and Lucia Specia. 2020. Unsupervised quality estimation for neural machine translation. *Transactions of the Association for Computational Linguistics*, 8:539–555.

Dedre Gentner. 1983. Structure-mapping: A theoretical framework for analogy. *Cognitive science*, 7(2):155–170.

Lorenz Kuhn, Yarin Gal, and Sebastian Farquhar. 2023. Semantic uncertainty: Linguistic invariances for uncertainty estimation in natural language generation. In *The Eleventh International Conference on Learning Representations*.

Kimin Lee, Kibok Lee, Honglak Lee, and Jinwoo Shin. 2018. A simple unified framework for detecting out-of-distribution samples and adversarial attacks. *Advances in neural information processing systems*, 31.

Zhen Lin, Shubhendu Trivedi, and Jimeng Sun. 2024. Generating with confidence: Uncertainty quantification for black-box large language models. *Transactions on Machine Learning Research*.

Amirabbas Majd, Mojtaba Vahidi-Asl, Alireza Khalilian, Ahmad Baraani-Dastjerdi, and Bahman Zamani. 2019. Code4bench: A multidimensional benchmark of codeforces data for different program analysis techniques. *Journal of Computer Languages*, 53:38–52.

Andrey Malinin and Mark Gales. 2021. Uncertainty estimation in autoregressive structured prediction. In *International Conference on Learning Representations*.

Alexander Nikitin, Jannik Kossen, Yarin Gal, and Pekka Marttinen. 2024. Kernel language entropy: Fine-grained uncertainty quantification for llms from semantic similarities. *Advances in Neural Information Processing Systems*, 37:8901–8929.

Chengwei Qin, Wenhan Xia, Tan Wang, Fangkai Jiao, Yuchen Hu, Bosheng Ding, Ruirui Chen, and Shafiq Joty. 2025. Relevant or random: Can llms truly perform analogical reasoning? *Preprint*, arXiv:2404.12728.

Vilayanur S Ramachandran. 2012. *Encyclopedia of human behavior*. Academic Press.

Stella Vosniadou and Andrew Ortony. 1989. *Similarity and analogical reasoning*. Cambridge University Press.

Yijun Xiao and William Yang Wang. 2021. On hallucination and predictive uncertainty in conditional language generation. In *Proceedings of the 16th Conference of the European Chapter of the Association for Computational Linguistics: Main Volume*, pages 2734–2744, Online. Association for Computational Linguistics.

Ling Yang, Zhaochen Yu, Tianjun Zhang, Shiyi Cao, Minkai Xu, Wentao Zhang, Joseph E Gonzalez, and Bin Cui. 2024. Buffer of thoughts: Thought-augmented reasoning with large language models. *Advances in Neural Information Processing Systems*, 37:113519–113544.

Michihiro Yasunaga, Xinyun Chen, Yujia Li, Panupong Pasupat, Jure Leskovec, Percy Liang, Ed H. Chi, and Denny Zhou. 2024. Large language models as analogical reasoners. In *The Twelfth International Conference on Learning Representations*.

Caiqi Zhang, Fangyu Liu, Marco Basaldella, and Nigel Collier. 2024. Luq: Long-text uncertainty quantification for llms. *arXiv preprint arXiv:2403.20279*.

Yufeng Zhang, Xuepeng Wang, Lingxiang Wu, and Jinqiao Wang. 2025. Enhancing chain of thought prompting in large language models via reasoning patterns. In *Proceedings of the AAAI Conference on Artificial Intelligence*, volume 39, pages 25985–25993.

A Data Examples

Dataset	GSM8K
Initial Problem	Mary does her grocery shopping on Saturday. She does her shopping only at a specific store where she is allowed a credit of $100, which must be paid in full before her next shopping trip. That week she spent the full credit limit and paid $15 of it on Tuesday and $23 of it on Thursday. How much credit will Mary need to pay before her next shopping trip?
Analogical Reasoning Answer (r_ar)	Analogous Problems: Q1: Sarah has a $200 store credit limit. She spends the full amount in one trip. She pays back $50 on Monday and $70 on Friday. How much does she still owe? A1: Sarah starts with $200 of debt. She pays back $50 + $70 = $120. So, the remaining debt is $200 - $120 = $\boxed{80}$. Solve the Initial Problem: Q: Initial Problem A: Mary spent the full credit: $100. She paid back $15 on Tuesday and $23 on Thursday. Total paid: $15 + $23 = $38. Remaining to pay: $100 - $38 = $\boxed{62}$
Direct Prompt Answer (r_dp)	Total credit used: $100. Payment on Tuesday: $15. Payment on Thursday: $23. Total paid so far: $15 + $23 = $38. Remaining credit to be paid: $100 - $38 = $62. Mary will need to pay $62 before her next shopping trip.
Extracted Analogical Section (r_an)	Q1: Sarah has a $200 store credit limit. She spends the full amount in one trip. She pays back $50 on Monday and $70 on Friday. How much does she still owe?A1: Sarah starts with $200 of debt. She pays back $50 + $70 = $120. So, the remaining debt is $200 - $120 = $\boxed{80}$.

Table 3: Example 1

Field	codeforces200 Example
Dataset	`codeforces200`
Initial Problem	Misha and Vasya participated in a Codeforces contest. Each of them solved one problem, submitted on first attempt. Misha solved a problem worth \$a\$ points at \$c\$ minutes, and Vasya solved one worth \$b\$ points at \$d\$ minutes. The final score is computed as: `score = max(3p/10, p - (p*t)/250)` Determine who scored higher.

Analogical Reasoning Answer (r_ar)	Analogous Problem: Alice solves a 200-pt question in 30min. Bob solves a 150-pt one in 20min.
	`Alice: max(3*200/10, 200 - 200*30/250) = max(60, 176) = 176`
	`Bob:   max(3*150/10, 150 - 150*20/250) = max(45, 138) = 138`
	Result: **Alice wins**.
	Mapping to Original Problem: This is analogous to comparing scores after time-adjusted penalties.
	Use the same scoring rule:
	`score = max(3p/10, p - (p*t)/250)`
	This is analogous to a disjoint set union (DSU) problem. We track original to current handle via mapping. E.g., given a sequence of changes `[("A", "B"), ("B", "C")]` we map original → final.
	Python3 Code:
	`def track_handle_changes(n, changes):`
	`original_to_current = {}`
	`current_to_original = {}`
	`for old, new in changes:`
	`original = current_to_original.get(old, old)`
	`original_to_current[original] = new`
	`current_to_original[new] = original`
	`current_to_original.pop(old, None)`
	`print(len(original_to_current))`
	`for orig, final in original_to_current.items():`
	`print(orig, final)`

Direct Prompt Answer (r_dp)	To determine who scored more, compute both scores using: `score = max(3p/10, p - (p*t)/250)` for both Misha and Vasya. Compare the two results.

Extracted Analogical Section (r_an)	**Analogous Problem:** Alice solves a 200-pt question in 30min. Bob solves a 150-pt one in 20min.
	`Alice: max(3*200/10, 200 - 200*30/250) = max(60, 176) = 176`
	`Bob:   max(3*150/10, 150 - 150*20/250) = max(45, 138) = 138`
	Result: **Alice wins**.

Table 4: Transposed example from codeforces200 showing reasoning and analogical mapping.

Meetalk: Retrieval-Augmented and Adaptively Personalized Meeting Summarization with Knowledge Learning from User Corrections

Zheng Chen[1] , Futian Jiang[2] , Yue Deng[1] , Changyang He[3] , Bo Li[1]

[1] Computer Science and Engineering, Hong Kong University of Science and Technology

[2] Data Science and Artificial Intelligence, The Hong Kong Polytechnic University

[3] Max Planck Institute for Security and Privacy

zchenin@connect.ust.hk, alexft@connect.hku.hk,
ydengbi@connect.ust.hk, changyang.he@mpi-sp.org, bli@cse.ust.hk

Abstract

We present **Meetalk**, a retrieval-augmented and knowledge-adaptive system for generating personalized meeting minutes. Although large language models (LLMs) excel at summarizing, their output often lacks faithfulness and does not reflect user-specific structure and style. Meetalk addresses these issues by integrating ASR-based transcription with LLM generation guided by user-derived knowledge. Specifically, Meetalk maintains and updates three structured databases, Table of Contents, Chapter Allocation, and Writing Style, based on user-uploaded samples and editing feedback. These serve as a dynamic memory that is retrieved during generation to ground the model's outputs. To further enhance reliability, Meetalk introduces hallucination-aware uncertainty markers that highlight low-confidence segments for user review. In a user study in five real-world meeting scenarios, Meetalk significantly outperforms a strong baseline (iFLYTEK ASR + ChatGPT-4o) in completeness, contextual relevance, and user trust. Our findings underscore the importance of knowledge foundation and feedback-driven adaptation in building trustworthy, personalized LLM systems for high-stakes summarization tasks.

1 Introduction

Large Language Models (LLMs) have shown impressive capabilities in performing summarization and generation tasks across a wide range of domains. However, a fundamental question remains: How do LLMs utilize knowledge, unstructured, in real-world applications, and how can we ensure that this knowledge is personalized, accurate, and faithful? This question is especially critical in the context of automated meeting minutes generation, where information needs to be not only complete and concise but also aligned with domain-specific writing norms and user preferences.

Although existing approaches have used LLM to generate abstractive meeting summaries, they often fall short in two key areas: (1) the inability to adapt to user-specific structural and stylistic knowledge and (2) the tendency to produce hallucinated or generic outputs due to weak grounding. Furthermore, traditional systems lack mechanisms for learning from user feedback, leading to repeated errors and suboptimal long-term performance in repetitive meeting contexts.

In this work, we propose **Meetalk**, an adaptive meeting minutes generation system that addresses these challenges by tightly integrating *retrieval-augmented generation* (RAG), user-driven knowledge modeling, and hallucination-aware design. Specifically, Meetalk builds and updates structured knowledge bases, including chapter allocation mappings and writing style templates, learning from user-provided examples and edits. At inference time, these personalized knowledge modules are retrieved and injected into LLM prompts to guide faithful and stylistically consistent generation. In addition, we incorporate uncertainty indicators such as "[Not Sure]" labels to make the confidence of the model interpretable to users, thus enabling human-AI collaboration in mitigating hallucinated content.

To evaluate Meetalk, we conducted a controlled user study in five real-world meeting scenarios. Compared to a strong baseline (iFLYTEK ASR + ChatGPT-4o), Meetalk consistently improves output completeness, contextual relevance, and user trust, while significantly reducing time and cognitive load. Our findings suggest that adaptively modeling and utilizing user-specific knowledge not only enhances generation quality, but also provides a promising paradigm for deploying trustworthy, personalized LLM-based systems in professional workflows.

Proceedings of the 3rd Workshop on Towards Knowledgeable Foundation Models (KnowFM), pages 94–110
August 1, 2025

2 Backgrouond

2.1 Text-to-Minutes: Evolution from Extractive Methods to Large Language Models

Early research on meeting summarization primarily employed extractive methods (Tur et al., 2008) (Riedhammer et al., 2008) (Tixier et al., 2017), though studies indicated a human preference for abstractive summaries in conversational content (Goyal et al., 2022) (Murray et al., 2010). The rise of LLMs has brought strong semantic capabilities to tasks like meeting minutes generation (Cao et al., 2024), but factual consistency remains a key issue. Studies show that nearly 30% of summaries generated by seq2seq models contain inaccuracies (Cao et al., 2018)(Kryściński et al., 2019). LLMs also face challenges in adapting to subjective preferences, crucial for meeting minutes. Biermann et al.(Biermann et al., 2022) found that users prefer tools that align with their writing styles, but Ippolito et al.(Ippolito et al., 2022)(Lin et al., 2024) noted LLMs struggle to maintain organizational or individual style and format, further complicating their use in this context. Therefore, to develop an accurate and personalized meeting minutes tool, we propose leveraging the capabilities of LLMs while implementing strategic system designs to enhance accuracy and adapt to personal preferences.

2.2 Adaptively Personalized Minutes: RAG and Summary-based Prompt Engineering

User preference modeling plays a crucial role in understanding and adapting to user preferences, thereby enabling the generation of personalized meeting minutes. Researchers have applied machine learning-based user preference modeling in various specific domains. Yang et al. proposed a kernel probability model for color theme evaluation (Yang et al., 2024). Ma et al. introduced CRNN-SA for extracting user music preferences from listening history (Ma et al., 2022). Ma et al. developed SmartEye, a deep learning system that generates real-time photo composition suggestions based on users' previous photos and feedback (Ma et al., 2019).

Recent advancements in LLMs have highlighted the potential of Retrieval-Augmented Generation (RAG) in user preference modeling (Lewis et al., 2020). RAG enhances LLM performance by providing relevant external information, reducing hallucinations, and improving response accuracy. Summary-based prompt engineering for adaptive personalization leverages the power of text summarization to create dynamic, user-tailored prompts (Ait Baha et al., 2023). This approach abstracts essential information conveniently without capturing sensitive details (Friedman et al., 2013). While users often struggle to distill key features to refine their prompts, employing LLMs to extract these features and automatically incorporate them into subsequent prompts offers a convenient solution (Ait Baha et al., 2023). Recent studies have shown that such adaptive systems can significantly improve engagement and satisfaction in various applications, from recommendation (Lyu et al., 2023) systems to personalized learning platforms (Ait Baha et al., 2023).

In the context of personalized meeting minutes, RAG and summary-based prompt engineering can be employed for retrieving users' sample meeting minutes and learning from user modifications on the minute's output.

3 System Design

3.1 Design Goals (DGs)

Motivated by the findings of formative study and existing research, we aim to design an adaptively personalized meeting minutes generation tool with the following **design goals (DGs)**:

DG1. To ***improve minutes quality*** while ***reducing time*** spent on meeting minute generation.

DG2. To integrate users' ***personal preferences*** in meeting minute formats and writing styles.

DG3. To leverage an adaptive approach that streamlines the process for repetitive meeting tasks, ***improving efficiency over time***.

DG4. To enhance the ***visualizations for trustworthiness***, increasing user confidence in the generated minutes.

3.2 Overall Workflow

Meetalk's workflow can be visualized in Figure 1, beginning with the user uploading a sample meeting minutes file and the meeting audio to be processed. The system analyzes the sample file to *suggest* three key components: the Table of Contents (ToC), Chapter Allocation Database, and Writing Style Database. These components serve as adaptive references for the subsequent processing steps, allowing Meetalk to tailor its output to each user's specific needs and preferences.

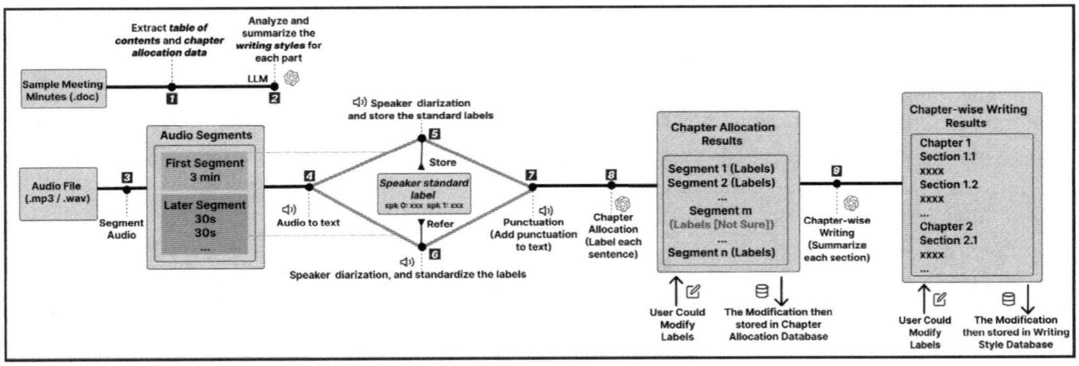

Figure 1: Meetalk's main process: Steps 1-2 sample file data analysis and suggestion, 3-7 transcribe audios, 8 allocates chapters, and 9 involves chapter-wise writing.

Next, Meetalk processes the meeting audio using ASR, dividing it into segments for *transcription, speaker diarization, and punctuation*. As each segment is processed, Meetalk performs *chapter allocation* by referring to the Chapter Allocation Database, labeling the text according to the existing ToC or creating new chapters or sections as necessary. If users find the chapter allocation results inaccurate, they can pause the process and *modify* the chapter allocation labels as easily as editing text. By confirming the modifications, these *changes are incorporated* into the Chapter Allocation Database for future reference.

Once all audio is processed and allocated, Meetalk *generates content for each section* based on the Writing Style Database and the allocated text. Similarly, if users are unsatisfied with the generated results, they can directly modify the content. By confirming the modifications, Meetalk will analyze the modified parts at a high level and *update the Writing Style Database* accordingly.

Throughout this process, Meetalk offers two LLM options: OpenAI ChatGPT API (supporting all available versions), and a locally hosted LLAMA3:8b. This flexibility allows users to choose their preferred LLMs for various needs, balancing factors such as performance, privacy, and cost.

3.3 Databases

Meetalk features three core databases. First, the **Table of Contents Database (ToC)** is responsible for storing the organizational structure of meeting records, specifically the chapters and sections. Second, the **Chapter Allocation Database** archives historical associations between contents and specific chapters and sections. Third, the **Writing Style Database** establishes guidelines and stores details for diverse writing styles. The writing styles for different sections are displayed alongside their corresponding sections in the ToC. These three components can be populated through three methods. *The first method is Referencing to Sample Files*: Meetalk processes reference documents by examining their chapter layouts, recognizing the content within, and summarizing the writing style characteristics. *The second method is Manual User Input*, where users can manually enter data for all three databases. *The third method involves Learning from User Modifications*, Meetalk learns and updates the databases based on user modification on the output. These processes will be explained in detail in a subsequent section.

3.3.1 Chapter Allocation Database

The Chapter Allocation Database is organized into three columns: content, Label A, and Label B. Both label columns follow the format "Chapter xx, Section xx," serving to denote the hierarchical chapter and section to which the content belongs. The inclusion of two labels is based on our rigorous testing results. We conducted a systematic study using a random sample of 200 sentences from meeting transcripts, analyzed in conjunction with their corresponding table of content. Two editors independently labeled each sentence, considering its contextual placement (Cohen's Kappa = 0.92, agreement ratio = 96.5%). Analysis of these labels revealed that 78% of sentences corresponded to a single section, while 22% belonged to two different sections. Therefore, we've included a second label column to accommodate these dual-labeled sentences. For content requiring more than two labels, users can split the same content item into multiple rows for input, allowing additional labels to be assigned to that content. For example, a content item needing 4 labels can be entered in two rows, with 2 labels assigned to each row.

To allow users conveniently update the databases, as shown in Figure 2, Meetalk provides users with the flexibility to edit table contents, add new entries, and modify chapter allocation outputs. While minor changes need to be made, our database can keep track on the preferences based on these changes. After editing and confirming the edits, users could click the "Save Data" button to upload the edited database and save it as the current chapter allocation database.

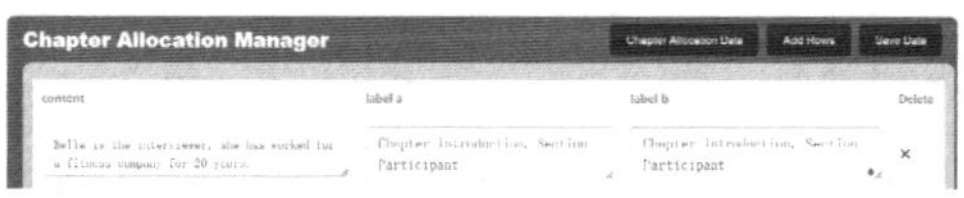

Figure 2: Chapter Allocation Databases, with buttons to get chapter allocation data, add rows, delete rows and save data.

The content column of the Chapter Allocation Database is stored as embeddings (referred to as "content embeddings" below). For each entry of the "content" column, an embedding is generated using the *large multilingual E5 text embedding model* (referred to as *"multilingual-e5-large"* below). The multilingual-e5-large model supports 93 languages, primarily English, enabling Meetalk to process meeting minutes in multiple languages, thereby enhancing its global applicability. These embeddings are crucial as they provide a mathematical representation of the text, facilitating later comparison and retrieval.

3.3.2 Writing Style Database

To empower users with the capability to utilize and preserve precise and tailored writing tags, we have defined eleven indicators categorized into three main types: Five for **Writing Context**, five for **Summary Variables**, and one **Difference**.

Figure 3: Writing Style Databases, with 11 columns and buttons to get writing style data, add rows, delete rows, and save data.

Writing Context encompasses the foundational elements necessary for creating the writing piece. These indicators were derived from a comprehensive formative study on meeting minutes requirements across diverse industries, including: **Input:** The scenario of the meeting. **Participant:** The individuals or groups involved in the meeting, including their roles and relevance to the discussion topics. **Writing Goal:** The primary objective of the meeting minutes, such as informing, decision-making, or action planning. **Writing Format:** The required structure or style of the meeting minutes, such as paragraphs, bullet points, or numbers. **Your role:** The viewpoints or roles that need to be represented in the minutes.

Summary Variables are mainly derived from LIWC 2022 definitions, including: **Analytical Thinking:** Measures logical and hierarchical thinking patterns. **Clout:** Reflects social status, confidence, or leadership abilities. **Authenticity:** Indicates honesty, personal disclosure, and genuineness. **Emotional Tone:** Assesses overall emotional tone of the writing. **Language:** *English, Spanish, Traditional Chinese, etc.*

And finally, the **Difference** variable is created to store comparisons between user modifications and original text.

The Writing Style Manager interface includes three main buttons to interact with the writing style data. The *"Get Writing Style Data"* button retrieves the current tag data from the database. Users may then add, delete, or edit rows, uploading their changes using the *"Save Writing Style Data"* button. With this approach, we enable dynamic and iterative improvements in writing style prediction and generation.

4 Knowledge Integration and Utilization in Meetalk

In the era of large language models (LLMs), the ability to effectively ground generation on structured and personalized knowledge is crucial to enhancing output accuracy and trustworthiness. Meetalk addresses this challenge by incorporating a retrieval-augmented and user-adaptive knowledge pipeline into its summarization workflow. This section details how Meetalk constructs, retrieves, and updates knowledge to enable personalized, faithful, and hallucination-aware meeting minutes generation.

4.1 Knowledge as Structured Memory

We conceptualize knowledge in Meetalk as a structured memory composed of three user-specific databases: the Table of Contents (ToC) database, the Chapter Allocation database, and the Writing Style database. These databases are derived from user-provided sample minutes or previous interactions, and encode the organizational structure, topical segmentation, and preferred linguistic style for each meeting domain. Unlike static templates, these knowledge modules dynamically evolve as users revise system outputs.

4.2 Retrieval-Augmented Prompting

To ensure faithful and stylistically consistent generation, Meetalk employs retrieval-augmented generation (RAG) techniques at multiple stages. During chapter allocation, each segment of transcribed audio is embedded and matched against prior content in the Chapter Allocation database to suggest contextual labels. Similarly, in the writing stage, the system retrieves style exemplars from the Writing Style database to construct section-specific prompts. These retrieved signals act as grounding knowledge, guiding the LLM to produce outputs aligned with both the user's structural expectations and domain-specific discourse.

4.3 Knowledge Updating via User Feedback

To support long-term adaptability, Meetalk treats user modifications as implicit knowledge updates. After each editing action—whether modifying chapter boundaries or rewriting section texts—the system summarizes the difference and updates the corresponding database entry. In doing so, Meetalk implements an interactive knowledge editing loop that enables continual refinement of the structured memory without requiring explicit reprogramming or prompt engineering from the user.

4.4 Hallucination Awareness and Uncertainty Markers

To further enhance trust and mitigate hallucinations, Meetalk integrates a lightweight hallucination-aware mechanism. When the system detects uncertain or low-confidence segment-label mappings—based on retrieval inconsistencies or model disagreement—it marks them with a "[Not Sure]" tag in the interface. This allows users to prioritize checking potentially unreliable content, offering a human-AI collaboration path for factuality verification. These uncertainty annotations can also be logged for future benchmarking or fine-tuning, supporting broader efforts in hallucination detection and correction in knowledge-intensive generation tasks.

In summary, Meetalk transforms user interactions into a dynamic knowledge lifecycle: acquiring knowledge from user examples, injecting it via retrieval-augmented prompting, refining it through feedback, and regulating output trustworthiness through uncertainty cues. This design provides a concrete pathway for realizing knowledgeable, user-aligned LLM applications in high-stakes domains such as meeting documentation.

5 Evaluation

To evaluate the effectiveness of Meetalk in supporting the generation of meeting minutes, we conducted a *within-subject study* comparing Meetalk with the conventional approach to automate meeting minutes. As our baseline, we selected *iFLYTEK real-time ASR combined with ChatGPT-4o*. Participants were asked to complete **two tasks**, using the baseline method and Meetalk respectively.

To validate the optimization of our system for handling the repetitive nature of meetings, participants in each task processed **three meeting audios** from a specific scenario, generating meeting minutes in a consistent format. To assess the generalizability of Meetalk, we selected **five different scenarios** and invited participants who were familiar with these scenarios to complete the tasks.

Through these comparisons, we seek to evaluate whether Meetalk outperforms the baseline method in addressing the design goals derived from literature and the formative studies.

Eighteen (N=18) participants are invited to this study, with five different real-world scenarios included: **legal consultations**, **study abroad counseling**, **academic discussions**, **mock interviews**, and **company pitches**. Participants generally span moderate to high levels of expertise within their respective fields.

It is noteworthy that all participants demonstrate high frequency of meetings and substantial usage of language models in their professional contexts, underscoring the relevance of this study to contemporary professional practices. If the audio contains private conversations, any mentions of real names have been cut out beforehand, and this removal does not affect the main content of the meeting.

5.1 The Baseline Method

The baseline method combines two powerful tools: Using iFLYTEK ASR to generate transcript from the meeting audios, and using OpenAI's ChatGPT-4o to write meeting minutes from transcripts. This approach requires users to switch between two separate tools and incurs significant costs.

5.2 Study Procedure

A remote study session for each participant lasted up to 3 hours, divided into three parts: **the pre-study survey, the main study itself, and the post-study interview.** Participants accessed Meetalk via a web browser on a researcher-provided computer through remote control software. Simultaneously, the experimenter communicated with the participants via Zoom or Lark video conferencing.

As for the main process, initially, communicate with the participant to ensure they understand the relationship and purpose of the above materials, as well as the workflow of using Meetalk. Then, proceed with two tasks while recording the time taken for each: ***Task 1:*** Using the three transcripts produced by iFLYTEK, create meeting minutes similar to the sample meeting minutes file using ChatGPT4o for each transcript. Instruct participants to pay close attention to the format and writing style, aiming to match the sample meeting minutes as closely as possible. Participants are allowed to use various tools within ChatGPT4o to accomplish this task. ***Task 2:*** On Meetalk, upload the sample meeting minutes file and click "suggest". Allow participants to freely modify the suggested database. Then, instruct them to click "submit" for chapter allocation, again allowing free editing. Finally, have them click "write" and permit further modifications as needed. Remind participants that their edits will be saved to the database, which may influence the processing of subsequent audio files.

6 Results

In this section, we analyzed objective and subjective results by combining the final study minutes, post-study questionnaires, and screen recordings captured during the process. The subjective ratings on minutes' quality and the ML GUI Heuristics are presented in Figure 4.

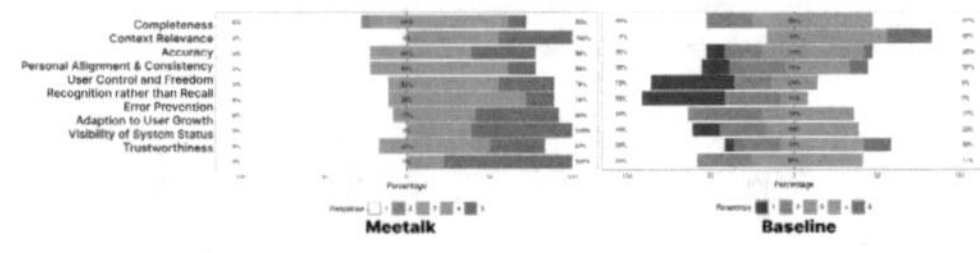

Figure 4: **Ratings for Meetalk(left) and the baseline(right) method** of the subjective 5-point Likert rating results on minutes' quality and user experience based on the ML GUI Heuristics.

6.1 Q1: Meetalk *improves writing quality* while *reducing time*

We recorded the time taken by 18 participants to complete two distinct tasks in this study. The average time for each scenario was calculated and visualized in Figure 5. Overall, Meetalk consistently utilizes less time than the baseline method across all scenarios, ($p = 0.0169$, Cohen's d = 1.7629), with an average time reduction of 33.9%.

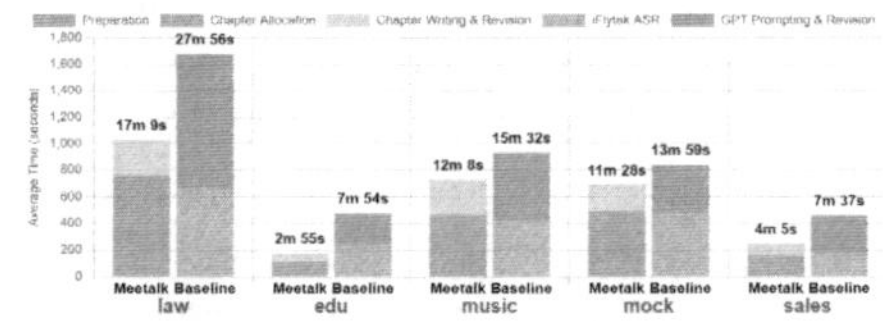

Figure 5: **Meetalk and the baseline method average time comparison** in five studied scenarios. Within a bar, the different colors show the specific time proportion of each stage. It is evident from the figure that the total time used by Meetalk is lower than that of the baseline method.

As shown in 1, the Flesch-Kincaid Reading Ease scores indicate that Meetalk's output has no significant difference on the readability level compared to the baseline's output ($p = 0.0688$, lower scores indicating easier-to-read text. Regarding word count, Meetalk consistently demonstrates a higher word count percentage across all domains compared to the baseline ($p = 0.0114$, Cohen's d = 1.9815). This substantial difference in word count percentages indicates that Meetalk consistently produces more extensive content than the baseline, suggesting more detailed or comprehensive responses in each domain.

Based on the participants' ratings of minutes quality, Meetalk-generated minutes generally outperformed those produced by the baseline method on **completeness** (Mean = 3.56 > 2.94, $p = 0.0022$, Cohen's d = 1.1093), **Context Relevance** (Mean = 4.44 > 3.94, $p = 0.0244$, Cohen's d = 0.7864), and **Accuracy**(Mean = 4.00 > 2.89, $p = 0.0010$,

Domain	Law		Edu		Music		Mock		Sales	
	Meetalk	Baseline	Meetalk	Baseline	Meetalk	Baseline	Meetalk	Baseline	Meetalk	Baseline
Flesch-Kincaid Reading Ease **Mean (SD)**	14.03 (0.23)	13.26 (0.55)	16.47 (1.72)	15.20 (2.08)	15.18 (2.83)	10.81 (1.69)	15.88 (1.92)	16.38 (2.87)	18.00 (1.44)	13.36 (2.27)
Word Count Percentage	3825/17945 =21.32%	869/17945 =4.84%	774/1500 =51.6%	476/1500 =31.73%	3566/13012 =27.41%	873/13012 =6.71%	841/4406 =19.09%	151/4406 =3.42%	1480/3595 =41.17%	551/3595 =15.32%

Table 1: Comparison of Meetalk and Baseline across **Flesch-Kincaid Reading Ease** (The lower, the easier to read) and the **word count**

Cohen's d = 1.1971).

• **Completeness:**

Meetalk's score generally outperforms the Baseline's score. Even though both methods cover the main idea, Meetalk provides more details and in-depth explanations, resulting in more comprehensive and complete content. This difference can be attributed to the different approaches Meetalk takes in processing the long transcript. Meetalk accurately extracts all sentences related to a specific section. Then, in a single LLM process, it focuses only on these sentences and rewrites them. By focusing on a specific section, Meetalk can provide richer, more relevant content within a limited generation space. In comparison, the baseline method adopts a full-text summarization, although it touches on the solution part, but only provides an overall summary. It is constrained by the token limit of the LLMs, resulting in limited space allocated to the solution part in the summary.

• **Conext Relevance:** Likert results show that Meetalk consistently achieves slightly higher context relevance scores compared to the baseline method. The low relevance in the baseline method may be attributed to overgeneralization. When processing large amounts of text, language models often attempt to synthesize broad summaries, resulting in vague or generic statements that lack specific, pertinent details (Liu & Lapata, 2019). This tendency towards overgeneralization leads to output that, while broadly related to the input, fails to address the nuances of the given query, significantly reducing its relevance and utility to the user.

• **Accuracy:** Users rated Meetalk's accuracy slightly higher than the baseline's. User feedback indicated that while both methods generally handle explicit numerical data well, the baseline often introduces logical errors that reduce overall accuracy. This issue likely stems from the limitations of traditional summarization techniques in handling long-form content (Liu & Lapata, 2019), which adapted by the baseline method.

6.2 Q2: Meetalk *allows user-driven customization to address personal preferences*

Two metrics in the ML GUI heuristics framework showed noteworthy results. The **Personal Alignment & Consistency** metric showed a positive trend favoring Meetalk over the baseline method (Mean = 3.72 vs. 2.83, p = 0.1887, Cohen's d = 0.4472), although the difference was not statistically significant. More compellingly, the **User Control and Freedom** metric demonstrated a highly significant advantage for Meetalk (Mean = 4.11 vs. 1.83, $p < 0.0001$, Cohen's d = 1.9031). These results strongly suggest that Meetalk effectively empowers users to tailor their reading experience according to individual preferences and habits, particularly in terms of providing enhanced control and freedom.

Through user-driven customization, the system achieves alignment consistency by ensuring that formats and writing styles are consistent with both sample files and user preferences. By allowing users to define their own formats and create writing style tags, the system maintains a seamless alignment with users' desired outcomes and expectations. By allowing users to edit or delete suggested content, and to modify Meetalk's output as needed, Meetalk ensures a high degree of user control and freedom.

6.3 Q3: Meetalk *streamlines repetitive meeting tasks with adaptive learning*

Given the repetitive nature of meeting minutes tasks, it's crucial for a system to leverage this characteristic to enhance efficiency. Our study revealed that Meetalk significantly outperformed the baseline method in three critical areas: **recognition rather than recall** (Mean 3.94 > 1.67, $p < 0.0001$, Cohen's d = 2.5820), **error prevention** (Mean 4.33 > 2.72, $p < 0.0001$, Cohen's d = 1.9437), and **adaptation to user modification** (Mean 4.67 > 2.61, $p < 0.0001$, Cohen's d = 2.2194). These results strongly indicate that Meetalk effectively empowers users to tailor their meeting minutes experience, leveraging the repetitive nature of the tasks to enhance overall efficiency and user satisfaction.

Function **suggestion** significantly enhances this aspect. P3 noted, *"Meetalk's ability to suggest table of contents and writing styles from sample files is incredibly helpful. I don't have to remember everything or keep separate databases."* P12 added, *"It's much easier than the baseline where we had to maintain our own databases and then figure out how to prompt ChatGPT correctly."* This automated suggestion feature allows users to focus more on minutes creation and understanding rather than tedious memorization and retrieval.

6.4 Q4: Meetalk *enhances visualizations for trustworthiness*

The trustworthiness of meeting minutes generation is paramount to its usefulness. Meetalk outperformed the baseline in both **Visibility of System Status** (Mean 4.00 > 3.28, p = 0.0198, Cohen's d = 0.8165) and **Trustworthiness** (Mean 4.78 > 2.89, $p < 0.0001$, Cohen's d = 2.2356), according to participant ratings.

• **Visibility of System Status:** Meetalk provides visibility into three key areas: databases, progress of the chapter allocation process, and final results. P5 commented, *"With Meetalk, I can see everything from the databases being used to how far along the process is. It's so much more transparent than just seeing input and output like with the baseline."* P11 added, *"Being able to track the chapter allocation process in real-time gives me a sense of control and understanding that I didn't have with ChatGPT."* The high degree of visibility allows to reduce uncertainty about system behavior. Users are better able to anticipate and adjust processes, resulting in greater efficiency and accuracy, making participants more confident and proactive in using LLMs.

• **Trustworthiness:** The enhanced visibility of system status, coupled with Meetalk's ability to indicate uncertainties, fosters a true collaboration between human and AI. P2 noted, *"I appreciate that Meetalk shows me what it's unsure about. It feels like we're working together, rather than me just correcting a finished product."* P14 elaborated, *"The constant feedback during the process makes me trust Meetalk more. It's not just a black box spitting out results."*

This approach to transparency and collaboration significantly increases trustworthiness. As P8 summarized, *"With Meetalk, I feel like I'm part of the process, not just an end-user. That makes me trust the results much more than I did with the baseline system."*

7 Conclusion and Discussions

Meetalk addresses the challenges of long meeting minutes generation through innovative chunking and adaptive personalization. By performing ASR on 30-second audio segments and labeling transcribed content for section allocation, Meetalk enhances completeness and relevance, allowing users to review and modify labels in real-time. This process reduces input length for LLMs, improving the quality of summaries. Additionally, the system's flexibility accommodates various data types and user preferences through RAG and summary-based prompt engineering, enabling natural adaptation to user behavior. Meetalk's design also includes an authenticity assessment mechanism that boosts user trust with feedback labels like "[Not Sure]." Overall, Meetalk's approach and principles can be generalized to other AI-driven applications beyond meeting note-taking, enhancing user engagement and facilitating multimodal processing tasks.

In conclusion, this study introduces Meetalk, an innovative adaptive AI system for personalized meeting minutes generation. By addressing key challenges in automated minute-taking, including effectively adapting to personal preferences, Meetalk represents a significant advancement. The system's unique features, such as chapter allocation, chapter-wise writing, and adaptive learning from user modifications, offer a flexible and user-centric approach to generate meeting minutes. Our comprehensive user study across diverse real-world scenarios demonstrates Meetalk's effectiveness in producing high-quality, personalized minutes while enhancing user experience and trustworthiness. These findings validate Meetalk's practical applicability, and further contribute valuable insights to the broader domain of personalized AI-assisted text processing and summarization. As organizations continue to rely heavily on meetings for information exchange and decision-making, systems like Meetalk have the potential to significantly improve productivity and communication effectiveness. Future research can build upon this foundation, further exploring the integration of adaptive personalization in various professional contexts and expanding the capabilities of AI-assisted documentation systems.

Limitations

One limitation for our work is that we chose personal computers as the primary device for Meetalk in the user study, since we consider their common use as meeting minute tools. However, we believe that one of Meetalk's core functionality, namely converting speech into structured meeting minutes, can be applicable to other devices, particularly smartphones, which might offer more convenience in audio recording and uploading. Nevertheless, using the system on smaller screens may require UI adjustments, and the user experience could differ. For instance, content review and manual editing might face more challenges, which potentially increases the need for automated support.

Another limitation lies in the failure to use locally deployed LLMs for the user study. Although we include LLAMA3:8b in the design of Meetalk, we still used GPT-4o in our user study in order to be consistent with the most commonly used methods mentioned by the participants in the formative study.This choice, while facilitating a direct comparison of the results, also limits our understanding of how the localized models perform in real-world applications. Future research could explore similar user studies using localized models such as LLAMA3:8b to validate the effectiveness of our proposed approach in real privacy-constrained environments.

Furthermore, we employed the Flesch-Kincaid Reading Ease score and word count percentage as objective measures to assess the quality of the meeting minutes produced. While readability is a crucial aspect of meeting minutes and it provides valuable insights, it does not include all dimensions of content quality. Additionally, word count percentage could somehow refelect the completeness of Meetalk's generated minutes, but we did not measure the quality of the large word counts. Both these two measures provide extra results to triangulate with the subjective assessment of text quality.

Lastly, Meetalk, as a research prototype, has inherent limitations. Our system relies on advanced LLMs like LLAMA3:8b or ChatGPT-4, both requiring significant computing resources. In our experiments, we either deployed LLAMA3:8b locally on a 24GB NVIDIA RTX 4090 GPU or used the ChatGPT-4o API. What's more, the 8k limit of one-sentence summarization, might lead to information gap, in concluding the meeting scenarios. Additionally, the ASR component lacks an interactive learning process, which means the transcription errors can't be automatically corrected based on user modifications. Currently, the system doesn't support real-time audio input, only allowing for audio file uploads. Furthermore, while powerful, the LLM-based text generation is not 100% accurate and can occasionally produce hallucinations or inaccuracies in the generated content.

References

Tarek Ait Baha, Mohamed El Hajji, Youssef Es-Saady, and Hammou Fadili. 2023. The power of personalization: A systematic review of personality-adaptive chatbots. *SN Computer Science*, 4(5):661.

Oloff C Biermann, Ning F Ma, and Dongwook Yoon. 2022. From tool to companion: Storywriters want ai writers to respect their personal values and writing strategies. In *Proceedings of the 2022 ACM Designing Interactive Systems Conference*, pages 1209–1227, New York, NY, USA. ACM.

Yupeng Cao, Zhi Chen, Qingyun Pei, Prashant Kumar, KP Subbalakshmi, and Papa Momar Ndiaye. 2024. Ecc analyzer: Extract trading signal from earnings conference calls using large language model for stock performance prediction. *arXiv preprint arXiv:2404.18470.*

Ziqiang Cao, Furu Wei, Wenjie Li, and Sujian Li. 2018. Faithful to the original: Fact aware neural abstractive summarization. In *Proceedings of the AAAI Conference on Artificial Intelligence*, volume 32.

Batya Friedman, Peter H Kahn, Alan Borning, and Alina Huldtgren. 2013. Value sensitive design and information systems. *Early engagement and new technologies: Opening up the laboratory*, pages 55–95.

Tanya Goyal, Junyi Jessy Li, and Greg Durrett. 2022. News summarization and evaluation in the era of gpt-3. *arXiv preprint arXiv:2209.12356.*

Daphne Ippolito, Ann Yuan, Andy Coenen, and Sehmon Burnam. 2022. Creative writing with an ai-powered writing assistant: Perspectives from professional writers. *arXiv preprint arXiv:2211.05030.*

Wojciech Kryściński, Nitish Shirish Keskar, Bryan McCann, Caiming Xiong, and Richard Socher. 2019. Neural text summarization: A critical evaluation. *arXiv preprint arXiv:1908.08960.*

Patrick Lewis, Ethan Perez, Aleksandra Piktus, Fabio Petroni, Vladimir Karpukhin, Naman Goyal, Heinrich Küttler, Mike Lewis, Wen-tau Yih, Tim Rocktäschel, et al. 2020. Retrieval-augmented generation for knowledge-intensive nlp tasks. *Advances in Neural Information Processing Systems*, 33:9459–9474.

Susan Lin, Jeremy Warner, JD Zamfirescu-Pereira, Matthew G Lee, Sauhard Jain, Shanqing Cai, Piyawat Lertvittayakumjorn, Michael Xuelin Huang, Shumin Zhai, Björn Hartmann, et al. 2024. Rambler: Supporting writing with speech via llm-assisted gist manipulation. In *Proceedings of the CHI Conference on Human Factors in Computing Systems*, pages 1–19.

Hanjia Lyu, Song Jiang, Hanqing Zeng, Yinglong Xia, Qifan Wang, Si Zhang, Ren Chen, Christopher Leung, Jiajie Tang, and Jiebo Luo. 2023. Llm-rec: Personalized recommendation via prompting large language models. *arXiv preprint arXiv:2307.15780*.

Shuai Ma, Zijun Wei, Feng Tian, Xiangmin Fan, Jianming Zhang, Xiaohui Shen, Zhe Lin, Jin Huang, Radomír Měch, Dimitris Samaras, et al. 2019. Smarteye: assisting instant photo taking via integrating user preference with deep view proposal network. In *Proceedings of the 2019 CHI conference on human factors in computing systems*, pages 1–12.

Xichu Ma, Yuchen Wang, and Ye Wang. 2022. Content based user preference modeling in music generation. In *Proceedings of the 30th ACM International Conference on Multimedia*, MM '22, page 2473–2482, New York, NY, USA. Association for Computing Machinery.

Gabriel Murray, Giuseppe Carenini, and Raymond Ng. 2010. Generating and validating abstracts of meeting conversations: a user study. In *Proceedings of the 6th international natural language generation conference*.

Korbinian Riedhammer, Daniel Gillick, Benoit Favre, and Dilek Hakkani-Tür. 2008. Packing the meeting summarization knapsack. In *INTERSPEECH*, pages 2434–2437.

Antoine Tixier, Polykarpos Meladianos, and Michalis Vazirgiannis. 2017. Combining graph degeneracy and submodularity for unsupervised extractive summarization. In *Proceedings of the workshop on new frontiers in summarization*, pages 48–58.

Gokhan Tur, Andreas Stolcke, Lynn Voss, John Dowding, Benoît Favre, Raquel Fernández, Matthew Frampton, Michael Frandsen, Clint Frederickson, Martin Graciarena, et al. 2008. The calo meeting speech recognition and understanding system. In *2008 IEEE Spoken Language Technology Workshop*, pages 69–72. IEEE.

Bailin Yang, Tianxiang Wei, Frederick W. B. Li, Xiaohui Liang, Zhigang Deng, and Yili Fang. 2024. Color theme evaluation through user preference modeling. *ACM Trans. Appl. Percept.*, 21(3).

A System Design

B Meetalk overall introduction

C Participant information

D System UI

E Meetalk and Baseline result comparison examples

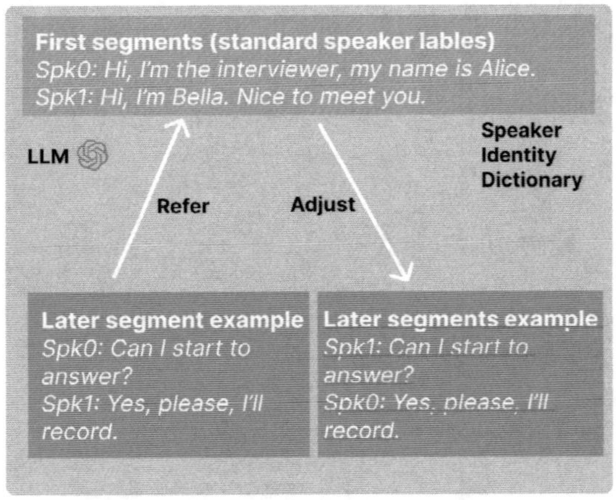

Figure 6: Meetalk's speaker diarization example in an interview scenario: The initial segment identifies Speaker 0 as the interviewer and Speaker 1 as the interviewee, storing their utterances in a **Speaker Identity Dictionary**. In later segments, even if speakers are initially mislabeled due to isolated analysis, the system corrects these labels by referencing the Dictionary, ensuring consistent speaker identification throughout the interview.

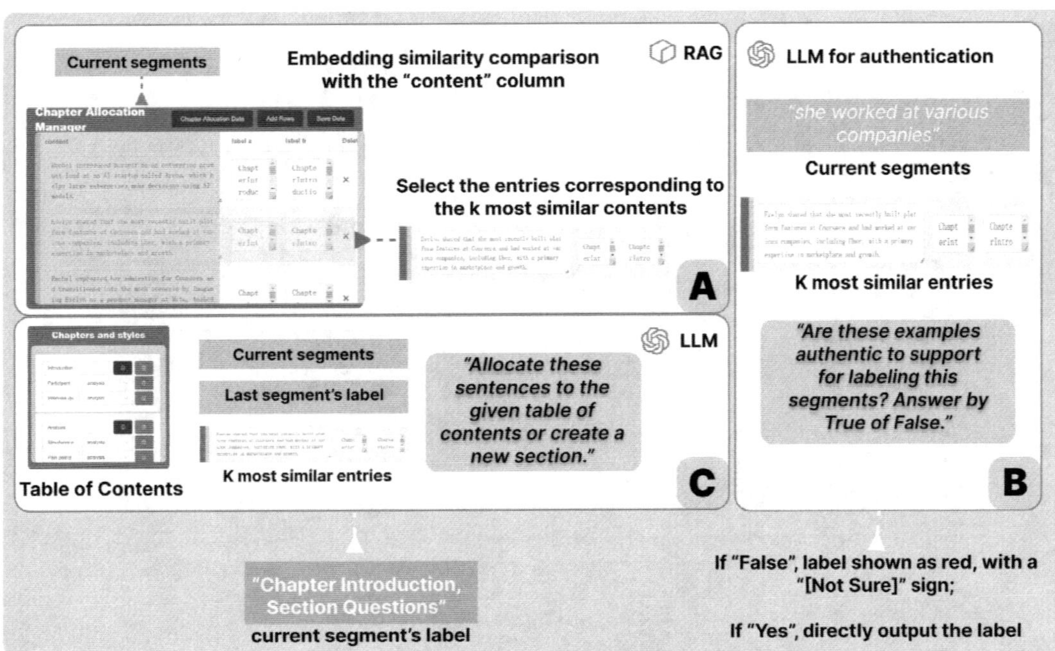

Figure 7: Chapter Allocation Procedure. **Step A**: Retrieve two entries with similar contents to the current segments. **Step B**. Leveraging an LLM to judge whether the retrieved two entries are authentic or not. If False, the label will be shown as red with a "[Not Sure]" sign. **Step C**. Request: Prompt ToC, current segments, last segment's label, and the retrieved two entries to an LLM, for generating the label for the current segment.

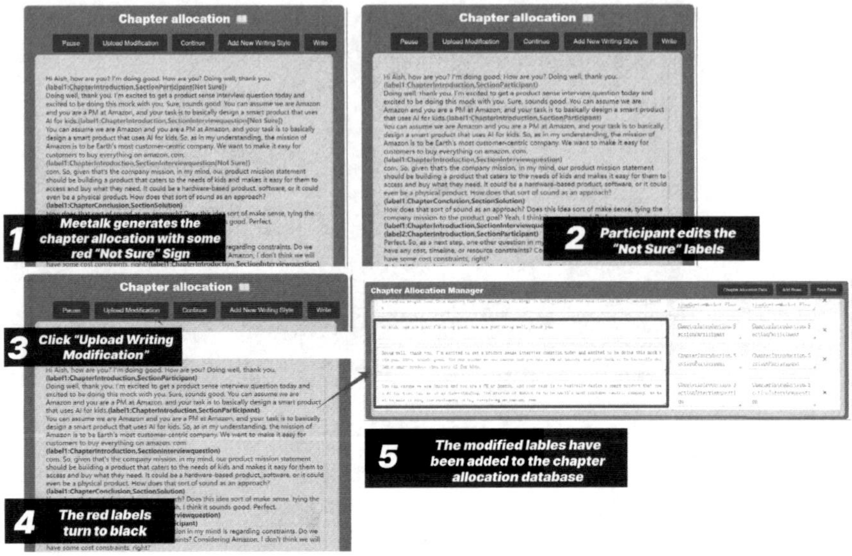

Figure 8: Chapter allocation modification procedure. Participants are notified with the unauthentic labels by a red "[Not Sure]" sign. By modifying these unauthenntic labels and clicking the "Upload Writing Modification" button, the modified labels turn black and been added to the chapter allocation database.

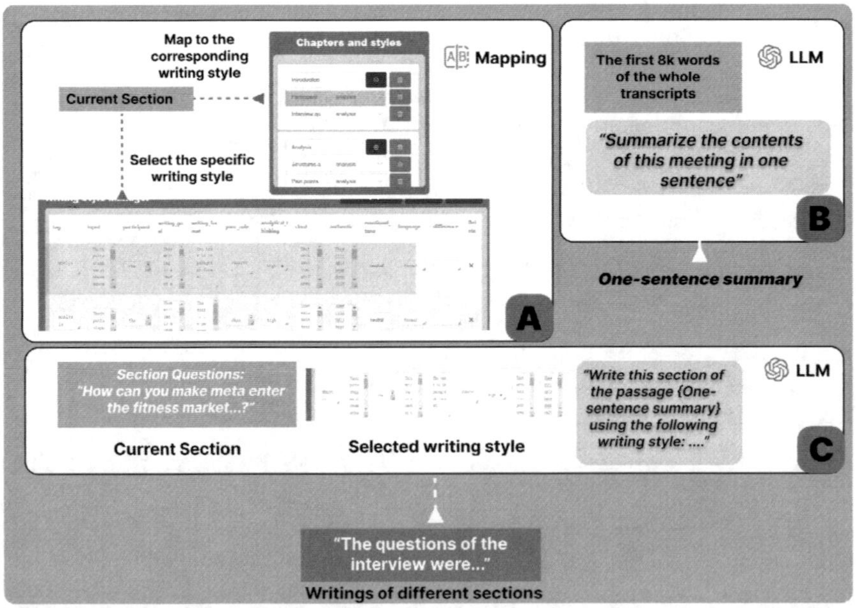

Figure 9: Chapter-wise Writing Procedure. **Step A**: Map the writing style with current section. **Step B**. Summarize the first 8k words (compatibility of the LLMs) of the whole transcripts with one sentence. **Step C**. Prompt current section and the writing style to an LLM for writing this section.

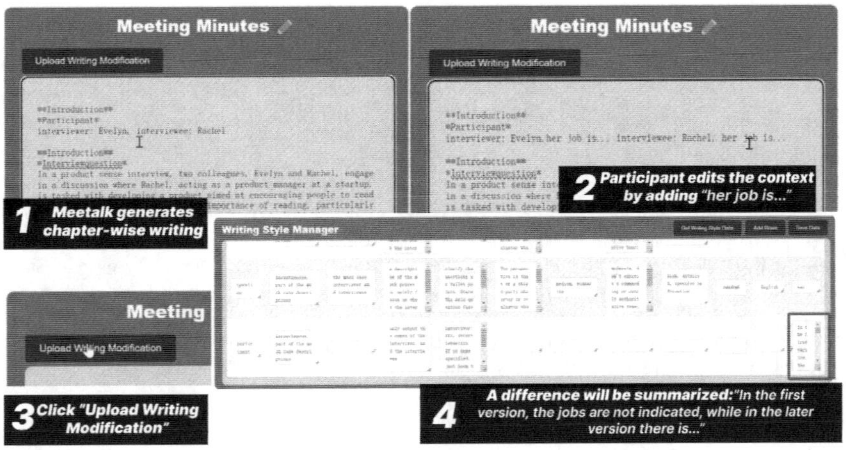

Figure 10: Chapter-wise writing revision procedure

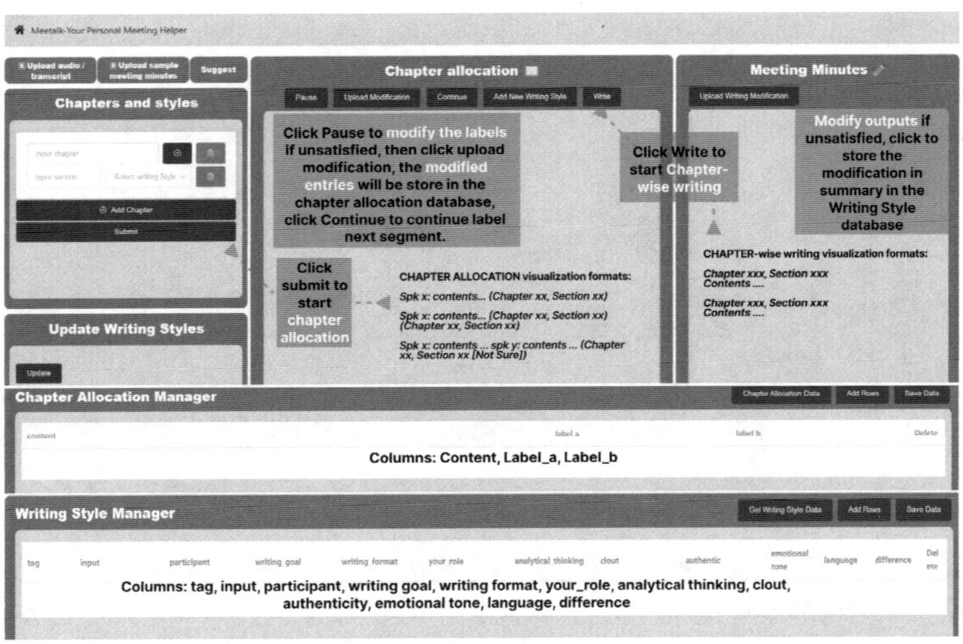

Figure 11: Meetalk, an adaptively personalized meeting minutes generation system. As illustrated in the Meetalk User Interface, after uploading meeting audio and a sample meeting file, Meetalk suggests a table of contents, chapter allocation data, and writing style data based on the sample file to personalize the meeting minutes. After that, Meetalk starts chapter allocation to label each segment according to the table of contents. Finally, meetalk write for each section to form a final meeting minutes. For both the chapter allocation and chapter-wise writing procedure, users could modify the outputs and Meetalk will learn the modifications to better adapt to user preferences.

Table 2: demographics, meeting frequency, and LLM usage of study participants

Scenario	ID	Age	Gender	Degree	Occupation	Meeting Freq.	LLM Usage
Legal consultations	P1	18-24	M	Bachelor	Lawyer trainee	Daily	Daily
	P2	18-24	F	Undergrad.	Law student	Weekly	Daily
	P3	25-34	M	Bachelor	Junior lawyer	Daily	Daily
Study abroad counseling	P4	25-34	F	Bachelor	Consultant	Weekly	Weekly
	P5	25-34	F	Master	Teacher	Weekly	Weekly
	P6	25-34	F	Bachelor	Teacher	Weekly	Weekly
	P7	25-34	M	Postgrad.	Senior postgraduate	Weekly	Daily
	P8	18-24	F	Postgrad.	Senior postgraduate	Monthly	Weekly
Academic discussions	P9	18-24	M	Undergrad.	Music major	Monthly	Daily
	P10	35-44	M	Ph.D.	Lecture tutor	Weekly	Daily
Mock Interviews	P11	25-34	M	Bachelor	HR intern	Weekly	Daily
	P12	25-34	M	Bachelor	HR intern	Weekly	Daily
	P13	25-34	F	Undergrad.	HR intern	Weekly	Daily
Company pitches	P14	35-44	M	Master	Sales manager	Weekly	Daily
	P15	24-34	M	Bachelor	Sales agent	Daily	Daily
	P16	35-44	F	Bachelor	Sales agent	Daily	Daily
	P17	35-44	F	Master	Venture Capital	Daily	Daily
	P18	35-44	M	Master	Venture Capital	Daily	Daily

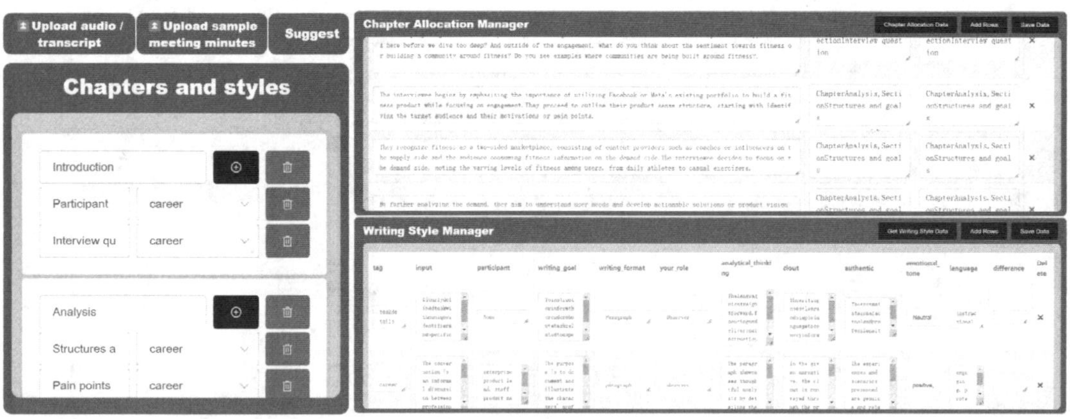

Figure 12: **Meetalk's Databases UI**: This comprehensive view showcases Meetalk's suggestions following document parsing in the databases' UI. The left panel displays a suggested Table of Contents, while the right side presents a Chapter Allocation Database (top) and Writing Style Database (bottom). These AI-generated recommendations offer a strategic starting point, with full user customization available to tailor the content structure and style to specific needs.

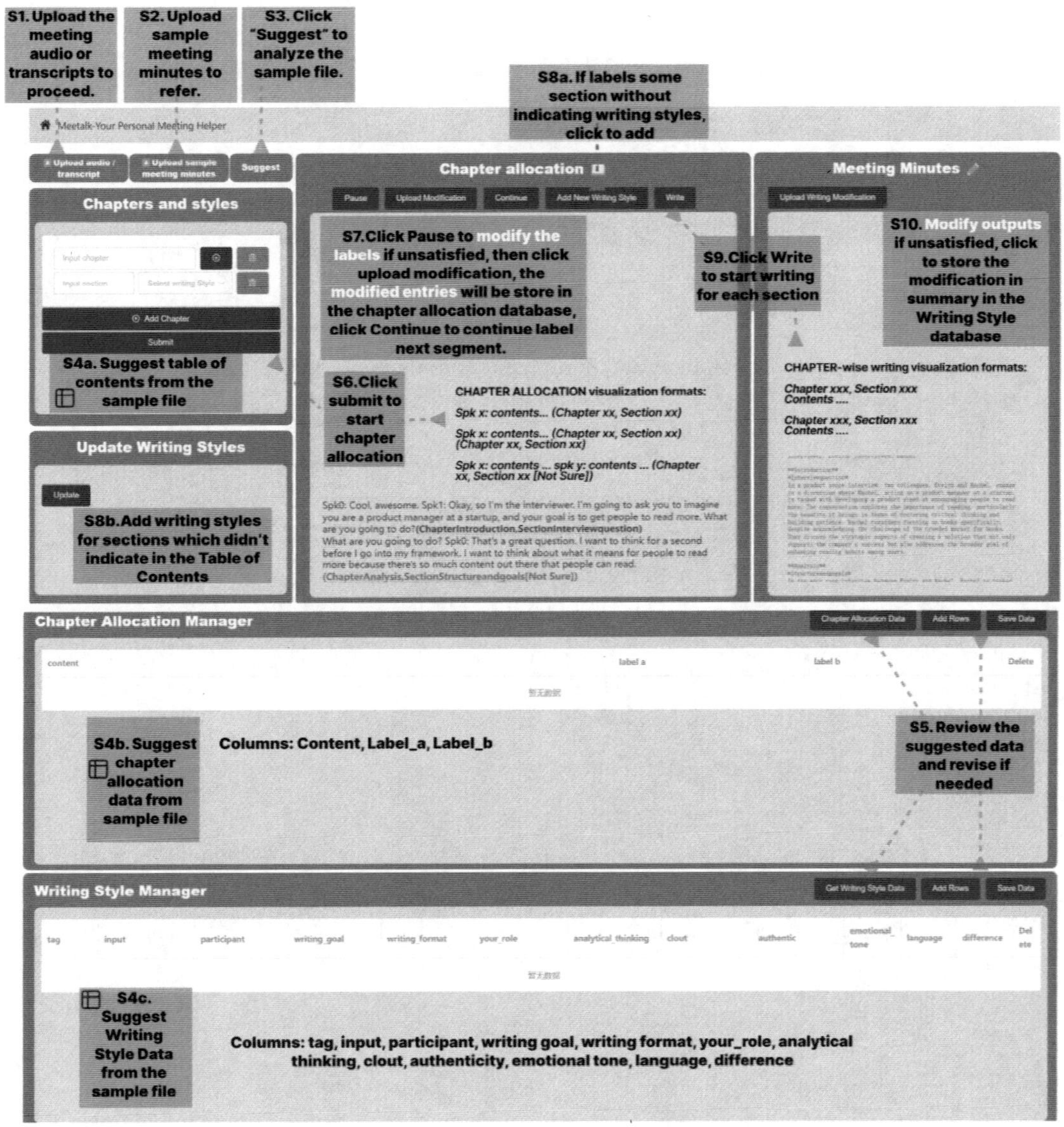

Figure 13: **Meetalk's Full UI illustration**: S1-2, upload meeting audios or transcripts to proceed, and upload sampe meeting minutes file to be referred by the system. After clicking on the suggest button in S3, Meetalk analyzes the uploaded files to suggest Table of Contents, chapter allocation data, and writing style data, as shown in S4. In S5, three buttons in each database are provided to reveiw and revise the suggested data if needed. In S6, while submitting the data to start chapter allocation, and could pause to modify the labels and store the modifications in the chapter allocation database. In S8, users could add writing styles if they are not specified in the table of contents. In S9, click write to start chapter-wise writing, and again in S10, if users are not satisfied with the outputs, modification is allowed and will be summarized in high level to store in the writing style database.

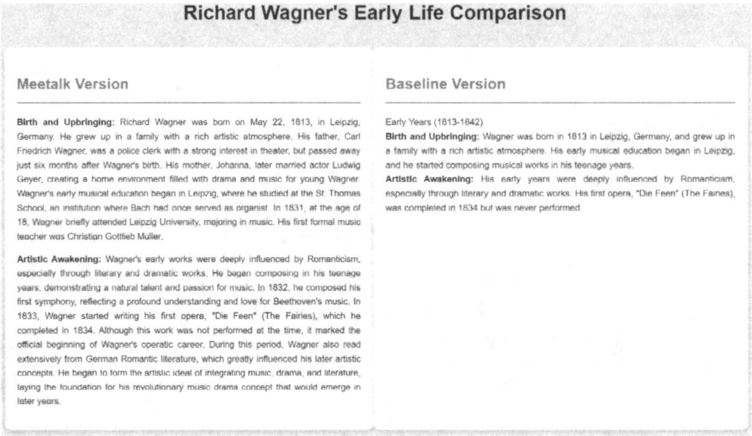

Richard Wagner's Early Life Comparison

Meetalk Version	Baseline Version
Birth and Upbringing: Richard Wagner was born on May 22, 1813, in Leipzig, Germany. He grew up in a family with a rich artistic atmosphere. His father, Carl Friedrich Wagner, was a police clerk with a strong interest in theater, but passed away just six months after Wagner's birth. His mother, Johanna, later married actor Ludwig Geyer, creating a home environment filled with drama and music for young Wagner. Wagner's early musical education began in Leipzig, where he studied at the St. Thomas School, an institution where Bach had once served as organist. In 1831, at the age of 18, Wagner briefly attended Leipzig University, majoring in music. His first formal music teacher was Christian Gottlieb Müller. **Artistic Awakening:** Wagner's early works were deeply influenced by Romanticism, especially through literary and dramatic works. He began composing in his teenage years, demonstrating a natural talent and passion for music. In 1832, he composed his first symphony, reflecting a profound understanding and love for Beethoven's music. In 1833, Wagner started writing his first opera, "Die Feen" (The Fairies), which he completed in 1834. Although this work was not performed at the time, it marked the official beginning of Wagner's operatic career. During this period, Wagner also read extensively from German Romantic literature, which greatly influenced his later artistic concepts. He began to form the artistic ideal of integrating music, drama, and literature, laying the foundation for his revolutionary music drama concept that would emerge in later years.	Early Years (1813-1842) **Birth and Upbringing:** Wagner was born in 1813 in Leipzig, Germany, and grew up in a family with a rich artistic atmosphere. His early musical education began in Leipzig, and he started composing musical works in his teenage years. **Artistic Awakening:** His early years were deeply influenced by Romanticism, especially through literary and dramatic works. His first opera, "Die Feen" (The Fairies), was completed in 1834 but was never performed.

Figure 14: High Readability Example: Audio Musician3

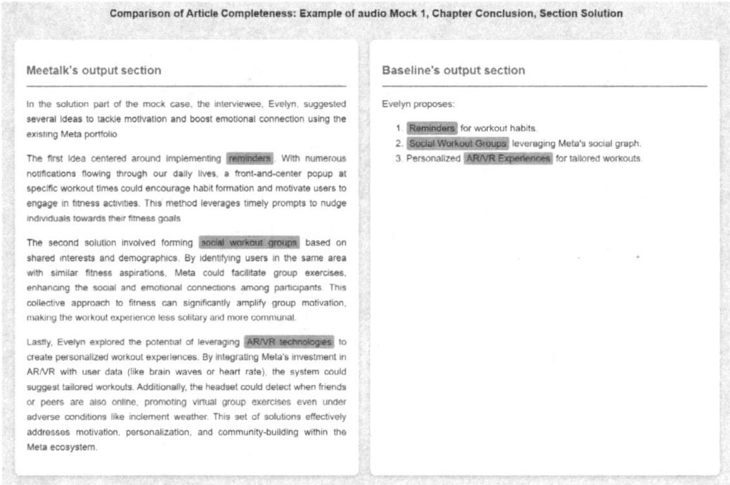

Comparison of Article Completeness: Example of audio Mock 1, Chapter Conclusion, Section Solution

Meetalk's output section	Baseline's output section
In the solution part of the mock case, the interviewee, Evelyn, suggested several ideas to tackle motivation and boost emotional connection using the existing Meta portfolio. The first idea centered around implementing reminders. With numerous notifications flowing through our daily lives, a front-and-center popup at specific workout times could encourage habit formation and motivate users to engage in fitness activities. This method leverages timely prompts to nudge individuals towards their fitness goals. The second solution involved forming social workout groups based on shared interests and demographics. By identifying users in the same area with similar fitness aspirations, Meta could facilitate group exercises, enhancing the social and emotional connections among participants. This collective approach to fitness can significantly amplify group motivation, making the workout experience less solitary and more communal. Lastly, Evelyn explored the potential of leveraging AR/VR technologies to create personalized workout experiences. By integrating Meta's investment in AR/VR with user data (like brain waves or heart rate), the system could suggest tailored workouts. Additionally, the headset could detect when friends or peers are also online, promoting virtual group exercises even under adverse conditions like inclement weather. This set of solutions effectively addresses motivation, personalization, and community-building within the Meta ecosystem.	Evelyn proposes: 1. Reminders for workout habits. 2. Social Workout Groups leveraging Meta's social graph. 3. Personalized AR/VR Experiences for tailored workouts.

Figure 15: Comparison of **Article Completeness**: Example of audio Mock 1, Chapter Conclusion, Section Solution

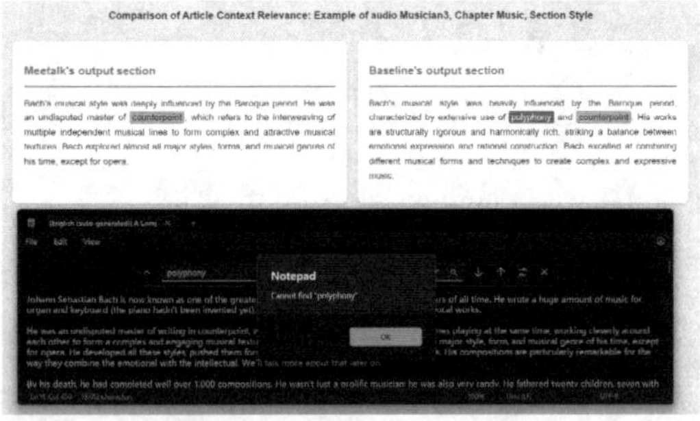

Comparison of Article Context Relevance: Example of audio Musician3, Chapter Music, Section Style

Meetalk's output section	Baseline's output section
Bach's musical style was deeply influenced by the Baroque period. He was an undisputed master of counterpoint, which refers to the interweaving of multiple independent musical lines to form complex and attractive musical textures. Bach explored almost all major styles, forms, and musical genres of his time, except for opera.	Bach's musical style was heavily influenced by the Baroque period, characterized by extensive use of polyphony and counterpoint. His works are structurally rigorous and harmonically rich, striking a balance between emotional expression and rational construction. Bach excelled at combining different musical forms and techniques to create complex and expressive music.

Figure 16: The image above is the **Comparison of Context Relevance** for Example of audio Mock 3, Chapter Music, Section Style. The screenshot below shows **no results for 'polyphony' in the audio Mock 3 transcript**, confirming its absence in the original text.

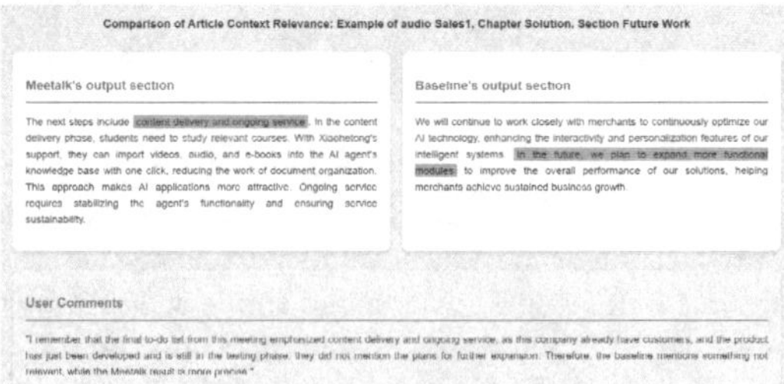

Comparison of Article Context Relevance: Example of audio Sales1, Chapter Solution, Section Future Work

Meetalk's output section	Baseline's output section
The next steps include content delivery and ongoing service. In the content delivery phase, students need to study relevant courses. With Xiaohetong's support, they can import videos, audio, and e-books into the AI agent's knowledge base with one click, reducing the work of document organization. This approach makes AI applications more attractive. Ongoing service requires stabilizing the agent's functionality and ensuring service sustainability.	We will continue to work closely with merchants to continuously optimize our AI technology, enhancing the interactivity and personalization features of our intelligent systems. In the future, we plan to expand more functional modules to improve the overall performance of our solutions, helping merchants achieve sustained business growth.

User Comments

"I remember that the final to-do list from this meeting emphasized content delivery and ongoing service, as this company already have customers, and the product has just been developed and is still in the testing phase. they did not mention the plans for further expansion. Therefore, the baseline mentions something not relevant, while the Meetalk result is more precise."

Figure 17: The image above is the **Comparison of Context Relevance** for Example audio Sales 1, Chapter Solution, Section Future work. The screenshot below shows **user comments**, proving the baseline results contain irrelevant information.

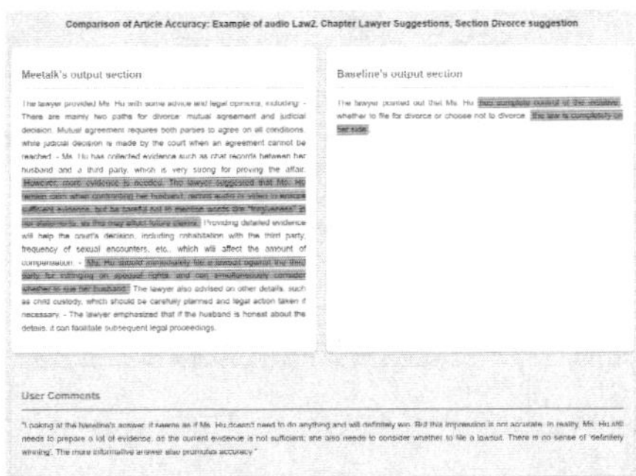

Figure 18: The image above is the **Comparison of Accuracy** for Example audio Law 2, Chapter Suggestion, Section Divorce suggestion. The screenshot below shows **user comments**, proving results of Meetalk are more accurate.

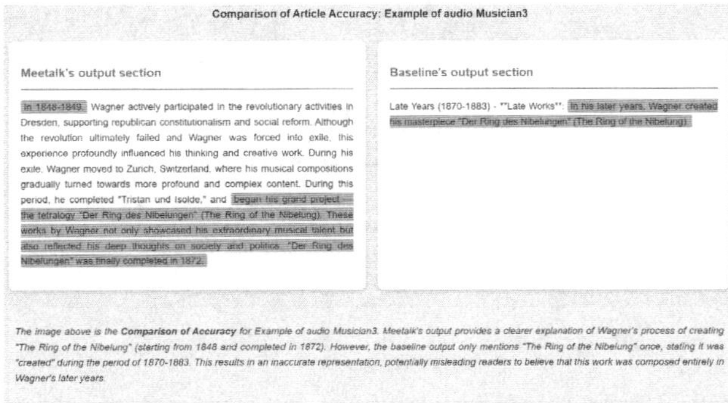

Figure 19: The image above is the **Comparison of Accuracy** for Example of audio Musician3.

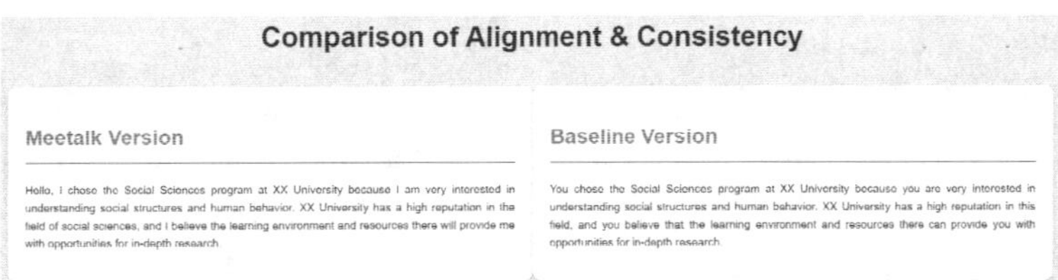

Figure 20: Alignment and consistency comparison, with Meetalk got the correct narrative perspective but the baseline method does not.

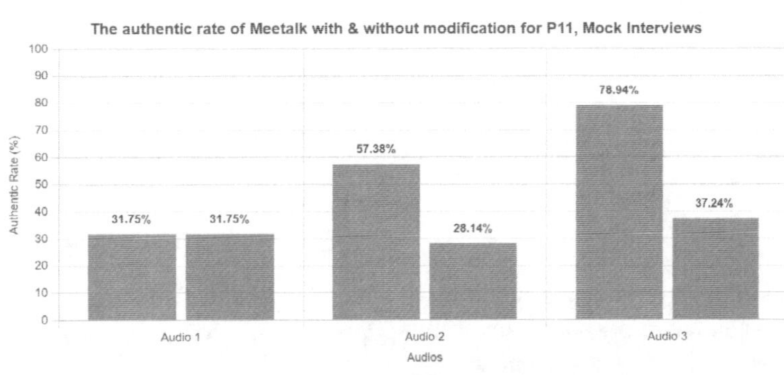

Figure 21: The authentic rate of Meetalk with & without modification for P11's mock interview audio tasks.

Theorem-of-Thought: A Multi-Agent Framework for Abductive, Deductive, and Inductive Reasoning in Language Models

Samir Abdaljalil[1], Hasan Kurban[2*], Khalid Qaraqe[2], Erchin Serpedin[1]
[1]Electrical & Computer Engineering, Texas A&M University, College Station, TX, USA
[2]College of Science and Engineering, Hamad Bin Khalifa University, Doha, Qatar

Abstract

Large language models (LLMs) have shown strong performance across natural language reasoning tasks, yet their reasoning processes remain brittle and difficult to interpret. Prompting techniques like Chain-of-Thought (CoT) enhance reliability by eliciting intermediate reasoning steps or aggregating multiple outputs. However, they lack mechanisms for enforcing logical structure and assessing internal coherence. We introduce **Theorem-of-Thought (ToTh)**, a novel framework that models reasoning as collaboration among three parallel agents, each simulating a distinct mode of inference: abductive, deductive, and inductive. Each agent produces a reasoning trace, which is structured into a formal reasoning graph. To evaluate consistency, we apply Bayesian belief propagation guided by natural language inference (NLI), assigning confidence scores to each step. The most coherent graph is selected to derive the final answer. Experiments on symbolic (WEBOFLIES) and numerical (MULTIARITH) reasoning benchmarks show that ToTh consistently outperforms CoT, Self-Consistency, and CoT-Decoding across multiple LLMs, while producing interpretable and logically grounded reasoning chains. Our findings suggest a promising direction for building more robust and cognitively inspired LLM reasoning. The implementation is available at `https://github.com/KurbanIntelligenceLab/theorem-of-thought`.

1 Introduction

Large language models (LLMs) have achieved impressive performance across a wide range of natural language understanding and generation tasks (Wang et al., 2024), enabled by advances in in-context learning (Sia et al., 2024), instruction tuning (Zhang et al., 2024), and chain-of-thought (CoT) prompting (Wei et al., 2022). These methods have extended LLMs' capabilities to handle complex forms of reasoning, including mathematical, logical, and commonsense inference.

Despite these advances, LLM reasoning remains shallow and unreliable. Existing approaches often rely on single-shot or sampling-based decoding along linear reasoning paths, making them susceptible to hallucinations (Abdaljalil et al., 2025), logical inconsistencies (Uceda Sosa et al., 2024), and weak generalization (Liu et al., 2025). Methods such as CoT and Self-Consistency (Wei et al., 2022; Wang et al., 2023) encourage intermediate steps and majority voting across sampled outputs, but lack mechanisms to verify internal coherence and model the logical structure of reasoning. As a result, outputs may appear fluent and plausible while remaining logically unsound.

This brittleness contrasts sharply with human reasoning, which is inherently multifaceted. Drawing on insights from cognitive science (Okoli, 2022), we observe that human inference typically blends three complementary modes—abduction, deduction, and induction—that support explanation, derivation, and generalization. However, LLMs typically conflate these distinct processes into a single, undifferentiated flow, limiting both interpretability and reliability.

To address this gap, we propose **Theorem-of-Thought (ToTh)**, a framework that models diverse reasoning strategies through structured, verifiable interactions. ToTh employs three specialized agents, each emulating a distinct cognitive mode:

- **Abduction**: inferring plausible explanations for observed facts;
- **Deduction**: deriving valid conclusions from given premises;
- **Induction**: generalizing from patterns or examples.

*Corresponding author: hkurban@hbku.edu.qa

Proceedings of the 3rd Workshop on Towards Knowledgeable Foundation Models (KnowFM), pages 111–119
August 1, 2025 ©2025 Association for Computational Linguistics

Each agent independently generates a reasoning trace, which is transformed into a Formal Reasoning Graph (FRG)—a directed graph where nodes represent intermediate conclusions and edges capture logical dependencies. We evaluate the internal consistency of each FRG using Bayesian belief propagation, with edge confidence scores calibrated via a Natural Language Inference (NLI) model. A composite score balancing average belief and logical entropy is used to select the most coherent graph, from which the final answer is extracted.

Contributions. The key results of this work are:

- We introduce ToTh, a structured reasoning framework that integrates abductive, deductive, and inductive inference into a modular LLM-based pipeline.
- We develop a belief propagation mechanism over reasoning graphs, leveraging NLI to assess and score logical coherence through Bayesian updates.
- We demonstrate that ToTh consistently outperforms state-of-the-art reasoning methods (e.g., CoT, Self-Consistency, CoT-Decoding) across multiple LLMs.
- Our evaluation on symbolic (WEBOFLIES) and numerical (MULTIARITH) benchmarks highlights ToTh's robustness on tasks requiring multi-step inference—settings where direct prompting often fails (Allen-Zhu and Li, 2025).

The remainder of the paper is organized as follows: Section 2 reviews related work. Section 3 presents the ToTh framework. Section 4 describes the experimental setup, and Section 5 analyzes the results obtained. Section 6 concludes with implications for structured reasoning in LLMs and future research directions.

2 Related Work

Prompt-based Reasoning in LLMs. A growing body of work explores prompting strategies to enhance the reasoning capabilities of LLMs. CoT prompting (Wei et al., 2022) encourages models to decompose problems into intermediate steps, guiding reasoning along a linear path. Building on this, Auto-CoT (Zhang et al., 2023) automates prompt generation by sampling diverse questions and producing corresponding reasoning traces, reducing manual effort. Beyond prompt generation, several works focus on optimizing prompt selection strategies. ActivePrompt (Diao et al., 2024) identifies high-uncertainty instances for annotation, improving data efficiency and reasoning robustness through active learning. More recent approaches introduce explicit structure into the reasoning process. Tree-of-Thought (ToT) (Yao et al., 2023) enables multi-path exploration with internal evaluation, while Graph-of-Thought (GoT) (Yao et al., 2024) structures reasoning as a graph to better model dependencies between steps.

Instruction Tuning for Reasoning. Instruction tuning and knowledge distillation offer alternative approaches to eliciting reasoning in LLMs without relying on explicit prompts (Lobo et al., 2025; Ranaldi and Freitas, 2024; Lai and Nissim, 2024). While effective, these methods typically require computationally intensive fine-tuning on large-scale datasets annotated with reasoning traces and CoT examples, which are often costly and domain-specific. Recent work has explored more indirect supervision strategies. For instance, Liu et al. (2024) introduce proxy tuning, which leverages auxiliary models to contrast a base LLM with its adapted variant. Although this approach reduces the need for direct supervision, it still assumes access to CoT-like outputs and pre-aligned reasoning benchmarks.

3 Methodology

ToTh is a graph-based reasoning framework designed to enhance the accuracy, interpretability, and generalization capabilities of LLMs on complex tasks. It decomposes reasoning into three modular agents, each simulating a classical inference paradigm—abduction, deduction, and induction. Each agent produces a structured reasoning trace, which is composed into a FRG. Final answers are derived via NLI-calibrated Bayesian belief propagation and composite graph scoring. The full pipeline is depicted in Fig. 1.

ToTh differs from prior reasoning paradigms along three axes: architecture, supervision, and verification. Prompt-based methods (e.g., CoT, ToT, GoT) elicit reasoning via linear or loosely structured traces, yet lack mechanisms for enforcing logical consistency. Instruction-tuned models embed reasoning behavior through fine-tuning on annotated traces, often requiring large datasets and

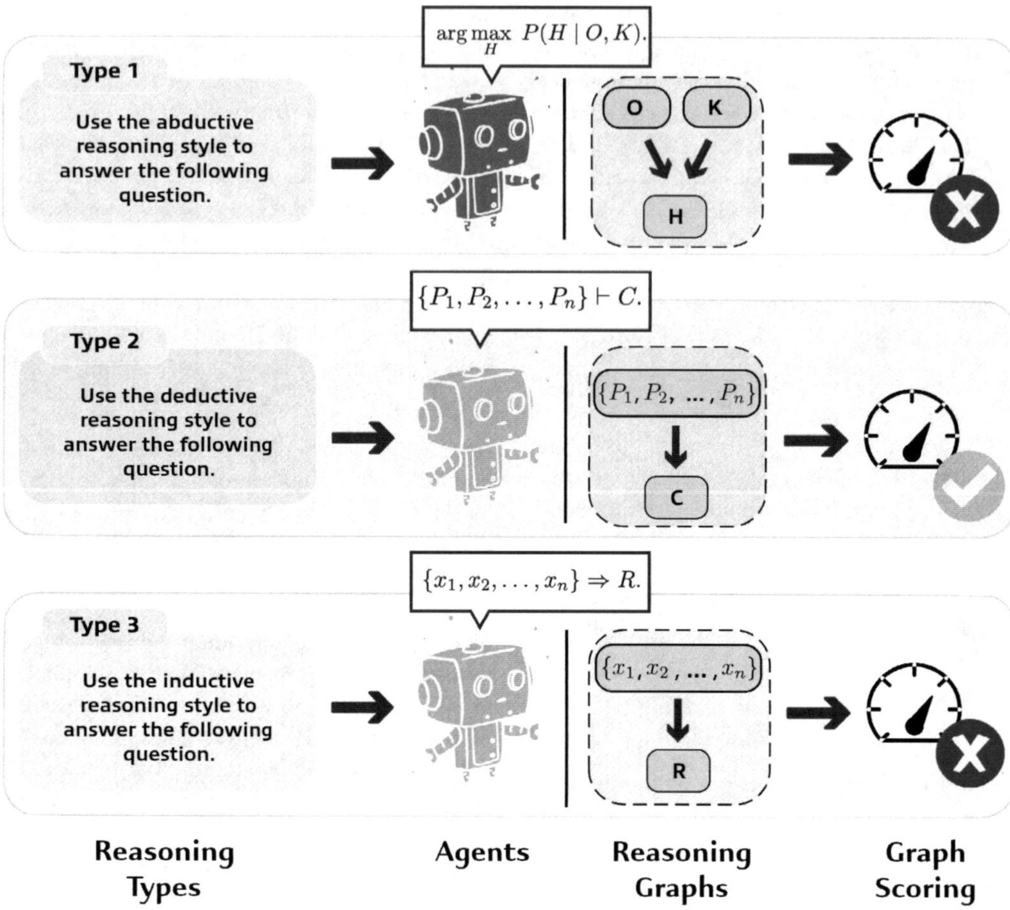

Figure 1: Overview of the Theorem-of-Thought (ToTh) reasoning pipeline. A question is independently processed by three agents, each using a distinct reasoning style: abductive (Type 1), deductive (Type 2), and inductive (Type 3). Each agent produces a structured reasoning graph, which is scored via Bayesian confidence propagation. Abduction infers the best hypothesis H given observations O and knowledge K (i.e., $\arg\max_H P(H \mid O, K)$); deduction derives a conclusion C from premises $\{P_1, \ldots, P_n\}$ (i.e., $\{P_i\} \vdash C$); induction generalizes from examples $\{x_1, \ldots, x_n\}$ to a rule R (i.e., $\{x_i\} \Rightarrow R$). The highest-scoring graph contributes its final node as the answer. ✓ and ✗ indicate whether a given agent's output was selected.

remaining opaque at inference time. While both families reflect growing interest in structured multi-step reasoning, they typically operate within monolithic or implicit architectures and do not support formal consistency checking. In contrast, ToTh instantiates distinct cognitive agents, integrates their outputs into an interpretable graph, and explicitly verifies reasoning coherence through NLI-guided Bayesian inference—enabling modular, transparent, and verifiable reasoning beyond the scope of existing methods.

Multi-Paradigm Reasoning Agents. Given a natural language question q, ToTh deploys three independent solver agents, each aligned with a distinct classical mode of inference: abductive, deductive, and inductive reasoning. These paradigms are formally defined as follows.

The abductive reasoning agent a_1 infers the most plausible hypothesis H given a set of observations O and background knowledge K, formalized as:

$$a_1 : \quad \arg\max_H P(H \mid O, K).$$

The deductive reasoning agent a_2 derives a conclusion C that logically follows from a set of premises $\{P_1, P_2, \ldots, P_n\}$, represented as:

$$a_2 : \quad \{P_1, P_2, \ldots, P_n\} \vdash C.$$

The inductive reasoning agent a_3 generalizes a rule

R from observed examples $\{x_1, x_2, \ldots, x_n\}$, expressed as:

$$a_3 : \quad \{x_1, x_2, \ldots, x_n\} \Rightarrow R.$$

Each agent $a_i \in \{a_1, a_2, a_3\}$ independently produces a reasoning trace

$$\mathbf{r}^{(i)} = \left[r_1^{(i)}, r_2^{(i)}, \ldots, r_{s_i}^{(i)}\right],$$

where $r_j^{(i)}$ denotes the j-th step in the agent's reasoning process.

Formal Reasoning Graph Construction. Each reasoning trace $\mathbf{r}^{(i)}$ is transformed into a directed graph $G^{(i)} = (V^{(i)}, E^{(i)})$, where $V^{(i)}$ denotes the set of nodes representing individual reasoning steps, and $E^{(i)}$ represents directed edges encoding inferential relationships between those steps. Edges $(v_u \rightarrow v_v) \in E^{(i)}$ are inferred using a pretrained NLI model, which assesses the semantic relationship between reasoning steps. Each edge is annotated with a trust score $\theta_{uv} \in [0, 1]$ based on the predicted label:

$$\theta_{uv} = \begin{cases} 0.95 & \text{if entailment} \\ 0.60 & \text{if neutral} \\ 0.10 & \text{if contradiction} \end{cases}$$

These scores quantify the strength of logical entailment between intermediate steps, providing a calibrated basis for probabilistic reasoning in the subsequent belief propagation stage.

Bayesian Confidence Propagation. To model belief flow across the graph, belief values are propagated using a Bayesian update rule, adapted from classical formulations of belief propagation in probabilistic graphical models (Pearl, 1988).

Each node $v \in V$ is initialized with a prior confidence $P(v) = 0.5$, reflecting maximum uncertainty. For a node v_c with a single parent v_p and associated trust score θ_{pc}, the updated belief is computed using a Bayesian update rule:

$$P(v_c) = \frac{P(v_p) \cdot \theta_{pc}}{P(v_p) \cdot \theta_{pc} + (1 - P(v_p)) \cdot (1 - \theta_{pc})}.$$

In the case of multiple parents $\{v_{p_1}, \ldots, v_{p_m}\}$, the belief for v_c is computed as the average of individual updates from each parent:

$$P(v_c) = \frac{1}{m} \sum_{j=1}^{m} f(P(v_{p_j}), \theta_{p_j c})$$

$$f(p, \theta) = \frac{p \cdot \theta}{p \cdot \theta + (1 - p)(1 - \theta)}.$$

This recursive formulation propagates confidence through the graph, amplifying agreement across consistent reasoning paths while attenuating belief when upstream uncertainty or contradiction is detected.

Graph Scoring. Each reasoning graph $G^{(i)}$ is evaluated based on a trade-off between average node confidence and logical uncertainty. We prioritize graphs that are both confident (high belief) and low in uncertainty (low entropy). The mean confidence is computed as

$$\mu^{(i)} = \frac{1}{|V^{(i)}|} \sum_{v \in V^{(i)}} P(v),$$

and the normalized binary entropy is given by

$$H^{(i)} = -\frac{1}{|V^{(i)}|} \sum_{v \in V^{(i)}} h(P(v))$$

$$h(p) = p \log p + (1 - p) \log(1 - p) .$$

The final score combines both terms:

$$\text{Score}(G^{(i)}) = \mu^{(i)} - H^{(i)}.$$

The reasoning graph with the highest score is selected as the final candidate:

$$G^* = \arg\max_i \text{Score}(G^{(i)}).$$

Answer Extraction. The final answer is extracted from the terminal node of the selected graph G^*, corresponding to the last step in the associated reasoning trace.

Theoretical Complexity. Let $k = 3$ denote the number of reasoning agents, and s the number of reasoning steps generated per agent. The ToTh framework involves three main stages of computation: trust estimation, belief propagation, and graph scoring. During trust estimation, each agent produces a sequence of reasoning steps, and an NLI model is applied to each adjacent pair to evaluate the strength of logical connection. Since each trace contains at most $s - 1$ such pairs, the total number of NLI evaluations across all agents is $\mathcal{O}(k \cdot s)$. In the belief propagation stage, each node in the constructed reasoning graphs is visited exactly once in topological order, and its posterior confidence is updated based on incoming trust scores using a Bayesian update rule, resulting in $\mathcal{O}(k \cdot s)$ total updates. Finally, graph scoring involves computing the average confidence and entropy over all nodes in each graph, which also requires $\mathcal{O}(k \cdot s)$ time. Therefore, the end-to-end complexity of the ToTh pipeline is $\mathcal{O}(k \cdot s)$, linear in both the number of agents and the number of reasoning steps per agent.

This makes ToTh substantially more efficient than sampling-based methods such as Self-Consistency or CoT-Decoding, which require $\mathcal{O}(n)$ decoding passes, where n is the number of sampled reasoning chains. In contrast, ToTh executes a single, structured reasoning pass per agent, followed by lightweight verification and scoring, offering a more scalable and interpretable alternative to stochastic decoding.

4 Experiments

Data. ToTh was evaluated on two representative reasoning benchmarks. MULTIARITH (Roy et al., 2015) targets compositional numerical inference through multi-step arithmetic word problems. WEBOFLIES (Suzgun et al., 2023), part of the BIG-BENCH-HARD suite, involves determining truth values among logically entangled symbolic statements. These datasets are known to challenge LLMs under direct prompting (Allen-Zhu and Li, 2025), making them suitable for testing structured reasoning capabilities.

Models. Three publicly available LLMs were selected to provide diversity in scale, alignment, and architecture: (1) MISTRAL-7B (Jiang et al., 2023)[1], a general-purpose decoder model with efficient scaling; (2) DEEPSEEK-7B (DeepSeek-AI et al., 2025)[2], an instruction-tuned model optimized for multi-turn reasoning and alignment; and (3) PHI-3.5 MINI (Abdin et al., 2024)[3], a lightweight model designed for educational, low-cost reasoning tasks. This selection spans compact inference-efficient models to instruction-aligned reasoning-focused systems.

Baselines. ToTh was compared with three strong baselines: CoT (Wei et al., 2022), Self-Consistency (Wang et al., 2023), and CoT-Decoding (Wang and Zhou, 2024). CoT prompts the model to generate intermediate reasoning steps before answering. Self-Consistency improves robustness by sampling $n = 20$ completions and selecting the most frequent answer. CoT-Decoding eliminates explicit prompting by using diverse decoding paths to stimulate latent reasoning behaviors.

Experimental Setup. All models were evaluated in their released form without fine-tuning. Decoding was performed with temperature 0.7 and a maximum output length of 526 tokens. RoBERTa-MNLI[4] was used for scoring reasoning coherence, consistent with prior work on NLI-based output validation (Farquhar et al., 2024). Inputs were uniformly formatted as "Q: [question] \n A:" across all methods for consistency with baselines (Wang and Zhou, 2024).

To direct reasoning behavior, the following instruction was prepended to each input, with the appropriate `{style}` keyword for each agent:

```
Use the {style} reasoning style
to answer the following question.
Follow these instructions
carefully:

• Break the problem into clear,
  numbered reasoning steps
  using {style}.
• Reference any known
  principles, patterns, or
  assumptions involved.
• Arrive at a final answer
  that directly responds to the
  question.
```

All experiments used a single decoding pass per input. Random seeds were fixed, and decoding settings were held constant for reproducibility.

5 Results

5.1 Main Experimental Results

Results are reported as answer accuracy (%) and summarized in Figure 2.

Performance Across Models. ToTh consistently outperforms all baseline methods on both tasks when evaluated with MISTRAL-7B and DEEPSEEK-7B, demonstrating clear gains in reasoning accuracy. On PHI-3.5 MINI, although CoT-Decoding marginally surpasses ToTh on certain

[1]https://huggingface.co/mistralai/Mistral-7B-Instruct-v0.3

[2]https://huggingface.co/deepseek-ai/deepseek-llm-7b-chat

[3]https://huggingface.co/microsoft/Phi-3.5-mini-instruct

[4]https://huggingface.co/FacebookAI/roberta-large-mnli

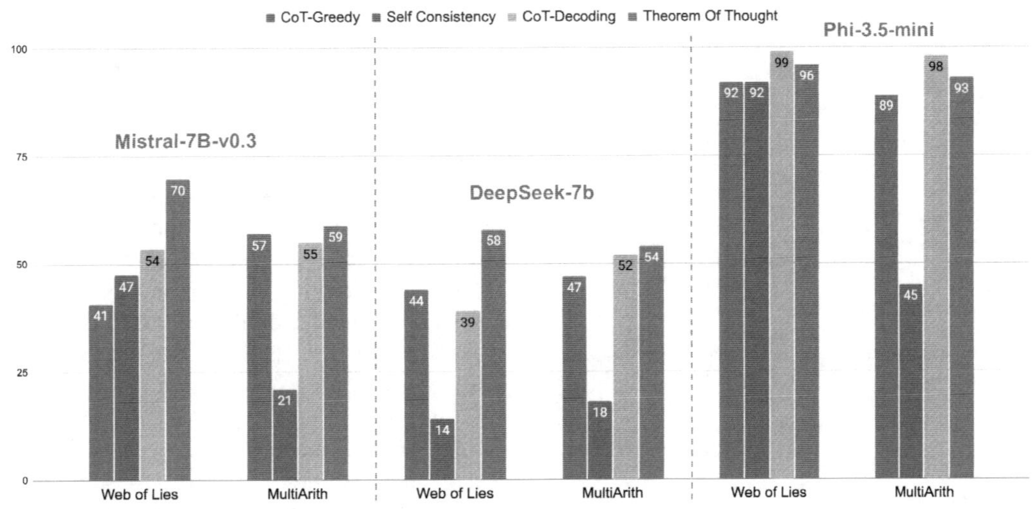

Figure 2: Accuracy (%) comparison across reasoning pipelines on two benchmark tasks (WEBOFLIES and MULTIARITH) using three open-source language models: MISTRAL-7B-V0.3, DEEPSEEK-7B, and Phi-3.5-mini. Each group of bars corresponds to a different reasoning method: CoT-Greedy (blue), Self-Consistency (red), CoT-Decoding (yellow), and our proposed Theorem-of-Thought (green).

instances, ToTh maintains consistently strong performance across both symbolic and numerical tasks. For example, on the WEBOFLIES dataset, ToTh improves over CoT-Greedy by 29% and 14% on MISTRAL-7B and DEEPSEEK-7B, respectively, and remains within 3% of the top-performing method on PHI-3.5 MINI. These results highlight ToTh's robustness and generalization across models of varying scale and alignment.

Comparison with CoT-Decoding. While CoT-Decoding performs strongly on Phi-3.5-mini, achieving near-perfect scores on WEBOFLIES (99%), ToTh achieves comparable or slightly lower performance (96%) while maintaining higher consistency across models. For example, on the MULTIARITH dataset, ToTh surpasses CoT-Decoding by 4–5 points on both MISTRAL-7B and DEEPSEEK-7B, indicating superior generalization in numerical reasoning.

Self-Consistency Under-performance. Surprisingly, Self-Consistency under-performs across all settings, particularly on symbolic tasks. For instance, it yields only 14% and 21% on WEBOFLIES and MULTIARITH with DEEPSEEK-7B and MISTRAL-7B, respectively. This suggests that majority-vote over stochastic generations fails to capture structured dependencies, especially in logic-heavy tasks.

Model Sensitivity. As expected, performance scales with model capability. Phi-3.5-mini achieves the highest absolute scores across all methods, reflecting its stronger alignment and training. However, ToTh's margin over baselines remains meaningful even at lower model scales, suggesting that the architecture contributes to reasoning robustness beyond just model size. While DEEPSEEK-7B is trained with reasoning capabilities in mind, its broader training objectives, including code generation and open-ended question answering, may diffuse its specialization in structured reasoning tasks. In contrast, Phi-3.5-mini benefits from a targeted curriculum focused on educational and step-by-step problem-solving, which likely accounts for its superior performance on both symbolic and mathematical benchmarks. Interestingly, MISTRAL-7B consistently outperforms DEEPSEEK-7B despite being similar in size. This may be attributed to Mistral's cleaner, reasoning-focused pretraining data and architecture-level optimizations, which enhance its ability to follow multi-step instructions and maintain logical coherence across token spans.

5.2 Robustness Under Reasoning Complexity

To evaluate the robustness of ToTh under increasing reasoning complexity, experiments were conducted using the MISTRAL-7B model on both symbolic and numerical tasks. Table 1 presents

	WEBOFLIES			MULTIARITH		
	3	4	5	d_0/l_3	d_0/l_4	d_2/l_3
CoT-G	41	32	19	57	26	14
SelfC	48	47	38	21	6	17
CoT-Dec	54	48	**46**	55	41	**24**
ToTh	**70**	**56**	<u>43</u>	**59**	**45**	<u>21</u>

Table 1: Accuracy (%) of MISTRAL-7B on symbolic (WEBOFLIES) and mathematical (MULTIARITH) reasoning tasks across increasing levels of difficulty. Columns 3–5 correspond to symbolic reasoning with 3, 4, and 5 interdependent statements, respectively. Columns d_0/l_3, d_0/l_4, and d_2/l_3 represent arithmetic reasoning problems categorized by depth and length: d denotes operation depth and l indicates sequence length. ToTh achieves the highest accuracy in 5 out of 6 settings and remains competitive even on the most complex instances, demonstrating consistent performance across symbolic and numerical domains. **Bold**: best performance; <u>Underlined</u>: second-best.

accuracy results stratified by problem difficulty: the number of interdependent statements (3–5) for WEBOFLIES, and operation depth/length combinations for MULTIARITH.

ToTh maintains strong performance across all difficulty levels, outperforming or closely matching leading baselines. In symbolic reasoning, ToTh achieves 43% accuracy on the most challenging setting (5 statements), significantly exceeding CoT-Greedy (19%) and Self-Consistency (38%), and closely approaching CoT-Decoding (46%). This trend persists across simpler instances, where ToTh attains the highest scores at 3 and 4 statements.

For numerical reasoning, ToTh delivers the strongest results at lower complexity levels—achieving state-of-the-art performance at d_0/l_3 (59%) and d_0/l_4 (45%)—and remains competitive even at higher complexity (d_2/l_3), with accuracy comparable to CoT-Decoding (21% vs. 24%). These findings highlight ToTh's capacity to generalize across task difficulty and suggest that its structured, multi-agent reasoning design offers a scalable advantage under increased inference load.

6 Conclusion and Future Work

This work presents Theorem-of-Thought (ToTh), a graph-based reasoning framework that integrates abductive, deductive, and inductive inference through a modular multi-agent design. Each agent generates structured reasoning traces, which are composed into formal graphs and verified using NLI-calibrated Bayesian confidence propagation. This approach supports both accurate prediction and interpretable, logically grounded reasoning. Empirical evaluations on symbolic and numerical benchmarks demonstrate that ToTh consistently outperforms strong prompting and decoding baselines, particularly in scenarios requiring structured logical inference.

ToTh introduces a new paradigm in reasoning with language models by treating inference as a verifiable, compositional process, rather than a monolithic generation task. Future research will explore dynamic agent routing based on input characteristics, inter-agent collaboration protocols, and adaptive trust estimation via fine-tuned and ensemble-based NLI models. Extending the framework to scientific hypothesis validation, law and policy reasoning, and multimodal domains such as visual question answering represents a promising direction for advancing general-purpose, verifiable reasoning in large language models.

Limitations

Fixed Reasoning Types. ToTh presumes a uniform decomposition into abductive, deductive, and inductive reasoning across all inputs. While this modularity improves interpretability, it imposes a fixed cognitive scaffold that may not align with tasks requiring hybrid or atypical inference patterns. For example, creative tasks or ambiguous prompts may benefit from dynamically blending reasoning types or emphasizing one over others. This rigidity can limit ToTh's adaptability and lead to suboptimal trace composition in such cases. Future work may explore data-driven and context-sensitive agent routing, allowing the framework to selectively instantiate and suppress reasoning paradigms based on input semantics.

Propagation Sensitivity. The Bayesian confidence propagation mechanism is sensitive to noise in low-confidence nodes, which may attenuate otherwise valid reasoning chains or distort belief estimates in deeper regions of the graph. This can occur in longer traces where errors in early reasoning steps propagate disproportionately, reducing the reliability of final predictions. Moreover, current propagation is uniform and unregularized, lacking robustness mechanisms against adversarial and inconsistent intermediate steps. Incorporating calibrated uncertainty modeling, edge dropout, and confidence smoothing—potentially informed by fine-grained entailment distributions—could enhance stability and mitigate the amplification of localized inconsistencies.

References

Samir Abdaljalil, Hasan Kurban, Parichit Sharma, Erchin Serpedin, and Rachad Atat. 2025. Sindex: Semantic inconsistency index for hallucination detection in llms. *Preprint*, arXiv:2503.05980.

Marah Abdin, Jyoti Aneja, Hany Awadalla, Ahmed Awadallah, Ammar Ahmad Awan, Nguyen Bach, Amit Bahree, Arash Bakhtiari, Jianmin Bao, Harkirat Behl, Alon Benhaim, Misha Bilenko, Johan Bjorck, Sébastien Bubeck, Martin Cai, Qin Cai, Vishrav Chaudhary, Dong Chen, Dongdong Chen, and 110 others. 2024. Phi-3 technical report: A highly capable language model locally on your phone. *Preprint*, arXiv:2404.14219.

Zeyuan Allen-Zhu and Yuanzhi Li. 2025. Physics of language models: Part 3.2, knowledge manipulation. In *Proceedings of the International Conference on Learning Representations (ICLR)*. ICLR 2025 Poster.

DeepSeek-AI, Daya Guo, Dejian Yang, Haowei Zhang, Junxiao Song, Ruoyu Zhang, Runxin Xu, Qihao Zhu, Shirong Ma, Peiyi Wang, Xiao Bi, Xiaokang Zhang, Xingkai Yu, Yu Wu, Z. F. Wu, Zhibin Gou, Zhihong Shao, Zhuoshu Li, Ziyi Gao, and 181 others. 2025. Deepseek-r1: Incentivizing reasoning capability in llms via reinforcement learning. *Preprint*, arXiv:2501.12948.

Shizhe Diao, Pengcheng Wang, Yong Lin, Rui Pan, Xiang Liu, and Tong Zhang. 2024. Active prompting with chain-of-thought for large language models. In *Proceedings of the 62nd Annual Meeting of the Association for Computational Linguistics (Volume 1: Long Papers)*, pages 1330–1350, Bangkok, Thailand. Association for Computational Linguistics.

Sebastian Farquhar, Jannik Kossen, Lorenz Kuhn, and Yarin Gal. 2024. Detecting hallucinations in large language models using semantic entropy. *Nature*, 630(8017):625–630. © 2024. The Author(s).

Albert Q. Jiang, Alexandre Sablayrolles, Arthur Mensch, Chris Bamford, Devendra Singh Chaplot, Diego de las Casas, Florian Bressand, Gianna Lengyel, Guillaume Lample, Lucile Saulnier, Lélio Renard Lavaud, Marie-Anne Lachaux, Pierre Stock, Teven Le Scao, Thibaut Lavril, Thomas Wang, Timothée Lacroix, and William El Sayed. 2023. Mistral 7b. *Preprint*, arXiv:2310.06825.

Huiyuan Lai and Malvina Nissim. 2024. mCoT: Multilingual instruction tuning for reasoning consistency in language models. In *Proceedings of the 62nd Annual Meeting of the Association for Computational Linguistics (Volume 1: Long Papers)*, pages 12012–12026, Bangkok, Thailand. Association for Computational Linguistics.

Alisa Liu, Xiaochuang Han, Yizhong Wang, Yulia Tsvetkov, Yejin Choi, and Noah A. Smith. 2024. Tuning language models by proxy. In *Proceedings of the Conference on Language Modeling (COLM)*.

Chaoqun Liu, Qin Chao, Wenxuan Zhang, Xiaobao Wu, Boyang Li, Anh Tuan Luu, and Lidong Bing. 2025. Zero-to-strong generalization: Eliciting strong capabilities of large language models iteratively without gold labels. In *Proceedings of the 31st International Conference on Computational Linguistics*, pages 3716–3731, Abu Dhabi, UAE. Association for Computational Linguistics.

Elita Lobo, Chirag Agarwal, and Himabindu Lakkaraju. 2025. On the impact of fine-tuning on chain-of-thought reasoning. In *Proceedings of the 2025 Conference of the Nations of the Americas Chapter of the Association for Computational Linguistics: Human Language Technologies (Volume 1: Long Papers)*, pages 11679–11698, Albuquerque, New Mexico. Association for Computational Linguistics.

Chitu Okoli. 2022. Inductive, abductive and deductive theorizing. *SSRN Electronic Journal*, Forthcoming.

Judea Pearl. 1988. *Probabilistic Reasoning in Intelligent Systems: Networks of Plausible Inference*. Morgan Kaufmann Publishers Inc., San Francisco, CA, USA.

Leonardo Ranaldi and Andre Freitas. 2024. Self-refine instruction-tuning for aligning reasoning in language models. In *Proceedings of the 2024 Conference on Empirical Methods in Natural Language Processing*, pages 2325–2347, Miami, Florida, USA. Association for Computational Linguistics.

Subhro Roy, Tim Vieira, and Dan Roth. 2015. Reasoning about quantities in natural language. *Transactions of the Association for Computational Linguistics*, 3:1–13.

Suzanna Sia, David Mueller, and Kevin Duh. 2024. Where does in-context learning happen in large language models? In *Proceedings of the 2024 Conference on Neural Information Processing Systems (NeurIPS)*. NeurIPS 2024 Poster.

Mirac Suzgun, Nathan Scales, Nathanael Schärli, Sebastian Gehrmann, Yi Tay, Hyung Won Chung, Aakanksha Chowdhery, Quoc Le, Ed Chi, Denny Zhou, and Jason Wei. 2023. Challenging BIG-bench tasks and whether chain-of-thought can solve them. In *Findings of the Association for Computational Linguistics: ACL 2023*, pages 13003–13051, Toronto, Canada. Association for Computational Linguistics.

Rosario Uceda Sosa, Karthikeyan Natesan Ramamurthy, Maria Chang, and Moninder Singh. 2024. Reasoning about concepts with llms: Inconsistencies abound. *Conference on Language Models (COLM)*. Published: 10 Jul 2024, Last Modified: 26 Aug 2024.

Qineng Wang, Zihao Wang, Ying Su, Hanghang Tong, and Yangqiu Song. 2024. Rethinking the bounds of LLM reasoning: Are multi-agent discussions the key? In *Proceedings of the 62nd Annual Meeting of the Association for Computational Linguistics (Volume 1: Long Papers)*, pages 6106–6131, Bangkok, Thailand. Association for Computational Linguistics.

Xuezhi Wang, Jason Wei, Dale Schuurmans, Quoc V. Le, Ed H. Chi, Sharan Narang, Aakanksha Chowdhery, and Denny Zhou. 2023. Self-consistency improves chain of thought reasoning in language models. In *The Eleventh International Conference on Learning Representations, ICLR 2023, Kigali, Rwanda, May 1-5, 2023*. OpenReview.net.

Xuezhi Wang and Denny Zhou. 2024. Chain-of-thought reasoning without prompting. In *Proceedings of the 2024 Conference on Neural Information Processing Systems (NeurIPS)*. NeurIPS 2024 Poster.

Jason Wei, Xuezhi Wang, Dale Schuurmans, Maarten Bosma, Brian Ichter, Fei Xia, Ed H. Chi, Quoc V. Le, and Denny Zhou. 2022. Chain-of-thought prompting elicits reasoning in large language models. In *Proceedings of the 36th International Conference on Neural Information Processing Systems*, NIPS '22, Red Hook, NY, USA. Curran Associates Inc.

Shunyu Yao, Dian Yu, Jeffrey Zhao, Izhak Shafran, Thomas L. Griffiths, Yuan Cao, and Karthik Narasimhan. 2023. Tree of thoughts: deliberate problem solving with large language models. In *Proceedings of the 37th International Conference on Neural Information Processing Systems*, NIPS '23, Red Hook, NY, USA. Curran Associates Inc.

Yao Yao, Zuchao Li, and Hai Zhao. 2024. GoT: Effective graph-of-thought reasoning in language models. In *Findings of the Association for Computational Linguistics: NAACL 2024*, pages 2901–2921, Mexico City, Mexico. Association for Computational Linguistics.

Shengyu Zhang, Linfeng Dong, Xiaoya Li, Sen Zhang, Xiaofei Sun, Shuhe Wang, Jiwei Li, Runyi Hu, Tianwei Zhang, Fei Wu, and Guoyin Wang. 2024. Instruction tuning for large language models: A survey. *Preprint*, arXiv:2308.10792.

Zhuosheng Zhang, Aston Zhang, Mu Li, and Alex Smola. 2023. Automatic chain of thought prompting in large language models. In *Proceedings of International Conference on Learning Representations (ICLR)*. Poster.

Reasoning or Memorization? Investigating LLMs' Capability in Restoring Chinese Internet Homophones

Jianfei Ma* and **Zhaoxin Feng*** and **Emmanuele Chersoni**
and **Huacheng Song** and **Zheng Chen**
Chinese and Bilingual Studies, The Hong Kong Polytechnic University
Computer Science and Engineering, Hong Kong University of Science and Technology
{jian-fei.ma,zhaoxinbetty.feng,huacheng.song}@connect.polyu.hk,
emmanuele.chersoni@polyu.edu.hk,
zchenin@connect.ust.hk

Abstract

Chinese homophones, prevalent in Internet culture, introduce rich linguistic twists to challenging language models. While native speakers disambiguate them through phonological reasoning and contextual understanding, the extent to which LLMs can effectively handle this task remains unclear, as does whether they rely on similar reasoning processes or merely memorize homophone-original word pairs in training.

In this paper, we propose **HomoP-CN**, the first Chinese Internet homophones dataset including systematic perturbations testing for evaluating LLMs' homophone restoration capabilities. With the benchmark, we investigated the influence of semantic, phonological, and graphemic features on LLMs' restoration accuracy, measured the memorization reliance levels of each model during restoration through consistency ratios under controlled perturbations, and assessed the effectiveness of various prompting strategies, including contextual cues, *pinyin* augmentation, few-shot learning, and thought-chain [1].

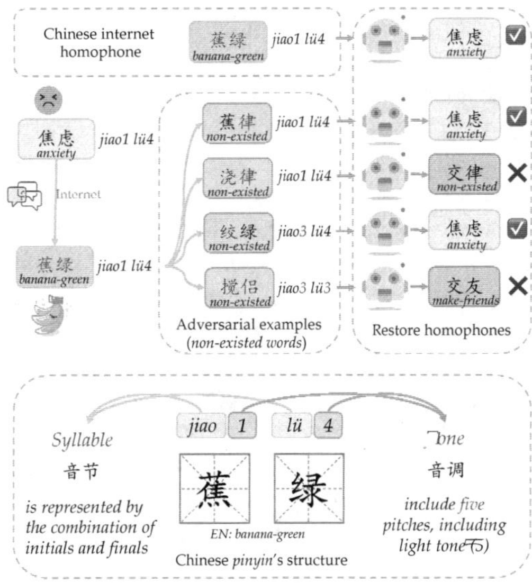

Figure 1: The upper figure illustrates an example of the homophonic word and its different adversarial perturbations in **HomoP-CN** dataset. The bottom figure demonstrates the structure of Chinese *pinyin*, which encompasses a syllable and a tone.

1 Introduction

Homophonic wordplay in Chinese Internet culture creatively utilizes phonological similarities between characters to construct new words and layered semantic meanings (Zhang et al., 2019). For example, the homophone "蕉绿" (*jiao1 lü4*, "banana-green") replaces the original word "焦虑" (*jiao1 lü4*, "anxiety"), reconfiguring a negative emotion into a playful and lighthearted expression. Unlike English puns, which rely on intralingual homophony (e.g., "a good pun is its own reword/reward") (Xu et al., 2024), Chinese homophonic wordplay creatively substitutes characters with similar pronunciations within the logographic writing system.

Recent advances in natural language processing (NLP), particularly through large language models (LLMs), have demonstrated substantial progress in disambiguating English homophones (Proietti et al., 2024; Xu et al., 2024; Mizrahi et al., 2024). However, due to the high homophone density in Chinese *pinyin*(e.g., *shi4* mapping to dozens of characters such as 是/事/市) and tonal complexity (identical syllables with different tones convey distinct meanings, e.g., *ma1*妈/*ma2*马/*ma3*码/*ma4*骂), LLMs encounter greater challenges in comprehending Chinese homophones than English.

Previous research has explored Chinese homophones in NLP tasks such as spelling correction (Liu et al., 2025, 2024; Li et al., 2024; Baluja, 2025), offensive language detection (Xiao et al., 2024), and humor generation (Xu, 2024). Nev-

* represents these authors contributed equally to this work.
[1] Our code and data are released at: https://github.com/sdmjf/Chinese_homophone_restoration_LLM.

Proceedings of the 3rd Workshop on Towards Knowledgeable Foundation Models (KnowFM), pages 120–139
August 1, 2025 ©2025 Association for Computational Linguistics

ertheless, there is no systematic study on LLMs' ability to understand and restore Chinese homophones, which is crucial for practical applications such as improving LLMs' ability to understand social media text and identifying offensive content. For instance, Chinese netizens may replace "太贱 (too mean)" with the same pronunciation "肽键 (peptide bond)" to use a non-offensive biological term conveying discriminatory and offensive content (Xiao et al., 2024).

It has been suggested that native Chinese speakers leverage their perceptual systems to retrieve original words from homophonic variants through phonological similarity-based reasoning and contextual information understanding (Samuel, 1981; Davis et al., 2005; Banfi and Arcodia, 2013; Mehta and Luck, 2020). Building upon this human cognitive paradigm, we propose the following research question: *How do LLMs perform in homophone restoration? Is this capability of LLMs driven by human-like reasoning through phonological similarity, or simply stem from memorization of homophone-original word pairs in pretraining? Additionally, can strategies like contextual information or providing pinyin*[2] *to enrich prompts enhance LLM performance in restoration?*

In this work, we comprehensively explored LLMs' effectiveness and enhancement in Chinese Internet homophone restoration by utilizing our **HomoP-CN** dataset. First, we analyzed the restoration capacity of LLMs by considering the differences between the original words and the homophones from semantic, phonological, and graphemic perspectives. Second, drawing inspiration from Xie et al. (2024), we designed a set of adversarial variations as perturbations to quantify the extent of memorization, as shown in Figure 1. Finally, we delved into the role of different prompting strategies, including context cues, *pinyin*-augmentation, few-shot, Chain-of-Thought (CoT) (Kojima et al., 2022), Memory-of-Thought (MoT) (Li and Qiu, 2023) in this task.

Our results demonstrate that LLMs exhibit substantial variation in restoring Chinese Internet homophones, with model scale emerging as a critical factor: larger models achieve reasoning-based restoration while smaller ones depend predominantly on memorization. This performance gap is further modulated by semantic, phonological, and graphemic disparities between original words and their homophone counterparts, which systematically affect both restoration accuracy and memorization dependence. While contextual cues, few-shot learning, and thought-chain strategies (CoT/MoT) prove effective for performance enhancement, *pinyin* augmentation shows limited utility. These findings provide valuable insights into LLMs' robustness in handling intralingual and user-generated content in Internet contexts.

2 Related work

2.1 Chinese Homophones

English homophones are words with distinct meanings that share the same pronunciation but differ in spelling. (HarperCollins, 2023). Similarly, in Chinese, homophones refer to a linguistic phenomenon where different words or phrases have similar or identical pronunciations (i.e., sharing the same or similar *pinyin*) but are represented by different Chinese characters[3]. On the Internet, homophones are frequently employed to substitute for or allude to the meanings of certain original words, often serving humorous or euphemistic purposes in communication (Xiao et al., 2024; Xu, 2024).

Current research on the ability of LLMs to comprehend Chinese homophones remains limited and is scattered across various NLP tasks. In spelling correction, LLMs face bottlenecks in coordinating phonological, graphemic, and semantic features when distinguishing between homophones (Liu et al., 2025, 2024; Li et al., 2024). For offensive language detection, LLMs demonstrate reduced effectiveness in identifying homophone-disguised toxic content, revealing vulnerabilities in understanding when confronted with phonological interference (Xiao et al., 2024). Additionally, LLMs exhibit challenges in semantic reasoning for humor generation involving homophones (Xu, 2024).

2.2 Language Perturbation

Researchers have proposed a wide range of perturbation techniques to explore the vulnerabilities of NLP models in adversarial scenarios, particularly

[2] *Pinyin*, a Latin-based phonetic notation system for Chinese, represents character pronunciation through syllables and tones shown in Figure 1.

[3] Chinese internet homophones include both perfect homophones and near-homophones (paronyms). Many of these words do not actually exist in standard Chinese, like "蕉绿" ("banana-green"). This encompasses: 1) Characters with identical pronunciation (same syllable + tone); 2) Characters with the same syllable but different tones; 3) Similar-sounding syllables where some phonetic feature differs (e.g., z/zh distinction between apical anterior and posterior consonants, ignoring tone differences).

through replacements or insertions at the character, word, and sentence levels (Alzantot et al., 2018; Jin et al., 2020; Ribeiro et al., 2020; Zhang et al., 2020; Garg and Ramakrishnan, 2020).

Recent studies have explored Chinese adversarial attacks through various language-specific perturbations, such as synonym substitution (Su et al., 2022), phonological and glyph swaps (Liu et al., 2023; Wang et al., 2024), and emoji replacement (Xiao et al., 2024). However, no studies have yet focused on the lexical perturbations for the Chinese homophone restoration task. Our work addresses this gap by introducing the **HomoP-CN** dataset, which provides different adversarial examples tailored to the unique characteristics of Chinese homophones.

2.3 Memorization in LLMs

The memorization capabilities of LLMs have been extensively studied across multiple domains, including copyright (Karamolegkou et al., 2023; Wei et al., 2024), logical reasoning (Xie et al., 2024), and performance on knowledge-intensive tasks (Hartmann et al., 2023). Previous studies have demonstrated that LLMs are capable of memorizing portions of their training data (Tirumala et al., 2022; Carlini et al., 2022).

In this paper, we focus on quantifying the extent of memorization in LLMs when performing the homophone restoration task. Inspired by Xie et al. (2024), we designed a set of adversarial variations to quantify the extent of memorization within a controlled setting: significantly worse performance on variants versus original homophones and suggests greater reliance on memorization[4].

3 Methodology

3.1 Problem Definition

Let $D = \{(X, Y)\}$ denote a dataset where each consists of a homophone X and the corresponding original word Y. The task of LLM is to analyze X and select a word $\hat{Y}$ which is most likely to be the original word Y. Formally, the output can be represented as:

$$\hat{Y} \sim \pi_\theta(X), \quad (1)$$

The goal of LLMs is to ensure $\hat{Y} = Y$, meaning that the LLMs correctly restore the target word. In this study, we use accuracy to represent the model's performance in the task of restoring homophones.

3.2 Dataset Construction

The **HomoP-CN** dataset involves extracting homophonic words from mainstream Chinese social media platforms as the control set, followed by a multi-faceted process of categorization and conversion. This enables a systematic comparison of the performance of LLMs across various dimensions and factors. Further details are outlined below.

3.2.1 Data Collection and Categorization

Given the prevalence of homophones particularly in creative and flexible online contexts, this study sourced target homophones from two mainstream Chinese social media platforms, namely, Weibo and Tieba[5]. After reviewing a random collection of user-generated posts and comments from these platforms first, spanning the period from 2010 to 2025 (before the data cutoff in March), a total of 365 highly frequent and representative homophonic words were filtered out by three native Chinese speakers with consensus, who also provided the original word and *pinyin* for each homophone. Besides, to explore the potential impacts of contexts, we augmented the homophones into sentences with sufficient contextual information by which humans can accurately infer their original words. All context sentences were generated by the DeepSeek-V3 model (DeepSeek-AI, 2024) with the prompts shown in Appendix A.4 and then validated by three native speakers (Appendix A.2).

Upon this preliminary dataset, we further grouped all homophones in line with three distinct taxonomies for fine-grained evaluation of LLMs' performance concerning their different semantic, phonological, and graphemic properties. The semantic categorizations were completed by three native speakers based on instruction guidance (Appendix A.2), and those at phonological and graphemic aspects were sorted through automated annotated methods by comparing the distinction in the form of the *pinyin* and characters in homophones and their origins (Appendix A.3). Examples are displayed in Figure 2.

[4]Borrowing intuition from human behavior: Students preparing for exams might not fully grasp underlying principles due to constraints. Yet, they can answer memorized exact questions correctly. A key trait of such memorization is high accuracy on identical questions but poor performance on slightly modified, similarly difficult ones.

[5]Weibo, managed by Sina company, is a popular Chinese microblogging platform similar to Twitter and Tieba, hosted by Baidu, is a large online community forum where users can engage in topic-based discussions, akin to Reddit.

Original word	Homophone	Original word pinyin	Homophone pinyin	Semantics	Phonology	Graphemics	Variant 1	Variant 2	Variant 3	Variant 4
什么 *Everything*	神马 *God-horse*	*shen2 me5*	*shen2 ma3*	1	4	3	神玛 *shen2ma3*	什玛 *shen2ma3*	神吗 *shen2ma1*	审妈 *shen3ma1*
Context sentence: <u>神马</u>都是浮云。*(Everything's just a puff piece.)*										
悲剧 *Tragedies*	杯具 *Cup*	*bei1 ju4*	*bei1 ju4*	2	1	3	碑具 *bei1ju4*	碑据 *bei1ju4*	贝具 *bei4ju4*	倍菊 *bei4ju2*
Context sentence: <u>杯具</u>总是让人心情沉重。*(Tragedies always make people feel heavy-hearted.)*										
压力 *Pressure*	鸭梨 *Ya pear*	*ya1 li4*	*ya1 li2*	2	2	3	鸭黎 *ya1li2*	鸦黎 *ya1li2*	鸭莉 *ya1li4*	讶利 *ya4li4*
Context sentence: <u>鸭梨</u>好大，我想去散步放松一下。*(I'm under so much pressure, and I want to go for a walk to relax.)*										

Figure 2: Data examples from our dataset. The numbers in the *Semantics*, *Phonology*, and *Graphemics* columns indicate the categories of homophones based on their differences from the original words in these three aspects, while *Variants* are adversarial perturbations. For detailed descriptions, refer to Section 3.2.

- **Semantic taxonomy** The first taxonomy labeled target homophones into two groups based on their semantic features on word level: 1) those are existing words and have meaning on their own and 2) those are pseudo words that are inherently meaningless.
- **Phonological taxonomy** Based on the phonological features of homophones, they were further grouped into: 1) homophones sharing matching syllables; 2) those with matching syllables but differing tones; 3) those with matching tones but differing syllables; and 4) those with differing syllables and tones, when compared to their corresponding original words.
- **Graphemic taxonomy** Refer to the difference in typing form and length of characters, all homophones were categorized into three groups, covering: 1) homophones with fewer characters (partially same or completely different) than their corresponding original words; 2) homophones sharing the same length and partially same characters with their origins; and 3) homophones with the same length but completely different characters compared to corresponding original words[6].

3.3 Task Formulation

This section delineates the design of progressive tasks aimed at evaluating the capabilities of LLMs in homophone restoration and uncovering the underlying patterns governing their performance. Considering the results from the ablation study in Appendix B.1, we selected Chinese as the language of prompts, whose detailed examples are presented in Appendix B.2.

Restoring Capability Under Zero-shot

To investigate whether popular LLMs can identify the profound relationships between pronunciations and meanings for Chinese characters in homophones, and the extent to which they can do so, we provided basic zero-shot prompts to each LLM, instructing them to restore the original forms from specific homophones. This task was conducted under three setups introduced in Section 3.2.1 to examine whether the semantic, phonological, and graphemic properties of homophones pose different challenges to LLMs and whether LLMs exhibit varying sensitivity to these properties. The metric of accuracy was employed to quantify performance by calculating the percentage of correct answers.

Patterns Behind Homophone Restoration

What follows the assessment of global restoration performance among LLMs is whether their capabilities are predominantly grounded on memorization of training data or reasoning derived from phonological similarity. To pursue this, we employed four adversarial variants as described in Section 3.4 with basic zero-shot prompts for perturbation. Besides, we define the Consistency Ratio (*CR*) to measure how robustly a model restores homophone variants. For each correctly restored case from basic homophones, we count how many of its four variants are also correctly returned to the original form, then average this count across the number of all restored cases from basic homophones. The final *CR* score (between 0 and 1) is obtained by normalizing this average against the maximum possible correct variants per homophone. Higher *CR* indicates less reliance on memorization and more on reasoning. Formally, *CR* can be represented as:

[6]Since each Chinese character covers a single syllable, the difference in character numbers between a homophone and its origin reflects elision or assimilation in their pronunciation.

Model	*Homophone*	*Variant1*	*Variant2*	*Variant3*	*Variant4*	*Variants Avg*
Llama3.1-8B	0.052	<u>0.025</u>	**0.030**	0.022	0.011	0.022
Qwen2.5-7B	0.216	**0.099**	0.060	<u>0.082</u>	0.019	0.065
OpenAI o3-mini	0.622	**0.422**	0.337	<u>0.386</u>	0.345	0.373
Deepseek-R1	0.833	**0.636**	0.515	<u>0.537</u>	0.370	0.514

Table 1: Results of the basic prompt experiments, including the accuracy of homophones, that of four types of adversarial variants, and the average value of variants. The best results among the variants are **bolded**, and the second-best results are <u>underlined</u>.

$$CR = \frac{1}{|D_C|} \sum_{X \in D_C} \left(\frac{1}{4} \sum_{i=1}^{4} \mathbb{I}[f(X_i') = Y_i'] \right) \quad (2)$$

Where $D_C = X \in D \mid f(X) = Y$ (set of successfully restored homophones), X_i' denotes the i-th variant of homophone X, Y_i' is the correct orginal word for variant X_i', and $\mathbb{I}[\cdot]$ is the indicator function.

Impacts of Context Cues and Other Strategies

In our final exploration, we investigate the impacts of several related knowledge and prompt strategies on LLMs' performance in homophone restoration. It is widely acknowledged that humans typically infer the meanings of homophones based on contextual cues at first glance (Xu et al., 2024). Hence, we first examine the effects of contextual information. The context sentences created in Section 3.2.1 were integrated into the basic zero-shot prompts, and the results were compared with those from the basic prompt. Improved performance indicates that contextual information positively contributes to homophone restoration, while degraded performance suggests the opposite.

Building on this exploration, we further investigate the impact of additional strategies, including: 1) Few-shot prompts: Provide examples to guide the model; 2) *Pinyin* annotations: Supply *pinyin* for sentences and homophones; 3) CoT: Encourage step-by-step reasoning; and 4) MoT: Leverage memory-enhanced reasoning, to provide comprehensive insights to this task.

3.4 Data Perturbation

To examine the underlying patterns of LLMs in restoring homophones, we created adversarial scenarios against the control homophones by introducing semantic, phonological, and graphemic perturbations through character modifications, as illustrated in Figure 1 and Figure 2.

We utilized a well-compiled dictionary[7] including 2,715 common Chinese characters with *pinyin* spellings, to enable automatic character retrieval and replacements. Using this dictionary, we introduced four types of adversarial variants with incremental distances away from the control homophones by replacing one character (or all characters) of the control homophone with a different character (or some different characters) sharing the same *pinyin* or the same syllables but differing in tones (Appendix A.5).

3.5 Model Selection

Models applied in current study include Qwen 2.5-7B (Qwen et al., 2025), Llama 3.1-8B (Grattafiori et al., 2024), OpenAI o3-mini[8] and Deepseek-R1 (DeepSeek-AI et al., 2025). Among these, the former two are open-sourced, while the latter two are not. These models rank at the top of current leaderboards and demonstrate remarkable performance across a diverse set of tasks, including reasoning, by leveraging extensive memorization capabilities developed during the pre-training phase (Zhang et al., 2024; Prabhakar et al., 2024). For all models, the temperature is set to 0, and other configurations are applied as default.

4 Results and Analyses

4.1 *Can LLMs Restore Chinese Internet Homophones to Original Words?*

As shown in Table 1, LLMs show significantly distinct performance in restoring homophones. Llama 3.1 and Qwen 2.5 show an overall weak performance. OpenAI o3-mini demonstrates superiority by outperforming the first two models, and Deepseek-R1 achieves the best performance with outstanding accuracy, showcasing its robustness correspondingly. The performance differences may

[7] https://github.com/5hwb/sort-hanzi-in-pinyin-order/

[8] https://openai.com/index/openai-o3-mini/

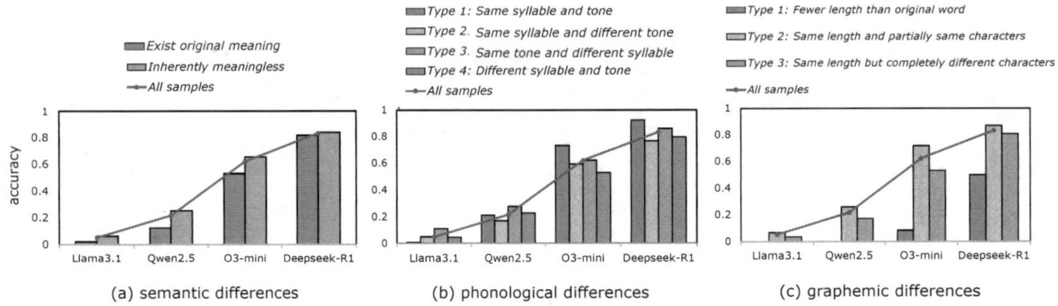

Figure 3: The impact of semantic, phonological, and graphemic disparities between homophones and their original words on LLMs' homophone restoration performance.

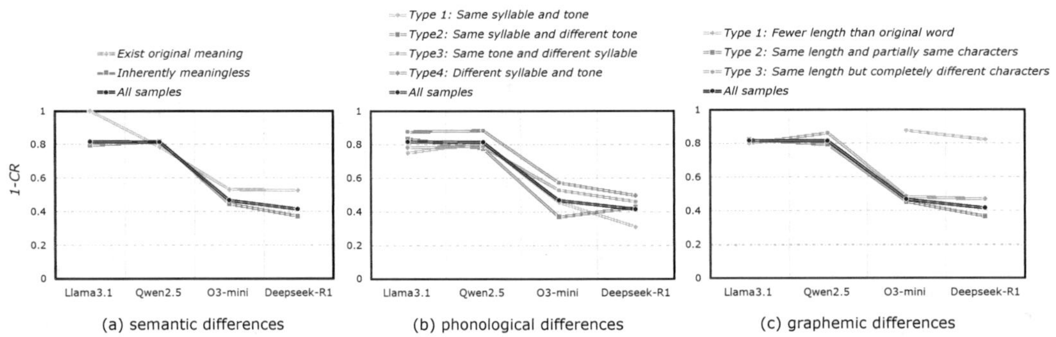

Figure 4: The influence of semantic, phonological, and graphemic differences between homophones and original words on the level of memorization dependence during homophone restoration. A higher (1-*CR*) value on the y-axis indicates greater reliance on memorization by LLMs.

stem from variations in training data and model size: Deepseek-R1 used more extensive Chinese corpora in training, outperforming the other models with the same scale. OpenAI o3-mini and Deepseek-R1, with larger parameter sizes and stronger inference capabilities, excel in this complex linguistic task than smaller models.

Also, we systematically categorized homophones based on differences between homophones and original words in terms of semantics, phonology, and graphemics to explore how these characteristics influence LLMs' ability to restore homophones. The results are shown in Figure 3.

For the semantic dimension, homophones were divided into two categories: those whose original word-level meanings exist and those that do not exist. The results in Figure 3 (a) reveal that all LLMs exhibit stronger restoration capabilities for homophones without existing meanings, suggesting that the inherent semantics in homophones may interfere with restoration, especially for small models.

For phonological differences, Figure 3 (b) shows significant accuracy differences in LLMs' homophone restoration across four types. Type 1 (consistent syllables+tones) outperformed others, except in large-parameter LLMs. Type 3 (same tone+different syllables) worked well in small models. Both types highlight the essentials of pinyin syllables and tones in homophone restoration. However, when comparing the performance of Type 2 and Type 3 to Type 1, it is emphasized that the same tone can benefit more than syllables in large models. Small models are highly dependent on the same tone, and syllables even negatively affect the accurate prediction of original words.

For the graphemics dimension, Figure 3(c) shows that Llama 3.1 and Qwen 2.5 completely fail to restore Type 1 homophones (shorter characters replacing original words, e.g., "酱紫" replaces "这样子", meaning "like this"). Even large models perform worst on Type 1 homophones, indicating that LLMs struggle most with pronunciation elision. In contrast, LLMs excel at Type 2 and 3 homophones, which have the same length with partial or total character substitutions, highlighting their sensitivity to word length and subtle surface graphemic changes.

4.2 *Reasoning or Memorization?*

To determine whether LLMs restore Chinese homophones primarily through memory or reasoning, we conducted experiments using four types of adversarial variants. Results are presented in Figure 4:

Deepseek-R1 and OpenAI o3-mini exhibit significantly less reliance on memorization compared to the other two models, likely attributable to their much larger scale and enhanced reasoning capabilities. Notably, Llama 3.1 demonstrates near-total reliance on memorization when the homophone carries their inherent semantic meanings.

Figures 4 (a) and (b) demonstrate that LLMs exhibit increased reliance on memorization under two conditions: 1) when homophones retain original semantic meanings, or 2) when phonological divergence between homophones and target words grows larger. Graphically, Figure 4 (c) reveals significantly stronger memorization dependence when homophones contain fewer characters than their corresponding original words.

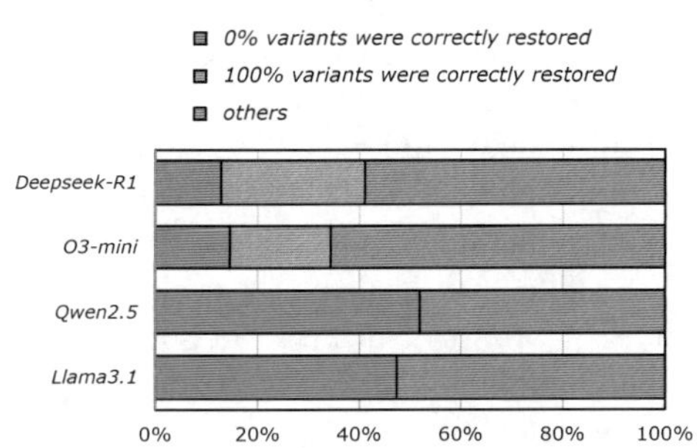

Figure 5: Percentage of different *CR* value homophones in the four LLMs.

We computed the *CR* for each successfully restored homophone, where *CR* = 1 indicates perfect variants restoration (100% accuracy) and *CR* = 0 denotes complete failure, as shown in Figure 5. Our results align with the pattern in Figure 4: smaller models demonstrate notably poorer performance on perturbation data compared to larger models.

Furthermore, based on the experimental results from Deepseek-R1 and OpenAI o3-mini, we selected homophones with different *CR* value, comparing their distributions across: 1) original word frequency[9] and 2) homophone-original word

[9]Calculated by Python library *wordfreq*, available at link.

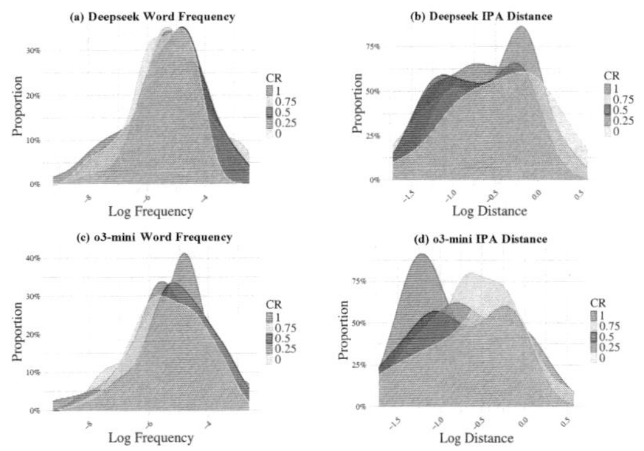

Figure 6: Comparison of homophone properties across *CR* values in Deepseek-R1 and OpenAI o3-mini. Analyzed distributions include: 1) original word frequency (log-scaled), and 2) IPA-based phonological distance between homophones and original words. Higher *CR* indicates less reliance on memorization.

phonological distance based on the *International Phonetic Alphabet* (see Appendix B.3). Intuitively, we hypothesize that LLMs rely more heavily on memorization when processing: 1) those derived from high-frequency original words (leveraging their prevalence in training data), and 2) those exhibiting substantial phonological divergence from their original words.

Results are shown in Figure 6. Contrary to our hypothesis, the original word frequency showed little correlation with memorization dependence during homophone restoration. Instead, phonological divergence between homophones and original words emerged as a more dominant factor (consistent with what we observed in Figure 4), particularly in OpenAI o3-mini.

4.3 *Can Contextual Cues Enhance Homophone Restoration in LLMs?*

The basic assumption for examining the effect of contextual information in homophone restoration is that, as for humans, contextual information can restrict and redirect potential choices in a more narrow range, facilitating accurate predictions. Thus, context-enhanced prompts (Appendix B.2) were employed to assess the role of context in improving LLMs' restoration performance.

As shown in Table 2 and Figure 7, the context-enhanced prompt can improve LLMs' restoration ability on Chinese homophones. Context imposes constraints, guiding LLMs to generate restored words relevant to the given semantic and pragmatic environment. As presented in Table 2, for all four

Model	*Homophone*	*Context*	*+Fewshot*	*+Pinyin*	*+CoT*	*+MoT*
Llama3.1-8B	0.052	0.058	0.156	0.036	0.099	**0.164**
Qwen2.5-7B	0.216	0.293	0.356	0.269	0.277	**0.400**
OpenAI o3-mini	0.622	0.723	0.732	0.723	0.718	**0.762**
Deepseek-R1	0.833	0.896	**0.910**	0.896	0.871	**0.910**

Table 2: Results of the context-enhanced prompt experiments. The best results among the *Fewshot*, *Pinyin*, *CoT*, and *MoT* are **bolded**, and the second-best results are underlined.

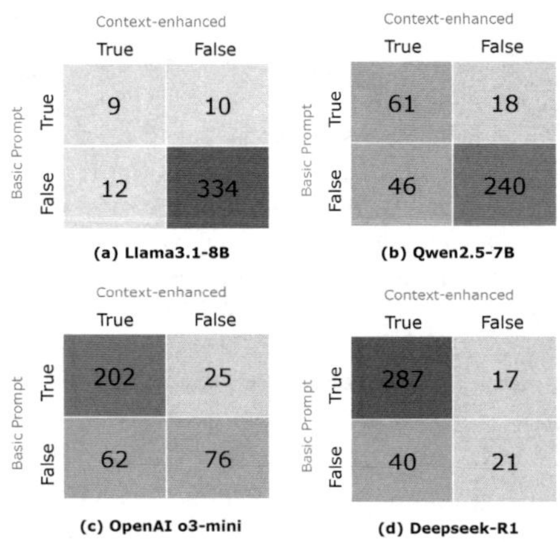

Figure 7: Comparison of the basic prompt and context-enhanced prompt experiments' results.

LLMs, contextual information can evidently improve their performance of restoring homophones into their original words (see the increased accuracy from *Homophone* column to *Context* column). However, in-depth results in Figure 7 uncover that this improvement is not universal. In other words, some cases correctly restored in the basic prompt experiment would be incorrectly handled after adding context. Specifically, for example, in Llama 3.1, 10 such cases can be observed (see upper right block), a phenomenon also seen in other models. This suggests that contextual information does not consistently impose a positive effect on each Chinese homophone for restoration and can sometimes disrupt comprehension or impair memorization in LLMs.

4.4 *Can Other Strategies Impact Homophone Restoration in LLMs?*

This study further examines if other strategies can enhance restoration ability. Table 2 summarizes the contributions of the different strategies.

Few-shot learning and MoT prompts can significantly enhance the restoration performance by presenting human-annotated examples to LLMs. Examples from few-shot learning can reveal linguistic patterns of homophones to LLMs, while MoT prompts explicitly provide human reasoning logic and *pinyin*-based knowledge. This enables LLMs to adopt these reasoning strategies, further improving their restoration capabilities.

***Pinyin* augmented prompts** result shows that LLMs have difficulty in explicitly adapting this knowledge alone to assist homophone restoration. This suggests that their orthography training may limit their effective leverage of *pinyin*.

CoT prompts realized various performance fluctuations among models. Specifically, Llama 3.1 improves with CoT, while Qwen2.5, OpenAI o3-mini, and Deepseek-R1 show declines. This discrepancy may arise from their default reasoning strategies. This task requires simultaneous pinyin and contextual information rationale. Without effective guidance for basic CoT prompts, Qwen2.5, OpenAI o3-mini, and Deepseek-R1 are prone to follow the default think flow, leading to errors in reasoning. In contrast, Llama 3.1 benefits from CoT as it compensates for its default lack of reasoning emphasis, improving restoration accuracy.

5 Conclusion

In this study, we present the first Chinese Internet homophones dataset with language perturbations to evaluate LLMs' restoration capabilities and their reliance on memorization. Our results show that LLMs exhibit significant differences in restoring homophones: larger models rely more on reasoning, while smaller ones depend on memorization. Performance variations are further influenced by semantic, phonological, and graphemic differences between original words and homophones, systematically affecting accuracy and memorization dependence. Although strategies like contextual cues, few-shot learning, and MoT improve performance, *pinyin*-based augmentation unexpectedly failed to enhance restoration. These findings shed light on LLMs' robustness with intralingual and user-generated online content.

Ethics Statement

We do not foresee any ethical risks related to our research.

Limitations

This study quantifies the extent of memorization in LLMs' restoration of Chinese homophones, though the underlying mechanisms of restoration remain unclear. A limitation is the use of DeepSeek-Chat to generate context sentences, which, despite human proofreading and optimization, may still impact experiments involving contextual prompts[10].

Additionally, our study is confined to four models (Llama3.1-8B, Qwen2.5-7B, OpenAI o3-mini, and Deepseek-R1), and results may vary with other models. Future work should expand to diverse languages and models to validate and refine these findings.

Moreover, character co-occurrence and character frequency are likely to influence the memorization and reasoning processes of LLMs during homophone restoration. Currently, there are no up-to-date datasets that incorporate Chinese Internet homophones along with data on character co-occurrence and character frequency. Future research efforts are expected to concentrate on collecting such data, with the aim of further exploring the impact of character co-occurrence and character frequency on homophone restoration.

References

Moustafa Alzantot, Yash Sharma, Ahmed Elgohary, Bo-Jhang Ho, Mani Srivastava, and Kai-Wei Chang. 2018. Generating natural language adversarial examples. In *Proceedings of the 2018 Conference on Empirical Methods in Natural Language Processing*, pages 2890–2896, Brussels, Belgium. Association for Computational Linguistics.

Ashwin Baluja. 2025. Text is not all you need: Multimodal prompting helps LLMs understand humor. In *Proceedings of the 1st Workshop on Computational Humor (CHum)*, pages 9–17, Online. Association for Computational Linguistics.

[10]To address this concern, we include supplementary real-world data evaluations in the Appendix C.1, where all LLMs demonstrate consistent performance trends between authentic and synthetic data, validating the reliability of our main synthetic-data findings.

Emanuele Banfi and Giorgio Francesco Arcodia. 2013. On line proceedings of the sixth mediterranean morphology meeting the shng/sheng complex words in chinese between morphology and semantics.

Nicholas Carlini, Daphne Ippolito, Matthew Jagielski, Katherine Lee, Florian Tramer, and Chiyuan Zhang. 2022. Quantifying memorization across neural language models. In *The Eleventh International Conference on Learning Representations*.

Matthew H Davis, Ingrid S Johnsrude, Alexis Hervais-Adelman, Karen Taylor, and Carolyn McGettigan. 2005. Lexical information drives perceptual learning of distorted speech: evidence from the comprehension of noise-vocoded sentences. *J. Exp. Psychol. Gen.*, 134(2):222–241.

DeepSeek-AI. 2024. Deepseek-v3 technical report. *Preprint*, arXiv:2412.19437.

DeepSeek-AI, Daya Guo, Dejian Yang, Haowei Zhang, Junxiao Song, Ruoyu Zhang, Runxin Xu, Qihao Zhu, Shirong Ma, Peiyi Wang, Xiao Bi, Xiaokang Zhang, Xingkai Yu, Yu Wu, Z. F. Wu, Zhibin Gou, Zhihong Shao, Zhuoshu Li, Ziyi Gao, Aixin Liu, Bing Xue, Bingxuan Wang, Bochao Wu, Bei Feng, Chengda Lu, Chenggang Zhao, Chengqi Deng, Chenyu Zhang, Chong Ruan, Damai Dai, Deli Chen, Dongjie Ji, Erhang Li, Fangyun Lin, Fucong Dai, Fuli Luo, Guangbo Hao, Guanting Chen, Guowei Li, H. Zhang, Han Bao, Hanwei Xu, Haocheng Wang, Honghui Ding, Huajian Xin, Huazuo Gao, Hui Qu, Hui Li, Jianzhong Guo, Jiashi Li, Jiawei Wang, Jingchang Chen, Jingyang Yuan, Junjie Qiu, Junlong Li, J. L. Cai, Jiaqi Ni, Jian Liang, Jin Chen, Kai Dong, Kai Hu, Kaige Gao, Kang Guan, Kexin Huang, Kuai Yu, Lean Wang, Lecong Zhang, Liang Zhao, Litong Wang, Liyue Zhang, Lei Xu, Leyi Xia, Mingchuan Zhang, Minghua Zhang, Minghui Tang, Meng Li, Miaojun Wang, Mingming Li, Ning Tian, Panpan Huang, Peng Zhang, Qiancheng Wang, Qinyu Chen, Qiushi Du, Ruiqi Ge, Ruisong Zhang, Ruizhe Pan, Runji Wang, R. J. Chen, R. L. Jin, Ruyi Chen, Shanghao Lu, Shangyan Zhou, Shanhuang Chen, Shengfeng Ye, Shiyu Wang, Shuiping Yu, Shunfeng Zhou, Shuting Pan, S. S. Li, Shuang Zhou, Shaoqing Wu, Shengfeng Ye, Tao Yun, Tian Pei, Tianyu Sun, T. Wang, Wangding Zeng, Wanjia Zhao, Wen Liu, Wenfeng Liang, Wenjun Gao, Wenqin Yu, Wentao Zhang, W. L. Xiao, Wei An, Xiaodong Liu, Xiaohan Wang, Xiaokang Chen, Xiaotao Nie, Xin Cheng, Xin Liu, Xin Xie, Xingchao Liu, Xinyu Yang, Xinyuan Li, Xuecheng Su, Xuheng Lin, X. Q. Li, Xiangyue Jin, Xiaojin Shen, Xiaosha Chen, Xiaowen Sun, Xiaoxiang Wang, Xinnan Song, Xinyi Zhou, Xianzu Wang, Xinxia Shan, Y. K. Li, Y. Q. Wang, Y. X. Wei, Yang Zhang, Yanhong Xu, Yao Li, Yao Zhao, Yaofeng Sun, Yaohui Wang, Yi Yu, Yichao Zhang, Yifan Shi, Yiliang Xiong, Ying He, Yishi Piao, Yisong Wang, Yixuan Tan, Yiyang Ma, Yiyuan Liu, Yongqiang Guo, Yuan Ou, Yuduan Wang, Yue Gong, Yuheng Zou, Yujia He, Yunfan Xiong, Yuxiang Luo, Yuxiang You, Yuxuan Liu, Yuyang Zhou, Y. X. Zhu, Yanhong Xu, Yanping Huang, Yaohui Li, Yi Zheng, Yuchen Zhu,

Yunxian Ma, Ying Tang, Yukun Zha, Yuting Yan, Z. Z. Ren, Zehui Ren, Zhangli Sha, Zhe Fu, Zhean Xu, Zhenda Xie, Zhengyan Zhang, Zhewen Hao, Zhicheng Ma, Zhigang Yan, Zhiyu Wu, Zihui Gu, Zijia Zhu, Zijun Liu, Zilin Li, Ziwei Xie, Ziyang Song, Zizheng Pan, Zhen Huang, Zhipeng Xu, Zhongyu Zhang, and Zhen Zhang. 2025. Deepseek-r1: Incentivizing reasoning capability in llms via reinforcement learning. *Preprint*, arXiv:2501.12948.

Siddhant Garg and Goutham Ramakrishnan. 2020. BAE: BERT-based adversarial examples for text classification. In *Proceedings of the 2020 Conference on Empirical Methods in Natural Language Processing (EMNLP)*, pages 6174–6181, Online. Association for Computational Linguistics.

Aaron Grattafiori, Abhimanyu Dubey, Abhinav Jauhri, Abhinav Pandey, Abhishek Kadian, Ahmad Al-Dahle, Aiesha Letman, Akhil Mathur, Alan Schelten, Alex Vaughan, Amy Yang, Angela Fan, Anirudh Goyal, Anthony Hartshorn, Aobo Yang, Archi Mitra, Archie Sravankumar, Artem Korenev, Arthur Hinsvark, Arun Rao, Aston Zhang, Aurelien Rodriguez, Austen Gregerson, Ava Spataru, Baptiste Roziere, Bethany Biron, Binh Tang, Bobbie Chern, Charlotte Caucheteux, Chaya Nayak, Chloe Bi, Chris Marra, Chris McConnell, Christian Keller, Christophe Touret, Chunyang Wu, Corinne Wong, Cristian Canton Ferrer, Cyrus Nikolaidis, Damien Allonsius, Daniel Song, Danielle Pintz, Danny Livshits, Danny Wyatt, David Esiobu, Dhruv Choudhary, Dhruv Mahajan, Diego Garcia-Olano, Diego Perino, Dieuwke Hupkes, Egor Lakomkin, Ehab AlBadawy, Elina Lobanova, Emily Dinan, Eric Michael Smith, Filip Radenovic, Francisco Guzm á n, Frank Zhang, Gabriel Synnaeve, Gabrielle Lee, Georgia Lewis Anderson, Govind Thattai, Graeme Nail, Gregoire Mialon, Guan Pang, Guillem Cucurell, Hailey Nguyen, Hannah Korevaar, Hu Xu, Hugo Touvron, Iliyan Zarov, Imanol Arrieta Ibarra, Isabel Kloumann, Ishan Misra, Ivan Evtimov, Jack Zhang, Jade Copet, Jaewon Lee, Jan Geffert, Jana Vranes, Jason Park, Jay Mahadeokar, Jeet Shah, Jelmer van der Linde, Jennifer Billock, Jenny Hong, Jenya Lee, Jeremy Fu, Jianfeng Chi, Jianyu Huang, Jiawen Liu, Jie Wang, Jiecao Yu, Joanna Bitton, Joe Spisak, Jongsoo Park, Joseph Rocca, Joshua Johnstun, Joshua Saxe, Junteng Jia, Kalyan Vasuden Alwala, Karthik Prasad, Kartikeya Upasani, Kate Plawiak, Ke Li, Kenneth Heafield, Kevin Stone, Khalid El-Arini, Krithika Iyer, Kshitiz Malik, Kuenley Chiu, Kunal Bhalla, Kushal Lakhotia, Lauren Rantala-Yeary, Laurens van der Maaten, Lawrence Chen, Liang Tan, Liz Jenkins, Louis Martin, Lovish Madaan, Lubo Malo, Lukas Blecher, Lukas Landzaat, Luke de Oliveira, Madeline Muzzi, Mahesh Pasupuleti, Mannat Singh, Manohar Paluri, Marcin Kardas, Maria Tsimpoukelli, Mathew Oldham, Mathieu Rita, Maya Pavlova, Melanie Kambadur, Mike Lewis, Min Si, Mitesh Kumar Singh, Mona Hassan, Naman Goyal, Narjes Torabi, Nikolay Bashlykov, Nikolay Bogoychev, Niladri Chatterji, Ning Zhang, Olivier Duchenne, Onur elebi, Patrick Alrassy, Pengchuan Zhang, Pengwei Li, Petar Vasic, Peter Weng, Prajjwal Bhargava, Pratik Dubal, Praveen Krishnan, Punit Singh Koura, Puxin Xu, Qing He, Qingxiao Dong, Ragavan Srinivasan, Raj Ganapathy, Ramon Calderer, Ricardo Silveira Cabral, Robert Stojnic, Roberta Raileanu, Rohan Maheswari, Rohit Girdhar, Rohit Patel, Romain Sauvestre, Ronnie Polidoro, Roshan Sumbaly, Ross Taylor, Ruan Silva, Rui Hou, Rui Wang, Saghar Hosseini, Sahana Chennabasappa, Sanjay Singh, Sean Bell, Seohyun Sonia Kim, Sergey Edunov, Shaoliang Nie, Sharan Narang, Sharath Raparthy, Sheng Shen, Shengye Wan, Shruti Bhosale, Shun Zhang, Simon Vandenhende, Soumya Batra, Spencer Whitman, Sten Sootla, Stephane Collot, Suchin Gururangan, Sydney Borodinsky, Tamar Herman, Tara Fowler, Tarek Sheasha, Thomas Georgiou, Thomas Scialom, Tobias Speckbacher, Todor Mihaylov, Tong Xiao, Ujjwal Karn, Vedanuj Goswami, Vibhor Gupta, Vignesh Ramanathan, Viktor Kerkez, Vincent Gonguet, Virginie Do, Vish Vogeti, V í tor Albiero, Vladan Petrovic, Weiwei Chu, Wenhan Xiong, Wenyin Fu, Whitney Meers, Xavier Martinet, Xiaodong Wang, Xiaofang Wang, Xiaoqing Ellen Tan, Xide Xia, Xinfeng Xie, Xuchao Jia, Xuewei Wang, Yaelle Goldschlag, Yashesh Gaur, Yasmine Babaei, Yi Wen, Yiwen Song, Yuchen Zhang, Yue Li, Yuning Mao, Zacharie Delpierre Coudert, Zheng Yan, Zhengxing Chen, Zoe Papakipos, Aaditya Singh, Aayushi Srivastava, Abha Jain, Adam Kelsey, Adam Shajnfeld, Adithya Gangidi, Adolfo Victoria, Ahuva Goldstand, Ajay Menon, Ajay Sharma, Alex Boesenberg, Alexei Baevski, Allie Feinstein, Amanda Kallet, Amit Sangani, Amos Teo, Anam Yunus, Andrei Lupu, Andres Alvarado, Andrew Caples, Andrew Gu, Andrew Ho, Andrew Poulton, Andrew Ryan, Ankit Ramchandani, Annie Dong, Annie Franco, Anuj Goyal, Aparajita Saraf, Arkabandhu Chowdhury, Ashley Gabriel, Ashwin Bharambe, Assaf Eisenman, Azadeh Yazdan, Beau James, Ben Maurer, Benjamin Leonhardi, Bernie Huang, Beth Loyd, Beto De Paola, Bhargavi Paranjape, Bing Liu, Bo Wu, Boyu Ni, Braden Hancock, Bram Wasti, Brandon Spence, Brani Stojkovic, Brian Gamido, Britt Montalvo, Carl Parker, Carly Burton, Catalina Mejia, Ce Liu, Changhan Wang, Changkyu Kim, Chao Zhou, Chester Hu, Ching-Hsiang Chu, Chris Cai, Chris Tindal, Christoph Feichtenhofer, Cynthia Gao, Damon Civin, Dana Beaty, Daniel Kreymer, Daniel Li, David Adkins, David Xu, Davide Testuggine, Delia David, Devi Parikh, Diana Liskovich, Didem Foss, Dingkang Wang, Duc Le, Dustin Holland, Edward Dowling, Eissa Jamil, Elaine Montgomery, Eleonora Presani, Emily Hahn, Emily Wood, Eric-Tuan Le, Erik Brinkman, Esteban Arcaute, Evan Dunbar, Evan Smothers, Fei Sun, Felix Kreuk, Feng Tian, Filippos Kokkinos, Firat Ozgenel, Francesco Caggioni, Frank Kanayet, Frank Seide, Gabriela Medina Florez, Gabriella Schwarz, Gada Badeer, Georgia Swee, Gil Halpern, Grant Herman, Grigory Sizov, Guangyi, Zhang, Guna Lakshminarayanan, Hakan Inan, Hamid Shojanazeri, Han Zou, Hannah Wang, Hanwen Zha, Haroun Habeeb, Harrison Rudolph, Helen Suk, Henry Aspegren, Hunter Goldman, Hongyuan Zhan, Ibrahim Damlaj, Igor Molybog, Igor Tufanov, Ilias Leontiadis,

Irina-Elena Veliche, Itai Gat, Jake Weissman, James Geboski, James Kohli, Janice Lam, Japhet Asher, Jean-Baptiste Gaya, Jeff Marcus, Jeff Tang, Jennifer Chan, Jenny Zhen, Jeremy Reizenstein, Jeremy Teboul, Jessica Zhong, Jian Jin, Jingyi Yang, Joe Cummings, Jon Carvill, Jon Shepard, Jonathan McPhie, Jonathan Torres, Josh Ginsburg, Junjie Wang, Kai Wu, Kam Hou U, Karan Saxena, Kartikay Khandelwal, Katayoun Zand, Kathy Matosich, Kaushik Veeraraghavan, Kelly Michelena, Keqian Li, Kiran Jagadeesh, Kun Huang, Kunal Chawla, Kyle Huang, Lailin Chen, Lakshya Garg, Lavender A, Leandro Silva, Lee Bell, Lei Zhang, Liangpeng Guo, Licheng Yu, Liron Moshkovich, Luca Wehrstedt, Madian Khabsa, Manav Avalani, Manish Bhatt, Martynas Mankus, Matan Hasson, Matthew Lennie, Matthias Reso, Maxim Groshev, Maxim Naumov, Maya Lathi, Meghan Keneally, Miao Liu, Michael L. Seltzer, Michal Valko, Michelle Restrepo, Mihir Patel, Mik Vyatskov, Mikayel Samvelyan, Mike Clark, Mike Macey, Mike Wang, Miquel Jubert Hermoso, Mo Metanat, Mohammad Rastegari, Munish Bansal, Nandhini Santhanam, Natascha Parks, Natasha White, Navyata Bawa, Nayan Singhal, Nick Egebo, Nicolas Usunier, Nikhil Mehta, Nikolay Pavlovich Laptev, Ning Dong, Norman Cheng, Oleg Chernoguz, Olivia Hart, Omkar Salpekar, Ozlem Kalinli, Parkin Kent, Parth Parekh, Paul Saab, Pavan Balaji, Pedro Rittner, Philip Bontrager, Pierre Roux, Piotr Dollar, Polina Zvyagina, Prashant Ratanchandani, Pritish Yuvraj, Qian Liang, Rachad Alao, Rachel Rodriguez, Rafi Ayub, Raghotham Murthy, Raghu Nayani, Rahul Mitra, Rangaprabhu Parthasarathy, Raymond Li, Rebekkah Hogan, Robin Battey, Rocky Wang, Russ Howes, Ruty Rinott, Sachin Mehta, Sachin Siby, Sai Jayesh Bondu, Samyak Datta, Sara Chugh, Sara Hunt, Sargun Dhillon, Sasha Sidorov, Satadru Pan, Saurabh Mahajan, Saurabh Verma, Seiji Yamamoto, Sharadh Ramaswamy, Shaun Lindsay, Shaun Lindsay, Sheng Feng, Shenghao Lin, Shengxin Cindy Zha, Shishir Patil, Shiva Shankar, Shuqiang Zhang, Shuqiang Zhang, Sinong Wang, Sneha Agarwal, Soji Sajuyigbe, Soumith Chintala, Stephanie Max, Stephen Chen, Steve Kehoe, Steve Satterfield, Sudarshan Govindaprasad, Sumit Gupta, Summer Deng, Sungmin Cho, Sunny Virk, Suraj Subramanian, Sy Choudhury, Sydney Goldman, Tal Remez, Tamar Glaser, Tamara Best, Thilo Koehler, Thomas Robinson, Tianhe Li, Tianjun Zhang, Tim Matthews, Timothy Chou, Tzook Shaked, Varun Vontimitta, Victoria Ajayi, Victoria Montanez, Vijai Mohan, Vinay Satish Kumar, Vishal Mangla, Vlad Ionescu, Vlad Poenaru, Vlad Tiberiu Mihailescu, Vladimir Ivanov, Wei Li, Wenchen Wang, Wenwen Jiang, Wes Bouaziz, Will Constable, Xiaocheng Tang, Xiaojian Wu, Xiaolan Wang, Xilun Wu, Xinbo Gao, Yaniv Kleinman, Yanjun Chen, Ye Hu, Ye Jia, Ye Qi, Yenda Li, Yilin Zhang, Ying Zhang, Yossi Adi, Youngjin Nam, Yu, Wang, Yu Zhao, Yuchen Hao, Yundi Qian, Yunlu Li, Yuzi He, Zach Rait, Zachary DeVito, Zef Rosnbrick, Zhaoduo Wen, Zhenyu Yang, Zhiwei Zhao, and Zhiyu Ma. 2024. The llama 3 herd of models. *Preprint*, arXiv:2407.21783.

HarperCollins. 2023. *Collins English Dictionary: Complete and Unabridged*, 14th edition. HarperCollins. ISBN 9780008511340, 1899 pages.

Valentin Hartmann, Anshuman Suri, Vincent Bindschaedler, David Evans, Shruti Tople, and Robert West. 2023. Sok: Memorization in general-purpose large language models. *Preprint*, arXiv:2310.18362.

Di Jin, Zhijing Jin, Joey Tianyi Zhou, and Peter Szolovits. 2020. Is bert really robust? a strong baseline for natural language attack on text classification and entailment. In *Proceedings of the AAAI conference on artificial intelligence*, volume 34, pages 8018–8025.

Antonia Karamolegkou, Jiaang Li, Li Zhou, and Anders Søgaard. 2023. Copyright violations and large language models. In *Proceedings of the 2023 Conference on Empirical Methods in Natural Language Processing*, pages 7403–7412, Singapore. Association for Computational Linguistics.

Takeshi Kojima, Shixiang Shane Gu, Machel Reid, Yutaka Matsuo, and Yusuke Iwasawa. 2022. Large language models are zero-shot reasoners. *Advances in neural information processing systems*, 35:22199–22213.

Xiaonan Li and Xipeng Qiu. 2023. MoT: Memory-of-thought enables ChatGPT to self-improve. In *Proceedings of the 2023 Conference on Empirical Methods in Natural Language Processing*, pages 6354–6374, Singapore. Association for Computational Linguistics.

Yuang Li, Xiaosong Qiao, Xiaofeng Zhao, Huan Zhao, Wei Tang, Min Zhang, and Hao Yang. 2024. Large language model should understand pinyin for chinese asr error correction. *arXiv preprint arXiv:2409.13262*.

Changchun Liu, Kai Zhang, Junzhe Jiang, Zixiao Kong, Qi Liu, and Enhong Chen. 2025. Chinese spelling correction: A comprehensive survey of progress, challenges, and opportunities. *arXiv preprint arXiv:2502.11508*.

Changchun Liu, Kai Zhang, Junzhe Jiang, Zirui Liu, Hanqing Tao, Min Gao, and Enhong Chen. 2024. ARM: An alignment-and-replacement module for Chinese spelling check based on LLMs. In *Proceedings of the 2024 Conference on Empirical Methods in Natural Language Processing*, pages 10156–10168, Miami, Florida, USA. Association for Computational Linguistics.

Hanyu Liu, Chengyuan Cai, and Yanjun Qi. 2023. Expanding scope: Adapting English adversarial attacks to Chinese. In *Proceedings of the 3rd Workshop on Trustworthy Natural Language Processing (TrustNLP 2023)*, pages 276–286, Toronto, Canada. Association for Computational Linguistics.

Anita Mehta and Jean-Marc Luck. 2020. Hearing and mishearings: Decrypting the spoken word. *Advances in Complex Systems*, 23(03):2050008.

Moran Mizrahi, Guy Kaplan, Dan Malkin, Rotem Dror, Dafna Shahaf, and Gabriel Stanovsky. 2024. State of what art? a call for multi-prompt LLM evaluation. *Transactions of the Association for Computational Linguistics*, 12:933–949.

Akshara Prabhakar, Thomas L. Griffiths, and R. Thomas McCoy. 2024. Deciphering the factors influencing the efficacy of chain-of-thought: Probability, memorization, and noisy reasoning. In *Findings of the Association for Computational Linguistics: EMNLP 2024*, pages 3710–3724, Miami, Florida, USA. Association for Computational Linguistics.

Lorenzo Proietti, Stefano Perrella, Simone Tedeschi, Giulia Vulpis, Leonardo Lavalle, Andrea Sanchietti, Andrea Ferrari, and Roberto Navigli. 2024. Analyzing homonymy disambiguation capabilities of pretrained language models. In *Proceedings of the 2024 Joint International Conference on Computational Linguistics, Language Resources and Evaluation (LREC-COLING 2024)*, pages 924–938, Torino, Italia. ELRA and ICCL.

Qwen, :, An Yang, Baosong Yang, Beichen Zhang, Binyuan Hui, Bo Zheng, Bowen Yu, Chengyuan Li, Dayiheng Liu, Fei Huang, Haoran Wei, Huan Lin, Jian Yang, Jianhong Tu, Jianwei Zhang, Jianxin Yang, Jiaxi Yang, Jingren Zhou, Junyang Lin, Kai Dang, Keming Lu, Keqin Bao, Kexin Yang, Le Yu, Mei Li, Mingfeng Xue, Pei Zhang, Qin Zhu, Rui Men, Runji Lin, Tianhao Li, Tianyi Tang, Tingyu Xia, Xingzhang Ren, Xuancheng Ren, Yang Fan, Yang Su, Yichang Zhang, Yu Wan, Yuqiong Liu, Zeyu Cui, Zhenru Zhang, and Zihan Qiu. 2025. Qwen2.5 technical report. *Preprint*, arXiv:2412.15115.

Marco Tulio Ribeiro, Tongshuang Wu, Carlos Guestrin, and Sameer Singh. 2020. Beyond accuracy: Behavioral testing of NLP models with CheckList. In *Proceedings of the 58th Annual Meeting of the Association for Computational Linguistics*, pages 4902–4912, Online. Association for Computational Linguistics.

A G Samuel. 1981. Phonemic restoration: insights from a new methodology. *J. Exp. Psychol. Gen.*, 110(4):474–494.

Hui Su, Weiwei Shi, Xiaoyu Shen, Zhou Xiao, Tuo Ji, Jiarui Fang, and Jie Zhou. 2022. RoCBert: Robust Chinese bert with multimodal contrastive pretraining. In *Proceedings of the 60th Annual Meeting of the Association for Computational Linguistics (Volume 1: Long Papers)*, pages 921–931, Dublin, Ireland. Association for Computational Linguistics.

Kushal Tirumala, Aram Markosyan, Luke Zettlemoyer, and Armen Aghajanyan. 2022. Memorization without overfitting: Analyzing the training dynamics of large language models. *Advances in Neural Information Processing Systems*, 35:38274–38290.

Ao Wang, Xinghao Yang, Chen Li, Bao-di Liu, and Weifeng Liu. 2024. Adaptive immune-based sound-shape code substitution for adversarial Chinese text attacks. In *Proceedings of the 2024 Conference on Empirical Methods in Natural Language Processing*, pages 4553–4565, Miami, Florida, USA. Association for Computational Linguistics.

Boyi Wei, Weijia Shi, Yangsibo Huang, Noah A. Smith, Chiyuan Zhang, Luke Zettlemoyer, Kai Li, and Peter Henderson. 2024. Evaluating copyright takedown methods for language models. In *Advances in Neural Information Processing Systems (NeurIPS 2024)*. Datasets and Benchmarks Track.

Yunze Xiao, Yujia Hu, Kenny Tsu Wei Choo, and Roy Ka-Wei Lee. 2024. ToxiCloakCN: Evaluating robustness of offensive language detection in Chinese with cloaking perturbations. In *Proceedings of the 2024 Conference on Empirical Methods in Natural Language Processing*, pages 6012–6025, Miami, Florida, USA. Association for Computational Linguistics.

Chulin Xie, Yangsibo Huang, Chiyuan Zhang, Da Yu, Xinyun Chen, Bill Yuchen Lin, Bo Li, Badih Ghazi, and Ravi Kumar. 2024. On memorization of large language models in logical reasoning. In *NeurIPS 2024 Workshop MATH-AI: The 4th Workshop on Mathematical Reasoning and AI*.

Rongwu Xu. 2024. Exploring chinese humor generation: A study on two-part allegorical sayings. In *2024 International Joint Conference on Neural Networks (IJCNN)*, pages 1–8. IEEE.

Zhijun Xu, Siyu Yuan, Lingjie Chen, and Deqing Yang. 2024. "a good pun is its own reword": Can large language models understand puns? In *Proceedings of the 2024 Conference on Empirical Methods in Natural Language Processing*, pages 11766–11782, Miami, Florida, USA. Association for Computational Linguistics.

Dongyu Zhang, Heting Zhang, Xikai Liu, Hongfei Lin, and Feng Xia. 2019. Telling the whole story: A manually annotated Chinese dataset for the analysis of humor in jokes. In *Proceedings of the 2019 Conference on Empirical Methods in Natural Language Processing and the 9th International Joint Conference on Natural Language Processing (EMNLP-IJCNLP)*, pages 6402–6407, Hong Kong, China. Association for Computational Linguistics.

Wei Emma Zhang, Quan Z Sheng, Ahoud Alhazmi, and Chenliang Li. 2020. Adversarial attacks on deep-learning models in natural language processing: A survey. *ACM Transactions on Intelligent Systems and Technology (TIST)*, 11(3):1–41.

Yizhuo Zhang, Heng Wang, Shangbin Feng, Zhaoxuan Tan, Xiaochuang Han, Tianxing He, and Yulia Tsvetkov. 2024. Can LLM graph reasoning generalize beyond pattern memorization? In *Findings of the Association for Computational Linguistics: EMNLP 2024*, pages 2289–2305, Miami, Florida, USA. Association for Computational Linguistics.

A About Dataset

A.1 Human Annotation

In our paper, two aspects require annotation: whether homophones have their meanings as existing words in Chinese and whether the sentence carriers generated by Deepseek-V3 are appropriate for the target homophone.

Regarding the first task, the Chinese homophones in the dataset are assigned to three native Chinese researchers in linguistics for annotation. When their opinions are not in agreement, we adopt the annotation results of the majority. For the latter task, we invited the same annotators to make them to determine the suitability of the homophone for the given sentence. Subsequently, sentences with different opinions will be further revised until a full agreement is reached for further implementation.

A.2 Instruction for Annotators

Judgment of Homophone Inherent Meaning

- Please check each of the homophones below and determine whether they have an inherent meaning in Chinese as an existing word. For example, "压力 (pressure)" and its homophone "鸭梨 (Chinese white pear)", where "鸭梨" has its original meaning as a fruit, and this kind of homophone should be marked as "1". Another example "焦虑 (anxiety)" and its homophone "蕉绿 (banana-green, which has no independent semantic meaning in standard language)", which should be marked as "0".

- In general, if the homophone is a word with a clear semantic meaning in regular language use, mark it as "1". If the homophone is just created as a homophone and has no actual semantic meaning, mark it as "0".

The Inter-Annotator-Agreement (IAA) reaches 92.88% (Fleiss' Kappa = 0.7215). Interannotators' inconsistent cases will finalize the label by the majority choice.

Judgment of Carrier Sentences Suitability

- Please review these given sentences that carry homophones. Your task is to determine whether each sentence conforms to the functions of Chinese homophones. If the sentence is appropriate, mark it as "1". If not (such as incorrect grammar or inappropriate context), mark it as "0".

A.3 Pseudo-code for Categorization

The pseudo-code of grouping words based on phonological and graphemic features is shown in Table 3. *Pinyin* can be accessible by involving the *pypinyin* package directly to transfer the character into Chinese *pinyin*. The pseudo-code demonstrates the logic of transferring words into Chinese *pinyin* and conducting the phonological taxonomy based on *pinyin* syllable and tone distinction. The package can transfer the neutral tone into label "5".

Pseudo-code for Categorization

Input: and $\begin{cases} \text{Original Word} & ow \\ \text{Homophone} & h \end{cases}$

Output: Result r

Procedure:

$py_or = f_{\text{char2pinyin}}(ow)$

$py_ho = f_{\text{char2pinyin}}(h)$

$(s_1, t_1) = py_or$

$(s_2, t_2) = py_ho$

$$r = \begin{cases} 0, & \text{if } s_1 = s_2 \text{ and } t_1 = t_2 \\ 1, & \text{if } s_1 = s_2 \text{ and } t_1 \neq t_2 \\ 2, & \text{if } s_1 \neq s_2 \text{ and } t_1 = t_2 \\ 3, & \text{if } s_1 \neq s_2 \text{ and } t_1 \neq t_2 \end{cases}$$

return r

Table 3: This table demonstrates the logic of phonological taxonomy based on *pinyin* syllables and tone.

A.4 Prompt for Carrier Sentence Generation

The carrier sentences are generated from the Deepseek-V3 based on the prompt shown in Table 4. Since Deepseek-V3 may not be able to understand the meanings of certain homophonies, we first input the original words into Deepseek-V3. This step allows Deepseek-V3 to generate carrier sentences based on the original words. Subsequently, we replace the original words with their corresponding homophones. Finally, we present these sentences with replaced homophonic words to annotators for verification and modification.

A.5 Pseudo-code for Adversarial Variants Generation

The pseudo-code of homophone variants generation is shown in Table 5.

Chinese original version
/*指令*/ 你是一位中文语言专家，擅长创作简单的句子。请你根据输入中的词创作符合逻辑的句子，要求结构简单，使用场景日常。 /*示例*/ 怎么了－>怎么了？身体不舒服吗？ /*输入*/
English translated version
/*Instructions*/ You are a Chinese language expert and you are good at writing simple sentences. Please create logical sentences based on the words in the input. The structure should be simple and the use situation should be daily. **/*Example*/** What's wrong－ >What's wrong? Don't you feel well? **/*Input*/**

Table 4: This table demonstrates the prompt design of Context Sentence Generation task. The input language is Chinese.

Pseudo-code for Varient Generation
Input: $\begin{cases} \text{Common Chinese Characters} & C \\ \text{Custom Homophones} & H \end{cases}$ Output: Result Variants V Procedure: $D = C \setminus H$ $(s_1, t_1) = f_{\text{char2pinyin}}(C)$ $(s_2, t_2) = f_{\text{char2pinyin}}(H)$ $r = \begin{cases} S_1, & \text{if } s_1 = s_2 \wedge t_1 \neq t_2 \\ S_2, & \text{if } s_1 = s_2 \wedge t_1 = t_2 \end{cases}$ Variants: $V_1 = \{v \mid p(v) = p(c) \wedge 0.5c \neq 0.5v\}$ $V_2 = \{v \mid p(v) = p(c) \wedge c \neq v\}$ $V_3 = \{v \mid 0.5p(v) = 0.5p(c) \wedge 0.5c \neq 0.5v\}$ $V_4 = \{v \mid p(v) \neq p(c) \wedge c \neq v\}$ return Variants V

Table 5: This table demonstrates the logic of categorization based on pinyin syllables, tone, and variant generation.

B About Experiments

B.1 Ablation Study

In order to explore performance fluctuations with prompts in Chinese or English, we conducted an ablation study before the formal experiment. We applied two open-source language models: Qwen2.5-7B and Llama3.1-8B. The result is shown in Figure 8. The results indicate that Qwen2.5-7B can achieve optimal performance with English prompts in limited strategy, while Chinese prompts yield better average performance. In contrast, Llama3.1-8B obtains more optimized performance when using Chinese as the prompt language. Considering the better performance of Chinese and the nature of Chinese linguistic exploration, in our main experiment, we used Chinese as the prompt language.

In details, we explored the output of Llama and its rationale when using English prompts. This approach tends to generate coding-type words, such as "\u5c0e\u9ed1\u62a8". Consequently, the performance in most tasks reaches 0 accuracy. Additionally, when using English prompts for the CoT task, Llama3.1-8B generates rationale similar to Python programming language. This information is provided to guide you in using Python code to achieve restoration. In that case, Llama also exhibits extremely weak performance.

B.2 Details of Prompts

The step-by-step investigation on LLMs' restoration of Chinese homophones requires highly structured prompts to make LLMs understand their tasks as well as avoid the performance influence by the different context information.

Basic Prompt Design

In the basic prompt, we do not give any related information but the homophone itself to instruct LLMs for restoring based on the given homophone alone. Prompts are shown in Table 6.

Context-enhanced Prompt with *Pinyin* and Few-shot learning Design

Due to context can assist in constructing meaning via the specific contextual cue offering, our study designs the context-enhanced prompt to explore its function in restoration. Additionally, the few-shot enhanced and *pinyin* are used to further examine their influence on restoration as the homophone source-target pattern and Chinese phonological spelling role are vital for this restoration task. The prompt is shown in Table 7.

CoT and MoT prompts Design

CoT and MoT can explicitly activate the rationale of LLMs by directly showing examples in prompts.

	Qwen_EN	Llama_EN	Qwen_CN	Llama_CN
Basic Prompt	0.000	0.000	0.000	0.000
Context Enhanced	0.059	0.000	0.098	0.000
Pinyin	0.059	0.000	0.039	0.020
Few-shot Learning	0.176	0.020	0.200	0.078
CoT	0.137	0.000	0.176	0.059
MoT	0.216	0.020	0.176	0.157
AVG	0.108	0.008	**0.114**	**0.052**

Figure 8: This table demonstrates the performance of different models using different languages in given tasks. Qwen_EN, Llama_EN, Qwen_CN and Llama_CN denote Qwen2.5-7B and Llama3.1-8B using English and Chinese Prompts. AVG refers to the average accuracy of specific model with one language.

Chinese original version
/*指令*/ 你是一位专业的中文语言分析专家。你会接收到一个中文谐音词作为输入内容，请准确将其还原为原本的词汇，然后只输出一个符合“原词”：“XXX”格式的JSON数据，这里的“XXX”就是你所输入的谐音词所对应的原本词汇。 //* 输入 */ 当前的输入是：
English translated version
/* **Instructions** */ You are a professional Chinese language analysis expert. When receiving a Chinese homophone word or phrase as input, accurately revert it to its original word or phrase, then only output a JSON object conforming to the format "originalWord": "XXX", where "XXX" represents the original word or phrase corresponding to the input homophone term. /* **Input** */ Current input is:

Table 6: This table demonstrates the basic prompt design of restoration task. The input language is Chinese.

The CoT can allow models to reason with the default chain, while the MoT can offer the human thinking chain to let models fit to restrict the chain more task-specific and similar to humans. The prompt design is demonstrated in Table 8.

B.3 Phonological Similarity Algorithm

We applied Panphon to calculate the phonological similarity between the homophone and its corresponding original word. The detailed procedure is demonstrated in Table 10. This method converts *pinyin* to IPA using the Dragonmapper package, then computes multiple distance metrics. Since different articulatory features contribute unevenly to phonetic perception, we adopt the weighted feature edit distance to account for these variations.

Chinese original version
/*指令*/ 你是一位专业的中文语言分析专家。你会收到含有一个谐音词的中文句子和该句子中的拼音，和该句子中的中文谐音词和谐音词的拼音作为输入内容，请准确将其中的谐音词还原为原本的词汇，直接输出且只输出一个符合“原词”：“XXX”格式的JSON数据，这里的“XXX”就是输入谐音词所对应的原本的中文词汇。输出中只能含有该json数据，而不能包含其他任何多余信息。 /* 示例 */ （1）句子输入：不要对我人参公鸡，否则我让管理员过来处理了。 谐音词：人参公鸡 输出为：“原词”：“人身攻击”(... with two more examples) //* 输入 */ 句子输入： 句子输入的拼音： 谐音词： 谐音词的拼音：
English translated version
/* **Instructions** */ You are a professional Chinese language analysis expert. When receiving Chinese sentence containing a homophone and the *pinyin* of the sentence, as well as the homophone in the sentence and the *magenta* of the homophone as the input, accurately revert the homophone part to the original word or phrase, then only output a JSON object conforming to the format "original word": "XXX", where "XXX" represents the original word or phrase corresponding to the input homophone term. /* **Examples** */ (1) Input sentence is: Don't ginseng male chicken to me, or I'll have the warden come and deal with it. Homophone is: ginseng male chicken Output is: "original word": "personal abuse"(... with two more examples) /* **Input** */ Input sentence is: *Pinyin* of input sentence is: Homophone is: *Pinyin* of homophone is:

Table 7: This table demonstrates the context-enhanced prompt design for restoration with two additional improvement strategies. The text with this text color denote the core addition of context-enhanced prompt. The text represents *pinyin* enhanced prompt. The text refers to few-shot learning enhanced prompt examples. The input language is Chinese while English translated version is a literal translation for understanding.

Chinese original version

/*指令*/

你是一位专业的中文语言分析专家。你会收到含有一个谐音词的中文句子和该句子中的谐音词作为输入内容，请首先给出思考推理的过程，然后准确地将句子的谐音词还原为原本的词汇，最后只输出样式为 "推理过程"："XXX"，"原词"："XXX" 的 JSON 数据，这里的第一个"XXX"是你推理的过程，第二个"XXX"就是你所输入的谐音词所对应的原本词汇。输出中只能含有该json样式的数据，而不能包含其他任何多余信息。

/* 示例 */

句子输入：不要对我人参公鸡，否则我让管理员过来处理了。

谐音词：人参公鸡

输出为："推理过程"："'人参公鸡'的拼音是[[ren2],[shen1],[gong1],[ji1]]，原词应该为'人身攻击'，拼音是 [[ren2],[shen1],[gong1],[ji1]]。这是属于完全的同音字置换形成的谐音词现象，拼音拼写（发声位置）以及音调没有发生任何变化。这个谐音词中的'参'，'公'和'鸡'字属于遭到置换的字。他们分别经历将'身'替换为'参'，将'攻'替换为'公'，将'击'替换为'鸡'。这一现象仅改变了汉字写法，保持发音一致形成了谐音效果"，"原词"："人身攻击"...(with two more examples)

//* 输入 */

句子输入：

谐音词：

English translated version

/*Instructions*/

You are a professional Chinese language analysis expert. When receiving a Chinese sentence with a homophone words/phrase as input: please first give the rationale, then accurately revert the word or phrase in the sentence back to original form with only output a JSON object conforming to the format "reasoning process": "XXX", "original word": "XXX", where the first "XXX" is the reasoning process you carried out, and the second "XXX" represents the original word or phrase corresponding to the input homophone term.

/* Examples */

Input sentence is: Don't ginseng male chicken to me, or I'll have the warden come and deal with it.

Homophone: ginseng male chicken

Output: "reasoning process": "*Pinyin* of 'ginseng male chicken' is [[ren2],[shen1],[gong1],[ji1]]. Original means 'personal abuse'. This is a homophonic phenomenon formed by complete homophone replacement, but no change in spelling or tone.'Seng', 'male', and 'chicken' in homophone belong to replaced words. They experienced replacing 'body' with 'seng', 'attack' with 'male', and 'strike' with 'chicken' respectively. This phenomenon only changed Chinese characters, keeping the pronunciation consistent to form homophonic effects.", "original word": "personal abuse"...(with two more examples)

/*Input*/

Input sentence is:

Homophone is:

Table 8: This table demonstrates the CoT and MoT prompt. The text is explict activation of LLMs' relationale. The content represents MoT with human rationale and true case. The input language is Chinese, while English translated version is given for understanding.

Model	Real Acc	Synthetic Acc
Llama3.1-8B	0.12	0.30
Qwen2.5-7B	0.64	0.80
OpenAI o3-mini	0.93	0.90
Deepseek-R1	0.99	1.00

Table 9: This table compares LLM performance using the MoT prompt on synthetic vs. real-world sentences. **Real Acc** represents the restoration accuracy for authentic homophone-included sentences, while **Synthetic Acc** denotes the accuracy for synthetic sentences with corresponding homophones.

Pseudo-code for Panphon-based Phonetic Distance

Input: $\begin{cases} \text{Pinyin}_1 & p\_t_1 \\ \text{Pinyin}_2 & p\_t_2 \end{cases}$

Output: Normalized Similarity $S \in [0, 1]$

Procedure:

1. **Phoneme Alignment**:
   Align p_t_1 and p_t_2 using IPA segmentation
2. **Panphon Distance**:
   $D \leftarrow \text{panphon.distance}(p\_t_1, p\_t_2)$ *(Weighted feature edit distance)*
3. **Similarity Conversion**:
   $S \leftarrow 1 - \frac{D - \min(D)}{\max(D) - \min(D)}$ *(Normalized to [0,1])*

Table 10: Phonetic similarity computation using Panphon's distance method. *Pinyin* was directly input with the spelling like ō and transferred into IPA to capture the articulation of sounds.

C Additional Results Analyses

C.1 Comparison between Sentences in Real-case and Synthetic Data

This study is constrained by its reliance on synthetic data generated by LLMs, leaving real-world cases untested. Owing to the scarcity of structured data on Chinese internet homophones, we randomly selected ten homophones and sourced corresponding sentences via an online Weibo corpus with a corpus retrieval function at link, establishing a 1:10 homophone-to-sentence mapping. These real-world sentences were then applied using the MoT strategy to validate its efficacy on synthetic datasets. The results and key distinctions are summarized in Table 9.

Although we did not test all homophone cases to calculate overall accuracy, the trends observed in real-world and synthetic sentences are consistent. This suggests that synthetic data can mirror outcomes similar to real-world data and validates the feasibility of using synthetic data in the main experiment. However, the significant discrepancy between the two also highlights that synthetic data may not fully capture the complexity of real-world scenarios, especially affecting the small models' performance a lot.

C.2 Confusion Matrices

This section reveals all confusion matrix of comparison between context-enhanced prompts with context and few-shot learning-enhanced, context and *pinyin* syllable-enhanced, context and CoT activating, and context and MoT activating prompts. Figure 9 shows the various strategies of prompts' effects on the case level. The confusion matrix highlights that the strategies of different prompts cannot consistently enhance or decline in each case. (A case can be correctly restored in one strategy, but it may be correctly or wrongly restored in subsequent strategies.)

C.3 Rationale in Error Cases Study

This session lists the original rationale in Chinese in Table 11 and Table 12.

D Experiment Details

During the experiments, we utilize one A100 GPU with 40GB of memory. Each experiment is configured to not exceed three hours in duration.

For the reasoning tasks of Deepseek-R1 and OpenAI o3-mini, we obtain access through the official API channels provided by the respective companies. As for Qwen2.5-7B and Llama3.1-8B, we download them from the official Hugging Face website and make use of the transformer package available there to integrate them into our experimental setup.

E Error Cases Study

Results from basic prompts and enhanced strategies reveal that LLMs can only restore a subset of Chinese homophones in our dataset, underscoring the challenges they face in restoration tasks. This section empirically investigates reasons behind their limitation by analyzing the rationale contents and restored words via CoT and MoT experiments. Through additional discussion of erroneous cases, we gain deeper insights into the underlying causes of these challenges. Detailed rationales for the examples are provided in Table 12 in Appendix C.3.

We manually reviewed homophones incorrectly restored by LLMs and categorized the errors into three types: 1) **Same Meaning Restoration**: The restored homophone has the same basic meaning as the original but is incomplete; 2) **Similar Meaning with Lost Elements**: The restored homophone conveys a similar meaning but loses some semantic elements of the original; 3) **Completely Wrong Restoration**: The restored word is entirely incorrect, bearing no meaningful relation to the original.

The Type 1 example, "石乐志" (*shi2 le5 zhi4*, literally "stone-happy-ambition"), was correctly restored as "失了智" (*shi2 le5 zhi4*, "lost one's mind") in the basic prompt experiment, relying on memorization. However, with CoT involvement, it was incorrectly restored as "失智" (*shi1 zhi4*, "lose mind"), omitting the past tense marker "了". This misalignment during reasoning highlights a limitation of CoT, where LLMs overthink meanings and neglect functional elements like tense markers. In contrast, the MoT prompt, which activates memorization and emphasizes proper alignment, ensures correct restoration. This suggests that LLMs' default CoT reasoning struggles to balance content words and functional elements, sometimes prioritizing meaning over structural accuracy.

The example of "雾化女性" (*wu4 hua4 nü3 xing4*, "atomization-women") in Type 2, is a partial homophone substitution and memory-relying restored homophoneme in the basic prompt experiment. However, CoT prompts incorrectly restores it as "物化" (*wu4 hua4*, "objectify"), neglecting the component of "woman", while MoT prompts can still capture all components correctly. This proves LLMs might lose their attention by CoT in dealing with multi-word tasks and tend to put the dominant focus on some key parts during restoration.

Type 3 is illustrated by the example of "非珠牛" (*fei1 zhu1 niu2*, "Non-jewelry cow"), which could be restored into "非主流" (*fei1 zhu3 liu2*, "non-mainstream") by using either memory or reasoning, as demonstrated in the basic prompt experiment. However, when guided by CoT prompts, it is incorrectly restored as "非洲鼓" (*fei1 zhou1 gu3*, "African drum"). The CoT rationale encounters two issues: incorrectly dividing the multiword term into two parts, "非珠" and "牛" instead of the correct pattern "非" and "珠牛", and excessively restoring the character "牛". In contrast, MoT prompts stress the entire word, facilitating correct restoration.

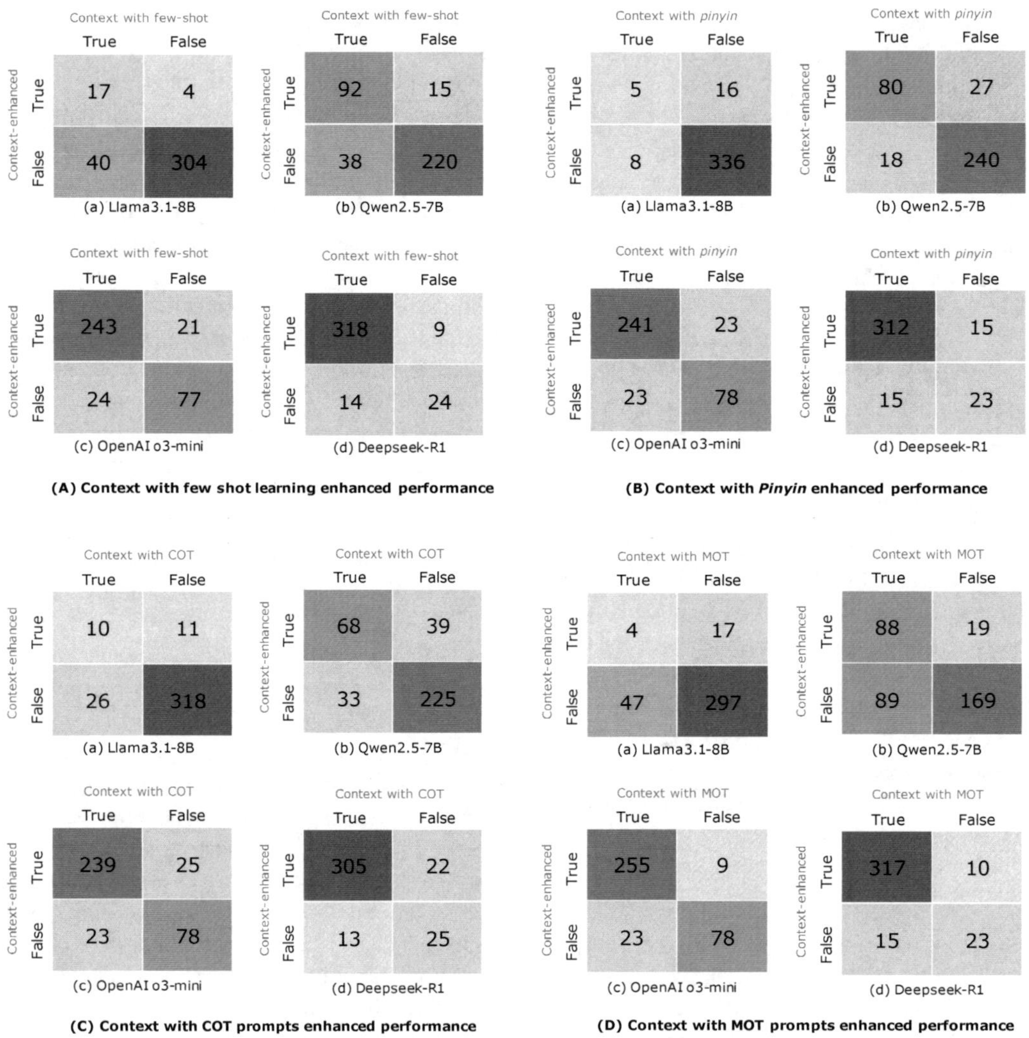

Figure 9: Comparison context-enhanced prompt between context enhanced with few-shot learning prompt, context enhanced with *pinyin* syllable prompt, context enhanced prompt with COT strategy, and context enhanced prompt with MOT experiments' results, in the form of confusion matrices.

Type	Homophone	CoT Rationale
Same semantic meaning restored word	石乐志 (shi2 le4 zhi4) (stone happy ambition)	{“推理过程”：“句子中的‘石乐志’发音与'失智'（shi1zhi4）相近，‘失智’指失去理智或精神恍惚，符合后文‘忘东忘西’的健忘语境。网络用语中常用‘石乐志’谐音表达这种状态。”,“原词”：“失智”}
Similar meaning with elements lost restored word	雾化女性 (wu4 hua4 nü3 xing4) (atomization female)	{“推理过程”：“原句中的‘雾化’与‘物化’发音相同，‘物化’指将人视为物品，常用于批评性别歧视行为，符合句意中对男性行为的负面评价。而‘雾化’的字面含义不符合语境，因此判断为谐音替换。”，“原词”：“物化”}
Complete wrong restoration	非珠牛 (fei1 zhu3 niu2) (Non jewelry cow)	{“推理过程”：“谐音词‘非珠牛’的发音为fei1 zhu3 niu1，需寻找与之发音相近且符合语境的音乐类型。‘非珠’与‘非洲’发音接近（zhu1与zhou1在某些方言中相似），‘牛’可能是‘鼓’的误写或方言发音(gu3与niu2可能存在地域性发音混淆)。结合‘非洲鼓音乐’在年轻人中流行的文化现象，判断原词应为‘非洲鼓’。”,“原词”：“非洲鼓”}

Type	Word	MoT Rationale
Same semantic meaning restored word	石乐志 (shi2 le4 zhi4) (stone happy ambition)	{“推理过程”：“‘石乐志’的拼音是shi2 le4 zhi4，原词应该为‘失了智’，拼音是shi1le5 zhi4。这是属于部分同音字置换形成的谐音词现象，其中‘石’与‘失’存在声调差异（阳平变阴平），‘乐’与‘了’属于同音字置换（仅改变汉字写法），‘志’与‘智’属于完全同音字置换。这种谐音现象通过调整部分字的声调（shi2→shi1）并配合同音字替换（le→le，zhi→zhi）来实现谐音效果，在保持整体发音近似性的同时形成网络用语的特殊表达方式。”,‘原词’：“失了智”}
Similar meaning with elements lost restored word	雾化女性 (wu4 hua4 nü3 xing4) (atomization female)	{“推理过程”：“‘雾化’的拼音wu4 hua4，原词应该为‘物化’，拼音为wu4 hua4。这是属于完全的同音字置换形成的谐音词现象，拼音拼写(发声位置)以及音调没有发生任何变化。这个谐音词中的‘雾’属于遭到置换的字。将‘物’替换为‘雾’。这一现象仅改变了汉字写法，保持发音一致形成了谐音效果”,“原词”：“物化”}
Complete wrong restoration	非珠牛 (fei1 zhu3 niu2) (Non jewelry cow)	{“推理过程”：“‘非珠牛’的拼音是fei1 zhu1 niu2，原词应该为“非主流”，拼音是fei1 zhu3 niu2。这是属于发音位置变化结合声调变化的谐音词现象。其中‘珠’字将原词‘主’(zhu3)的声调从第三声改为第一声，‘牛’字则将‘流’(liu2)的声母从[l]改为[n]，在部分方言区存在n/l不分现象。这一谐音词通过调整声母发音位置(n/l替换)和改变声调(第三声转第一声)，在保持整体音节相似度的同时形成了该谐表达效果”,“原词”：“非主流”}

Table 11: This table shows the three types of words and examples, which represent three kinds of restoration error. The Chinese original CoT and MoT prompts are listed in the right part of the table with the rationale procedure and restored words.

Type	Homophone	CoT Rationale
Same semantic meaning restored word	石乐志 (shi2 le4 zhi4) (stone happy ambition)	Reasoning process: The term "石乐志" in the sentence has a similar pronunciation to "失智", shi1 zhi4. "失智" means losing one's rationality or being in a trance, which is consistent with the context of forgetfulness described as "forgetting things here and there" later. In Internet lang, "石乐志" is often used as a homophonic way to express this state. Original term: "失智" (loss of wisdom) (shi1 zhi4)
Similar meaning with elements lost restored word	雾化女性 (wu4 hua4 nü3 xing4) (atomization female)	Reasoning process: In the original sentence, the pronunciation of "雾化" (atomization) is the same as that of "物化", wu4 hua4. It aligns with the negative evaluation of men's behavior in the meaning of the sentence. However, the literal meaning of "雾化" does not fit the context. Therefore, it is determined that it is a homophonic substitution. Restored word: "物化"(objectify) (wu4 hua4)
Complete wrong restoration	非珠牛 (fei1 zhu3 niu2) (Non jewelry cow)	Reasoning process: The homophonic word "非珠牛" is pronounced as fei1 zhu1 niu2. We need to find a musical genre with a similar pronunciation that fits the context. "非珠" has a pronunciation close to fei1 zhu1 (the pronunciation of zhu1 and zhou1 can be similar in some dialects), and niu2 might be a miswriting of or a dialectal pronunciation of "鼓" (there could be a confusion in regional pronunciations between gu3 and niu2). Considering the cultural phenomenon that African drum music is popular among young people, it is judged that the original word should be "非洲鼓" (African drum), fei1 zhou1 gu3. Restored word: "非洲鼓" (African drum) (fei1 zhou1 gu3)

Type	Word	MoT Rationale
Same semantic meaning restored word	石乐志 (shi2 le4 zhi4) (stone happy ambition)	Reasoning process: The *pinyin* of "石乐志" is shi2 le4 zhi4, and the original phrase should be "失了智" with the *pinyin* shi1 le5 zhi4. This is a phenomenon of homophonic words formed by replacing some homophonic characters. Among them, there is a difference in tone between "石" (shi2) and "失" (shi1); "乐" and "了" are homophonic character replacements(only the written Chinese characters are changed); "志" and "智" are completely homophonic character replacements. This kind of homophonic phenomenon is achieved by adjusting the tones of some characters (shi2→shi1) and matching with homophonic character replacements (le→le, zhi→zhi). While maintaining the approximate similarity of the overall pronunciation, it forms a special expression in Internet slang. Restored word: "失了智" (loss of wisdom)(shi1 le5 zhi4)
Similar meaning with elements lost restored word	雾化女性 (wu4 hua4 nü3 xing4) (atomization female)	Reasoning process: The *pinyin* of "雾化" (atomization) is wu4 hua4, and the original word should be "物化" (objectify), with the *pinyin* also being wu4 hua4. This is a phenomenon of homophonic words formed by a complete replacement of homophonic characters, where neither the *pinyin* syllables spelling (place of articulation) nor the tone has changed at all. In this homophonic word, the character "雾" (wu4) is the one that has been replaced. The character "物" (wu4) has been substituted with "雾" (wu4). This phenomenon only changes the written form of the Chinese character while keeping the pronunciation consistent, thus creating a homophonic effect. Original word: "物化" (objectify) (wu4 hua4)
Complete wrong restoration	非珠牛 (fei1 zhu3 niu2) (Non jewelry cow)	Reasoning process: The *pinyin* of "非珠牛" is fei1 zhu1 niu2, and the original word should be "非主流" with the *pinyin* fei1 zhu3 liu2. This is a phenomenon of homophonic words that combines changes in the place of pronunciation and tone changes. Among them, for the character "珠" (zhu1), the tone of the original character "主" (zhu3) has been changed from the third tone to the first tone. As for the character "牛" (niu2), the initial consonant of "流" (liu2) has been changed from [l] to [n]. There is a phenomenon of confusion between "n" and "l" in some dialect areas. This homophonic word forms a humorous expression effect while maintaining the overall similarity of syllables by adjusting the pronunciation position of the initial consonant (replacement of "n" and "l") and changing the tone (changing from the third tone to the first tone). Original word: "非主流" (non-mainstream)(fei1 zhu3 liu2)

Table 12: This table shows the three types of words, which represent three kinds of restoration error. The English-translated CoT and MoT prompts are listed in the right part of the table with the rationale procedure and restored words.

Superfluous Instruction: Vulnerabilities Stemming from Task-Specific Superficial Expressions in Instruction Templates

Toma Suzuki, Yusuke Sakai, Justin Vasselli, Hidetaka Kamigaito, Taro Watanabe
Nara Institute of Science and Technology (NAIST), Japan
{suzuki.toma.ss5, sakai.yusuke.sr9, vasselli.justin_ray.vk4, kamigaito.h, taro}@is.naist.jp

Abstract

Large language models (LLMs) achieve high performance through instruction-tuning, which involves learning various tasks using instruction templates. However, these templates often contain *task-specific expressions*, which are words that frequently appear in certain contexts but do not always convey the actual meaning of that context, even if they seem closely related to the target task. Biases inherent in such instruction templates may be learned by LLMs during training, potentially degrading performance when the models encounter superficial expressions. In this study, we propose a method that incorporates additional instructions to FLAN templates, without altering the base instruction to produce **"superfluous instructions"**. This allows us to investigate the vulnerabilities of LLMs caused by overfitting to task-specific expressions embedded in instruction templates. The experimental results revealed that the inclusion of superficial words strongly related to each task in the instruction text can alter the output, regardless of the intended meaning.

1 Introduction

Large language models (LLMs) adopt a training method called instruction-tuning (Wei et al., 2022a; Longpre et al., 2023), which enables them to respond appropriately to a wide range of user queries based on given instructions. To perform instruction-tuning, it is necessary to construct datasets consisting of instruction-output pairs. Instruction templates are typically designed to structure existing natural language processing tasks so that generative LLMs can produce relevant outputs. Furthermore, diverse templates for each task are crucial to avoid overfitting to any single template. Providing multiple templates during instruction-tuning is important for improving the model's generalization (Sakai et al., 2024). However, templates designed for specific tasks often contain task-specific words, which may introduce biases related to those tasks. Table 1

	trivia qa	wmt16 translate	multi news	math dataset	true case
1	**answer**	**translate**	**article**	**problem**	**capitalize**
2	**question**	to	summary	**math**	**case**
3	the	language	this	**solution**	proper
4	**trivia**	in	true	**solve**	correctly
5	be	not	context	the	**low**

Table 1: The five most words with high TF-IDF scores in instruction templates for each task in the FLAN dataset.

presents the five most significant words, based on TF-IDF (Ramos, 2003), for each task in the instruction template dataset FLAN (Wei et al., 2022a), showing a strong connection between the words used in the templates and their associated tasks.

In this study, we focus on surface-level biases arising from the presence of task-specific words in instruction templates. By leveraging FLAN, a widely adopted instruction template dataset that allows for precise control over word occurrences, we can rigorously evaluate the influence of such task-specific words. Furthermore, we propose **"superfluous instructions"** which incorporate unrelated text into FLAN templates, while preserving the original task-solving intent of the instructions. For example, we add expressions such as *"Answer the following question* ***without generating unrelated text****"*. These expressions are carefully designed not to interfere with the original intent. Therefore, we expect that they will not affect the model's output from a task-solving perspective.

We evaluated three models tuned by FLAN instructions using 80 superfluous instructions tailored to each task. The results show that adding superfluous instructions, particularly those containing task-specific superficial expressions, negatively impacted performance. This suggests that instruction-tuned LLMs are vulnerable to superficial cues in the instructions, which degrade performance even when the instruction's meaning remains unchanged.

Proceedings of the 3rd Workshop on Towards Knowledgeable Foundation Models (KnowFM), pages 140–152
August 1, 2025 ©2025 Association for Computational Linguistics

These findings provide important insights for developing more robust instruction-tuning methods.

2 Background and Related Work

Instruction-Tuning Datasets. FLAN (Wei et al., 2022a; Longpre et al., 2023) is a widely used English resource for instruction-tuning, designed to cover a broad range of natural language processing tasks. By adapting these templates to each task, diverse data can be generated for instruction tuning. In addition to FLAN, other datasets have been proposed that use different templates for instruction-tuning (Wang et al., 2022; Zhang et al., 2023; Chen et al., 2024). However, there are concerns that datasets created using templates might merely lead models to memorize the superficial patterns of the templates (Kung and Peng, 2023). As a result, LLMs may struggle to follow instructions that deviate from the patterns found in their training data, failing to produce the expected output. Alternatives to template-based approaches include generating instruction-tuning data from LLM outputs (Xu et al., 2024, 2023; Peng et al., 2023), or efficiently producing large datasets through methods like crowdsourcing (Wang et al., 2022; Mishra et al., 2022; Köpf et al., 2023). However, such data can inherit generation biases from the LLMs used (Kavumba et al., 2022; Zellers et al., 2019; Tamborrino et al., 2020; Omura et al., 2020) or include low-quality artifacts from crowdsourcing, known as Annotation Artifacts (Gururangan et al., 2020; Poliak et al., 2018; Tsuchiya, 2018). Training models with such data may cause them to develop strong biased responses toward certain characteristic words.

Vulnerabilities to Specific Instructions. LLMs can achieve enhanced performance through prompt engineering (Wei et al., 2022b; Kojima et al., 2022; Zhong et al., 2023; Yang et al., 2024; Zhou et al., 2023; Yao et al., 2023; Chen et al., 2025), or via prompt tuning (Lester et al., 2021; Liu et al., 2024; Li and Liang, 2021). While well-designed prompts can maximize their potential, there is also a concern that language models might not understand the meaning of the text but rather rely on characteristic tokens in the input, guiding their outputs solely based on the superficial expressions of prompts (Du et al., 2023; Kavumba et al., 2022; Zellers et al., 2019; Tamborrino et al., 2020; Omura et al., 2020; Zheng et al., 2025). This issue has also drawn attention from the perspective of instruction-following (Moon et al., 2025; Sakai et al., 2025; Qin et al., 2024; Zeng et al., 2024), consistency (Sakai et al., 2024; Lee et al., 2025; Raj et al., 2025), and safety (Dong et al., 2024; Li et al., 2024). Thus, while specific tokens can enhance a model's performance, they may also cause the model to behave differently than usual when encountering certain tokens. For instance, popular instruction-tuning datasets like FLAN include only positive instructions in their templates. As a result, it has been questioned whether language models can properly handle instructions involving negation, such as *"does not contain the keyword"* or *"does not imply the meaning"* (Kassner and Schütze, 2020; Jang et al., 2023; Hosseini et al., 2021; Hossain et al., 2020; Ye et al., 2023). These studies evaluated models' ability to reverse answers in tasks like NLI (Williams et al., 2018) by making minor changes to evaluation templates, e.g., replacing "plausible" with "implausible" or "correct" with "incorrect." Their findings suggest that language models struggle with handling negation. However, these analyses focus on introducing negation by simply replacing words in templates, which leaves it unclear whether LLMs are inherently vulnerable to semantic negation, or merely biased due to the disproportionate presence of positive over negative instructions in training templates.

3 Superfluous Instructions

We introduce "superfluous instructions" that contain target words for analysis but provide no new semantic information. By adding superficial expressions without semantic changes, we investigate how superficial expressions, such as task-specific words, affect model output. We use FLAN (Wei et al., 2022a)[1] as seed instruction templates.

3.1 Design of Base Superfluous Instructions

Superfluous instructions are phrases added to instructions in a way that does not change their meaning. For instance, the phrase *"without generating unrelated text"* is a superfluous instruction in Figure 1. Such phrases are natural yet do not alter the purpose of the tasks due to the presence of a double negative. To generalize this structure, we create variations such as *"without generating **{unrelated} {text}**"*, where ***{unrelated}*** is replaced with synonyms and ***{text}*** with task-specific words.

[1] https://github.com/google-research/FLAN/blob/main/flan/templates.py

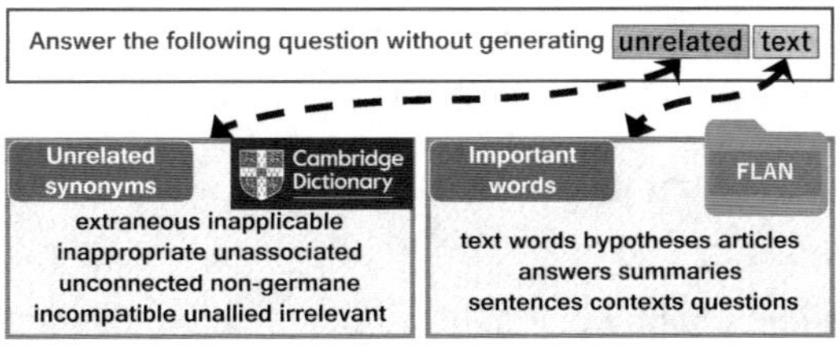

Figure 1: Base template of the superfluous instruction. The superfluous phrase **"without generating {unrelated} {text}"** includes placeholders, where **{unrelated}** is replaced with adjectives and **{text}** with nouns, using all possible combinations from the respective candidate sets. This allows us to add superficial expressions without introducing any semantic changes.

This approach allows us to generate multiple superfluous instructions per task. Since the core task instruction remains unchanged, the model's output should, in theory, also remain the same. If the output changes, it suggests that the superfluous instruction is influencing the model's behavior. For simplicity, "superfluous instructions" refers to the entire instructions containing the superfluous phrase: **"without generating *{unrelated} {text}*"**.

3.2 Word Selection for {Unrelated} Part

We fill the **{unrelated}** placeholder in the base superfluous instruction with synonyms of the word "unrelated" to evaluate the model's ability to generalize. By comparing the results across multiple instructions, we assess how the model responds to variations in the instruction. To identify appropriate synonyms, we consulted the Cambridge Dictionaries Online[2] and found 11 synonyms for "unrelated". We used 10 synonyms[3]: "unrelated," "extraneous," "inapplicable," "irrelevant," "unassociated," "incompatible," "unconnected," "unallied," "non-germane," and "inappropriate." We confirmed with native English speakers that all 10 variations are grammatically correct and preserve the original instruction's meaning. We then generated multiple instructions by replacing the ***{unrelated}*** placeholder in the phrase *"without generating* ***{unrelated}*** *text"* with each of these synonyms.

3.3 Important Word Selection from Instruction Templates

We replaced the **{text}** placeholder in the superfluous instruction with task-specific important words from each instruction to evaluate their effect on model performance. To identify these important words, we used TF-IDF (Ramos, 2003). For each task, we treated the set of templates associated with that task as a single document and computed TF-IDF scores. Since instruction tuning aims to improve model performance across multiple tasks, it is important to consider word importance not only within individual tasks but also across all templates. The TF-IDF calculation of our study is as follows:

$$tf(t,d) = \frac{n_{t,d}}{\Sigma_{s \in d} n_{s,d}}, \text{ where } d \in D, \quad (1)$$

$$df(t,D) = |\{d \in D : t \in d\}|, \quad (2)$$

$$idf(t,D) = \log \frac{|D|}{df(t,D)} + 1, \quad (3)$$

$$tfidf(t,d,D) = tf(t,d) \cdot idf(t,D). \quad (4)$$

Here, D denotes the collection of documents, d is a single document, t is the target word, and n is the raw count of the word t in d. For our TF-IDF calculation, we treat the entire collection of templates as D, where each task d_i is considered a document consisting of multiple templates. Each individual template within a task is denoted as d_{ij}.

Next, the TF-IDF scores for each word t were summed across the dataset D. To reduce bias from differences in word usage across tasks, we normalized these scores by dividing the sum by the number of tasks in which the word appears:

$$Importance(t, d_i, D) = \frac{\Sigma_{j=1}^{N} tfidf(t, d_{ij}, D)}{df(t,D)}. \quad (5)$$

This approach balances *word importance* across the dataset while mitigating bias from infrequent words. We calculated TF-IDF scores after lemmatizing[4] the words in each template. The importance of each word, based on its TF-IDF score, is normalized by its occurrence count, as shown in Equation 5. However, words that appear very infrequently may yield artificially high importance scores. To address this, we consider only words with above-average occurrence counts. We define such frequently occurring words across the FLAN templates as high-importance words (henceforth, "important words").

Table 2 shows the top 15 important words. As indicated in Table 2, some of these words belong to parts of speech other than nouns. Therefore, to

[2]`https://dictionary.cambridge.org/`

[3]We exclude "foreign" because it did not strongly align with the meaning of "unrelated."

[4]For lemmatization, we used the "`en_core_web_sm`" model from the spaCy library: `https://spacy.io/`.

Rank	Word	TF-IDF	Importance
1	same	2.877	0.4795
2	**question**	7.601	0.4751
3	**hypothesis**	2.245	0.4491
4	**article**	5.226	0.4355
5	**answer**	6.246	0.3123
6	**summary**	2.426	0.2696
7	true	2.032	0.2540
8	we	1.800	0.2250
9	if	2.185	0.2185
10	two	1.706	0.2133
11	**word**	1.268	0.2114
12	next	2.240	0.2037
13	**sentence**	7.615	0.1953
14	**context**	1.533	0.1917
15	paragraph	1.519	0.1898

Table 2: Top 15 words that appear more frequently than average and have high importance scores. Words highlighted in bold were used in this study. Note that words with high TF-IDF scores do not always have high importance scores, e.g., "sentence".

maintain the correct structure of the superfluous instruction, we selected only nouns with an importance score of 0.19 or higher. The final eight words used in our experiments are highlighted in bold in Table 2. For consistency, countable nouns were used in their plural forms.

4 Experimental Setup

LLMs. We used three instruction-tuned LLMs based on FLAN templates, with different parameter sizes: FLAN-T5 XL (3B) based on T5-XL (Raffel et al., 2020); FLAN-T5 XXL (11B) based on T5-XXL (Raffel et al., 2020); FLAN-UL2 (20B) (Tay et al., 2023) based on UL2 (Chung et al., 2024).

Datasets. We selected MMLU (Hendrycks et al., 2021) and BBH (Suzgun et al., 2023). MMLU covers 57 subjects with varying difficulty, including STEM, law, medicine, and ethics. BBH focuses on 23 particularly challenging tasks for language models, derived from the broader BIG-Bench dataset (Srivastava et al., 2023), which spans 204 categories, including linguistics and software knowledge. These datasets are reserved for evaluation and not trained for each model.

Evaluations. We used 8-bit quantized inferences (Dettmers et al., 2022) with greedy decoding in a zero-shot setting[5]. We evaluated the models using accuracy as the evaluation metric. We apply simple post-processing to remove whitespace and newline characters, convert the text to lowercase, and then evaluate using exact match accuracy.

5 Experimental Results

Table 3 shows the evaluation scores for each model and task with superfluous instruction.

5.1 Effect of Adding Superfluous Instructions

In Table 3, where the **{unrelated}** part of the instructions was replaced with synonyms, all models exhibited a performance drop compared to the standard instructions, indicating that superfluous instructions negatively impact performance. BBH showed a larger score decrease than MMLU, which can be attributed to BBH's more varied answer formats. This suggests that the models are highly fitted to the concise style of FLAN instructions and struggle to handle the redundancy introduced by the added phrases. Furthermore, contrary to expectations based on scaling laws, the standard deviation increased with larger model sizes. This suggests that improving generalization requires not only scaling up model size, but also careful selection of instruction templates.

5.2 Impact of Superfluous Instructions with Important Words

In Table 3, when the **{text}** part was replaced with important words, the scores dropped even further. This suggests that the presence of important words in FLAN templates can introduce vulnerabilities, affecting model behavior regardless of context. As in Section 5.1, the score drop was larger for BBH than for MMLU and became more pronounced with increasing model size. These results further support the hypothesis of overfitting to instruction templates, as discussed in Section 5.1.

5.3 Impact of Combining Superfluous Instructions and Important Words

When both **{unrelated}** and **{text}** were replaced, the score drops, with FLAN-T5 XXL and FLAN-UL2 being as high as when only the {text} part was replaced. This suggests that replacing important words {text} consistently led to substantial performance degradation, regardless of the accompanying {unrelated} term. Additionally, although BBH features tasks with diverse answer formats, while MMLU consists solely of multiple-choice questions, MMLU exhibited higher standard deviations. This indicates that replacing important

[5]This was implemented using HuggingFace Transformers (Wolf et al., 2020) and used a single A6000 GPU.

Replacement		Score	FLAN-T5 XL		FLAN-T5 XXL		FLAN-UL2	
{unrelated}	{text}		MMLU	BBH	MMLU	BBH	MMLU	BBH
Standard Instruction		acc.	47.1	33.7	52.5	41.0	53.1	34.5
✓		acc.	46.8±0.3	30.3±3.0	49.1±2.4	33.1±3.6	48.8±5.1	20.9±5.6
✓		Δ	↓0.3 (0.7%)	↓3.4 (10.1%)	↓3.4 (6.5%)	↓8.0 (19.4%)	↓4.4 (8.2%)	↓13.5 (39.3%)
	✓	acc.	45.8±1.5	26.3±4.3	45.8±9.1	31.2±5.0	33.3±14.3	14.7±8.9
	✓	Δ	↓1.3 (2.7%)	↓7.4 (22.1%)	↓6.7 (12.8%)	↓9.9 (24.1%)	↓19.8 (37.3%)	↓19.7 (57.2%)
✓	✓	acc.	46.3±1.5	27.3±4.8	46.9±6.3	30.7±5.7	37.1±13.8	16.7±8.8
✓	✓	Δ	↓0.8 (1.7%)	↓6.4 (19.0%)	↓5.6 (10.7%)	↓10.4 (25.3%)	↓16.1 (30.2%)	↓17.8 (51.6%)

Table 3: Average scores per model and instruction type across tasks. Checkmarks indicate which part of the instruction *"Answer the following question without generating* ***{unrelated} {text}****."* was replaced. When present, a checkmark means {unrelated} was replaced with synonyms and {text} with important words. The ± symbol denotes the standard deviation, and Δ indicates the change in score relative to the version with no replacements.

Replacement: {text}	MMLU	BBH
Standard Instruction	53.1	34.5
words	↓22.0 (41.4%)	↓14.7 (42.6%)
hypotheses	↓22.3 (41.9%)	↓21.3 (61.9%)
articles	↓16.3 (30.6%)	↓21.3 (61.7%)
answers	↓ 1.2 (2.2%)	↑ 0.6 (1.8%)
summaries	↓ 3.7 (7.0%)	↓17.8 (51.6%)
sentences	↓21.5 (40.4%)	↓21.9 (63.5%)
contexts	↓18.2 (34.2%)	↓23.5 (68.1%)
questions	↓35.1 (66.1%)	↓26.6 (77.1%)

Table 4: FLAN-UL2's average scores for each replaced important word across all **{unrelated}** replacements.

words disrupted the model's ability to select correct answers, even in the constrained format of multiple-choice tasks. These findings suggest potential overfitting to the instruction templates used during tuning. Moreover, contrary to expectations from scaling laws, FLAN-T5 XL showed smaller variations in score and standard deviation compared to FLAN-T5 XXL and FLAN-UL2, reinforcing the idea that improving generalization depends not only on model size, but also on factors such as the instruction templates used during tuning.

5.4 Analysis of the Relationship Between Important Words and Scores

To identify which important words had the greatest impact on performance, Table 4 presents FLAN-UL2's average scores for each replaced important word, averaged over all {unrelated} replacements. The word "answers" caused the smallest change in scores, suggesting minimal influence on model behavior. In contrast, "questions" led to the largest score drop in both BBH and MMLU. Additionally, while "summaries" had little effect on MMLU, it caused a noticeable drop in BBH, similar to the behavior observed when using "text" in the base instruction. In summary, compared to both the standard instruction and the basic "text" prompt, the use of important words resulted in larger score decreases, confirming that these words have a strong influence on model behavior.

6 Discussion

6.1 Analysis of Score Decrease by Each Task

To understand how each important word affects model behavior, we analyzed task-level score changes in MMLU and BBH. Figures 2 and 3 show the scores without the superfluous instruction (w/o), and with replacements to {unrelated} (U), {text} (T), or both (U/T). Tasks are ordered by the standard deviation of scores across these conditions, from highest (top left) to lowest (bottom right).

MMLU. In most MMLU tasks shown in Figure 2, the scores for all three models are quite similar when standard instructions (column w/o) are used. However, superfluous instructions lead to noticeable variations in scores across tasks. For tasks with high standard deviation (top left), FLAN-UL2 (green line) shows a significant score drop when the prompt is altered. Similarly, FLAN-T5 XXL also shows a decline, especially in tasks with greater score variability, while FLAN-T5 XL exhibits minimal score changes. We also examined the impact of replacing {unrelated} and {text}. For FLAN-UL2, scores declined when {unrelated} was replaced, but an even larger drop occurred when {text} was substituted. This suggests that, for certain tasks, replacing {text} has a greater impact on performance than replacing {unrelated}.

BBH. In BBH tasks shown in Figure 3, even with standard instructions (column w/o), score trends varied across models, in contrast to the MMLU

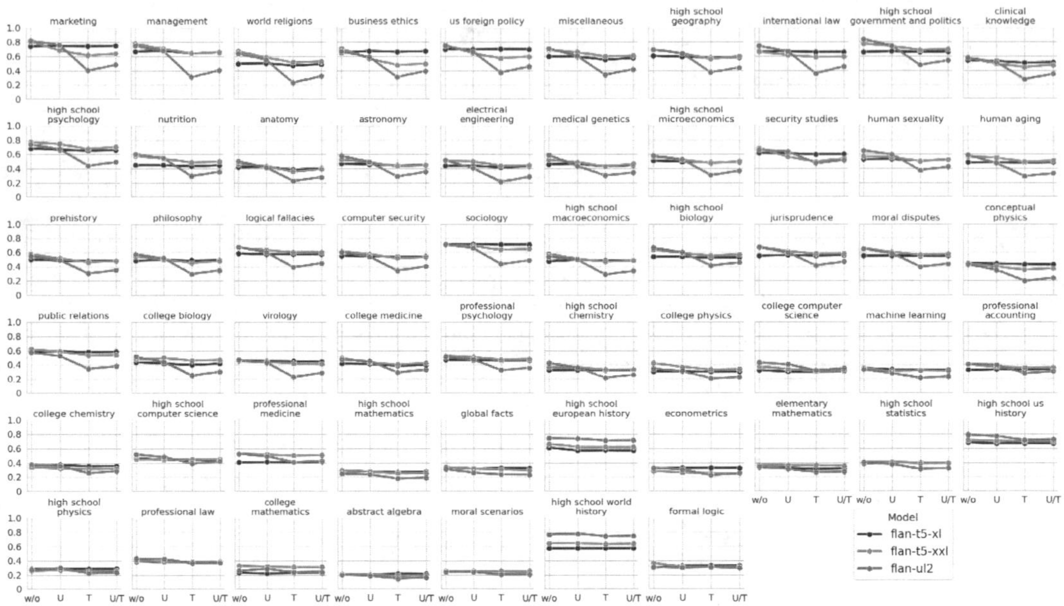

Figure 2: Accuracy for each task in MMLU. "w/o" indicates values without superfluous instructions, "U" indicates values with changes to {unrelated}, "T" indicates changes to {text}, and "U/T" indicates changes to both. Results are arranged from top left to bottom right in order of decreasing standard deviation for each task.

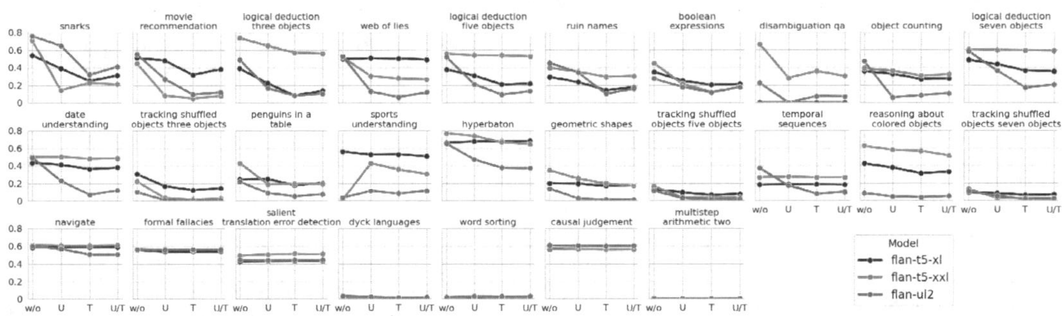

Figure 3: Accuracy for each task in BBH. "w/o" indicates values without superfluous instructions, "U" indicates values with changes to {unrelated}, "T" indicates changes to {text}, and "U/T" indicates changes to both. Results are arranged from top left to bottom right in order of decreasing standard deviation for each task.

case. Additionally, the score variations introduced by superfluous instructions were quite diverse. For FLAN-UL2, replacing {text} led to substantial score drops in many tasks. However, in tasks such as snarks and movie recommendation, the drop from {unrelated} replacements was relatively small compared to {text}, indicating that {text} played a stronger role in influencing model behavior in these tasks. For FLAN-T5 XXL, tasks such as snarks, disambiguation_qa, and sports understanding showed higher scores when {text} was replaced than when {unrelated} was, suggesting that important words had a positive effect on performance in these cases. FLAN-T5 XL, similar to its performance on MMLU, showed relatively little change in scores. The four tasks with the lowest standard deviations, except for causal judgement, consistently showed low accuracy across all prompts, indicating their difficulty for the models. BBH appears to contain many tasks that are highly sensitive to prompt variations. While MMLU consists entirely of multiple-choice questions (A to D), BBH includes tasks with various answer formats, such as valid-invalid, true-false, sorting, and symbol-based answers, leading to substantial variation in response quality depending on the prompt.

Case Analysis 1: To clarify how the replaced important words specifically impacted model behavior, we conducted a detailed analysis of several tasks from MMLU and BBH where the score decreased more significantly when {text} was replaced than when {unrelated} was replaced. We also examined BBH tasks that exhibited notable changes. For example, in the movie recommendation task, FLAN-UL2's score decreased further when important words were replaced after adding superfluous instructions. The frequent occurrence of the word "movie" in this task, which also appears in some FLAN template tasks, may suggest overfitting. While the movie recommendation task involves label selection, some FLAN template tasks require summary or sentence generation, often using words like "summarize" or "sentence". This overlap in terminology likely contributed to overfitting, resulting in a substantial drop in performance.

Case Analysis 2: Another noteworthy example is the sports understanding task. FLAN-T5 XL achieved around 60% accuracy, but the larger models, FLAN-T5 XXL and FLAN-UL2, showed lower performance even with standard instructions. Interestingly, FLAN-T5 XXL's score improved to 40% when superfluous instructions were added. In this task, the word "plausible" appears frequently, and the correct responses are "yes" or "no". The FLAN template task Copa also uses "plausible", but it involves multiple-choice answers. With standard instructions, FLAN-T5 XXL often responded in choice format, e.g., "(II)", but with superfluous instructions, correct yes-no responses increased. This suggests that FLAN-T5 XXL was overfitting to the word "plausible" in the prompt, and that the insertion of superfluous expression helped reduce this overfitting. These observations further support the hypothesis of word-level overfitting within the FLAN templates. This overfitting appears to influence both score performance degradation and improvement, depending on the specific task and prompt structure.

6.2 Impact of Low-Importance Words

Motivation and Settings. We examine whether the performance decrease attributed to high-importance words in Section 3.3 can also be observed with "low-importance words". We define low-importance words as those ranked among the lowest in importance scores. Table 5 lists the words with low importance. The final seven noun words used in our experiments are highlighted in bold. For consistency, countable nouns were replaced with their plural forms. To test this, we created similar instructions using low-importance words and calculated task scores for each model and instruction type. From the bottom 36 words in importance listed in Table 5, the nouns that appear in the FLAN templates include: "messages," "potentials," "terms," "definitions," "examples," "opinions," and "contents". These words were substituted into the {text} part of the instructions, while the {unrelated} part was also replaced with its synonyms, resulting in a total of 70 generated superfluous instructions.

	Word	TF-IDF	Impo-rtance		Word	TF-IDF	Impo-rtance
1	your	0.043	0.043	19	give	0.523	0.065
2	means	0.043	0.043	20	one	0.917	0.065
3	out	0.043	0.043	21	otherwise	0.131	0.066
4	resemble	0.043	0.043	22	tell	0.536	0.067
5	closely	0.043	0.043	23	so	0.068	0.068
6	try	0.050	0.050	24	second	0.277	0.069
7	else	0.050	0.050	25	first	0.277	0.069
8	impossible	0.050	0.050	26	return	0.209	0.070
9	**messages**	0.053	0.053	27	type	0.070	0.070
10	**potentials**	0.053	0.053	28	at	0.142	0.071
11	propose	0.053	0.053	29	embody	0.071	0.071
12	**term**	0.225	0.056	30	**example**	0.356	0.071
13	generate	1.186	0.059	31	perceive	0.072	0.072
14	follow	2.255	0.063	32	**opinion**	0.072	0.072
15	here	1.157	0.064	33	whether	0.146	0.073
16	another	0.065	0.065	34	above	1.404	0.074
17	**definition**	0.065	0.065	35	think	0.151	0.075
18	both	0.065	0.065	36	**contents**	0.303	0.076

Table 5: List of 36 low-importance words, ranked by importance score from lowest to highest. The seven bolded nouns were used in our experiments.

Relationship Between Low-Importance Words and Scores. Table 6 presents the task scores for each model and instruction type. When using instructions with low-importance words, particularly in BBH, the rate of score decline tended to increase with larger model sizes. However, this decline was smaller for FLAN-UL2 compared to the case with high-importance words. Similar trends were observed in the other models, though the changes were generally smaller. Furthermore, Table 7 shows the average scores for each low-importance word. Except for "terms" and "definitions", most words caused only minimal score changes across all models, indicating limited impact on performance. However, "terms" and "definitions" led to substantial drops in FLAN-T5 XXL and FLAN-UL2, despite being classified as low-importance. This may be due to "definitions" appearing only once in the original FLAN templates used for

Replacement		Score	FLAN-T5 XL		FLAN-T5 XXL		FLAN-UL2	
{unrelated}	{text}		MMLU	BBH	MMLU	BBH	MMLU	BBH
Standard Instruction		acc.	47.1	33.7	52.5	41.0	53.1	34.5
	✓	acc.	46.8±0.2	27.6±3.3	46.3±7.0	33.1±6.7	48.3±7.5	24.2±7.1
	✓	Δ	↓0.2 (0.5%)	↓6.1 (18.2%)	↓6.2 (11.9%)	↓8.0 (19.4%)	↓4.8 (9.1%)	↓10.3 (29.9%)
	✓	acc.	46.9±0.4	28.6±3.4	47.7±7.0	34.1±6.6	48.8±6.9	25.0±7.0
✓	✓	Δ	↓0.2 (0.5%)	↓5.2 (15.3%)	↓4.9 (9.2%)	↓6.9 (16.9%)	↓4.4 (8.2%)	↓9.4 (27.4%)

Table 6: Average scores per model and instruction type across tasks using lower importance words. Checkmarks indicate which part of the instruction *"Answer the following question without generating **{unrelated} {text}**."* was replaced. When present, a checkmark means {unrelated} was replaced with synonyms and {text} with important words. The ± symbol denotes the standard deviation, and Δ indicates the change in score relative to the version with no replacements.

Replacement: {text}	MMLU	BBH
Standard Instruction	53.1	34.5
messages	↓ 0.6(1.2%)	↓ 5.8(16.8%)
potentials	↓ 0.5(1.0%)	↓ 2.3(6.7%)
terms	↓ 14.8(27.9%)	↓ 15.0(43.5%)
definitions	↓ 9.3(17.5%)	↓ 19.4(56.3%)
examples	↓ 2.6(4.9%)	↓ 8.5(24.6%)
opinions	↓ 0.8(1.5%)	↓ 5.5(16.0%)
contents	↓ 1.8(3.4%)	↓ 9.7(28.0%)

Table 7: FLAN-UL2's average scores for each replaced low important word across all {unrelated} replacements.

TF-IDF computation, but being used frequently in the natinst_v2 task included in the updated FLAN-v2 templates[6]. At the task level, FLAN-UL2 again showed greater score variability, consistent with observations for high-importance words. In MMLU, scores remained stable across different low-importance words, whereas BBH showed slightly more variation, though still less than when high-importance words were used. These results support the use of our importance score as an indicator of words that may cause overfitting.

6.3 Low-Importance Words by Tasks

Figures 4 and 5 show task-level results using low-importance words. Since the word "text" is not among the selected low-importance words, the "U" column contains no values. Tasks are ordered by standard deviation from top left to bottom right, following the same order as in Figures 2 and 3.

MMLU. In Figure 4, MMLU shows minimal score variation when low-importance words are used. When {text} is replaced (T), tasks that previously showed large drops with high-importance words now exhibit only slight decreases. When both {unrelated} and {text} are replaced (U/T), scores remain nearly the same as when only {text} is replaced, suggesting that {unrelated} has a limited impact. This trend aligns with the earlier results using high-importance words.

BBH. In Figure 5, similar patterns are observed. For most tasks, excluding "sports understanding", FLAN-T5 XL and FLAN-T5 XXL show little to no score change, in contrast to the greater variations seen with high-importance words in Figure 3. FLAN-UL2 displays some variability, but again, to a lesser extent. These results support the claim that high-importance words more strongly affect model behavior and task performance. Interestingly, in the "sports understanding" task, replacing {text} led to a score increase to about 30% for FLAN-T5 XXL, while FLAN-UL2 remained mostly unchanged. This contrasts with the high-importance condition in Figure 3, where FLAN-T5 XXL improved by about 40% and FLAN-UL2 by 10%. These findings highlight the importance of task-specific prompt design.

6.4 What Does Importance Score Capture?

We analyze why certain words that strongly influence model behavior tend to have high importance scores. First, we calculated TF-IDF scores within FLAN templates to assess how distinctive a word is in contexts requiring specific answer formats (Table 1). Next, we identified task-specific important words using the importance score and confirmed which words were generally characteristic across tasks (Figure 1). Finally, we filtered out words with high scores that appeared only a few times, as described in Section 3.3.

This process allowed us to **efficiently identify** words that are both strongly tied to output formats and frequently encountered during training. These

[6]https://github.com/google-research/FLAN/blob/main/flan/v2/templates.py

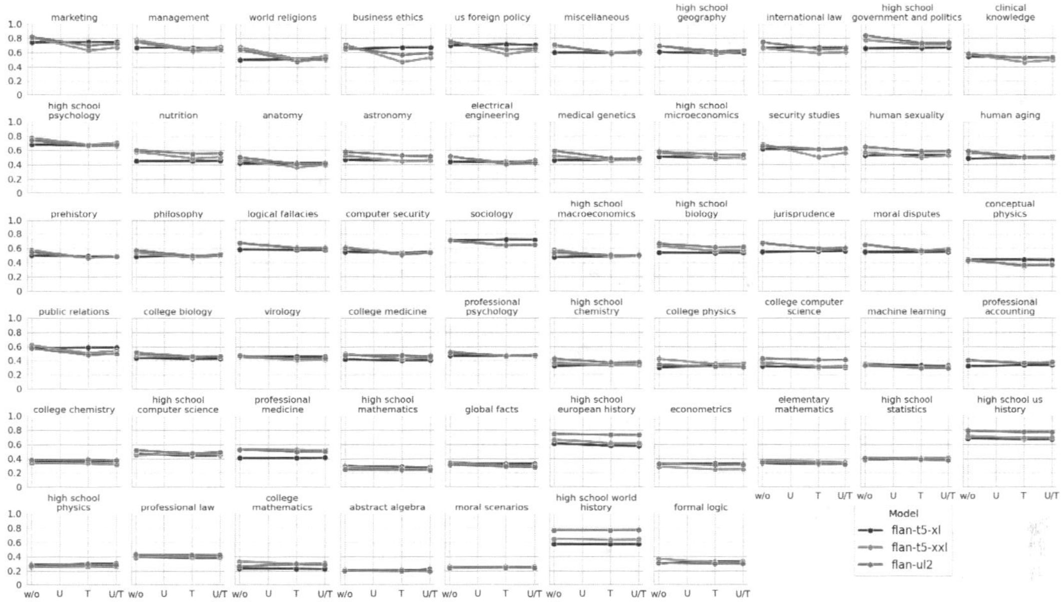

Figure 4: Accuracy for each task in MMLU. The notation and order in each table are the same as in Figure 2. "w/o" indicates values without superfluous instructions, "U" indicates values with changes to {unrelated}, "T" indicates changes to {text}, and "U/T" indicates changes to both. In contrast to Figure 2, the word "text" is not among the low TF-IDF words, so there are no values in the "U" column.

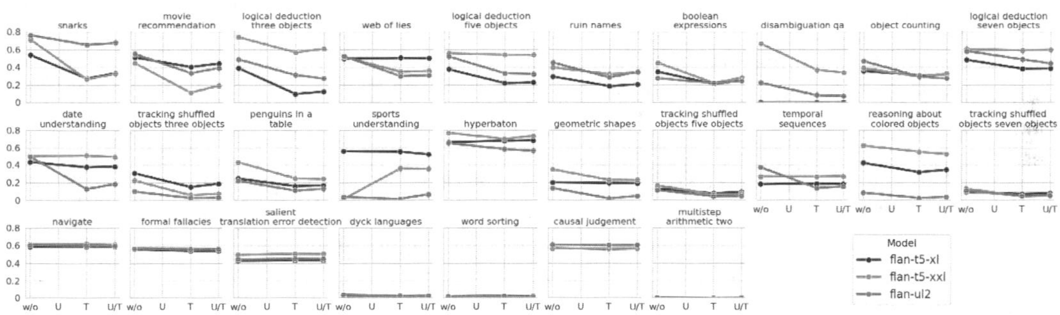

Figure 5: Accuracy for each task in BBH. The notation and order in each table are the same as in Figure 3. "w/o" indicates values without superfluous instructions, "U" indicates values with changes to {unrelated}, "T" indicates changes to {text}, and "U/T" indicates changes to both. In contrast to Figure 3, the word "text" is not among the low TF-IDF words, so there are no values in the "U" column.

results suggest that such words are more likely to cause overfitting and that heuristic methods like TF-IDF-based importance scores may be useful for identifying vulnerabilities in deep learning models.

7 Conclusion

In this study, we proposed a novel method for designing instruction templates to analyze the impact of task-specific superficial expressions found in instruction-tuning templates on the performance of large language models. Using this method, we generated instructions based on the FLAN templates and conducted evaluations on both MMLU and BBH tasks. The results revealed that the performance of LLMs is affected by task-specific superficial expressions included in the instructions. This insight is essential for developing more robust instruction-tuning methods. In future work, we plan to explore solutions such as replacing these superficial expressions during instruction-tuning to address the issues identified in this study.

8 Limitations

Language Models. Our study validated the findings using a limited set of open models instruction-tuned on the FLAN dataset. Due to resource constraints, we could not train models on the full FLAN datasets and instead relied on widely used instruction-tuned models. This choice allowed us to isolate the impact of word biases in the FLAN templates. However, our conclusions may not generalize to all large language models. Future work could involve comparisons among models with similar architectures to further examine these effects.

Generality of Dataset. In this study, we used only two datasets, MMLU and BBH, which were explicitly labeled as held-out tasks in the original paper (Longpre et al., 2023). This choice was made to create an ideal environment for isolating the influence of words in the FLAN templates by mitigating other variables. Whether the results observed with these two tasks can be replicated in other datasets remains an open question for future research. However, the in-depth analysis at the task level within BBH could help clarify the potential impact of similar effects in other datasets. In the future, we could also explore broader impacts in datasets like MMMLU[7], which includes multilingual tasks and might provide insights similar to those seen in our held-out tasks.

Datasets for Instruction-Tuning. Although we investigated the influence of word bias in templates, other methods have been developed to reduce word-related biases, such as allowing language models to generate diverse prompts (Wang et al., 2023; Taori et al., 2023; Kojima et al., 2021; Nayak et al., 2024). This approach may increase the variety of tasks and phrases used. However, as previous research has repeatedly shown, biases in the words and ideas produced by language models remain a concern. Techniques like TF-IDF, which count word frequency, continue to be effective in detecting such biases early on. Additionally, there are restrictions on how data generated by models like Llama2 (Touvron et al., 2023) can be used, such as limitations on usage outside of Llama 2 or derivative works[8]. Considering these constraints, instruction-tuning with templates remains valuable, and efforts to mitigate bias in this context are still essential.

[7]https://huggingface.co/datasets/openai/MMMLU

[8]https://github.com/metallama/llama/blob/main/LICENSE

9 Ethical Considerations

Dataset. We used public datasets and modified them. These datasets are allowed to be used and modified under their respective licenses. Therefore, our dataset does not raise ethical considerations.

Use of AI Assistants. In this study, we have used GitHub Copilot and ChatGPT as an AI assistant for coding and writing support.

References

Banghao Chen, Zhaofeng Zhang, Nicolas Langrené, and Shengxin Zhu. 2025. Unleashing the potential of prompt engineering for large language models. *Patterns*, 6(6):101260.

Lichang Chen, Jiuhai Chen, Tom Goldstein, Heng Huang, and Tianyi Zhou. 2024. InstructZero: Efficient instruction optimization for black-box large language models. In *Proceedings of the 41st International Conference on Machine Learning*, volume 235 of *Proceedings of Machine Learning Research*, pages 6503–6518. PMLR.

Hyung Won Chung, Le Hou, Shayne Longpre, Barret Zoph, Yi Tay, William Fedus, Yunxuan Li, Xuezhi Wang, Mostafa Dehghani, Siddhartha Brahma, Albert Webson, Shixiang Shane Gu, Zhuyun Dai, Mirac Suzgun, Xinyun Chen, Aakanksha Chowdhery, Alex Castro-Ros, Marie Pellat, Kevin Robinson, and 16 others. 2024. Scaling instruction-finetuned language models. *Journal of Machine Learning Research*, 25(70):1–53.

Tim Dettmers, Mike Lewis, Younes Belkada, and Luke Zettlemoyer. 2022. GPT3.int8(): 8-bit matrix multiplication for transformers at scale. In *Advances in Neural Information Processing Systems*.

Zhichen Dong, Zhanhui Zhou, Chao Yang, Jing Shao, and Yu Qiao. 2024. Attacks, defenses and evaluations for LLM conversation safety: A survey. In *Proceedings of the 2024 Conference of the North American Chapter of the Association for Computational Linguistics: Human Language Technologies (Volume 1: Long Papers)*, pages 6734–6747, Mexico City, Mexico. Association for Computational Linguistics.

Mengnan Du, Fengxiang He, Na Zou, Dacheng Tao, and Xia Hu. 2023. Shortcut learning of large language models in natural language understanding. *Commun. ACM*, 67(1):110–120.

Suchin Gururangan, Ana Marasović, Swabha Swayamdipta, Kyle Lo, Iz Beltagy, Doug Downey, and Noah A. Smith. 2020. Don't stop pretraining: Adapt language models to domains and tasks. In *Proceedings of the 58th Annual Meeting of the Association for Computational Linguistics*, pages 8342–8360, Online. Association for Computational Linguistics.

Dan Hendrycks, Collin Burns, Steven Basart, Andy Zou, Mantas Mazeika, Dawn Song, and Jacob Steinhardt. 2021. Measuring massive multitask language understanding. In *International Conference on Learning Representations*.

Md Mosharaf Hossain, Venelin Kovatchev, Pranoy Dutta, Tiffany Kao, Elizabeth Wei, and Eduardo Blanco. 2020. An analysis of natural language inference benchmarks through the lens of negation. In *Proceedings of the 2020 Conference on Empirical Methods in Natural Language Processing (EMNLP)*, pages 9106–9118, Online. Association for Computational Linguistics.

Arian Hosseini, Siva Reddy, Dzmitry Bahdanau, R Devon Hjelm, Alessandro Sordoni, and Aaron Courville. 2021. Understanding by understanding not: Modeling negation in language models. In *Proceedings of the 2021 Conference of the North American Chapter of the Association for Computational Linguistics: Human Language Technologies*, pages 1301–1312, Online. Association for Computational Linguistics.

Joel Jang, Seonghyeon Ye, and Minjoon Seo. 2023. Can large language models truly understand prompts? a case study with negated prompts. In *Proceedings of The 1st Transfer Learning for Natural Language Processing Workshop*, volume 203 of *Proceedings of Machine Learning Research*, pages 52–62. PMLR.

Nora Kassner and Hinrich Schütze. 2020. Negated and misprimed probes for pretrained language models: Birds can talk, but cannot fly. In *Proceedings of the 58th Annual Meeting of the Association for Computational Linguistics*, pages 7811–7818, Online. Association for Computational Linguistics.

Pride Kavumba, Ryo Takahashi, and Yusuke Oda. 2022. Are prompt-based models clueless? In *Proceedings of the 60th Annual Meeting of the Association for Computational Linguistics (Volume 1: Long Papers)*, pages 2333–2352, Dublin, Ireland. Association for Computational Linguistics.

Noriyuki Kojima, Alane Suhr, and Yoav Artzi. 2021. Continual learning for grounded instruction generation by observing human following behavior. *Transactions of the Association for Computational Linguistics*, 9:1303–1319.

Takeshi Kojima, Shixiang Shane Gu, Machel Reid, Yutaka Matsuo, and Yusuke Iwasawa. 2022. Large language models are zero-shot reasoners. In *Advances in Neural Information Processing Systems*.

Andreas Köpf, Yannic Kilcher, Dimitri von Rütte, Sotiris Anagnostidis, Zhi Rui Tam, Keith Stevens, Abdullah Barhoum, Duc Minh Nguyen, Oliver Stanley, Richárd Nagyfi, Shahul ES, Sameer Suri, David Alexandrovich Glushkov, Arnav Varma Dantuluri, Andrew Maguire, Christoph Schuhmann, Huu Nguyen, and Alexander Julian Mattick. 2023. Openassistant conversations - democratizing large language model alignment. In *Thirty-seventh Conference on Neural Information Processing Systems Datasets and Benchmarks Track*.

Po-Nien Kung and Nanyun Peng. 2023. Do models really learn to follow instructions? an empirical study of instruction tuning. In *Proceedings of the 61st Annual Meeting of the Association for Computational Linguistics (Volume 2: Short Papers)*, pages 1317–1328, Toronto, Canada. Association for Computational Linguistics.

Noah Lee, Jiwoo Hong, and James Thorne. 2025. Evaluating the consistency of LLM evaluators. In *Proceedings of the 31st International Conference on Computational Linguistics*, pages 10650–10659, Abu Dhabi, UAE. Association for Computational Linguistics.

Brian Lester, Rami Al-Rfou, and Noah Constant. 2021. The power of scale for parameter-efficient prompt tuning. In *Proceedings of the 2021 Conference on Empirical Methods in Natural Language Processing*, pages 3045–3059, Online and Punta Cana, Dominican Republic. Association for Computational Linguistics.

Xiang Lisa Li and Percy Liang. 2021. Prefix-tuning: Optimizing continuous prompts for generation. In *Proceedings of the 59th Annual Meeting of the Association for Computational Linguistics and the 11th International Joint Conference on Natural Language Processing (Volume 1: Long Papers)*, pages 4582–4597, Online. Association for Computational Linguistics.

Zekun Li, Baolin Peng, Pengcheng He, and Xifeng Yan. 2024. Evaluating the instruction-following robustness of large language models to prompt injection. In *Proceedings of the 2024 Conference on Empirical Methods in Natural Language Processing*, pages 557–568, Miami, Florida, USA. Association for Computational Linguistics.

Xiao Liu, Yanan Zheng, Zhengxiao Du, Ming Ding, Yujie Qian, Zhilin Yang, and Jie Tang. 2024. Gpt understands, too. *AI Open*, 5:208–215.

Shayne Longpre, Le Hou, Tu Vu, Albert Webson, Hyung Won Chung, Yi Tay, Denny Zhou, Quoc V Le, Barret Zoph, Jason Wei, and Adam Roberts. 2023. The flan collection: Designing data and methods for effective instruction tuning. In *Proceedings of the 40th International Conference on Machine Learning*, volume 202 of *Proceedings of Machine Learning Research*, pages 22631–22648. PMLR.

Swaroop Mishra, Daniel Khashabi, Chitta Baral, and Hannaneh Hajishirzi. 2022. Cross-task generalization via natural language crowdsourcing instructions. In *Proceedings of the 60th Annual Meeting of the Association for Computational Linguistics (Volume 1: Long Papers)*, pages 3470–3487, Dublin, Ireland. Association for Computational Linguistics.

Hyeonseok Moon, Jaehyung Seo, Seungyoon Lee, Chanjun Park, and Heuiseok Lim. 2025. Find the intention of instruction: Comprehensive evaluation of instruction understanding for large language models. In *Findings of the Association for Computational Linguistics: NAACL 2025*, pages 5944–5964, Albuquerque, New Mexico. Association for Computational Linguistics.

Nihal Nayak, Yiyang Nan, Avi Trost, and Stephen Bach. 2024. Learning to generate instruction tuning datasets for zero-shot task adaptation. In *Findings of the Association for Computational Linguistics: ACL 2024*, pages 12585–12611, Bangkok, Thailand. Association for Computational Linguistics.

Kazumasa Omura, Daisuke Kawahara, and Sadao Kurohashi. 2020. A method for building a commonsense inference dataset based on basic events. In *Proceedings of the 2020 Conference on Empirical Methods in Natural Language Processing (EMNLP)*, pages 2450–2460, Online. Association for Computational Linguistics.

Baolin Peng, Chunyuan Li, Pengcheng He, Michel Galley, and Jianfeng Gao. 2023. Instruction tuning with gpt-4. *Preprint*, arXiv:2304.03277.

Adam Poliak, Jason Naradowsky, Aparajita Haldar, Rachel Rudinger, and Benjamin Van Durme. 2018. Hypothesis only baselines in natural language inference. In *Proceedings of the Seventh Joint Conference on Lexical and Computational Semantics*, pages 180–191, New Orleans, Louisiana. Association for Computational Linguistics.

Yiwei Qin, Kaiqiang Song, Yebowen Hu, Wenlin Yao, Sangwoo Cho, Xiaoyang Wang, Xuansheng Wu, Fei Liu, Pengfei Liu, and Dong Yu. 2024. InFoBench: Evaluating instruction following ability in large language models. In *Findings of the Association for Computational Linguistics: ACL 2024*, pages 13025–13048, Bangkok, Thailand. Association for Computational Linguistics.

Colin Raffel, Noam Shazeer, Adam Roberts, Katherine Lee, Sharan Narang, Michael Matena, Yanqi Zhou, Wei Li, and Peter J. Liu. 2020. Exploring the limits of transfer learning with a unified text-to-text transformer. *Journal of Machine Learning Research*, 21(140):1–67.

Harsh Raj, Vipul Gupta, Domenic Rosati, and Subhabrata Majumdar. 2025. Improving consistency in large language models through chain of guidance. *Transactions on Machine Learning Research.*

Juan Ramos. 2003. Using tf-idf to determine word relevance in document queries.

Yusuke Sakai, Hidetaka Kamigaito, and Taro Watanabe. 2025. Revisiting compositional generalization capability of large language models considering instruction following ability. *Preprint*, arXiv:2506.15629.

Yusuke Sakai, Adam Nohejl, Jiangnan Hang, Hidetaka Kamigaito, and Taro Watanabe. 2024. Toward the evaluation of large language models considering score variance across instruction templates. In *Proceedings of the 7th BlackboxNLP Workshop: Analyzing and Interpreting Neural Networks for NLP*, pages 499–529, Miami, Florida, US. Association for Computational Linguistics.

Aarohi Srivastava, Abhinav Rastogi, Abhishek Rao, Abu Awal Md Shoeb, Abubakar Abid, Adam Fisch, Adam R. Brown, Adam Santoro, Aditya Gupta, Adrià Garriga-Alonso, Agnieszka Kluska, Aitor Lewkowycz, Akshat Agarwal, Alethea Power, Alex Ray, Alex Warstadt, Alexander W. Kocurek, Ali Safaya, Ali Tazarv, and 431 others. 2023. Beyond the imitation game: Quantifying and extrapolating the capabilities of language models. *Transactions on Machine Learning Research.* Featured Certification.

Mirac Suzgun, Nathan Scales, Nathanael Schärli, Sebastian Gehrmann, Yi Tay, Hyung Won Chung, Aakanksha Chowdhery, Quoc Le, Ed Chi, Denny Zhou, and Jason Wei. 2023. Challenging BIG-bench tasks and whether chain-of-thought can solve them. In *Findings of the Association for Computational Linguistics: ACL 2023*, pages 13003–13051, Toronto, Canada. Association for Computational Linguistics.

Alexandre Tamborrino, Nicola Pellicanò, Baptiste Pannier, Pascal Voitot, and Louise Naudin. 2020. Pretraining is (almost) all you need: An application to commonsense reasoning. In *Proceedings of the 58th Annual Meeting of the Association for Computational Linguistics*, pages 3878–3887, Online. Association for Computational Linguistics.

Rohan Taori, Ishaan Gulrajani, Tianyi Zhang, Yann Dubois, Xuechen Li, Carlos Guestrin, Percy Liang, and Tatsunori B. Hashimoto. 2023. Stanford alpaca: An instruction-following llama model. `https://github.com/tatsu-lab/stanford_alpaca`.

Yi Tay, Mostafa Dehghani, Vinh Q. Tran, Xavier Garcia, Jason Wei, Xuezhi Wang, Hyung Won Chung, Dara Bahri, Tal Schuster, Steven Zheng, Denny Zhou, Neil Houlsby, and Donald Metzler. 2023. UL2: Unifying language learning paradigms. In *The Eleventh International Conference on Learning Representations*.

Hugo Touvron, Louis Martin, Kevin Stone, Peter Albert, Amjad Almahairi, Yasmine Babaei, Nikolay Bashlykov, Soumya Batra, Prajjwal Bhargava, Shruti Bhosale, Dan Bikel, Lukas Blecher, Cristian Canton Ferrer, Moya Chen, Guillem Cucurull, David Esiobu, Jude Fernandes, Jeremy Fu, Wenyin Fu, and 49 others. 2023. Llama 2: Open foundation and fine-tuned chat models. *Preprint*, arXiv:2307.09288.

Masatoshi Tsuchiya. 2018. Performance impact caused by hidden bias of training data for recognizing textual entailment. In *Proceedings of the Eleventh International Conference on Language Resources and Evaluation (LREC 2018)*, Miyazaki, Japan. European Language Resources Association (ELRA).

Yizhong Wang, Yeganeh Kordi, Swaroop Mishra, Alisa Liu, Noah A. Smith, Daniel Khashabi, and Hannaneh Hajishirzi. 2023. Self-instruct: Aligning language models with self-generated instructions. In *Proceedings of the 61st Annual Meeting of the Association for Computational Linguistics (Volume 1: Long Papers)*, pages 13484–13508, Toronto, Canada. Association for Computational Linguistics.

Yizhong Wang, Swaroop Mishra, Pegah Alipoormolabashi, Yeganeh Kordi, Amirreza Mirzaei, Atharva Naik, Arjun Ashok, Arut Selvan Dhanasekaran, Anjana Arunkumar, David Stap, Eshaan Pathak, Giannis Karamanolakis, Haizhi Lai, Ishan Purohit, Ishani Mondal, Jacob Anderson, Kirby Kuznia, Krima Doshi, Kuntal Kumar Pal, and 16 others. 2022. Super-NaturalInstructions: Generalization via declarative instructions on 1600+ NLP tasks. In *Proceedings of the 2022 Conference on Empirical Methods in Natural Language Processing*, pages 5085–5109, Abu Dhabi, United Arab Emirates. Association for Computational Linguistics.

Jason Wei, Maarten Bosma, Vincent Zhao, Kelvin Guu, Adams Wei Yu, Brian Lester, Nan Du, Andrew M. Dai, and Quoc V Le. 2022a. Finetuned language models are zero-shot learners. In *International Conference on Learning Representations*.

Jason Wei, Xuezhi Wang, Dale Schuurmans, Maarten Bosma, brian ichter, Fei Xia, Ed H. Chi, Quoc V Le, and Denny Zhou. 2022b. Chain of thought prompting elicits reasoning in large language models. In *Advances in Neural Information Processing Systems*.

Adina Williams, Nikita Nangia, and Samuel Bowman. 2018. A broad-coverage challenge corpus for sentence understanding through inference. In *Proceedings of the 2018 Conference of the North American Chapter of the Association for Computational Linguistics: Human Language Technologies, Volume 1 (Long Papers)*, pages 1112–1122, New Orleans, Louisiana. Association for Computational Linguistics.

Thomas Wolf, Lysandre Debut, Victor Sanh, Julien Chaumond, Clement Delangue, Anthony Moi, Pierric Cistac, Tim Rault, Remi Louf, Morgan Funtowicz, Joe Davison, Sam Shleifer, Patrick von Platen, Clara Ma, Yacine Jernite, Julien Plu, Canwen Xu, Teven Le Scao, Sylvain Gugger, and 3 others. 2020. Transformers: State-of-the-art natural language processing. In *Proceedings of the 2020 Conference on Empirical Methods in Natural Language Processing: System Demonstrations*, pages 38–45, Online. Association for Computational Linguistics.

Can Xu, Qingfeng Sun, Kai Zheng, Xiubo Geng, Pu Zhao, Jiazhan Feng, Chongyang Tao, Qingwei Lin, and Daxin Jiang. 2024. WizardLM: Empowering large pre-trained language models to follow complex instructions. In *The Twelfth International Conference on Learning Representations*.

Canwen Xu, Daya Guo, Nan Duan, and Julian McAuley. 2023. Baize: An open-source chat model with parameter-efficient tuning on self-chat data. In *Proceedings of the 2023 Conference on Empirical Methods in Natural Language Processing*, pages 6268–6278, Singapore. Association for Computational Linguistics.

Chengrun Yang, Xuezhi Wang, Yifeng Lu, Hanxiao Liu, Quoc V Le, Denny Zhou, and Xinyun Chen. 2024. Large language models as optimizers. In *The Twelfth International Conference on Learning Representations*.

Shunyu Yao, Jeffrey Zhao, Dian Yu, Nan Du, Izhak Shafran, Karthik R Narasimhan, and Yuan Cao. 2023. ReAct: Synergizing reasoning and acting in language models. In *The Eleventh International Conference on Learning Representations*.

Mengyu Ye, Tatsuki Kuribayashi, Jun Suzuki, Goro Kobayashi, and Hiroaki Funayama. 2023. Assessing step-by-step reasoning against lexical negation: A case study on syllogism. In *Proceedings of the 2023 Conference on Empirical Methods in Natural Language Processing*, pages 14753–14773, Singapore. Association for Computational Linguistics.

Rowan Zellers, Ari Holtzman, Yonatan Bisk, Ali Farhadi, and Yejin Choi. 2019. HellaSwag: Can a machine really finish your sentence? In *Proceedings of the 57th Annual Meeting of the Association for Computational Linguistics*, pages 4791–4800, Florence, Italy. Association for Computational Linguistics.

Zhiyuan Zeng, Jiatong Yu, Tianyu Gao, Yu Meng, Tanya Goyal, and Danqi Chen. 2024. Evaluating large language models at evaluating instruction following. In *The Twelfth International Conference on Learning Representations*.

Shengyu Zhang, Linfeng Dong, Xiaoya Li, Sen Zhang, Xiaofei Sun, Shuhe Wang, Jiwei Li, Runyi Hu, Tianwei Zhang, Fei Wu, and Guoyin Wang. 2023. Instruction tuning for large language models: A survey. *Preprint*, arXiv:2308.10792.

Xiaosen Zheng, Tianyu Pang, Chao Du, Qian Liu, Jing Jiang, and Min Lin. 2025. Cheating automatic LLM benchmarks: Null models achieve high win rates. In *The Thirteenth International Conference on Learning Representations*.

Qihuang Zhong, Liang Ding, Juhua Liu, Bo Du, and Dacheng Tao. 2023. Can chatgpt understand too? a comparative study on chatgpt and fine-tuned bert. *Preprint*, arXiv:2302.10198.

Yongchao Zhou, Andrei Ioan Muresanu, Ziwen Han, Keiran Paster, Silviu Pitis, Harris Chan, and Jimmy Ba. 2023. Large language models are human-level prompt engineers. In *The Eleventh International Conference on Learning Representations*.

Author Index

Association for Computational Linguistics
209 N. Eighth Street
Stroudsburg, Pennsylvania 18360

ISBN 979-8-3313-2410-0

9 798331 324100

CURRAN ASSOCIATES INC.
proceedings
.com